Ministering to Education

A Reformer Reports

Leighton Andrews

Foreword by Sir Michael Barber

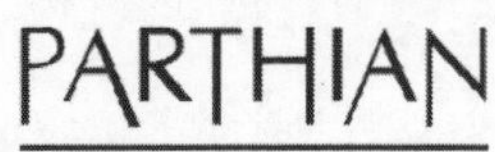

Parthian, Cardigan SA43 1ED
www.parthianbooks.com
First published in 2014

ISBN 978-1-909844-83-4
Editor: Susie Wild
Cover design by www.theundercard.co.uk
Photography by Keith Morris with kind permission of Ysgol Uwchradd Aberteifi
Typeset by Elaine Sharples
Printed and bound by Gomer Press, Llandysul, Wales

Ministering to Education
A Reformer Reports

Leighton Andrews has been the Assembly Member for the Rhondda since 2003. A former Head of Public Affairs at the BBC in London, he has been a visiting professor at the University of Westminster and an Honorary Professor at Cardiff University. He was Carwyn Jones' campaign manager in the Welsh Labour leadership election in 2009, and convened the steering group for the Yes campaign in the 2011 referendum.

For the leaders of change in our schools, colleges, universities and local authorities

Contents

Foreword by Sir Michael Barber ix
Introduction 1

Appointed Minister for Children, Education and Lifelong Learning 7
Setting the Direction 22
Leading Change 38
Removing Distractions – Funding the Future 52
Avoiding Distractions: No Academies 64
Three Clear Priorities 81
From School Effectiveness to School Improvement 100
Local Delivery 129
A World-Class Workforce 149
Qualifications Reform 167
Michael Gove and the war on Wales 187
English Language GCSE 207
Curriculum reform and cultural choices: unfinished business 231
Learning in a digital world 252
A Living Language 264
Adapt or Die 284
The New Higher Education Policy 312
Tuition Fees and Funding 331
Skills for Employment 353
Devolution, Difference – and Delivery 370

Acknowledgements 381
Glossary 384
Bibliographical Essay 386
Chronology 394
Index 398

Foreword

Sir Michael Barber

Ministering to Education is an important and highly readable contribution to the literature on reforming education systems. It will of course be of great interest to those involved in the education system in Wales, whether as politicians, officials, teachers or parents. I also believe it will be of interest around the world because it enables the reader to see education reform from a minister's perspective, as very few books have done before.

The appointment of Leighton Andrews as Minister for Education in the Welsh Assembly Government was a powerful signal from Carwyn Jones, the First Minister, that for the education sector business as usual in Wales was over and transformation would begin. As is recounted in the book, I first met Leighton shortly after his appointment and was impressed by his grasp of the state of affairs. He knew that the performance of the education system in Wales was unacceptably poor – and was willing to speak plainly about the way things were. I also recognised a politician who had the courage to act, even if some sacred cows would need to be slaughtered along the way.

In the decade or so between the creation of the Welsh Assembly and Leighton's appointment, in relation to education, the government in Wales had in effect chosen to be 'not England'. Tests and published test results abolished. No targets. No new forms of school such as academies. Power in effect left firmly in the hands of traditional local authorities and teachers. The result, as international comparisons began to show, was that Wales fell behind. Wales's performance at secondary level in 2010 was worse than that of the lowest performing English region. Leighton was determined to change that – he knew what every progressive citizen of Wales knew – that the success of Wales in the twenty-first century would depend more than anything on the education of its people.

He also knew, given the distinctive culture and qualities of Wales, that the solution could not and should not be to ape what England had done. Instead, he chose to learn from it, adapt it where appropriate and ignore it where it did not make sense for Wales. Moreover, he recognised that England was just one country from which Wales could learn. What you find in these pages is a minister who is globally aware and shows an unusually deep knowledge of the research and writing on reforming education systems around the world.

I would highlight three major aspects of the book, though there is much else of interest including the stand-off with the government in England over GCSE, especially GCSE English, and changes in higher education too.

First, throughout the story Leighton's determination to challenge the status quo, to reject mediocrity and to stand up for aspiration and standards shines through, even when on occasions it gets him into trouble. For example, in establishing a firm focus on literacy, numeracy and narrowing gaps in performance, Leighton learnt from England's experience between 1997 and 2001 but also from Ontario's experience between 2003 and 2013. He never wavered in pursuit of those goals even when the going got tough.

Second, while he knew it would be very difficult, he also refused to accept the status quo in relation to local government. In the mid-1990s, the government (in London) had, in an act of administrative madness, created twenty two local authorities in Wales when ten or twelve would have been quite sufficient. Most of them became mediocre institutions rarely willing to provide real challenge to the education system. They drained resources that might otherwise have been in the schools and smothered innovation. Until Leighton no one had been willing to tackle the problem, with the result that reform was long overdue.

Again he examined the path England had taken but refined and adapted it. He recognised that the stronger sense of social solidarity in Wales was a potential asset and therefore wanted a stronger middle tier rather than doing without one. In Blaenau Gwent he showed a willingness to intervene where necessary, sending a signal to the whole country that he expected more. The report he commissioned from Robert Hill gave him a constructive way forward which is now being implemented under his successor, Huw Lewis.

Third, in addition to making bold decisions, on the basis of a global evidence base and the needs of the hour, Leighton also concerned himself with implementation. He knew that unless reform had a real impact in classrooms across Wales, as well as in policy circles, the lives of children and young people would not be changed and his efforts would be in vain.

The ultimate outcomes – whether students learn more and achieve more – of his tenure as Minister of Education will be the acid test. Here, as Leighton recounts, there is some promising progress but as he would be the first to admit what we've seen so far is only the beginning and not nearly enough to fulfil the aspiration he has for Wales. Three years is not long enough to deliver irreversible reform, and the impact of, for example, the changes he made to GCSE cannot be known for years to come. My judgement would be that Leighton set education in Wales on a new and much more promising path and, whether that results in the much-hoped-for transformation, will depend on whether his successors pursue the path with the same vigour, determination and courage as Leighton did.

Either way, this book is instructive and tells a great story. It reveals vividly the challenges of being a minister; for example, being able to master the evidence base, the political context, the policy detail and the ability to communicate with stakeholders and the public not just over a period of time but also sometimes within a single day. As Leighton tells the story, he plays out the arguments he lived through and is often self-critical in ways that few contemporary memoirs do.

I hope that *Ministering to Education* will be widely read. Even more, I hope that Wales will build on the achievements recounted in these pages and create an education system that becomes the envy of the world.

Sir Michael Barber

June 2014

Introduction

Education, as the Welsh cultural critic Raymond Williams reminded us in *Culture & Society*, is one of those words which gained its modern meaning during the Industrial Revolution. If I were writing a book on educational philosophy in Wales, I would draw on the writings of Raymond Williams and the even earlier pioneers of adult education, the founders of the Plebs' League, the Central Labour Colleges, which gave Aneurin Bevan one of his first routes to publication, and the Workers' Educational Association (WEA). Amongst their observations and disputes many of the great questions about educational practice were addressed in ways which are still relevant today. Their debates around adult education were communitarian in focus, unsurprisingly, given how many of their leaders, such as Noah Ablett and W.H. Mainwaring, were drawn from the Unofficial Reform Committee in the Rhondda which gave birth, just over a century ago, to *The Miners' Next Step*. The community socialist traditions of the South Wales valleys sit uncomfortably with the often libertarian individualism of much of educational philosophy, even today, and would find some of it self-indulgent and lacking in rigour.

This is not, however, a book on educational philosophy. Nor is it intended to be an academic book. But I hope that it will be useful to academics as well as practitioners. I hope it will be of interest to anyone who wants to know more about the shaping of education policy in Wales. I hope that the book will also provide insights into the operation and culture of devolved policy-making and public administration in Wales, as well as the interaction between a devolved government and a UK government at a time of significant policy divergence.

I believe that I am the first former minister in any of the Welsh governments since 1999 to write a book-length account of any of their periods as a minister. I hope others will follow. We need more reflection on devolved politics – on what has gone well and on what has gone wrong – away from the self-important rhetoric of the Assembly Chamber and the glib simplicities of a TV studio. I began work on this book a few weeks after I left the Welsh Government on 25th June 2013. I had always intended to write an account of my time as Education Minister in Wales at some stage in the future. I just didn't expect the opportunity to come so soon!

Inevitably, much has had to be left out. I have focused on the main areas of reform – schools, further and higher education, qualifications, the Welsh language – as well as key responsibilities in my own portfolio where there were specific policy differences with London. Even here, I have had to edit ruthlessly. I have sketched in outline matters where there is more to do, such as the curriculum.

Like any former minister, I am restricted by the Ministerial Code, and have therefore principally relied on published sources. Anyone hoping for juicy titbits from Cabinet meetings will be disappointed. However, the period of the book covers some interesting moments in the development of devolution in Wales.

The story begins during the One Wales Coalition government of Labour and Plaid Cymru. Carwyn Jones's leadership victory in December 2009 had enabled us to refresh the image of Welsh Labour eighteen months before the Assembly election. Our ambition in 2009 was to build on the leadership election victory and deliver a full victory in the Assembly elections of 2011. Positioning Carwyn as a Leader for the whole of Wales was key to this, of course, but his own decision to make education a key plank of his leadership election manifesto gave us new energy in the 2011 Assembly election in which education policy featured strongly, and in which we won an additional four seats, taking us from twenty six to thirty out of the sixty seats in the National Assembly.

Our election preparations began in 2010, alongside the referendum campaign which delivered full law-making powers for the National Assembly in March 2011. Our key 2011 campaign theme – *Standing up for Wales* – was firmly in our minds by the summer of 2010. In December 2010 at Carwyn's request I attended a meeting of Ed Miliband's Shadow Cabinet where electoral strategy for 2011 – English local elections, Welsh and Scottish elections – was being discussed. I was amused to find that the same theme – *Standing up for Communities* – had been developed in England as well, after significant investment in focus group research. I said that we had also determined our slogan through a focus group in Wales – in our case, a focus group of Welsh Government ministers and advisers in a pub near the Assembly.

In May 2010 the Conservative-led UK coalition government was elected, meaning we had a very different policy context within which to operate. Manifesto options for the 2011 Assembly election were outlined at the Welsh Labour special policy conference in November 2010. The education section of the policy platform highlighted Carwyn's central commitment to raising the funding going into schools. In introducing this section of the document I highlighted the dividing lines now emerging between Welsh Labour and the coalition in England, such as the development of free schools. I was able to confirm that local authorities had also committed to delegate more of the money they received from the Welsh Government to their schools. This pre-manifesto document, however, appeared before we published our plans on tuition fees and before the Programme for International Student Assessment (PISA) 2009 results were published in December 2010. The final manifesto in 2011 had much more detail in these areas in particular. Some of our key commitments became central Labour campaign pledges – including the commitment that no Welsh student should pay higher tuition fees in real terms than if they had been a student in 2010-11, and the commitment to raise funding to schools by 1 per cent above the percentage increase in the block grant to Wales.

Of course, policies do not arrive fully-formed overnight. There is a cycle of policy development. This can involve the shaping of an initial idea, sometimes by a minister or an official, or a political party or a think tank, or a lobby group such as a union or charity. Then there is the process of manifesto preparation and adoption. After the election, if the proposal makes it into the legislative programme, there will be consultation, policy instructions to government lawyers, the preparation of legislation, then the passage of that legislation through the Assembly, and finally the preparation of regulations or statutory guidance deriving from the legislation. Not all policies require legislation. Some programmes, such as Jobs Growth Wales can be developed and delivered quickly. But others, such as my reforms to the procedures which governed the closure of schools, took three and a half years from conception to final implementation.

It was only after May 2011 that we were able to embark on a fully Labour education policy, with the ending of the One Wales coalition government. Even then we were, in practice, a minority government. In the run-up to the 2011 Assembly election, Plaid Cymru had started to distance themselves from us on education policies. Their leader, Ieuan Wyn Jones, in June 2010, and their education spokesperson, Nerys Evans, in March 2011, both made keynote speeches on education. I got on well with Nerys, but I was amused when she tried to claim Plaid was responsible for the Foundation Phase, 14-19 Learning Pathways and the Welsh Baccalaureate, as those had been developed before the One Wales government. I joked in the Assembly 'I was interested to see that all the things that had been done in education that she liked had been carried out by a Plaid Government and that all the things that she did not like had been carried out by Labour Ministers.' Amongst other things, Plaid made it clear that they would not go along with our proposal for a national grading system for schools if they were in government in the next Assembly term.

On my reappointment as Education Minister following the 2011 election, the *Western Mail* editorial was headlined

'Leighton's a tough teacher, but he has the right lessons for our schools.' I was very clear that I had unfinished business. I was able to carry through many of the key elements of our manifesto before I left the government in June 2013, and put in place the plans for legislation to underpin a number of other areas.

You rapidly find, as a minister, that when Opposition parties are not criticising you for not doing enough and not having done it by yesterday, they are criticising you for doing too much and doing it too fast. Sometimes you simply have to put your head down and drive forward, ignoring the bufferings from all sides. You have to hold your nerve and stick to your strategy.

I was pleased to be succeeded by Huw Lewis, who had been my Deputy Minister from the period following Carwyn's victory in the leadership election in December 2009 until the May 2011 Assembly election. I knew he shared my commitment to high standards for all, meaning that the impetus behind our reforms would be carried forward, supplemented by Huw's personal commitment to addressing issues of tackling deprivation and inequality.

I was fortunate as Education Minister to work with some very talented people in government, in schools, colleges and universities in Wales, and in the education inspectorate, Estyn. I wish there were more space to thank the hundreds who were involved.

As Aneurin Bevan famously said, 'This is my truth. Tell me yours.'

Appointed Minister for Children, Education and Lifelong Learning

As we waited for the official announcement of the Welsh Labour leadership result on the 1st December 2009, I looked across at Carwyn Jones, sitting in the rows opposite. He and his agent Mick Antoniw had been given the result earlier, in private. As his campaign manager, with the rest of the campaign team, I had just arrived at the Wales Millennium Centre (WMC). We didn't know the result, though we were highly optimistic given our telephone canvassing returns. While we waited for the announcement, Carwyn mouthed something at me. I thought he was saying 'effing lost'. It turned out later he had been saying 'First ballot'. I will never make it as a lip-reader.

Carwyn undertook a long round of interviews after the official ceremony and speeches, then as we were about to leave the WMC to join Carwyn's assembled supporters in the Eli Jenkins pub just across the way, a call came in. It was 10 Downing Street, with the Prime Minister on the line. Carwyn received Gordon Brown's congratulations standing in the public space of the foyer of the WMC. There were few there to witness it.

Carwyn's election came just over ten years after the opening of the National Assembly. It offered a chance to set a clear direction for the second decade of devolution. It certainly helped to renew the appeal of Welsh Labour. There was just one problem. We didn't have a majority Labour government – we were in coalition with Plaid Cymru.

Carwyn had set out his own manifesto for the leadership of Welsh Labour during the campaign, under the slogan, *Time to*

Lead. A number of us had contributed to the ideas in that manifesto, which was eventually pulled into shape by former Welsh Labour special adviser Cathy Owens. At the launch of the manifesto, well-managed by Cathy, David Taylor and Steve Jones, there was a focus on a specific pledge – that spending on education would rise each year by 1 per cent above the total percentage change in grant received by the Welsh Government from the UK government. I had never been entirely certain how that pledge arose. I understood it had been developed by Carwyn, together with Jane Davidson, then Environment Minister and formerly Education Minister from 2000-2007. I interrogated Carwyn on the pledge as we planned the launch of the manifesto. 'One per cent of what?', I asked him when the idea was first aired. I was worried that we would be pulled up on the cost of the commitment and also not clear whether we could honour it during the lifetime of the One Wales government. We nailed down what it meant. The one per cent commitment, once clarified, helped to give Carwyn's campaign clear definition – and it was obvious that education would be a priority for the government he led.

Carwyn was aware that I hoped to take on the education brief in his Cabinet. By then I had served for two and a half years as a Deputy Minister, first with responsibility for housing, in the six or seven weeks of Rhodri Morgan's minority Labour government established in late May 2007. Once the One Wales coalition with Plaid Cymru was formed in early July that year, I had become the Deputy Minister for Regeneration, working across the two government departments of Economy and Transport, as deputy to Plaid Cymru leader Ieuan Wyn Jones, and Social Justice and Local Government, as deputy to Labour Minister Dr Brian Gibbons. I had thoroughly enjoyed this portfolio, which addressed issues I had worked on earlier in my life when I was the UK Campaign Director for the 1987 UN International Year of Shelter for the Homeless.

I'd had some experience of the education department in the course of Cabinet Committee and other ministerial meetings on public service delivery and welfare reform. My officials in Regeneration and in Communities First had had to develop relationships with the department as getting people into paid work was a key task in regenerating communities. We saw regeneration as being about people as much as it was about place. The JobMatch programme, operating under the City Strategy pathfinder programme, established by UK Labour ministers in the Department of Work and Pensions, was one element where Regeneration officials had been in the lead. Relations with the education department had not always been harmonious while this programme was being developed. I had also had some serious doubts about the department's analytical capability, having seen their calculations around childcare needs in the welfare reform area.

Over the previous decade of devolution, the education department had developed a number of creative and pioneering policies, particularly around curriculum development, including the Foundation Phase, the Welsh Baccalaureate and the 14-19 Learning Pathways. The Foundation Phase, initial work on which began under Rosemary Butler, as Assembly Secretary for pre-16 Education and Children, and developed under Jane Davidson, provided a new approach to the education of 3 to 7-year-olds relevant to their development, placing great emphasis on learning by doing, aiming to develop young people's self-esteem and confidence through play and active involvement in problem-solving, and to inculcate a positive approach to learning. My predecessor as Education Minister, Jane Hutt, had delivered additional funding for the programme because its reliance on large numbers of teaching assistants absorbed more revenue than had originally been budgeted.

The Welsh Baccalaureate gave young people broader experiences than simply vocational qualifications or academic study. It combined personal development skills with existing qualifications and was designed to give young people experience of the world of work, community projects, and personal research-based investigation.

The 14-19 Learning Pathways were designed to ensure that all young people had tailored support whatever course they took, with a wide choice of options, designed to break down the barriers between vocational and academic learning, and to boost the number of young people going on to higher level qualifications. The plans were developed by Jane Davidson with additional work by her Deputy Minister Christine Chapman in 2005, and were taken forward in the Learning and Skills Measure piloted through the Assembly by the Deputy Minister for Skills, John Griffiths, in 2008-9.

The first decade of the Assembly had therefore been one where a new Welsh education agenda was developed – what Professor David Reynolds had called 'a distinctive Welsh way for our education policies'. Jane Davidson's White Paper *The Learning Country* set out the outline of that approach in 2001 – its title borrowed from a 1999 paper on adult education by Hywel Francis and Rob Humphreys.

The first two Welsh Assembly Governments, as they were called at the time, had also made significant policy departures in other areas in the first decade – reinstating student grants, with the introduction of the Assembly Learning Grant, the development of a more generous approach to tuition fee support for Welsh students studying in Wales from 2005, and approaches to intensive early years support in some of Wales's poorest communities, through the Flying Start programme.

My philosophy of education was very simple. It was that a child in Maerdy in my Rhondda constituency, one of the most deprived communities in Wales, should have the same life chances as a child in Monmouth, one of the richest parts of Wales. To achieve this demanded activist politics – but then, that is why we in the Labour Party are in politics. I was fed up of excuses and alibis. Too often we heard the most blatant and outrageous socio-economic determinism – that you couldn't expect kids from these backgrounds to do well, that poverty would always hold these communities back, or you couldn't expect schools to overcome the challenges of a chaotic or dysfunctional family environment. That just made me angry. Sometimes excuses came in a more sugar-coated form: academic results might be poor, but the school surveys of wellbeing were terrific, or they had a top-rating for their pastoral care.

Yet there were teachers and head teachers out there who were performing extraordinarily well in schools in deprived communities. In Treorchy in my own constituency, first under Bethan Guilfoyle and now Rhys Jones. In Sandfields in Neath Port Talbot. In St. Mary Immaculate in Cardiff under Marc Belli's leadership. In 2013, in Llanwern High in Newport under Peter Jenkins. In Rhyl High, under Claire Armitstead. In primary schools like Hafod in Swansea, led by Rachael Webb; Barry Island then Cadoxton under Janet Hayward; Herbert Thompson Primary in Ely, led by Bethan Hocking and Rhos y Medre near Wrexham under Liz Edwards. These heads took responsibility: they didn't duck it or find excuses. When Ferndale Community School, based in the Maerdy ward, became the first secondary school in Wales to move from Band 5 to Band 1 in 2013, under the dynamic leadership of head teacher Heather Nicholas, I felt we were really getting somewhere.

Of course, we had to intervene in the community as well – and we needed a team around the family approach, like that of On Track in Tylorstown in the Rhondda Fach, pioneered by the late Mick Millman, not one that expected families to trek to a variety of services in a variety of locations. Huw Lewis pioneered the roll-out of the Families First programme. We made the commitment in the 2011 manifesto to double the spending on the Flying Start programme for 0 to 3-year-olds. We recognised the imbalances of wealth and power. We invested in parenting strategies. We stressed the importance of parents talking to children. We had results which showed that children who had been through the Flying Start programme were more likely to be attentive and well-behaved. We also supported free school breakfasts, to ensure that young people had a good start to the day, with research showing the link between good nutrition and better learning outcomes. As young people progressed through the system, we maintained support for the poorest, keeping the EMAs (Educational Maintenance Allowances) for the poorest young people post-16, maintaining Assembly Learning Grants for the poorest students, and later introducing the Pupil Deprivation Grant, aimed at breaking the gap between poverty and poor attainment levels.

But we knew that issues of power and wealth extended to access to information also. If our ambition was that every school should be a good school – and aspiring to be great – then we had to ensure parents and governors had some sense of what made a good school, and what each school should be capable of achieving, just as their children needed access to information on career options and the qualifications necessary to achieve those. Parents, particularly in deprived communities, often with few educational qualifications themselves, were not always in the best position to challenge professionals over performance. Too often, it seemed to me, local authority school improvement staff colluded in complacency rather than challenging it on behalf of parents. That was why we needed buy-in from local authority political leaderships to drive up standards. The state has a responsibility to equalise access to power, including information on performance and what it means. There were almost too many statistics in our system, making judgement for non-professionals difficult. We needed a simple range of measures which told communities what we thought their schools were capable of achieving and what they were actually achieving, and how progress was being measured over time. Secondary banding was to give us that. The problem remains in our primary schools, but now at least local authorities have measures which are meaningful and challenging.

At the core of my philosophy then, was that we should demand high standards for all – we should never tolerate a system which condemned any young people to failure in Wales. We believed in the comprehensive system. We had far fewer middle-class withdrawals from the state system than in England. The English system, inherited by New Labour in 1997, had division built into it from the start.

If we believed in the comprehensive system, then we had a duty to make it work. We had to ensure successful schools with a balanced intake. That meant, by the way, tough decisions on closing poorly-performing schools that had been neglected for years by local authorities, since the evidence was that young people's performance overall would generally be raised by switching them to a school which had higher standards; it also meant tough decisions on catchment areas to ensure social balance in the intakes.

It wasn't only young people from deprived backgrounds who suffered from poorly performing schools. In 2011, David Cameron railed against coasting schools in the leafy suburbs of England. We had similar problems, and that was part of the reason why Monmouth's education system was put into special measures by Estyn in 2013. They may have been getting good results on an all-Wales measure, but on the basis of what they should have been achieving, they were well behind the pace. Banding, particularly in the first two years, made parents think about performance. When Radyr Comprehensive in Cardiff was placed in Band 3 in the first year of banding, that sent a short sharp shock though the system. It had good GCSE scores on paper but should have been performing much better.

I made it clear in the first weeks of January 2010 that I wanted 'a big emphasis on standards', saying that we faced challenges on attainment and that I was more concerned about standards than structures. Although education was devolved, we deliberately flagged up some planned Welsh Labour initiatives in the 2010 UK General Election manifesto. These included a National Literacy Programme aimed at 7 to11-year-olds, recognising that improved literacy rates would increase school attendance and help pupils engage more widely with their learning as they progressed through school, and committing ourselves to 'raise educational attainment' overall.

In our 2011 Assembly manifesto, we set out a clear standards agenda for the first time, going into detail on our plans for grading of schools on a national basis, our clear focus on literacy and numeracy for all, backed by nationwide tests, the production of statutory guidance on school improvement, and our high aspirations for education workforce development including the new Master's programme and the introduction of Teach First. In the 2007 Welsh Labour election manifesto, the word 'standards' did not feature. Attainment issues were raised only in the context of inequality in respect of gender or race or deprivation – there was no sense of this being a system-wide issue. In our 2003 manifesto, there had been talk of action that had been taken in the first Assembly term to reduce the gap between the best and worst-performing secondary schools and a vague promise to extend this to primary schools including a brief reference to 'driving up standards' through more literacy and numeracy schemes and by extending out-of-school and homework clubs. This gave the impression that attainment and standards issues could be tackled through isolated initiatives, not a national system-wide focus.

Perhaps I should say a word about my own educational experiences. I went to state schools in Wales and then England. I started in primary school in Barry Island on 3rd September 1962, just a few weeks after my fifth birthday. As an August baby, initially I must have been one of the oldest in my year, but after a couple of years a policy change led me to being bumped up a year and I ended as one of the youngest in the class. I enjoyed Barry Island. Taking the school bus daily from the Knap where we lived was something of an adventure. In 1967, after my father had been ill for two years, finally dying in September when I was just 10, my younger brother and I moved to Romilly School.

The next year my mother decided to move away from South Wales, to the town of Broadstone in Dorset where she had other relatives. Dorset was a selective county.

Instead of going to Barry Comprehensive, I found myself one of the few pupils in Romilly to have to sit the 11-plus. I sat the test on my own and remember the headmaster, Mr Morgan, discussing my reading preferences so that he could send a report to the powers that be. He teased me for still reading books by Enid Blyton. I passed the 11-plus and duly entered Poole Grammar, a single-sex school.

We arrived in Dorset a week or so before term started. Unlike other boys who had come up to the grammar school with friends from primary, I knew no one. Poole, I soon learned, was a very affluent area – Sandbanks and Branksome these days are where millionaires from football and entertainment often have homes. After my father's death, throughout my secondary schooling, I was entitled to free school meals. I can bear out the stigmatistion of this experience – what the Child Poverty Action Group in the 1980s called the 'Badge of Poverty'. As I told ITV Wales Political Editor Adrian Masters on the *Face to Face* programme in December 2012, there was some verbal bullying, when a couple of boys in the art class decided to start calling me, a few months after Enoch Powell's 'Rivers of Blood' speech, a 'Welsh wog'.

I also knew nothing of the local area, so the early geography lessons which assumed a knowledge of Poole Harbour – one of the largest natural harbours in the world – were alien to me. In my first term I finished twenty-eighth out of thirty. I remember one boy asking me how my mother had reacted when I told her the result. The next term I was twenty-sixth out of thirty. By the end of the year I had clawed my way up to fifteenth in the year. In the fourth form – what we would now describe as year 10 – pupils were streamed into five classes – 4 Arts, 4 Science, the middle stream 4 General, and 4 Design and 4 Engineering (if I remember these accurately). After my third year exams, the head teacher recorded in my annual report 'he has won his place in 4 Arts'. The school practised what we would now term 'early entry' for O levels, and I sat three in the fourth form in English, Maths and French, passing them all.

My brother, four years younger than me, did not pass the 11-plus, largely, I think, due to exam anxiety. I have hated selective education ever since. The 11-plus divides families, separates young people on the basis of an absurdly early judgement, and is an arbitrary test that people can fail for all sorts of reasons on the day. Confidence, as academics from the London School of Economics (LSE) have recently shown, is key to academic success.

I therefore agreed wholeheartedly when, in December 2013, the chief inspector of schools in England, Sir Michael Wilshaw, attacked the concept of state-funded grammar schools, saying that they served only the top 10 per cent of the population at the expense of the poorest, with a tiny percentage of their pupils on free school meals (FSM) – 3 per cent and were 'stuffed full of middle-class kids'. Indeed, Sutton Trust figures released in November 2013 put the figure at 2.7 per cent FSM against 17.5 per cent in other state schools in England.

My brother never got on with his secondary education, leaving school at sixteen. Subsequently he started an Open University course and won a place at Ruskin College with the assistance of his trade union. He then went to Cardiff University and got a First. Dr Geoff Andrews is now the author of several books, including one on Berlusconi's Italy, and another on the Slow Food Movement, a senior fellow at the Open University frequently appearing on the BBC and Sky or the Italian media to talk about Italian politics or on the Radio 4 *Food Programme* to discuss local food initiatives, or championing the rights of football fans through the organisation Philosophy Football.

My mother, Peggy, bravely retrained as a primary school teacher, in the 1970s, while bringing us up on her own, taking courses first at Poole Technical College then at Teacher Training College in Salisbury. We were and are very proud of what she achieved. Her work as a teacher took place mainly in Dorset, though later in Wales, including as a supply teacher in some of the most deprived schools in Cardiff.

I realise now that throughout my secondary schooling I was clinging on to the lost but remembered cultural moorings of Wales, cheering Welsh success at rugby, Glamorgan's county championship victory in 1969, and the occasional pop-chart appearances of a variety of Welsh icons, and sharing from afar the general disappointment of John Toshack's move to Liverpool from Cardiff in 1970. The road back to Wales commenced when I was accepted at University College, Cardiff, to study English: but I messed up my English A level despite gaining an S-Level in the same subject. Cardiff were prepared to take me to study History – but I knew a couple of people who were going to the University College of North Wales, Bangor, and I thought that I might have a chance of switching to English and History if I took up a place there through clearing. So it proved. Clearing worked for me, just as it works for thousands of other young people every year. I drove to Bangor with a friend who had also suffered over the 11-plus, Bill Gow. His twin brother had passed the exam and been a fellow pupil of mine from the first-form at Poole, while Bill only joined us in the sixth form. How many talents were wasted by that divisive 11-plus exam? We will never know.

Because of our circumstances, growing up in a one-parent family, I went to Bangor on a full grant. At Bangor, I came into contact with the Welsh language – not for the first time, but certainly for the first time on a meaningful basis – being heavily involved in protests against the college's bilingual policy in 1976, along with Vaughan Roderick, now Welsh Affairs Editor at BBC Wales, and the first woman President of UCNW Bangor Students' Union, Ann Beynon – now BT's Director for Wales, amongst her many different roles.

I became heavily involved in student politics, active in the students' union, a sabbatical officer in 1978 and elected in 1979 to the national executive of the National Union of Students in the UK, serving first as a part-time officer then as the sabbatical Vice President Welfare. My NUS contemporaries included former Equality and Human Rights Commission (EHRC) chair and TV producer Trevor Phillips, *The Times* columnist and former BBC Editor David Aaronovitch, current Labour MPs Fiona MacTaggart and Richard Burden, former Scottish First Minister Jack McConnell, current Pontypridd AM Mick Antoniw and current Conservative Minister Anna Soubry MP.

My first degree was in English and History, where I found that the joint honours structure failed adequately to synthesise the two disciplines. I became interested in the agenda of cultural studies and people's history, and the work of cultural critics such as Raymond Williams and historians like E.P. Thompson and Christopher Hill. I then found a Master's course at Sussex University, with modules based on Raymond Williams' cultural *Keywords*, and began there in the autumn of 1979, leaving Wales for the second time not long after the referendum defeat and Mrs Thatcher's election victory. At the same time I had started to discover a generation of iconoclastic Welsh historians, to a degree grouped around the journal *Llafur*, whose writings had helped me understand what it was to be Welsh in the late twentieth-century, and whose rooted communitarian socialist philosophy had no truck with the vacuous romantic libertarian individualism so prevalent on the British left in the 1980s and 1990s. One of those historians, whom I had already 'read' with great enthusiasm and personal recognition, Dai Smith, was to pop up in the BBC at the other end of the M4 while I was getting my intellectual grounding in public service reform at the Corporation's headquarters in London in the early 1990s.

State education served me well. I am determined it should serve all our young people well.

One of the things that I came to find most irritating when I became education minister was how often the media sought to personalise the politics of education, trying to force me into criticisms of my predecessors. I defended them and their achievements throughout. This is part of the modern media's attempt to simplify every policy in terms of personality. The truth is that ministers face different challenges at different times. They have to conduct policies in the context of collective responsibility. They are bound by legislation, by the funding available, by the arithmetic of seats in the Assembly, by party policy, by Cabinet agreement. In terms of our education policies between 1999 and 2009, when I took over, and the period until my departure in 2013, there were far more continuities in policy terms than fractures – not least, for example, in terms of policy towards higher education. It is these fractures or revisions which interest the media, not the continuities. In general, I believe individuals as ministers can make a difference. But context, often, is all.

Consider this: In Rosemary Butler's year as Minister for pre-16 education, the Assembly was a corporate body barely sure of its own powers. During Jane Davidson's entire period as Education Minister, while education responsibilities in many areas were devolved, primary law-making powers of the kind we obtained in stages under the 2006 Government of Wales Act did not exist, and much of education was, for most of Jane's period, under the direction of non-governmental public bodies or quangos, such as the curriculum and assessment quango, ACCAC, and the education and training quango, ELWA – and she had to put up with the corporate body model of the Assembly throughout her entire time as Education Minister, as well as a coalition with the Lib-Dems from 2000-2003 and a minority Labour government after 2005. Her successor, Jane Hutt, and her Deputy Minister John Griffiths, had to operate under the One Wales coalition government with the complicated model of obtaining authorisation to legislate in new fields by first getting a Legislative Competence Order approved through the Assembly and through Parliament, and then passing a Measure through the Assembly. That was the model in operation when I became Education Minister, and we only gained the power to legislate in all areas of the 2006 Act after the March 2011 referendum – in practice, after the May 2011 Assembly election. The Education (Wales) Measure was the final Measure under the pre-referendum system. The School Standards and Organisation Act 2013 was Wales's first Education Act.

Even then, policy autonomy can be circumscribed, as we shall see. The interpretation of European law by the Office of National Statistics had implications for our desired policy objectives on further education governance; the close integration of our higher education system with that of England, based on the choices of students from Wales and England, limited the range of realistic policy options open to us after the UK government decided to raise tuition fees in England; and the sharing of qualifications with England and Northern Ireland meant difficult negotiations with regulators in those jurisdictions, particularly with Ofqual in England after 2010.

After the leadership election, Carwyn had been working on his cabinet appointments for a few days with former Welsh Government Special Adviser Jane Runeckles. Jane had privately told Carwyn a year or so before that if he wanted to be elected First Minister, then he needed me as his campaign manager. We had met for lunch to discuss Carwyn's chances. Knowing the complexity of the electoral college for the leadership, he needed broad support. 'Can he get any backing from the unions?' I asked. 'UNISON will back him', Jane replied confidently. So it proved.

Ministerial appointments generally take place in the First Minister's office on the first floor of the Welsh Government offices in Cathays Park – the old CP1 building, as it is known internally. It was there that Rhodri Morgan had asked me to become Deputy Minister for Social Justice and Public Service Delivery in 2007 – though subsequently when the One Wales coalition was formed, my appointment as Deputy Minister for Regeneration was made by telephone, as I was in the Rhondda at the time. A number of us were in touch when we found out we had been asked to go and see the First Minister on Thursday 10th December. Carl Sargeant, Lesley Griffiths and I met in the Hilton Hotel, just down the road from Cathays Park. When my turn came to see him, Carwyn asked me, with Jane Runeckles in attendance, to take on the role of Minister for Children, Education and Lifelong Learning. Huw Lewis was to be my deputy, with responsibility for Children specifically. I soon learned Carl was taking over Local Government, and Lesley would be Deputy Minister for Science and Skills. The news was released at around 4 p.m. and a Ministerial photocall followed not long after.

Cabinet Ministers are supported by a Private Office, headed normally by a Senior Private Secretary. Mine was Helen Childs, who had been working in the same capacity for Jane Hutt, and knew the department well. She had also in the past worked for Carwyn when he was Environment Minister. The team under Helen included two further Private Secretaries, one of whom supported Huw, a Diary Secretary and two Assistant Diary Secretaries, again one supporting Huw. I asked that Rhian Atkinson, who had been my Private Secretary when I was Deputy Minister for Regeneration, join Helen's team, as she was accustomed to working with me.

My first priority was to get a grip on the diary. I realised that I would be taking over meetings and events previously scheduled not just for Jane Hutt, but also for John Griffiths who had been Deputy Minister for Skills. I went through the diary with Helen and Rhian late that afternoon because I wanted to get a strong hold on the issues facing the department at the outset. In his entertaining book *How to be a Minister*, Gerald Kaufman wrote: 'He who controls the minister's diary controls his life. So it had better be you.' Out went a long list of forward engagements that I scrapped as I determined to keep a focus on the big picture.

Special advisers, technically *temporary* civil servants exempt from certain requirements of the civil service code – with a brief to undertake political work – finished in their posts on the resignation of a First Minister. A number had been renewed for an initial three months and the special adviser supporting me was Ian Butler, a professor at Bath University, who worked part-time. That evening he sent me through some suggestions on what he thought I should discuss with the Director General of the department the next day. I had a long list of my own. Ian's issues included the School Effectiveness Framework, which he saw as key to raising standards (I was glad to see that word), school closures and funding, the funding of the Foundation Phase, childcare, the national bursary framework for students, youth service funding and the children's plan. My priorities were Carwyn Jones's manifesto commitments, particularly funding, literacy and the department's policy and delivery capacity. We had run Carwyn's campaign on a series of themes headed '*Time to…*,' culminating in *Time to Lead*. Now, it was Time to Deliver.

Setting the Direction

I arrived at my fifth floor office in Ty Hywel, Cardiff Bay on Friday December 11th with a firm view of the challenges. First, establishing a clear direction and priorities for the department itself; making a start on delivering Carwyn's funding commitment; a strong drive forward on the new higher education strategy; starting to examine the delivery of education through the twenty two local education authorities; and finally, beginning to communicate the new focus for the department to all those working in the education system in Wales, and to the wider Welsh public.

Ministers need to be able to lead on policy, and to do that they need to have a sound view of their priorities, a close eye on their budgets, clear understanding of the legal boundaries to their powers, a real overview of the issues likely to come at them from within the department and good intelligence on what is happening within the sector, both in Wales and at a UK level. Ministers also need to know how to turn policy into delivery. That requires a sound grasp of forward planning, setting clear timescales and demanding precise critical paths from officials as to when a policy announcement will actually come into force, and clarity on the processes and work-streams and key stages involved in delivering that. Take tuition fees as an example – the policy, announced at the end of November 2010, only began to benefit the first cohort of Welsh students in the autumn of 2012. The policy I announced on school closures in June 2010 was not completed until the passage of the School Standards and Organisation Act in early 2013.

I commissioned a great deal of reading material in my first few days and my in tray was soon filled with lilac MB (Ministerial

Briefing) folders, light green SFs (Submission Folders) and, new to me, as I hadn't had legislation to deal with as a Deputy Minister, orange LFs (Legislative Folders). Dark green correspondence folders filled up rapidly and I made myself unpopular with some officials when I complained about grammar, syntax and basic literacy issues in my correspondence. But if the Education Minister didn't complain about the written standard of draft correspondence, then who would? I made Huw Lewis laugh when I described myself in ironic terms as 'the guardian of the nation's literacy'.

My first meeting with the Director General of the department, David Hawker, would, I knew, set the tone. David had been Assistant Chief Executive of the Qualifications and Curriculum Authority, and before that the School Curriculum and Assessment Authority, from 1995-1999. Immediately prior to joining the civil service, David was Deputy chief executive and Director of Children's Services at Westminster City Council (2007-2008) and Director of Children's Services in Brighton & Hove (2001-7), where he started as Director of Education in 1999. He was a former modern languages teacher. He ran through the issues that were on his agenda, including forthcoming legislative and funding issues. He was one of a group of new Director Generals appointed by the then Permanent Secretary, Gill Morgan.

Having heard him out, I made it clear that I felt there was a real lack of urgency in the department. It was dysfunctional and not operating in a strategic fashion. I felt that there were too many empires within it, and insufficient focus on One Wales and Ministerial priorities. I thought some of the papers I had seen going to Cabinet Committees were weak. I wanted a moratorium on strategies and non-statutory consultations. I requested a line-by-line examination of the department's budget, and set up a meeting for the following Monday to go through budgets with David and his senior directors, with the objective of identifying £100 million of savings which could be redeployed to key priorities, not least to free up funds for a stronger literacy programme. Privately I didn't expect them to find £100 million, but setting a target would force everyone to look forensically at what was feasible. This forward commitments review uncovered some £88 million of uncommitted spend in the 2010-11 financial year, including £25 million capital. I made it clear that I was open to alternative sources of funding for school-building, and for further and higher education capital projects. I said I did not rule out the central financing of schools, and commissioned some policy work on that.

I also told David that I would be establishing a monthly policy board to examine thorny issues. The first item to be tackled would be policy on school closures, and I would expect all policy leads to attend. I wanted to ensure all key departmental policy leads shared in the collective challenges facing the department, to break down what I was already learning was something of a silo mentality.

I was determined that the department would improve its implementation. I worried that it suffered from the same disease that Michael Barber had identified in Whitehall: 'When asked for a plan, Whitehall's traditional response is to write some thoughtful prose, and if it really wants to impress the recipient, to enclose the prose in a glossy cover.'

My mantra for the department in that first year – soon to be obvious to all from the whiteboard in my office – was 'Better implementation; fewer initiatives; keep it simple'. As I said in interviews and articles in my first few weeks, 'Wales is a small country. I'm sure we can be simpler and smarter in the way we make things happen in education'. I told David that I wanted to reduce the number of consultations, reduce the paperwork going out to schools, and stop the production of what were usually called strategies – though too often were simply aspirational policy statements. I asked how many publications to schools were planned between December and June, and from then until the May 2011 election. The answer that came back to me was '186, minister, 93 before June'. I ordered a 50 per cent reduction. Arbitrary, I know, but sometimes you simply have to make a clear decision to stop people wasting time haggling.

Meetings had been arranged with the divisional directors in the department: Chris Tweedale, who led on children, schools and young people, a cheerful, bearded northerner, ex-head teacher and geography teacher; Lynne Hamilton, highly competent Scotswoman, full of insight, who headed the department's finance, corporate planning and student finance departments; Dennis Gunning, director of SHELL (Skills, Higher Education and Lifelong Learning) another Scot, wiry, pragmatic and with vast experience of post-16 education in the UK and internationally. Sadly, I never got to meet Mike Clancy, who headed the Curriculum division, husband of the Assembly Commission's chief executive Claire Clancy, as he was already seriously ill and tragically died in February 2010.

It was obvious from the beginning that Chris Tweedale enjoyed working around politicians and knew the value of what, in US Presidential politics, is called 'face time' with them. Chris had been seconded to work with the Department for Education in London and had also served time in the delivery unit run by Michael Barber. I had already begun to explore the possibility of getting Michael Barber in to run a seminar on priority-setting for my senior officials. I had read and enjoyed his book *Instruction to Deliver* on his time running the Prime Minister's Delivery Unit. The ebullient Dr Tim Williams, who had served me as specialist adviser on regeneration, had worked with Michael when they were both NUT staffers, and again when Tim was special adviser to David Miliband, and had already opened up lines of communication for me. Tim – *Dr. No* in the 1997 Welsh referendum campaign – had become a convert to devolution by the time of the 2011 referendum and was a constant source of rewarding, entertaining and creative ideas in the regeneration field and later in education too.

My first discussion of substance was with Lynne Hamilton in Cathays Park. As I walked into CP2, the more modern end of the Welsh Government Cathays Park complex, I ran into a mid-ranking civil servant whom I knew from another government department. He told me the message had got out clearly that the times were changing, expectations were different and there was no question who was setting the agenda for the department. Early in January 2010, Dennis Gunning told me candidly that the department needed time to adjust to my style. 'You must let us get used to your approach. It's very different. I'm not saying that's bad, but it is very different,' he told me. I told officials 'My biggest weakness is my impatience. But my impatience is also my biggest strength.' It gets things done.

I have always hated bureaucracy. My background before coming into elected politics in Wales in 2003 had principally been in charities focused on campaigning and in small businesses providing direct and immediate services to clients. Even during my time at the BBC, I had the privilege of running a small unit which was able to operate in guerrilla style to put across the BBC's corporate policies to Westminster and Brussels. Within bureaucracies – and you will see this all the time in Welsh local government, the land of little empires – too often you find process stifling creativity, slowing down decisions, with power trips preventing effective collaboration and innovation. I was determined the Education Department would work speedily, effectively and openly.

Lynne Hamilton came to see me in the spare meeting room allocated at the time to Ministers just down the corridor in CP1 from the First Minister's office. She had already heard that alternative sources of finance could now be considered for school buildings, and that I was looking for serious savings in departmental budgets. She warned me that would be difficult to do, as the department was already carrying 'pressures' – civil service-speak for unfunded costs – which would need to be met, not least in the student finance area, which of course was largely demand-led. I discussed with her a programme for line-by-line review of budgets, going through the full detail and getting to understand precisely how much was being spent on each item. A series of meetings were held before Christmas which made it crystal clear to me that not all senior officials had a tight grip on every expenditure heading in their divisions. If they didn't know what the money was being spent on, I mused, how could I be confident it was being used for the right purposes. I couldn't see how they could demonstrate that budgets were aligned with One Wales or Ministerial priorities. There were to be further budget meetings, one of them stormy and short, over the next few months.

There were initially ministerial boundary issues to resolve – Lesley Griffiths as deputy minister for Science and Skills, was responsible to Deputy First Minister Ieuan Wyn Jones. We had to work out quickly a modus operandi which gave us both clarity over our areas of responsibility. That was never a problem for Lesley and myself, but we were wary in case our Plaid Cymru coalition partners wanted to re-direct the work we had started to implement.

I was greatly relieved that Carl Sargeant had responsibility for Local Government. Carl had a similar view to me about local government performance. Early in 2010 he gave a clear message to the Welsh Local Government Association's Chief Executive, Steve Thomas – local authorities needed to demonstrate more actively that they were capable of working together, or they would face re-organisation. He had given out similar messages in early meetings with local government chief executives. He had also warned his own officials that work on the Local Government Agreements had been too slow.

Local authorities were critical to delivery of education. Less than a week into the job, I had to produce my first *Western Mail* column as Education Minister. I used the column to set out the core educational messages of Carwyn Jones's manifesto, which I described as putting 'flesh on the bones' of the One Wales programme for government. I also repeated some of the internal messages I had given the department:

> I have already made it clear to my officials that I want to see fewer strategies – and I want to reduce the burden of paperwork as well. The strategy and consultation development industry doesn't need any more government

> subsidies. I don't need more glossy documents landing with a thud on my desk. Nor does anyone else in education.

This was also an opportunity to send a signal to local government: 'Nobody would have invented 22 Education Authorities if we already had a National Assembly for Wales'. I was even blunter in my first interview with the *Western Mail* a month later, saying 'nobody sensible would have invented 22 local education authorities. John Redwood did.' This was an issue to which we would return.

During Carwyn's campaign I had begun privately to formulate some of the issues which I felt were missing from the Welsh Assembly Government's education agenda. Viv Thomas, a Carwyn supporter from Neath, had been helpful in this. Viv was a former secondary head teacher and had also served as Corporate Director for Education, Leisure and Lifelong Learning at Neath Port Talbot County Borough Council. Neath Port Talbot (NPT) was widely recognised as one of the best-performing local education authorities in Wales. Viv had regularly berated me whenever we had met about the fact that we only had a small number of local education authorities in Wales classed as good by the Welsh education inspectorate, Estyn.

One of Viv's early contributions to Carwyn's campaign identified the need to disseminate the good practice that already existed in parts of Wales; the need for local authorities to be held to account for performance; the need for clarity between the different delivery mechanisms of local education authorities, 14-19 consortia, and the regional forums looking after the school effectiveness programme; clarity and transparency on funding of schools; and the need to ensure effective provision through the medium of Welsh. Viv stressed, 'the experience from NPT shows that it's not the amount of money/resources that you have that's really important but the effective and efficient use that you make of your resources, financial and human.'

In my first term in the Assembly, I had served on the Education and Lifelong Learning Committee from 2003 until early 2005. I had pretty much hated it. This was the Assembly under the old corporate body model. It was not really a scrutiny committee, but broadly speaking a policy committee, with the minister as a member. The committee and its agenda seemed to me to be suffering from a soggy consensus owing more to libertarian values of choice and prizes for all, than quality and standards. It was certainly a world away from the traditional pride, evident in valleys communities, about educational achievement. The traditions of working-class education in Wales – whether of the WEA or Central Labour College varieties – would have tested that soggy consensus and found it wanting.

It also seemed a world away from the sharp focus on standards which Labour governments in London had introduced, notably under David Blunkett, as Tony Blair's first Secretary of State for Education and Employment. I had met Blunkett only briefly, when he addressed the Rhondda Labour Party annual dinner shortly after I was selected as their Assembly candidate in 2002. But his diaries make clear his commitment to the standards agenda in education, as did his actions at the time. In his book *Instruction to Deliver*, Michael Barber states very clearly David Blunkett's sense of moral purpose in education: 'With his roots in working-class Sheffield, he understood this challenge viscerally. All around him he saw that children were being betrayed by an education system characterized by low expectations and a refusal to accept any definition of what was best practice in teaching.'

The committee also had an obsession with 'strategies'. As I wrote in my first *Western Mail* column:

> I felt at first I had wandered into an alien world with its own language – without the benefit of *Doctor Who*'s universal translator machine. It was a lifelong learning experience all of its own, with a strategy for this and a strategy for that.

I'm afraid I share Andrew Adonis's view on this: 'strategy is too often an excuse for higher waffle'.

The One Wales Government had an education agenda, based around the proposals in the Labour and Plaid Cymru manifestos. There were many important and worthwhile ideas. It was strong on Welsh-medium education from school to higher education. It sought a fairer approach to school funding across Wales, and a new capital building programme for schools. The proposals included items adapted from the Plaid Cymru manifesto, such as a pilot programme for laptops for pupils, and from the Labour manifesto, such as legislation on 14 to 19 provision. There were specific commitments in respect of pupil disengagement, Physical Education in schools and a radical reduction in class sizes from 3 to 7 years, in respect of the Foundation Phase. The document also looked ahead to potential changes in higher education tuition fees if the cap on student fees was lifted, promising that the government would do what it could to mitigate this for Welsh-domiciled students. The document contained a specific promise to 'meet the challenge of improving the level of qualifications attained by our children, young people, and adults too'.

Carwyn's election manifesto for the Welsh Labour leadership had had to be formulated in the context of Carwyn himself being a member of the One Wales Government. The most fundamental education proposal in Carwyn's manifesto was the funding commitment but there was a range of other educational policies outlined there too.

So there was a full agenda, with an Assembly election less than eighteen months away. There wasn't a blank slate. A new higher education strategy had just been launched. A review of careers was underway. Legislation was already in train in one or two areas such as children's rights and school governance. A UK General Election was on the horizon. How quickly could we get movement on Carwyn's key agenda items? Would it be possible to shape a distinctive Welsh Labour agenda within the context of the One Wales government?

What I really wanted to focus on, however, was educational standards. I had been impressed with the early focus of the UK Labour government after 1997 in its drive to raise standards. I was less keen on what had been done subsequently with the shift to structures and the development of academies. I told the *Western Mail* in my first interview:

> I will be putting a big emphasis on standards... I think the issue for us is, are there challenges on attainment? Yes, there are. Can we do more in that area, in the area of performance? I think we can. I'm someone who's more concerned about standards than I am about structures, on the whole.

Developing an effective programme on school improvement required more consensus than I felt we had at that time, given the tone of One Wales, the history of education policy development in Wales since devolution, and the culture within the Welsh education system. I certainly felt we had to challenge three obvious libertarian myths that floated around our system:

- that we should simply let children develop at the pace they decided
- that if we simply expanded learner choice, everyone would want to learn
- that we should let teachers teach as they saw fit

Radical cultural change was necessary, in my view. That could not be done overnight, but I knew who could help us start to shape the agenda.

Before he had been head of the delivery unit in 10 Downing Street under Tony Blair, Sir Michael Barber was head of the standards and effectiveness unit in the Department of Education under David Blunkett. The unit was key in ensuring strategic delivery of the department's goals throughout the education system in England and driving the focus on standards. Michael set out clearly in *Instruction to Deliver* how their public service reform agenda was driven forward. Michael starkly expressed what he called the modern politician's dilemma: 'You have to have a long-term strategy but unless it delivers short-term results no one will believe you.' Michael rightly also identified that in terms of the public services, four years is a *very* short period to bring about and demonstrate significant reform. Drawing on the change management specialist John Kotter, whom I had personally had the privilege of hearing in the mid-1990s when I worked in the BBC in London during that immense period of change under John Birt, Michael set out the principles for driving successful change programmes in public service delivery, beginning with the need to establish a sense of urgency and to build a coalition to guide change.

Political life, especially life in a coalition government, is not quite so straightforward as implementing change in a corporate body, but there is a lot to be gained from thinking through this process. In his book, Michael Barber says that reform needs not more initiatives, but 'relentless implementation'. He rightly identifies that:

> Stubborn persistence, relentless monotony, attention to detail and glorying in routine are vastly underestimated in the literature on government and indeed political history.

The former *Sunday Telegraph* editor, Charles Moore, recognised that this focus bypasses most journalists. In an article early in 2010 he said:

> We want fireworks, war-cries, blood on the decks. We are bored by strategy, consistency, plugging on. But we don't have to fight elections, let alone govern the country.

In the middle of January 2010, barely a month after I had become minister, we arranged a seminar with Michael, myself, Huw Lewis and our senior officials, to identify a consensus across the department on our core challenges. I had an early telephone chat with Michael on a snowy day in the first week of January to prepare the ground for the seminar, which we agreed would focus on developing the levers for change. I was delighted that we had been able to get him to come down to Cardiff. Huw told me it was 'a real coup'.

I gave a presentation at the seminar on how I saw the first four weeks in the role, looking at strengths, weaknesses, opportunities and threats. In terms of strengths, I saw some excellent work and knew that strong and unique policies had been developed in a number of areas – the Foundation Phase, the Welsh Bac, the ProAct scheme to help companies retain and train staff in the recession, the student finance policy, Flying Start and many others. I knew there were good people, passionate and committed about education. But on the downside, I said I thought that the department lacked focus, lacked a sense of priority and a sense of urgency. It needed clear leadership and a clear sense of direction, with an absolute focus on delivery. I quoted from Professor Sir Adrian Webb's report on Further Education, *Promise and Performance*, where he had said in 2007 that in its early days, the new devolved government had had to develop the capacity for policy-making, and now it needed a capacity for delivery. I said that I felt that it was a sprawling department, not properly integrated since the 2006 mergers with the different quangos, amongst them ELWA and ACCAC. I said that I thought that the alignment of internal departmental divisions and strategies was not always clear, and that budgetary alignments did not always follow One Wales or ministerial priorities. I thought that there were too many initiatives, strategies, and policies. I pointed out that the department seemed to lack a corporate memory – there were targets set in legacy documents like *The Learning Country* which were due for fulfilment in 2010, but no one had volunteered these when I took office – I'd had to ferret them out myself. It was not clear who owned these policy commitments and who was monitoring their success or failure.

Beyond this, I felt that there was too much reliance on consensus in policy-making, rather than clear decisions.

I was concerned about what I called the quango mentality of sweetheart deals with local authorities. I also felt that people in the system saw the education department budget as a kind of Christmas tree with presents for everyone, and that had to stop.

In terms of opportunities, I cited the First Minister's commitment to an additional 1 per cent spending, a new ministerial team with an education minister impatient for results, with a strong relationship with a local government minister also focused on delivery. The department's transformation agenda I felt was genuinely challenging to local authorities. The review of administration costs we were shortly to announce was another opportunity. Partners in the sector were looking for leadership. If we could free up funds through the forward commitments review I had initiated, then we would have scope for creative change.

However, there were threats – including an impatient new minister. Could we get the systems of accountability for delivery right? Could we get enough money to the frontline? UK budget priorities could affect us, and we had short-term budget challenges of our own, with demand-led budgets such as student grants strangling our own current spending. Our own targets might distort outcomes, and it might be that our partners only wanted the kind of leadership that suited them.

Michael's presentation to us began by stressing that the future of Wales lay in the talent of its people. In words that echo the later OECD report in 2014, he said we should be benchmarking ourselves not so much against England but against our history, against the best in the world, against similar systems, developing bench-marking within our own system, and against organisations which had similar processes. He noted that performance in Wales had improved over time, but that there were some significant problems when we looked at PISA data, GCSE performance against regions of England with similar socio-economic challenges, the number of young people who were not in education, employment or training, variance within schools and between schools in Wales was particularly high, social class variability was greater than it should be, and boys' performance was significantly worse than that of girls. But contrary to what was often said, the money invested in education in Wales was at an all-time high and was growing faster than in many OECD countries, whatever the comparison with England.

Michael identified our key challenge as making rapid improvements in a time of austerity budgets. He urged us to set clear goals, offering the comparison of Ontario, which had set clear goals of improving literacy and numeracy, increasing high school graduation rates, and building confidence in the school system. To achieve high performance, Wales needed to set the right balance of support and challenge. We needed to learn from the best systems, setting clear standards with transparency of data, and accountability, programmes focused on every child, strengthening workforce development and attainment, particularly school leadership, with clear leadership within the system, appropriately functioning central and local government agencies, and budgets and responsibilities devolved as far as possible to school level.

It was particularly important, Michael felt, to ensure that the system was functioning well. That meant establishing clear priorities, defining what success would look like, strengthening the delivery chain, creating routines that drove delivery, reviewing the system's capacity to deliver, and tackling problems rigorously as they arose. We needed to challenge complacency and drive cultural change. Michael encouraged us to set goals for Wales five and fifteen years out. In five years, we wanted to see improved PISA performance, addressing the gender gap, reducing within school variation and starting to close the gap with England, improving literacy and numeracy, and developing more reliable measurement systems at eleven. In fifteen years, we wanted to be demonstrably world-class, with 95 per cent of young people achieving Level 3 qualifications, far fewer young people not in education, employment or training, with a stronger and more highly skilled education workforce, and increased aspirations overall.

At the seminar, we collectively identified the opportunities and challenges we faced. We should use the challenge of austerity to refocus priorities. The School Effectiveness Framework needed a greater focus on implementation and delivery. We needed better data.

We were very clear about the challenges. There had been a historical unwillingness to confront difficult issues, and the search for a consensus often added to that. There were also too many policies and targets; and leadership was blurred through the twenty two local education authorities. The delivery chain was lengthy and lethargic and resources were being stripped out along the way. There were too many silos – not only in the education department, but often in local authorities and schools, setting different priorities that didn't contribute to system-wide goals. There were challenges in the analysis and utilisation of data throughout the system. It took time to change legislation and move from policy to implementation. There were clearly processes and practices we needed to stop – and we needed to be very clear that we would no longer tolerate poor performance.

After the seminar, Michael sent me a note which summarised what he felt were the three core areas I needed to focus on as Minister:

1 **Developing and communicating your vision for the future.** This should be something which provides clarity to all stakeholders and forms the core of all initiatives and communications going forward.

2 **Prioritising a few core themes and delivering results** – as per above, this is likely to focus on initiatives to improve literacy, reducing variance in performance within schools and cutting administrative budgets. Work out the delivery chain for each initiative and focus time and energy on ensuring this handful of high priorities are moving at pace.

3 **Setting goals and measuring yourselves against international peers** – be clear internally and externally how you will measure success over the coming years and how various aspects of policy will contribute towards this.

Michael ended by saying 'One of the big questions is **"What will you do in the short term to signal this new direction?"** You have a unique opportunity to set a bold new direction for education in Wales. You probably won't need me to encourage you to be bold in your plans and your communication of them!'

Michael's seminar energised senior officials in the department to think across divisional boundaries and to be clear about goals. We began work on his proposals. I had already begun to communicate the new approach in articles in the Welsh and educational press but I considered direct communications with the profession to be critical. As Andrew Adonis says, you need to lead and explain, lead and explain. The right occasion was needed to take the agenda forward – and if we were to develop a successful coalition for change, then we needed to demonstrate that we were delivering on what Carwyn had promised. That meant that while we worked on refining the standards agenda, we needed also to be making good on the funding pledge. That work needed to start now.

Leading Change

The department I led, of course, had to be at the centre of our plans for school improvement. The Canadian educationalist Michael Fullan, whom I met early in 2010, formulated the theory of 'tri-level reform' which underpinned the School Effectiveness Framework I inherited. I disliked the term 'tri-level reform', as I disliked most phrases redolent of technocracy. But essentially Michael was talking about the need for reform across the system – in central government; in the 'middle tier' of the system – usually local government; and at the level of the school. I was certainly clear that we did have challenges in our system at all three levels – at the centre, in my own department and in the education inspectorate; in local government; and in schools.

I was broadly pleased at the development of the department after 2010, thanks principally to the new director general Emyr Roberts and his successor from 2013, Owen Evans. After two years driving reform in the department, Emyr left to be the first chief executive of Natural Resources Wales in the autumn of 2012. He told staff that those two years had been the most stimulating of his career so far. By the time Emyr left, the staff surveys showed that the department was achieving the highest scores within the Welsh Government for staff satisfaction and this continued under Owen. We had successfully built capacity within the department – a key task identified for central government by Michael Fullan, who says 'it takes capacity to lead capacity'.

There was one general problem affecting the approach of the department when I arrived which related to the post-Welsh Office culture of the Welsh civil service. The Permanent Secretary was the head of the civil service in Wales, and the civil service director generals who worked to her, not in all cases but in some, saw themselves as accountable to her, rather than to ministers. With the appointment of the new Permanent Secretary Derek Jones in 2012, there was also much greater clarity about what the civil service was there to do, even down to the branding on civil service computer screens, that the civil service was 'delivering for ministers'. Derek immediately began work on trimming the senior civil service structure while finding additional resources to support ministers in delivering their priorities. That was a relief, and a change from previous practice. I had raised early on why it was that we didn't get the financial benefit in our department from reductions in civil service staffing in our departments which we could transfer to the front line – instead, savings on civil service staffing remained under the control of the Permanent Secretary.

David Hawker had left us in the summer of 2010 to head a new initiative for the Department for Education in London, which allowed him to be closer to his family after his wife had suffered ill health. Emyr Roberts took on the role, initially in addition to being director general of the department for local government and communities.

In my February 2011 speech, *Teaching makes a difference*, which set out the 20-point plan for school reform, I was very critical of how my own department had performed historically. I said my impression as a minister was of a department that had been culturally and geographically fragmented without a clear focus. Several quangos had merged with it in 2006. I did not know if those mergers were ever culturally integrated. I did know that a single departmental culture had yet to emerge. There had been a lack of alignment of performance measurement, including qualifications in particular. Implementation of policy had been weak. Historically civil servants had been strong on policy design, but less good at policy implementation and embedding. However, I said that under Dr Emyr Roberts' leadership, a clear focus and sense of direction was developing. I had made it clear that I expected the focus of the department to be one which seeks to raise standards of performance for all, so that all can reach their potential. Performance would be our driver. All other matters – curriculum, qualifications, professional development, governor support, capital programmes, would be subservient to that.

Emyr Roberts had great civil service experience and understood the need to work closely with his departmental minister to ensure that the minister's agenda was delivered and departmental priorities were aligned with those of ministers and the government's legislative programme. Emyr put in place a more logical departmental structure that gave clarity to external stakeholders as to how policy, funding and delivery were integrated, and took care to explain those changes to the outside world. The overall size of the department reduced from 773 to 640 people. It was, I said in June 2011, 'a leaner department with a sharper focus.'

Speaking to our *Raising our Sights* event in March 2013, Michael Barber recalled that when he started working for the Prime Minister, in 2001, plans 'tended to be thought of as a kind of beautifully-written essay with a glossy cover that then gets ignored after it's published'. What was needed, he said, were plans 'with marmalade on the corners and coffee stains that got used daily and were used to plan the changes and help you anticipate whether you were on track or not'. I said early on that one of the key parts of my mantra was 'better implementation'. As Michael said 'one of the most common mistakes that politicians around the world make is this… they think it's 90 per cent getting the policy right and then implementation takes care of itself. Actually, I think it's pretty much the reverse.'

In my first months, I was very concerned that I wasn't getting the right kind of guidance on the pressures we faced, and that the department was not approaching the overall agenda strategically, with minor and inconsequential issues too often coming forward to me. There seemed to be no sensible management of papers to go to Cabinet or Cabinet committees, and insufficient forward thinking about what was to be taken for plenary discussion in the Assembly. There was also clearly a problem of under-staffing in some highly visible areas – school closure assessments, youth unemployment and 14 to 19 education amongst them. In the area of school improvement, there was a real capacity issue. I withdrew a number of papers in my early months from the cabinet Children and Young People's Committee which I chaired. Some were too technical and jargon-ridden – others I felt simply weren't rigorous enough. I had to ask constantly in my first three months for a reduction in the number of strategy and consultation documents due to issue. Meanwhile, analyses I requested of critical issues such as the school funding gap with England took far longer than they should have done.

My first special adviser, Ian Butler, who was a professor of social policy at Bath University, had a clear view of how things should work and the facility to express this in civil service language when it was needed. We discussed what we really wanted in terms of the leadership, management and organisation of the department. We wanted to see – in early 2010 – amongst other things:

- Budgets and staffing aligned with One Wales and Ministerial priorities
- A clear line of sight for ministers and external stakeholders between the government's priorities and the work of those providing services to learners in Wales
- Administrative efficiencies to free up resources for the front line
- A better balance between staff with an outward-facing role and those who managed the internal business of the department
- Simplification of delivery and better accountability of external partners responsible for delivery

It was obvious both to us and to external stakeholders at that time that there were weaknesses, including the continuation of a silo mentality in which civil servants in particular areas did not understand the linkages between their areas of responsibility and wider departmental goals and objectives. Ian and I spent some time in the first half of 2010 working on these issues with the Director General and his senior team and the Permanent Secretary. We set out in clear terms what we expected the director general and department to deliver, including regular updates on staffing levels which presented a risk; assurances on quality of information coming through to ministers; and higher quality and more timely support for ministerial speeches and statements. We made it clear that we wanted the department to understand that its objectives were determined by ministerial and One Wales priorities and its job was to deliver for ministers. By the time Matt Greenough replaced Ian Butler as my special adviser after the 2011 election, most of the key departmental issues had been gripped. Matt's superb political and communication skills allowed him to help me shape the broader communication of our policy as we began the process of minority government and the implementation of our manifesto. While our press operation had always been immensely sharp and professional, our overall marketing required attention, and Emyr attended to that.

One of the things that did most to break down the silo mentality that still prevailed was the creation of the monthly Policy Board, where as well as assessing tricky areas of policy, we also looked at departmental performance, including financial performance. Our school closure policy was the first issue gripped at the first Policy Board meeting in January 2010, leading to a Ministerial Statement in June that year and the final elements implemented in the School Standards and Organisation Act of 2013. The meetings also looked at key initiatives such as the review of the cost of administering the education system, and the work-streams generated by that, the review of the structure of delivery of education, and the 20-point plan, assessing progress in delivering against these issues against a traffic-light grading system of red, amber or green. Officials who would not otherwise have had input or understanding of areas of work outside their immediate division now had a wider perspective on the issues facing the department as a whole. I subsequently renamed the Policy Board as the Policy and Delivery Board.

One issue which specifically benefitted from the ability to take a wider departmental perspective was our approach to young people in danger of finding themselves not in education, employment or training. When I arrived in the department I felt that this issue was only being tackled as people approached the age of sixteen or beyond, when in fact many of the challenges could be identified earlier. Thus began an approach of bringing together a series of officials from different divisions to identify better how we could ensure intervention at an earlier age prevented young people ending up out of education, employment or training, rather than simply picking up the pieces through a range of programmes post-16. This is obviously a long-term approach but one which I believe will ultimately pay off.

We tracked the implementation of the 20-point plan carefully, and I reviewed progress every month at the Policy Board. Some of the proposals required legislation, such as our plans on reform of the General Teaching Council for Wales, stronger intervention powers for local authorities and the creation of statutory guidance on school improvement. The Master's programme had to be tendered, modules devised, and then recruitment could take place. The national reading and numeracy tests also had to be tendered. Other policies required changes to regulations and significant background work. The banding system had to be worked through in detail – and primary banding, or grading, was a real challenge.

When I arrived, the department had in place a Ministerial Advisory Board (MAB) including a number of senior education specialists as well as the chair of HEFCW, Roger Thomas, the Estyn chief inspector, Ann Keane, and the chair of the Wales Employment and Skills Board (first Sir Adrian Webb, then Scott Waddington), and independent members such as early years specialist Professor Iram Siraj. Senior officials also attended, as did my special advisors, and my specialist advisor on HE to

2011, Professor Merfyn Jones. I wanted someone on the MAB who had a good understanding of school developments in England, and I was delighted when we secured the journalist Fiona Millar, who not only wrote for *The Guardian* on education issues but was a serving chair of school governors with years of experience in London, and had an insider's view of the early developments in education policy under the New Labour government from her period in 10 Downing Street. She brought clarity and incisive questions – and reminded us not to talk our system down as the English system was heading into fragmentation. The MAB allowed us to range widely and innovatively over areas of policy and it provided me with an independent form of challenge to established thinking within the department.

Michael Barber had stressed the importance of communicating clearly the vision for education at the core of our strategy. Viv Thomas's task and finish group on the structure of delivery of education in March 2011 said that we needed to establish the mission in education for the term of the next Assembly after the May 2011 election, and this I did in front of a wide range of stakeholders at the end of June that year. I regarded speeches to stakeholder audiences as a key means of communicating to the profession and to the public, and always took questions after them so that no one could feel that they had not had a chance to put their view to the Minister. We developed strong working relationships with the key journalists. Constant communication of our key themes was critical – most people in Wales get daily newspapers published in London, which were likely to be leading with the latest from Michael Gove, which could be confusing for parents and teachers, so it was important that the BBC Wales and ITV Wales early evening news bulletins, which were the most important outlets in terms of eyeballs and ears reached, had strong stories from us. There was also considerable noise from within other parts of the Welsh education system itself. Education became a staple of the news diet.

We worked hard to build capacity. The creation of the School

Standards Unit in 2011 was a major step forward for the department and meant, at long last, that we had a vehicle to engage directly with schools and to hold local authorities, and the regional consortia, to account for local performance. Another recommendation of the review of the Task and Finish group on the structure of delivery of education, was that it fulfilled the objective which Ian Butler and I had set down of ensuring that there was a clear line of sight from ministers to those delivering on the ground. Modelled on the Number Ten Delivery Unit, under its first Head, Dr Brett Pugh, it began the process of using the mass of data which we had available to challenge effectively and proactively what we were being told by local authorities and consortia through regular stocktakstock-takes identifying where schools needed both challenge and support. Professor Ken Reid had rightly said publicly that it was the job of leadership within DCELLS, as the department was then called, 'to get a grip on Welsh data, analyse it properly and deliver the results to Welsh schools, colleges and local authorities'. After all, he said, how could the School Effectiveness Framework (SEF) work without it? The work of Brett and his team took on that task and demonstrated to all working in Welsh education what needed to be done.

Of course, I needed evidence and allies to take things forward. Evidence depended largely on the reports from our education inspectorate, Estyn. The work done by Bill Maxwell (whom I met in early 2010 just before he returned to Scotland), and then Ann Keane, in reforming the education inspectorate, Estyn, had been widely welcomed. It was clear that there was a more rigorous approach under way. Bill had made significant changes, dropping the tick-box methodology, which came into effect in September 2010 as the new Common Inspection Framework. Speaking to me in December 2012 in Edinburgh, where he now led Education Scotland, Bill said that he had essentially adapted many of the key elements of the Scottish system. Ann Keane, who took over from Bill during 2010, said publicly in March 2012 that 'Estyn was part of the complacency that affected the education sector.' She stated that there had been complacency in Estyn's inspections of local authorities:

> We were not sharp enough. We are now more robust and rigorous and we focus much more strongly on outcomes for learners and how local authorities get to grips with improving those outcomes.

The new Common Inspection Framework was a result, she said, of internal debates within Estyn in the years before she became the chief inspector. The plans to re-orientate Estyn began under Bill in the autumn of 2008. Ann carried this through after Bill left. She had reviewed the previous inspection cycle from 2004 to 2010 and found that a consistently robust attitude to data and performance was lacking. There had been no follow-up for mediocre or weak schools, and too many schools seemed to earn the accolade 'good, with outstanding features'. That inspection cycle had focused too much on the curriculum and subject content. There was now a focus on skills with literacy a mandatory line of enquiry. In respect of local authorities, she said that one of their particular concerns was the speed at which local authorities recognised that a school was in difficulties. There was an issue of quality control when so many inspections had been reliant on lay inspectors in the previous cycle. By September 2012 Estyn had moved to 100 per cent Estyn-led school inspections.

Not everything went as swiftly or as smoothly as I would have liked. I became immensely frustrated in late 2011 at the slow rate of progress in developing national resources of high quality case studies of the best performing schools in Wales, and support for the most-challenged schools. I encouraged criticism to be directly expressed to me and I was receiving independent feedback from experienced people in the field that there was frustration with the pace of delivery within the department over this and other matters. Schools, I was being told, were feeling the accountability and challenge, particularly after the publication of secondary school banding, but they were not seeing the support elements of the 20-point programme. The best practice materials were one very visible element of this, along with the online resource to ensure that they, and the materials on professional learning communities on which Professor Alma Harris had been working, were widely available. The consortium developments, including the appointment of system leaders, were also slow, and I continued to crack the whip with local authorities over that. In the end, I made it clear to the department that if the best practice examples did not appear, I would write them myself. I told Emyr that I felt we needed greater capacity to provide evidence of good practice, support to more challenged schools, simple explanation of successful continuous professional development activity including peer support through professional learning communities, and nationally produced resources for school effectiveness. That seemed to do the trick, and in time for my speech *Learning from the Best* in February 2012, which reported back on progress against the 20-point plan, I had the case studies available – and online.

I was certain we needed to show we were listening to the feedback, and demonstrating our willingness to rethink the child development assessment profile, and postponing primary banding until later (though I felt a lot of our key problems were in the primary sector), were two ways of doing that. I was pleased that union officials like Anna Brychan of the NAHT, Rebecca Williams of UCAC and Phil Dixon of the ATL publicly recognised that. But the feedback I was getting also influenced my desire to get a Practitioners Panel in place to provide me with more direct feedback from schools on a regular basis, and to ensure we had additional financial support for the schools in bands 4 and 5. With the creation in early 2012 of the Practitioners' Panel, chaired by Ysgol Bro Morgannwg head Dr Dylan Jones, made up of leading and experienced head teachers, I felt we had good structures to allow us not only to develop policy but also to think through the practical issues of implementation.

It also became clear in late 2011 that we had got the Child Development Assessment Profile (CDAP) for the Foundation Phase wrong and that was another issue I addressed in the February 2012 speech. I had appointed Professor Iram Siraj to review the CDAP and she did an excellent job. Meanwhile guidance on the operation of professional learning communities was published without being brought to me for sign-off. The guidance drew serious criticism on publication, and I told officials to look at it again. Internally, there was something of a shake-up after this, and it was one of the factors leading to the establishment of the Workforce Unit within the department, which built new capacity in this area. I was also concerned at the pace of progress on additional learning needs and areas such as dyslexia. Emyr Roberts, then Owen Evans, took steps to strengthen these areas. Owen, a shrewd and calm problem-solver originally recruited by David Hawker to lead the Skills, Higher Education and Lifelong Learning division, had the great advantage of having worked outside the civil service, and brought with him a powerful network of contacts across industry and civic society in Wales from his working life in business, academia and the third sector.

It was clear by 2013 that as we headed towards a review of curriculum and assessment, and the major new development of an external exam regulator and awarding body in Qualifications Wales, this was an area which would require greater capacity. Following Chris Tweedale's decision to take a job as Director of the leading educational consultancy CfBT, Owen decided we would need a directorate focusing on these issues. Jo-Anne Daniels, who had worked as Deputy Director for two years, and had a great grasp of policy with significant experience from the Department for Education in England, took over this area as Director. Meanwhile, Brett Pugh was promoted to Director of School Standards and Workforce.

By 2013, we could look back with some success at how the department had made progress. But there were still some difficulties in implementation even in 2013. I was disappointed at the management of the implementation of the contract for the National Support Programme for the Literacy and Numeracy Framework when I had made it clear on more than one occasion that this was one of the most important policies we had to implement. I was also disappointed when it became apparent that the draft reading tests had not been shared across the whole department which would have improved the design, presentation and suitability for the younger age groups. I had already shared with the relevant officials criticisms I had received from head teachers from RCT regarding the pilots of the test. Owen Evans took steps to rectify these omissions subsequently. Anna Brychan, Welsh director of the National Association for Head Teachers, who had come into government as an adviser, brought additional focus to the National Support Programme.

Sharing information on the significant reform programme that is under way is a big challenge for the department, particularly in the schools field. In HE and FE, the lines of communication with the sector leadership are simpler and more direct. In the school system, communication is both direct to over 1650 schools through the department's newsletter – though how widely this is shared within schools is open to conjecture – and via local authorities and consortia, which is where messages often become confused and overlaid with conflicting priorities. This is why it is essential that the minister repeatedly reinforces the core messages about priorities. But even within the Education Department, it is critical to reinforce messages to departmental officials on a regular basis, and to ensure that senior officials are sharing information with each other and across their divisions. I never found a problem that was ever the result of too much communication. Too little communication – from officials to me, or from officials to each other – was much more likely to cause problems.

It was also critical to listen to dissident voices. They wouldn't always be right, and they wouldn't always agree with each other, but I found that some who had occasionally been amongst the most critical of the department were actually very happy to pitch in and help if they could see that their views were being heard – even when not all they said was embraced uncritically. For example, Professors Ken Reid and David Reynolds, past critics of the department, had ideas that could be developed and drawn on. We made good use of them and a wide range of other senior educationalists, including head teachers on secondment.

The Organisation for Economic Co-operation and Development (OECD) report, *Improving Schools in Wales*, published in April 2014, could be an important basis for future consensus, and I hope that it will be seen as such across Wales. I commissioned the report when I visited the OECD with Jeff Cuthbert, Deputy Minister for Skills, Owen and Chris Tweedale in December 2012, where we met Andreas Schleicher, Michael Davidson and others who worked on The Programme for International Student Assessment (PISA). The OECD report has noted 'strong support among the profession and general public for the policy directions set out under the current reforms', and said that the Welsh government was 'already on the path to strengthening and improving the equity and quality of its schools'.

The OECD document recognised that the reform programme had been driven from the top, and there was now a need for greater ownership within the profession through the building of capacity. The creation of a longer-term vision of the Welsh learner and the education system as a whole would be key to that, and, said the OECD, 'some of the elements that can help inform the vision are already in place'. However, I make no apology for the pace of change. We had a lot to do. Whenever there is change in education there are always complaints about its pace. The curriculum review will allow some of the rough edges to be smoothed out.

The OECD rightly says that it is a mark of successful systems that they grow their own capacity and bring that to bear within the executive branch of government. We did that with our school improvement work, particularly in turning round local authorities. Those involved included, along with former Directors of Education Nick Jarman and Gareth Williams (from England),

Karl Napierella and Viv Thomas (ex-Neath Port Talbot), former Wigan and Monmouthshire Chief Executive Joyce Redfearn, current Ceredigion Education Director Eifion Evans, former Social Services Director Phil Robson, current and former head teachers such as Jano Owen, Geraint Rees and Bethan Guilfoyle, former Estyn Inspector Betsan O'Connor, and academic leaders such as Professor Mel Ainscow, former Head of the Manchester Challenge, Professor Karen Graham of Glyndwr University, and Professor Sue Davies of Trinity St David's, and industry figures such as Sony's Wales Managing Director, Steve Walton.

While there is a degree of political naivety in the OECD document – Wales is not Alberta, with the same government in place for forty years, or Singapore, with the same government since its foundation – the organisation was right to identify that the curriculum review could provide a vehicle for the development of a future vision. I would say myself that I hope that is allied to the plans which Huw Lewis has for the development of teacher training, building on the suggestions by Ralph Tabberer for a senior expert adviser on initial teacher training. I am encouraged by the fact that Professor Graham Donaldson, who is leading on the curriculum review, was also involved in Scotland on its review of teacher training, and therefore understands these matters. I think that we need to look at the development of the curriculum for Wales alongside the development of our initial teacher training, and if I have one proposition for my successors as they move forward, it is that they should consider a senior role within the department for a Director of Teaching and Learning – someone who is abreast of the contemporary research on the best teaching methods, and who understands the need to reflect those within our developing Curriculum for Wales.

Over recent years, the department has had to be focused on dragging the system into reality, as the next chapters explain. Building a vision for teaching and learning is an exciting challenge and can provide the impetus that Wales needs in the next phase of reform.

Removing Distractions – Funding the Future

During the Welsh Labour leadership campaign in the autumn of 2009, the National Union of Teachers (NUT) had been running a determined campaign in Wales to highlight the per-pupil spending gap they said existed between Wales and England. They lobbied assembly members and argued their case in the media. Evidence to the Assembly's Education, Lifelong Learning and Skills committee that autumn suggested almost two-thirds of local authorities were spending less than their indicator-based assessment suggested they should. I had felt the One Wales government response to the NUT campaign had been somewhat weak. It was right, of course, to remind people that education budgets were scheduled to go up by 2.5 per cent in the next financial year. It was also right to say that the Assembly Government has to allocate resources according to an assessment of priorities and needs in Wales – it should not be case of simply following English decisions. It was right to point out the additional funding that had been found for the Foundation Phase. No one could doubt that devolution and the growing diversity of policy and practice also made comparisons very difficult and there are different funding methods between England and Wales. In the English system there were also larger elements of private finance for capital and to support the new academies programme.

However, Carwyn Jones's campaign had accepted that there was a funding gap, and that something had to be done about it. His commitment to raise schools spending by 1 per cent a year above the block grant received from the UK government would begin to address the problem. Carwyn reiterated his commitment to the policy in his first BBC interview following his appointment as First Minister, saying 'I want to make sure that that money is channelled into ensuring that we spend more money per head on children in Wales than we do at the moment and we will look to catch up with England'. We also knew we needed to move on local authorities who were holding back money from schools – what was known as the 'delegation rate'. Professor David Reynolds had pointed out in the *Times Educational Supplement* (*TES)* that the delegation rate had fallen from 81 per cent in 2002-3 to a planned 74.8 per cent in 2010-11. David called this 'educational lunacy'. No one would argue all the money going to local authorities for educational purposes should immediately be passported to schools – there were some services which were delivered more efficiently centrally – but we had to turn this round. As David said, across the world, people believed change was being driven by giving greater control of resources to those at the front line.

We began discussions on the detail of the 1 per cent pledge, which if it was to reach schools would have to be distributed through local authorities. This would mean an additional £20 million. There were early meetings, commencing in a snowy January 2010, to work through how we would do this from the 2011-12 financial year, and by March we had our plans in place. My departmental budget of roughly £1.7 billion was not where the bulk of school funding came from – that was Carl Sargeant's local government budget which funded the Revenue Support Grant.

Funding of schools had been a big issue from the beginning of the Assembly, with concerns raised about the differences between individual local authorities – for example, Ceredigion in 2009 spent £1,172 per secondary pupil more than its neighbour Powys; the additional funding needs of schools in deprived areas or in rural areas; the operation of the funding formula in the local government budget and many other areas. These had been explored in a series of reports by Assembly Committees and others. I asked my private office to dig out all of these reports so that I could review them in more detail.

Carwyn's 1 per cent commitment could not come into effect until the 2011-12 financial year, as the budget for 2010-11 had been passed before his appointment as First Minister. But his manifesto had also included a commitment to ensure that the funding invested into the system actually reached the front-line, and I was determined that we should do something about that at an early stage. Over the weekend following my appointment, I came up with the idea of a review of the cost of administering the education system. I felt we needed stronger analytical skills than the department possessed, and it seemed to me, based on my experience of working at the BBC, that this was precisely one of those areas where management consultants might have the skills we lacked. I discussed the idea with my colleagues and with officials in the week beginning 14th December. As Minister for Local Government, Carl Sargeant was for it, as long as we could sort out the politics. Being in coalition, officials in the Cabinet Secretariat thought it might have to go to Cabinet for discussion, but Mark Drakeford, then a Ministerial special adviser, helpfully suggested it could be circulated to other ministers through a letter from me – dealing with it 'in correspondence' in the jargon.

I pushed hard for the review and it came together surprisingly quickly. By the morning of 18th January I was ready to announce it. I had not met Professor David Reynolds before, but I ran into him the night before the announcement. He was going on BBC Radio Wales's *Good Morning Wales* in the early slot to talk about it. I was going on later. David had already told the *TES* in early January that he saw Carwyn's pledge to increase school spending by at least 1 per cent above the block grant settlement as 'the very first time that anyone in Welsh politics has acknowledged the gap exists.' Spending figures released later in January were to show that the spending gap continued to grow.

Professor Reynolds also said that there needed to be a redistribution within government budgets towards education, and local authorities which held cash back from schools needed to be tackled – the delegation rate issue. This was an important point. Government figures showed that local authorities were keeping more and more of the money given to them by the Welsh Government in central budgets.

The announcement of the review was largely well-received. Colette Hume, the BBC's education correspondent, was effusive, and the story ran on their bulletins from *Good Morning Wales* right through to their evening television news programme, *Wales Today*. I did interviews in both English and Welsh. The union response was supportive as were organisations like Colegau Cymru representing the further education colleges. AMs from other parties also welcomed it. The announcement came the Monday after our seminar with Michael Barber, and was the first stage in cementing a coalition for change behind us. It enabled us to demonstrate that we were taking the sector's funding concerns seriously.

The first stage was an internal exercise looking at the costs of administering education using information collected by the Welsh Assembly Government. Recommendations for making savings and opportunities to move resources to front line services would be made by the end of March. I said: 'We need to ensure our funding reaches the education front lines'. The review would be conducted in two stages by external consultants with experience and expertise in the field to ensure complete objectivity and impartiality.

I elaborated on the review in my regular *Western Mail* column:

> The Education budget should not be a Christmas tree with presents for everyone. Investment must lead to performance improvement in the areas that matter. That means a line-by-line review of all our budgets to ensure money is going on the people's priorities, not bureaucratic process. Some will be disappointed.

I didn't want our additional investment disappearing into County Hall budgets or college administrations.

I made it clear that the review would be strategic and would consider the way in which money reached the front-line. I told the *Western Mail* I wanted to ensure 'that the pipeline doesn't have too many blockages in it.' I also made it clear that the review had the backing of the First Minister and the Local Government Minister – a deliberate signal to local authorities that they needed to be thinking about the implications for them. In evidence to the Assembly Finance Committee early in 2010 I said that the role of local education authorities in funding schools could come under scrutiny, and there were other models we would consider if necessary, such as direct funding of schools.

In March 2010, I took new school funding regulations through the Assembly which made local authorities give schools a three-year budget forecast. The regulations also enabled local authorities to intervene when schools were carrying excessive surpluses. There were surpluses across Wales of some £74 million in school budgets at the end of the 2008-9 financial year. Nearly half of all secondary schools were carrying surpluses of £100,000.

PriceWaterhouseCoopers won the contract to deliver the review and I took their report to Cabinet on May 17. PwC had held widespread discussions with stakeholders. They identified a clear need for a national impetus to the reforms, creating an effective coalition for change across the system. I stressed to Cabinet colleagues that this was not about cuts in budgets, or about fundamental structural change in local government at this time, but relied on driving collaboration, using the local authority Outcome Agreements (which Local Government Minister Carl Sargeant and I were starting to doubt would ultimately drive delivery) and changes to the remit of the Higher Education Funding Council for Wales.

As we told Cabinet, PwC had assessed:

> direct support for learning and teaching, and appropriate educationally-focused support (for example, professional support to educators and research) as making up 68 per cent overall of the £4.5 billion expenditure on education.

> It is the remaining 32 per cent – made up of elements such as back office, access and assessment, service management and administration – where they see the real opportunity for savings, and suggest that this is where we should focus our attempts to release investment for the front line.
>
> PwC proposed a number of hypotheses through which some of these administration costs may be released and this provides a significant and important opportunity for the Assembly Government and, indeed its delivery partners, to pursue. It is difficult, without being overly simplistic, to attach a figure to this opportunity.... a conservative estimate of the overall benefits available through the implementation of PwC's hypotheses – achieving a shift of about 2 per cent in the balance between front line and back office – could produce a sum of around £100 million.

There were differences in different sectors. Over 80 per cent of school spending was front-line, whereas less than half of higher education spend was:

	Support: Service split
Delegated schools	17:83
LEA retained	34:66
Further Education	41:59
Higher Education	52:48
Estyn	41:59
Careers Services	41:59

The paper also raised some broader strategic questions, but I was mindful of the constraints of the One Wales agreement:

> I have no doubt that discussion of the review will give rise to questions as to whether the education system in Wales is optimally configured – inter alia, should we continue with the current arrangements for the funding and delivery

> of the service, or institute change. However, these are matters for political parties properly to consider in the development of manifestoes for the 2011 Assembly elections. My focus at this point is on delivering change within the current system by driving collaboration by local authorities and other delivery partners such as higher education institutions.

PwC's recommendations highlighted major scope for savings if local authorities in particular could deliver some of their services to schools on a regional basis.

Cabinet supported the paper and the review, and I made a statement to the National Assembly the next day. I made it clear that I wanted to see a commitment across the entire education system that this was a direction of change which they supported.

Following the publication of the PwC review, we embarked on a fundamental sector-by-sector search for savings under our Front Line Resources Review. This took up PwC's suggestion of a national challenge to stakeholders to deliver savings, which we called the 'summer challenge'. We estimated we would be able to find around £20 million of savings in the financial year 2010-11, and the savings ultimately delivered could exceed PwC's estimates. I had to keep pushing on this, telling the Assembly in October 2010 that some of the proposals coming forward simply did not go far enough. The savings required some structural changes in the FE, HE and local authority sectors. We also identified savings in our own department's budgets. I reported on these savings to Cabinet in March 2011, noting that we had identified opportunities for some £200 million of savings when the full cost shift from support to front-line functions had been achieved. My own department also reduced its administrative costs by £2.6 million in 2010-11 with further reductions planned in future years.

In July 2010, it was clear that we still had an issue with local authorities in relation to delegating resources to schools as estimates suggested that the percentage delegation rate was due to fall further to 74.76 per cent. I took this issue up directly with local authorities as part of my 'summer challenge'. Tough talking over the summer period resulted in a written commitment from local authorities, in advance of my first annual meeting with all local authority education cabinet members and Directors of Education in late November 2010 under the auspices of the Welsh Local Government Association, to seek to raise the delegation rates to at least 80 per cent. I told them I expected them to find an additional £20 million from the efficiency savings identified by PwC. I had to take action in spring 2010 to challenge the then Liberal Democrat-controlled Swansea City Council when it cut its spending on education. I eventually had a commitment from the WLGA to raise delegation rates to 80 per cent by September 2012 and to 85 per cent by September 2014. The 80 per cent rate was largely achieved on time. What rapidly became clear as the Association of Directors of Education in Wales worked through the implications was the variation between authorities in how they calculated central support and other costs.

By now, of course, we had other challenges. The UK coalition government had come to power, and its austerity policies proposed serious cuts in the Welsh Government's budget, with £6 billion of public spending cuts announced that month for the immediate financial year. The Welsh share was £162 million, £113 million in revenue. Delivering Carwyn's commitment to the 1 per cent would mean disproportionate cuts in spending in other budgets – not easy in times of rising spending, but even more difficult now. Cabinet discussions had commenced on the 2011-12 budget. These were made even more difficult by the late publication of the UK government's first Comprehensive Spending Review (CSR) in October 2010, meaning the publication of the Welsh Government's draft budget occurred more than a month later than normal. In the 2011-12 financial year the Welsh block received a reduction in funding and therefore the commitment became a protection of 1 per cent rather than an absolute increase. Accordingly, a stipulation was placed in the terms of the Local

Government Revenue Settlement, with authorities asked to ensure that school spending was protected.

Wales had the worst outcome of all the devolved administrations with total spending set to fall by 9.9 per cent over the three years of the CSR, and lower in real terms by £1.8 billion. We were able to protect budgets for schools – both within the education department and through the revenue support grant to local authorities – by 1 per cent above the rate of change in the Welsh budget, and we managed to find additional money for the Foundation Phase and for teachers' continuing professional development, as well as for skills. The additional 1 per cent would mean an extra £60 million for schools by 2013-14. But the higher education budget in 2011-12 was to be cut by about 9 per cent.

Our capital budgets were the worst hit by decisions at Westminster, with cuts of around 40 per cent. I therefore created what was essentially a single capital pool across all sectors of education. It was very important that we were able to ensure that capital was used when we needed it. We could only do that if we had direct control of all the capital budgets, so that we could if necessary switch capital from one sector to another because there had been some slippage – as there very often is in capital programmes. The department was also successful in attracting funds from the central capital resources of the Assembly Government, for school repairs and refurbishment, amongst other things.

Funding cuts from the UK government continued. I left the Welsh Government the day before the 2013 CSR was published. The Chancellor's budget in March 2013 had already imposed in-year spending cuts on the Welsh Government and the CSR added further cutbacks.

Jane Hutt had created the groundwork for the twenty-first century schools fund, which was a much more strategic approach to developing investment in the school infrastructure over time. As we developed our plans for it, we had to demand more of local authorities. We did that in partnership with the Welsh Local

Government Association (WLGA), which was immensely supportive of that initiative. I co-chaired the programme board with the WLGA leader responsible for education. The WLGA had written to the Permanent Secretary to say that it thought that this was a good model of partnership working between local government and the Assembly Government. Local authorities had borrowing powers, the Welsh Government did not. Initially we expected them to provide 30 per cent of the cost of schemes – this had to be raised to 50 per cent when in December 2011 I announced the £1.4 billion budget for the programme over seven years, to take effect from 2014 – the largest ever education capital programme. This was in addition to the £415 million of transitional spending that had been previously provided during the One Wales Government. I worked with Finance Minister Jane Hutt to establish a way of extending the Welsh Local Government Borrowing Initiative (WLGBI) to provide additional alternative finance for school-building, and the result was that in December 2013, Jane was able to announce that an additional £200 million would be provided in this way and the twenty-first century schools programme would be completed two years earlier, in 2018-19.

One further consequence of UK government policy was the way in which the rapid expansion of academies under Michael Gove made it harder for the Office of National Statistics (ONS) to publish comparisons of educational spending between Wales and England. The then chief statistician, Kate Chamberlain, said that the 'changing educational policy landscape in England' made the comparisons impossible to carry out. I was profoundly disappointed by this, as we were protecting school spending under Carwyn's pledge, and the Office of National Statistics (ONS) decision made it impossible for us to demonstrate the difference we were making. The ONS had essentially been given independence in law by the UK Labour government prior to 2010. But inevitably, the Welsh Government got the blame for the ONS decision.

I also moved to reform the National Planning and Funding

System for post-16 education in schools and colleges, unchanged since the days of the quango Education and Learning Wales (ELWA) first freezing the funding for three years, then moving to a system funded at the level of a programme for learning for an individual, rather than individual qualifications. Funding would be allocated on a three-year basis to aid stability and future planning. We would maintain uplifts for deprivation, rurality and Welsh-medium education. The old system may have equalised funding between colleges and schools, but it had encouraged competition for students and also provided incentives to recruit students on courses that were not necessarily the best for them. The new focus would be on outcomes not outputs. I also sought to protect funding for post-16 special educational needs. Funding for this sector had doubled between 2003 and 2010, and I set up a task and finish group to look at how we were allocating services. Funding for SEN was enshrined in the local authorities' Revenue Support Grant following the passage of the 2013 School Standards and Organisation Act. We also found additional funding for schools in bands 4 and 5 after the banding system came into effect. Following the budget deal with the Liberal Democrats in 2011, we received significant increase for the 2012-13 financial year which allowed us to create the pupil deprivation grant, designed to address the gap in performance between pupils on free school meals and those not on free school meals. This was increased in the budget for the 2014-15 financial year to £918 per child from its previous £450.

Delivering action on funding was important to building the coalition for change in our schools. It also showed that we were serious about tackling the lack of commitment in local government. According to figures from my successor, Huw Lewis, between 2011-12 to the end of the 2013-14 financial year, the Welsh Government had made available an additional £115m to schools through the Revenue Support Grant (RSG) and the Department for Education and Skills budget, which includes funding for the School Effectiveness Framework. Together with the additional funding for the Pupil Deprivation Grant in 2012-

13 and 2013-14, schools have benefitted from over £155m additional funding in this period. The 1 per cent pledge was met.

However, the real issue on funding is how it is used, not how much there is. In August 2011 even Professor David Reynolds, a sharp critic of under-funding by Welsh Governments prior to Carwyn's, felt able to tell the *Western Mail* 'I think personally I made an error in talking about money as if it was the sole issue. I've given Welsh education an excuse. That isn't to say there's nothing in it.' In January 2013 he told the *TES* 'I wonder now whether it's as big an issue as I once thought.' Indeed, the OECD has noted that high education spending levels could not automatically be equated with strongly-performing education systems. Countries which spent less on education than Wales, such as Poland and New Zealand, outperformed us. We identified in 2011 that Ceredigion and Blaenau Gwent were the highest spenders on education but ranked only tenth and twenty-first out of the twenty two local education authorities in terms of performance at the end of Key Stage 2. Blaenau Gwent was one of the two highest per-head spenders when it was put into special measures by Estyn. As evidence came to show, standards and spending are two different issues.

Avoiding Distractions: No Academies

In March 2014, as part of the Conservative led 'war on Wales', *The Times* said in an editorial that we should be following England over academies to improve performance. The introduction of academies had been ruled out early in the life of the Assembly by Jane Davidson and Rhodri Morgan, and I agreed with them. I confirmed this in my first six months as Minister; shortly after the Conservative-Liberal Democrat UK coalition government came to power, ruling out free schools as well. Even if I had been convinced of their worth in the Welsh context, which I wasn't, the political effort that would have been required would have taken energy away from building the consensus necessary on standards; there would have been no political support from our coalition partners, Plaid Cymru, and I didn't think there would have been political support within Welsh Labour either.

There were people I respected on both sides of the Academies argument. David Blunkett's former special adviser, Conor Ryan, wrote in 2008 about how Blunkett came to announce the idea of city academies which would eventually lead to the academies programme:

> The city academies were to be part of a wider programme to extend diversity within the state sector and raise standards where existing provision is inadequate. They were to offer a real change and improvement in pupil performance, for example by innovative approaches to management, governance, teaching and learning from other local schools, including a specialist focus in at least

> one curriculum area. Academies would replace schools which were either in special measures or underachieving.

Andrew Adonis has set out his story of developing the Academies programme in his book *Education, Education, Education*. I have also had the opportunity of a couple of brief conversations with him and others about them over recent years.

Initially in England there was simply a small number of sponsored academies – a few hundred schools by May 2010, designed as replacements for failing schools in the most deprived areas. Academies are, in the words of the Department for Education in England 'publicly funded independent state schools... directly accountable to the Department for Education'. They are outside local authority control, run by 'academy trusts' – charitable companies limited by guarantee, accountable to the Secretary of State for Education through an individual funding agreement which sets their operating framework. They are now counter-posed, ideologically, by the Department for Education, to what are called 'council-run schools', as the education journalist Warwick Mansell noted in 2014.

The critics of academies whom I respect are largely gathered around the Local Schools Network, a web-based campaign for those with positive experiences of state education in England and who want to find ways to improve it rather than disparage or dismantle it, as Melissa Benn describes it in her book, *School Wars*. Fiona Millar, one of its founders, interviewed for the book *Reinventing Schools, Reforming Teaching* by John Bangs, John MacBeath and Maurice Galton, recalls during her time at Number Ten how the term 'comprehensive' had been viewed pejoratively by some of the younger advisers around Tony Blair: 'all it means is an all abilities school, but it's become a phrase that was used to brand something else, which was failing inner city schools, basically, made up of very tough kids.' Peter Hyman, former Head of the Number Ten Strategic Communications Unit, who left the political world to train as a teacher and now heads the Free School School 21, confirms this in his fascinating book

1 out of 10: From Downing Street Vision to Classroom Reality, 'whatever it was meant to mean, the word "comprehensive" was contaminated. People, particularly in London and other major cities, associated it with failing inner city schools.'

When I worked in London in the 1980s and particularly the 1990s, I lost count of how many of my friends were rejecting the state school route for their children. It was refreshing to return to South Wales to live and to find that state schools were the route of choice for all except a very tiny minority. In the English context, it has been the need to assuage London middle-class opinion which seems to have dominated the drive for new forms of school structure, creating new forms of public service contestability. As Professor Sir Adrian Webb wrote in his 2007 report for the Welsh Government on post-14 education, *Promise and Performance*, contestability:

> requires confident, well-informed consumers who can choose between many competing providers. However, public services were invented, in part, because such conditions are often absent; for example, in large parts of Wales where rurality or poor communications prevail. A market in public services is essentially an urban, even metropolitan, idea.

While I did, in effect, later create a form of contestability by legislating so that local authorities had to measure parental demand for Welsh-medium education in their areas, I have no doubt that Adrian's analysis is broadly right.

History, of course, tends to be written by the winners. So the narrative of school improvement in England now is that academies were the reason for improving standards. After 2010, the academy programme was taken on by Michael Gove and the coalition government. By 2013 more than half of all English secondary schools were academies. In 2010, David Miliband warned that the coalition government's plan was 'to extend the academy model to existing successful schools' which taught 40 per cent fewer poor pupils than the national average, meaning that new academies were overwhelmingly in suburban and rural districts. Indeed, as Stephen Twigg pointed out in the Caroline Benn memorial lecture in November 2012, the worst-performing school in England that year was St. Aldhelm's Academy in Poole, Dorset – a school formerly known, when I attended Poole Grammar School from 1968 to 1975, as Kemp-Welch Secondary Modern. After the 2011 Education Act all new schools had academy status and all schools were able to convert to academy status. This was no longer a targeted programme aimed at improving standards in deprived areas, but a mass programme of conversion to academies. As Fiona Millar has said to me, the Labour government did not appreciate what a different party in government might do with the programme. The converter academy programme under Michael Gove has proved expensive and the department seriously underestimated its cost, as the National Audit Office demonstrated in November 2012, having to find hundreds of millions from other budgets. The Department for Education's accounts were qualified in 2014 due to concerns about academy spending.

I understand why successful school head teachers might want to adopt academy status, free, as they see it, of the constraints of local authority bureaucracy and, as the argument goes, greater freedom to innovate – coupled, of course, with what Fiona Millar called in 2011 'hefty bribes' to convert. However, I do not believe that the existing state system cannot provide the flexibility to innovate, in terms of the curriculum, for example, as has happened at Glyn Derw in Ely in one of the most deprived areas of Cardiff, where the Year 7 lessons now have a fundamental focus on literacy and numeracy. Or in the organisation of the school environment, such as at Newport High School, a newly built school which replaced the former Bettws Comprehensive, a massively under-achieving school. Newport High has created an environment where Year 7 pupils operate in a system more akin to the primary school they have just left, based in a classroom where they stay and where subject teachers come to them, separate from the rest of the school.

I do not agree with the proposition that changing the fundamental structure of schools, particularly secondary schools, is essential to driving up performance. Take Tower Hamlets. There, performance outstripped most other parts of the country between Tower Hamlets' damning Ofsted report in 1998 and 2010 – and in that period, Tower Hamlets had no academies. They also had a far lower achievement gap between pupils on Free School Meals and those not on Free School Meals; and they did better than the national averages for looked-after children and those with statements of special needs, and primary school pupils also achieved well above the national average. Only since the advent of the coalition government have academies and free schools appeared in Tower Hamlets.

There is some evidence that some of Labour's original sponsored academies have transformed outcomes in specific school settings. But there is limited evidence to suggest that academies have been responsible for system-wide improvement (similar debates are now under way in the United States in respect of charter schools). Professor Dylan Wiliam has pointed out that the early sponsored academies were starting from a lower base than other schools, and says 'when we compare the improvements in the results of academies with other schools starting from similar baselines, we find no difference.' Recent evidence to the House of Commons Select Committee on Education suggests it is simply too early to even consider evaluating the UK coalition's academies programme.

The academy narrative tends to drown out other school improvement programmes which Labour introduced in England. The Local Schools Network in 2010 pointed to the Ofsted Report on the London Challenge which showed that when schools co-operate, everyone is a winner. The London Challenge allowed schools to work with each other and share best practice and pool resources – good schools got better and under-performing schools significantly raised their game. Since the introduction of London Challenge, secondary schools in London improved at a faster rate than secondary schools in the rest of England. London Challenge, said Professor Tim Brighouse, had 'articulated a vision of what schooling could, should and would be like based on a moral purpose that brooked no denial', with committed teachers and school leaders enabling schools to learn from one another and use data intelligently. Ofsted chief inspector, Sir Michael Wilshaw, acknowledged in the *TES* in September 2012 that in London 'standards have radically improved since the 1970s, when I started teaching', and acknowledged that London was now leading the country.

The National Challenge, which in 2008 named the 638 schools in England where fewer than 30 per cent of pupils were getting five GCSE grades A*-C including English and Maths, had ended 'denial in the system' said Professor David Woods, the adviser to the Labour Government on the issue. Researchers at London Metropolitan University found in July 2012 that it was the City challenge programmes that contributed most to raising attainment between 2008 and 2011 in terms of pupils gaining five A*-C GCSE grades including English and Maths. The Local Schools Network produced evidence based on Department for Education figures in 2012 that non-academies were performing as well as academies and to suggest that academies made more use of GCSE-equivalents to achieve these results than non-academies. While academies played an important role in Hackney, the key intervention there, as Fiona Millar pointed out in *The Guardian* in November 2012, was arguably the creation of the not-for-profit Learning Trust, accountable to the local authority but with a largely independent board focused on standards and community re-engagement. Reviewing the evidence overall on academies in *The Guardian* in January 2014, Fiona wrote:

> in both the primary and secondary sector the improvement in similar maintained schools – starting from a low base and with relatively high numbers of children on free school meals – is as good as in academies. And if you strip out the GCSE-equivalent qualifications used by many

sponsored secondary academies, the improvement in non-academy results appears to be better. In short, you don't need to be an academy to improve.

There is, of course, international evidence, including from the OECD, that introducing competition into the school system does not significantly improve performance and may bring other penalties. As Fenton Whelan says in *Lessons Learned:*

> School systems which employ market models tend to suffer a range of problems: they fail to leverage choice and competition as real drivers of improvement, they are unable to quickly or preventively tackle underperformance, they divide the system into units which are too small to innovate, they inhibit the spread of best practices, and they often increase academic, ethnic, and social stratification in the system. More fundamentally the power of choice and competition as drivers of improvement has generally been overstated.

We do not yet know what will be the overall outcome of the academies programme as it is now being pursued in England since 2010. Indeed, as former UK Education Secretary Estelle Morris argued in April 2013, the range of new schools opening in the English state sector, including free schools, university technical colleges, studio schools and independent schools joining the state sector, and new providers including private companies, meant new surplus capacity based on a free-for-all with no effective oversight for planning of places and admissions. Market forces would therefore rule in the English system, she argued, with schools opening and closing faster than before. UK government figures indicated in July 2013 that free school primaries were being opened in areas where there was no need for additional schools. As competition took hold, she warned, there would be less incentive for schools to support one another in the advancement of a self-improving system, as all sought to maximise their competitive position. She argued that the result would be greater instability, incoherence and less sharing of good practice. As Michael Barber has said to me, at least the academy chains offer some hope of consistency and mutual learning. But beyond them the position is likely to be less satisfactory – and some academy chains have themselves been questioned seriously about their performance.

Conservative educational philosophy under Michael Gove sees no role for local authorities, whatever Conservative councils like Westminster might think, and possibly, given the criticisms of certain groups on the Tory right, no need for a national inspection system either, on the basis that market forces and parental choice will determine all. It is a strangely Leninist route to a free market, forcing or bribing schools into academy status and rigging the market for future ventures through directing subsidies to free school development, reserving hundreds of millions in capital spend specifically for academies, and dictating that all new schools would be academies or free schools. As Fiona Millar has said to me 'the nature of the academy funding agreements means that they must all be run from the DFE (and now the very overworked Education Funding Agency). Of course it was do-able with a few hundred schools, but utterly impossible with thousands.'

Even Michael Gove has had to concede the difficulty of managing all schools from the centre, introducing a system of regional commissioners. The head of the OECD's PISA programme, Andreas Schleicher, warned the House of Commons Education Select Committee in 2014 that 'You need a very strong education system to make autonomy work, you can't leave it to market forces alone.' In April 2014, following a review by David Blunkett, Labour announced a new system to bring back local engagement in schools imrpovement. Blunkett told *The Guardian*: 'We need to build on what we know works – local oversight of schools to keep a check on performance, timely interventions in schools to support those at risk of failing, and partnerships between schools to help each one to improve.'

The academies debate is for England, already riddled with significantly more inequalities in its school system than Wales had even before the advent of academies and now free schools.

Ofsted now wants to inspect academy chains, and some have already been told not to take on more schools. There have been scandals over certain free schools where issues of religious extremism have been alleged. The anarchy of the English system is coming to light, with overt rows breaking out between the UK government coalition partners over free schools in particular. Simon Jenkins said in *The Guardian* in early May 2014 that the free school system 'was blatant ideological favouritism', and warned 'were it to bed down, the free school would replicate in English cities the sectarian and social divisiveness still experienced in Ulster.' As the First Minister told the Welsh Labour Conference 2014:

> how is Michael Gove's Free Schools project faring? Schools are being set up in the wrong place, inside substandard buildings, with unqualified teachers at the helm. Some have been closed down already. This is a free market experiment in education, with choosy parents having the most buying power.

By mid-2014, the UK coalition partners appeared deeply divided over free schools and a significant challenge was mounting over the costs of the programme.

Sadly, there is no simple, compelling, analytical, one-volume account of the other things that Labour did for education while in government during the 1997-2010 period. This means to some extent that the academies story has become the legacy narrative of Labour's period running education in England.

The challenges facing New Labour in England in 1997 illustrate fundamentally the differences between the Welsh and English systems. As David Blunkett said in his autobiography *On a Clear Day*, around a fifth of secondary schools had voted for grant-maintained status under the Conservatives, subsequently to become foundation schools under Labour (Professor Sally Tomlinson in her book *Education in a post-welfare society* records the numbers as 1000 of the 4460 secondary schools).

In Wales, there were only a dozen or so foundation schools when I came into office, with four of these being primary schools. Fewer than ten out of 200 plus secondary schools were foundation schools – around 4 per cent compared to 20 per cent in England. Nor did we have the kind of middle-class withdrawal from the state system that England – and particularly, London – experienced, with only around 2 per cent in private schools in Wales compared to around 8 per cent in England. The debates on private schools which still surface from time to time in the *New Statesman* and other journals of the left are largely irrelevant to us. We had no grammar schools. Our system was, in essence, more equal, and, like Scotland, community-based comprehensives had parental buy-in from all classes. Our job in Wales is to demonstrate that we can deliver sustained and sustainable improvements in standards within our comprehensive system. If we believe in comprehensive education, then we have to ensure that it is of the highest standard. We also have to raise standards throughout our primary schools at the same time.

Michael Barber's book *Instruction to Deliver* says a little more about Labour's policy development in Opposition and the Standards and Effectiveness Unit in the Department for Education and Employment from 1997-2001, including the early development of two key phrases which became guiding principles – 'Intervention should be in inverse proportion to success' – meaning the freedom a school could have would depend on its performance; and 'standards matter more than structures' – meaning that the focus should be on the quality of teaching, not changing structures. The advent of school inspection judgements of 'failing' or 'struggling' in the mid-1990s allowed Barber to identify how many failing and struggling schools there might be – and the moral purpose to turn that situation around so that young people did not lose out. Michael was a member of the team which recommended the closure of Hackney Downs in 1995:

> While of course there was a risk in this course of action – such disruption could hardly be considered ideal – it was one of those cases I found so common later in government, where the risk of acting was far less than the risk of doing nothing.... It was also good for the education system: a line had been drawn; catastrophic, ongoing failure was morally unacceptable.

I felt the same way when I took the decision to close Llanrumney High School in 2013. Michael said that 'the symbolic value of the announcement was the shock it gave to the system'. By 2000, the UK Department was intervening in poorly-performing local authorities. In the first term, with the literacy and numeracy programmes, significant improvement had happened in primary schools in England. As David Reynolds and Tony Kelly observed in a paper for the Royal Society in 2013, the National Numeracy and Literacy Strategies had phases of very rapid growth in scores from 1998 to 2002, though sustaining this over time was more difficult. The next period was to be about secondary schools, and then the Academy programme started in earnest.

One problem in politics is that physical structures can often leave more of a lasting and identifiable legacy than statistics or personal testimony. So, as Michael writes in *Instruction to Deliver*, 'The magnificent, high-achieving Mossbourne Community Academy, standing on what was the site of Hackney Downs, is perhaps the most powerful symbol of Blair's legacy in education.' Yet magnificent school buildings that do not look like traditional school settings are being built in many places – I recall visiting, shortly before it opened, the new £29 million Llanwern High in Newport, which replaced the crumbling Hartridge comprehensive, with its atrium-style reception and inspiring quotations on walls all over the school. That was the most improved school in Wales in 2013 on the basis of its GCSE results.

Michael himself notes that Tony Blair began to focus more on structures than standards from the end of his first term onwards. He recalls confessing to the Prime Minister that he had been the author of the phrase 'standards not structures'. In his own autobiography, Tony Blair writes 'structures beget standards. How a service is configured affects outcomes', and says later 'the whole point was that without the different structure, there was no possibility of achieving the higher standards'. I disagree. I think it is about leadership. Tower Hamlets' experience belies Tony Blair's claim. The danger of attributing success principally to the Academies programme is that it undermines the real impact of Labour's other reforms which resulted in improvements in educational standards in England in the 1997-2010 period. After all, there were 3,500 secondary schools in England and by 2010 only a few hundred were academies. Additionally, as Fenton Whelan writes, 'while structural reform may enable other changes, it rarely improves performance in and of itself.'

One of the strengths of the pre-2010 sponsored academies, Andrew Adonis explains, has been the recruitment of governors with a stake in the success of the schools. Governing boards usually had a dozen or so governors, with a majority appointed by the sponsor. These original sponsored academies had school governing bodies with a real stake in the success or failure of their schools. As Andrew says: 'academy sponsors know that they will reap the consequences of poor planning and management into the indefinite future.' Too often, I found, Estyn found, and my Assembly colleagues from all parties found that school governing bodies acted more like parent-teacher associations and cheerleaders for their schools, almost whatever they did, than serious governing bodies with a commitment to real school development and progress measured against the best.

That criticism extended to local authority appointed governors as well. Too many were councillors anxious to retain control of their local school, or alternatively anxious to be on good terms with parents at the school or with the head teacher as a key local opinion-former, and not prepared to ask the right questions. There was no culture of leadership, seeking to be the best. Instead, excuses were found and accepted for below par performance. In some cases, Estyn found that governors simply did not know what should be expected of them or of their schools, or how to look at the key data available on performance. In her 2010-11 report, chief inspector Ann Keane found that governors were sometimes 'under an illusion' about their schools' performances and were surprised when inspectors raised problems; in too many cases, head teachers present school performance data and other information 'in a way that hides the real issues'. She concluded that this could result in a degree of complacency that is typical of 'coasting' schools. The Viv Thomas review also made demands for governor training. In January 2014, the Department for Education in England said it too had concerns about school governors.

To counter these problems of governance, my predecessor Jane Hutt had embarked on a programme of governor reform. I had inherited from Jane a Legislative Competence Order (LCO) on School Governance, designed to allow the Assembly to take powers to reform the conduct and governance of schools, to secure collaboration between school governing bodies, and others. The LCO was the device under the 2006 Government of Wales Act which paved the way for powers to be transferred to the Assembly on a case by case basis in certain areas, enabling us then to legislate in those new areas. It was a cumbersome process reformed by the 2011 Referendum outcome. The LCO was approved by the Assembly in February 2010.

The Education (Wales) Measure, using the powers gained through the LCO, introduced proper clerking of governing bodies and compulsory training of governors, which had been the original purpose. By then, I had also decided to use the Measure to prevent the creation of more Foundation Schools, following the decision of Whitchurch High School in Cardiff to go down that route after it fell out with the then Liberal Democrat/Plaid

Cymru coalition which was running Cardiff City Council. I had been frustrated that I had no option other than to sign off on their application, though I regarded it as counter-productive to our approach to school reform, giving the school control over its own admissions, thereby adding to the complexity of local authority planning for school places. The eventual measure placed a duty on local authorities, school and FE governing bodies to collaborate, allowed local authorities to federate school governing bodies, with a streamlined procedure for the federation of very small schools.

The need for the measure was clear. Governors were not on the whole playing a challenging enough role in respect of school performance. They needed to understand the data on school performance; and they needed to understand that they were not there simply to take on trust everything they were told by the head teacher. In respect of federation, there had been powers for schools to federate voluntarily since 2002 in the early days of devolution, but it wasn't happening. Giving local authorities the power to federate was another element in the school improvement portfolio. The measure passed through the Assembly on 29th March 2011, the penultimate day of the Third Assembly, and received Royal Assent in May. It was the final Measure of the Third Assembly, and, following the referendum result on 3rd March 2011, it was the final ever Assembly Measure, because in future the Assembly would scrutinise Bills which would become Acts. It was a historic moment to acknowledge in the developing process of devolution in Wales.

Despite the Education Measure, I was still not clear, in 2012, that school governance was operating well in all settings. I spoke regularly at events organised by Governors Wales around Wales which gave me an opportunity to explain our agenda directly to members of school governing bodies. But I suspected that we reached only a small number. I was struck by the fact that Scotland did not have governing bodies but instead a system of parents' forums when I visited there in December 2012. I established a Task and Finish group on school governance, chaired by former ITN Political Editor Glyn Mathias, from 2001-2008 the Electoral Commissioner for Wales, himself chair of a school governing body in Powys, who had written to me at length on the subject. Other members of the group were Professor Catherine Farrell of the University of Glamorgan, Marc Belli, head teacher of Mary Immaculate High School, and the chair of the National Governors Association in England, Stephen Adamson. Glyn, unfortunately, had to step down from that role through illness in 2013, and some of the work was in any case superseded by the Robert Hill review.

Robert Hill's review of the delivery structure of education in Wales, which I commissioned in 2013, has generally been read more in the context of local government reform, but in practice, Robert outlined a route forward for Wales on school improvement without academies. His most important comments concerned the quality of teaching and school leadership. Robert Hill rightly said in his review that this was 'a key moment in the improvement journey for schools in Wales.' He made it clear that he had been struck by 'the shared commitment to improve standards of education in Wales.' Effectively acknowledging that by then we had built the necessary consensus for change.

As Robert noted, greater autonomy did not on its own result in school improvement, but it could boost performance if schools had greater control over managing staff, curriculum and budgets, provided leaders were supported and subject to clear accountability. We had increased the autonomy of schools with an increase in the delegation of funding to schools. We needed in particular to make greater use of the best schools – Lead Practitioner Schools – to support weaker or emerging schools. Resources should be delegated from local authorities to federations and hard clusters of schools. But there was a dependency culture within the primary sector in particular which inhibited taking responsibility for performance, and variable quality of school governing bodies. Partnership culture was shallow and there were too few federations or hard clusters in place with shared governance led by an executive leader, though we had commenced some federation pilots alongside the Measure. Robert said that there was a strong case for the majority of, and potentially all, schools in Wales to be part of a formal federation or hard cluster, which could be primary to primary or secondary to secondary or an all-through cluster covering primary and secondary. We should enforce that through the new statutory guidance on school improvement to indicate that federation with a high-performing school should form the core of a recovery programme. I had asked Robert to consider the role of co-operative schools. He said that the Co-operative Trust approach offered one organisational model for hard clusters of schools. More grants, including capital grants, should be awarded through clusters and federations, and the accountability and inspection frameworks should be adjusted to recognise their role.

Robert said that what academies could do, maintained schools could also do. What Robert proposed for us could also have been a model in England if the political will had been there rather than the desire by Michael Gove to turn most schools into academies. The National Governors Association in 2014 argued that pooling resources through federations was one of the best ways to help school improvement, using the 2002 federation model developed by the then Labour Government to create non-academy federations. The Dartmoor federation, for example, has five schools sharing one governing body. The four primaries are rated as good by Ofsted and Okehampton College, a secondary school, is rated outstanding. This structure could work well in Wales, where we have had difficulty in obtaining enough high quality governors. Federated governing bodies such as this can be successful in raising standards throughout and can attract a wider range of expertise than can a single school.

So we did start to explore the prospect of co-operative schools, which we saw as being entirely in line with Welsh traditions of mutuality dating back over a century. I had asked Robert Hill to look at this model in his review. In 2008, Ed Balls as Secretary of State for Children, Schools and Families, had made available money to enable Trust schools to become co-operatives, with the intention that the schools be owned and controlled by the local community. By summer 2013 there were over 450. Co-op schools were the third-biggest association of schools in England, after the Church of England and the Roman Catholic Church. Schools could become single co-operatives or a cluster of co-operatives. It was clear that many were going down this route to escape enforced academy status.

In 2012, the Welsh think tank, the Bevan Foundation, produced a report on co-operative education. Meanwhile, we held a seminar at Transport House in Cardiff hosted by the Co-operative party in February 2013, addressed by Mervyn Wilson of the Co-operative college and Dave Boston of the Co-operative Schools Society, where we explored the opportunity they offered. Dave Boston made it clear that they could be an excellent vehicle for raising standards collectively across a local school system. In the summer of 2013 the Institute of Welsh Affairs held a further seminar on the subject.

The attractions of the co-operative model are that they are based on the principle of sharing values such as self-help, self responsibility, democracy, equality, equity and community solidarity. Their ethos is reinforced and acknowledged in their governance documents that is drawn from the globally shared co-operative values. They have governance mechanisms that engage key stakeholder groups, particularly parents and carers, staff, learners and the local community in the governance of the school through membership of the co-operative. Their curriculum and pedagogy embraces co-operation, using the global co-operative movement as a learning resource across the curriculum, and drawing on co-operative approaches to teaching and learning. They could be a Welsh alternative to academies.

Three Clear Priorities

Following the seminar with Michael Barber, I had decided early on in January 2010 that literacy and numeracy, along with tackling the impact of poverty on educational achievement, would be the key priorities for the department as far as schools were concerned. If we didn't get literacy and numeracy right in primary school, then we were storing up trouble for secondary – not only in terms of attainment, but also behaviour and attendance. In its 2014 report on Wales, the OECD team explicitly said:

> The school leaders, teachers, students, trade union representatives and others the OECD team met recognised the need for change and supported the government's three education objectives – improve students' literacy and numeracy performance, and reduce the impact of deprivation on performance – as being appropriate for improving learning in Wales. This is a strong starting-point to build on.

In 1971, Dr Julian Tudor Hart, a GP living and working in the South Wales valleys, wrote in *The Lancet* about a problem he had identified as the Inverse Care Law:

> The availability of good medical care tends to vary inversely with the need for it in the population served.

The same could be said about education – it could be argued that we suffered from an inverse learning law.

Research showed that children who were not fully literate at eleven had only a 25 per cent chance of improving their skills by age fourteen. The Wales Millennium Cohort Study showed that by the age of five, the vocabulary of children from disadvantaged backgrounds could be as much as a year behind those from better-off families. At eleven, 75 per cent of those from the most deprived backgrounds achieve expected levels compared to 97 per cent from the most affluent quintile. By the age of fifteen, children living in deprived circumstances were two and a half times less likely to achieve five good GCSEs including English or Welsh and Maths. The gap between those on free school meals (FSM) and those not on FSM in 2011 was 33 per cent. If young people didn't have the basic skills of literacy and numeracy, how could they access the rest of the curriculum? Was it any wonder that some of those without those key skills would switch off – and sometimes, bunk off or kick off?

In its first term, the Assembly had begun the development of an important agenda around children's rights, with the appointment of the first Children's Commissioner in the UK. I came to learn that, if pursued as a collective approach, the children's rights agenda was a powerful tool in challenging vested interests within education in the drive to raise standards. However, too often it was described in highly individualistic terms. I was worried that it was too often emphasising a naïve Rousseau-esque natural development model of childcare and early years learning, which some might see as 'anything goes', leaving children to develop as they saw fit rather than being challenged consistently to grow and progress. All that did was entrench the advantages of privilege. Estyn said studies on child poverty tell us that the gap between children from richer and poorer backgrounds widens especially quickly during primary school. Disadvantaged children in primary schools are more likely to lack ambition and self-esteem and to have behavioural problems. Boys as young as nine in disadvantaged schools become disenchanted with school and start to disengage. Young people living in poverty were more likely to be deprived of access to the arts, to sports opportunities, and to ICT – issues which three of the curriculum review areas I commissioned work on could help to tackle.

Estyn also said that amongst learners from disadvantaged backgrounds were those more likely to have a poor attendance record; to perceive the curriculum as irrelevant; less likely to accept the school culture; more likely to have additional learning needs; have parents who are less likely to be involved in their children's education; have parents who are more likely to have a negative perception and experience of school and education; be less healthy; more likely to be not in employment, education or training; more likely to have a child in their teenage years; and in the case of white working-class boys, less likely to achieve their potential than any other group.

In more socially-deprived areas teachers faced challenging circumstances overall. In early 2012 the newspaper *Wales on Sunday* splashed on what it called 'shocking revelations' that 'children in Wales are starting primary school without basic skills like toilet training and the ability to speak'. This came as no surprise to me. Primary teachers had been telling me that ever since I became an Assembly Member. Professor Iram Siraj's stock-take of the Foundation Phase reported similar issues in 2014. Sadly, we were dealing with the consequences of the children and grandchildren of Thatcherism, where the doctrine that 'there's no such thing as society' and the tolerance of long-term unemployment and economic inactivity led to an undermining of basic social and community values, with for some a consequential loss of dignity, self-esteem, time-discipline and a culture of respect for others, and the abandonment sometimes of core family values learned over generations in place of rights without responsibilities.

As a government we supported the rights of the child. Children have a right to proper parenting. Most parents, including those in the most deprived areas of Wales, provide that. But there are some who do not take their responsibilities seriously. If the parental home is not providing the necessary learning environment; if children are not getting the stimulation they require; if they are not getting the right parental engagement in their development – from talking to toilet-training – then the government must give those children their second chance, and the support they are not getting at home. And teachers, teaching assistants and other staff are at the front line of delivery on this. Our system has to deliver for children from the most disadvantaged backgrounds who sometimes are dependent on their schools to give them what other parents can provide.

This requires cultural change in some parts of the system. I have considerable sympathy with what Sir Michael Wilshaw, chief inspector of Ofsted, and former head teacher of the Mossbourne Academy in Hackney, has said about this: 'you can't be woolly. It's about meticulous standards'. He cited the importance of clear boundaries, respect for teachers, no excuses and high expectations. Head teachers turning round schools in areas of disadvantage in Wales have said similar things to me – including the need sometimes to move on staff who have essentially given up on the children in their schools, and use socio-demographics as an excuse for low performance outcomes, with the excuse 'what can you expect with kids like this?' Representing the Rhondda, a series of communities where education has been valued over time, but acute social disadvantage is obvious in places, I am not prepared to see the young people in my constituency let down in that way.

It is too often the case that those who need the most support do not get it. That is the inverse learning law – places where there is a high proportion of pupils whose family circumstances are themselves significantly more challenging, their school buildings are frequently the worst, leadership has sometimes been weak and where in some schools poor standards of teaching went unchallenged, pupil outcomes have been poor and consequently their school numbers were trapped in a spiral of decline with resources reducing year-on-year. Sickness levels amongst teachers in these areas were sometimes higher than average and there was less stability for pupils than in other places. One secondary school in South Wales, now closed, was allegedly running a budget to cover staff absence of around £25,000 *per month* – whereas the expectation of another school in a similar area of deprivation in an adjoining authority was more like £35,000 *a year*. Some schools in deprived areas, however, outperformed expectations thanks to good leadership, and effective local authority and community support. They are the schools who can teach us all how our system can succeed.

Early on, Estyn provided evidence of the way forward. One of its first thematic reports to cross my desk in January 2010 was on tackling poverty and disadvantage. Estyn looked back at the impact of the Welsh Assembly Government's RAISE-funding between 2008 and 2009, a programme to combat under-achievement amongst the most deprived. The evaluation of RAISE showed that many disadvantaged pupils did not directly benefit from RAISE and few average or more able disadvantaged pupils benefitted from RAISE. In the main, schools took the easier option of tackling low performance of borderline pupils rather than those from deprived backgrounds. During the development of the grant conditions for the Pupil Deprivation Grant in 2012, the experience of RAISE was taken into account.

Perhaps Estyn's most important finding was that some schools succeed despite facing challenging circumstances and that *these successful schools tend to do well by doing the same kinds of things that all successful schools do*. What is different in the schools that do well in disadvantaged areas, said Estyn, is that they have highly effective leadership and consistently good teaching, and place an emphasis on particular activities or combination of activities. For instance, they:

- attach great importance to extra-curricular and out-of-school-hours provision, including cultural and sport enrichment, as well as extra educational support such as homework clubs, at lunchtimes or after school;

- have high expectations of standards and behaviour and a zero tolerance of excuses for poor provision or underachievement;
- work closely with parents and the wider community to reinforce expectations; and
- give substantial attention to developing pupils' social and emotional skills, and improving their confidence and self-esteem.

In other words, these schools did not have a culture of socio-demographic determinism – they didn't take the view, nor did they allow teachers to take the view, that just because their children came from deprived backgrounds they were not capable of doing well. Speaking to head teachers during my time as Education Minister, those who had made significant strides in addressing issues of performance in schools in the most deprived communities sometimes made it clear that they had had to move teachers on, not because they lacked traditional teaching skills – though some did – but because their attitude was wrong – they had low expectations of their pupils and reinforced a culture of low expectation. Recognising the potential of every pupil required a different approach – and could lead to different results. The dynamic head teacher of Rhyl High, Claire Armitstead, now a member of the Welsh Government's new National Leadership Development Board for Wales, explained how she had worked to re-engage young people with the help of outside agencies including the army and Rhyl Football Club. She told me when I visited her school 'These kids gave us a second chance.' Rhyl High was in special measures in 2008 and the expected percentage of pupils getting five GCSEs was 25 per cent – it is now over 90 per cent. The percentage getting five good GCSEs including English or Welsh and Maths has risen from 36 per cent in 2011 to over 50 per cent in 2013. Leadership matters.

Estyn found that some local authorities were better than others in tackling these issues. Estyn also argued rightly that schools alone could not break the link between poverty and underachievement. Research stresses the need for integrated and broad-based approaches that involve a number of agencies working together.

It became clear that the excellent practice that did exist was not being shared sufficiently across Wales. The biggest variation in performance that we faced was between those on free school meals and those not. Looked-after children had the worst outcomes. There were other equality issues we had to address, of course, and we protected investment in funding designed to lift attainment amongst ethnic minority children and gypsies and travellers, and developed work based on the Equalities Task and Finish Group chaired by Bethan Guilfoyle. Alan Evans from Bethan's group was an expert on literacy and the performance of boys and produced excellent work for us.

Professor Chris Taylor, from The Wales Institute of Social and Economic Research, Data & Methods (WISERD) at Cardiff University, while accepting that there is a need to raise levels of literacy and vocabulary development between the wealthiest and poorest children in Wales, says that Welsh children in the early years actually out-perform parts of the UK in many areas of educational development. He argues, from the Millennium cohort study, that differences in society outside education may have more to do with outcomes in early years. We certainly accepted the need for wider programmes beyond school.

We sought to integrate family and school approaches to addressing poor attainment. We used research to inform our policy development – and to this end focused on whole-family approaches through Families First and investing in the early years to give children the best possible start in life. In 2013, for example, Carl Sargeant, as Minister for Local Government and Communities, launched a new £2 million fund to support greater co-operation and joint working between schools and Communities First Clusters. The Communities First Pupil Deprivation Match Fund will enable a significant number of Clusters in Wales to secure additional funding if they can show

how they will work with schools. The fund runs from April 1st 2013 until March 31st 2015.

We also made our extra investment in Early Years, supporting young children and families through Flying Start, doubling the reach of the programme. Flying Start was making a difference. In evaluating the programme, the feedback was positive: parents said:

- their confidence as a parent has increased;
- they feel better able to make decisions about how to look after their baby and have a better understanding of their child's general development;
- there have been positive changes in their child's behaviour since attending Flying Start parenting courses; and
- importantly, many parents of them are now engaged in home learning activities with their children.

Flying Start is beginning to have a real, positive impact on these children – when they go to school they are ready to learn, better behaved and more confident at mixing with other children.

Research by the Joseph Rowntree Foundation in 2011 and 2012 challenged the widespread presumption that poorer children and their parents have low aspirations. It found that poorer children (along with their families) often have high aspirations and that many want to go to university or get professional, managerial and skilled jobs. Professor Stephen Gorard of the University of Birmingham, who led the work, noted the research found little evidence of unrealistic aspirations among poorer young people and their families. It also found little evidence of fatalism among people faced with depressed local labour markets, nor of beliefs that not working was acceptable. Indeed, it indicated that most poorer young people attached great importance to school and that their parents did what they could to support them.

However, the study stressed that the real difficulty for many children was in knowing *how* to fulfil their ambitions. Rather than raising aspirations in order to raise attainment, there was a real need for children and parents to be offered support to learn more about educational and career options so they could make more informed decisions about their future. Indeed, the Rowntree research concludes that what might look like low aspirations might be high dreams beaten down by negative experience. What looks like parental disengagement may be real commitment let down by lack of school support. Programmes of parental engagement which helped parents understand how to help their children achieve were more valuable. The research also had implications for our careers service as well.

LSE Professor Ruth Lupton has argued for a contextualised school improvement policy which enables schools in deprived areas to have the flexibility to innovate in respect of the curriculum to address underperformance and raise standards, and has also argued that schools in areas of deprivation may require different teaching approaches to raise performance than schools in more affluent areas that do not face the same challenges. I believe that a contextualised policy is starting to emerge in Wales, based on the sharing of good practice between schools facing similar challenges, underpinned by the availability of the Pupil Deprivation Grant.

The Sutton Trust has provided some of the most effective guides on what really works in tackling poor attainment amongst pupils from deprived backgrounds, working with the Education Endowment Foundation (EEF) and Durham University. In 2012, it set out what existing international evidence says about the effectiveness of approaches from improving the attainment of pupils from deprived backgrounds in order to help schools make best use of resources targeted at these pupils. The top five approaches with a high impact for a low-moderate cost include:

- Effective feedback – information given to the learner or teacher about the learner's performance relative to learning goals which then redirects or refocuses the learning action to achieve the goal. The estimated impact is equivalent to nine months of progress in a year.

- Self-regulation strategies – teacher approaches which make learners manage their own motivation towards learning and learners think about their own learning more explicitly in the classroom. The estimated impact is equivalent to eight months of progress in a year.
- Peer tutoring/peer assisted learning – approaches in which learners learn in groups to provide each other with explicit teaching support. The estimated impact of this approach is equivalent to six months of progress in a year.
- Homework – reading and preparing for work to be done in class or practising and completing that already taught or started, extended activity to develop pupils' inquiry skills or revision for tests. Estimated impact is again significant and equivalent to at least five months of progress in a year.
- Assessment for learning – developing a clear understanding of what it is learners need to learn and evidence about their current level of performance. The estimated impact of this approach is equivalent to at least three months of progress in a year.

I saw such approaches in place, utilising the Sutton Trust toolkit, when I visited Glyn Derw school in Ely, part of a new federation with Michaelston Community College under then executive head teacher, and now Welsh Government adviser, Geraint Rees. The Sutton Trust research also sets out those approaches that do not achieve significant benefits for learners. The two approaches most to be avoided are reducing class sizes and basic deployment of more teaching assistants.

It was our job to maximise the performance within the school system. The advent of the Pupil Deprivation Grant (PDG) from the 2012-13 financial year gave us a new lever – an additional £32 million or so – to drive this work forward, and we published guidance on how the grant could be used to deliver long-term sustainable improvements that last beyond the lifetime of the grant. Guidance required schools to demonstrate how they were using evidence-based approaches such as the EEF Sutton Trust Toolkit.

I surveyed schools in my own constituency in 2012 to find out how they were using the PDG. Schools in the Rhondda used the Grant to fund a variety of initiatives including literacy and numeracy intervention programmes such as phonics resources and Spotlight Maths. Additional staff were employed in several schools such as Learning Support Assistants, support teachers and learning coaches. Schools throughout the Rhondda also used the grant to fund well-being and nurture programmes. Several schools also used the fund to engage with families and strengthen links between the home and school through initiatives such as Investors in Family Assessment and employing Family Liaison Officers. Others used the Grant to create family rooms and cafés where parents and pupils can work together on reading skills.

Estyn published a good practice guide for headteachers in November 2012 which gave further illustrations. This set out ten key areas in which successful schools excelled, including data tracking, literacy and learning skills, targeting attendance, punctuality and behaviour, developing social and emotional skills, tailoring the curriculum to the needs of disadvantaged learners, providing enrichment experiences that more advantaged pupils take for granted, such as cultural experiences, engaging parents and carers, developing skills of staff, including listening skills. Transition arrangements between primary and secondary could also make a difference. Schools had to prepare transition plans.

Estyn gave fifteen examples of best practice throughout Wales. I was pleased that the best practice outlined included that of Llwynypia Primary School in my own Rhondda constituency, where at Key Stage 1, results have improved and are in the top half of those for similar schools, and in the top quarter for Key Stage 2. In the last two years, the performance of learners entitled to free school meals (FSM) at both Key Stages had improved. These learners have achieved better-than-average for FSM learners in the family of schools and the Welsh average.

Estyn reported further in December 2013 that the most recent data shows there has been a slight narrowing in the gap between the performance of learners who are eligible for free school meals and those who are not. However, learners eligible for free school meals still do not perform as well as their peers against all key performance indicators. Estyn identified a range of factors that still needed to be addressed.

There were other initiatives which we maintained which helped to address issues of poverty, including the school uniform grant and free breakfasts. Some teachers told me that there had been an upsurge in the desire to wear school uniform, which they put down to the success of the Harry Potter books and films. The school uniform grant had been the result of campaigning by Huw Lewis when he was a backbencher. The free breakfast policy, launched in 2004, was protected in our manifesto. 73 per cent of primary schools took part in it, backed by £12.7 million of Welsh Government funding. This initiative was intended to help improve the health and concentration of pupils, to assist in the raising of standards of learning and attainment. It was opposed by the Welsh Conservatives, whom I dubbed the 'cereal killers' for their opposition to it. It supported the provision of healthy breakfasts, not Coco Pops, as some ignorant journalists believed. Our Healthy Eating measure underpinned quality provision for food in schools. In Wales, we kept the Educational Maintenance Allowance (EMA), giving financial support to the most deprived pupils to stay in school or college after sixteen. It was abolished by the UK coalition government in England. This area of policy was one of the most difficult to get right. As the UK coalition government's welfare reforms worsened, it was likely to get tougher, with an increase in child and family poverty and a growth in those on free school meals.

There was no question that tackling problems of literacy and numeracy were key to addressing the impact of poverty on attainment. This was a social justice issue. When I arrived as Minister, I found we had a number of initiatives, but they seemed uncoordinated and run by different teams. I once had two meetings on literacy on the same day with completely different teams involved. We had confusing terminology. Sometimes we spoke of Basic Skills. Other times, it was Key Skills. We had catch-up programmes, campaigns to encourage boys to read, since there was a significant gender gap in literacy levels, aimed at getting boys to read with other boys and with male family members. There was nothing wrong with these programmes per se, which were often grounded in the best research available. But ensuring consistency across the curriculum required better strategic planning.

Early on, I asked the director general of my department to find me an additional £1 million for literacy programmes. That was done. But it was just the start. I was being told by some head teachers that skills of literacy and numeracy were being lost in the Foundation phase. That had never been the intention. Newport Director of Education, Dr Brett Pugh, whose authority was widely seen to be amongst the best at delivering primary education, confirmed that in the best primary schools literacy and numeracy was integrated throughout the Foundation Phase delivery. It had never been intended to be just 'learning through play' – there had always been the intention that it would be directed learning, not 'anything goes'. But the evidence from Estyn and others was that this was not being applied consistently. Estyn reported in September 2011 that in a significant minority of schools there was not enough direct teaching of reading. Targeted early intervention was critical. Catch-up programmes, used consistently, worked. Over 6000 primary pupils in Wales were benefitting from such programmes in the 2009-2010 academic year. But reporting on the 2010-11 academic year, in February 2012, Ann Keane said that 40 per cent of primary pupils had a reading age of six months behind their chronological age – and half of these were eighteen months behind. Given that teacher assessment since 2008 had consistently been telling us that around 80 per cent of young people were meeting the desired level for their age (level 4) at the end of primary, this was deeply worrying in several ways.

We needed to learn from best practice. I told the National Assembly in May 2010, West Dunbartonshire in Scotland had focused on a twelve-year plan to develop an approach that was used in every school, using consistent measures, and tracking every pupil, resulting in a tiny percentage leaving primary school without functional literacy skills. We involved Professor Tommy Mackay, who had led the West Dunbartonshire programme, in our national steering group developing the National Literacy Plan. This was focused on the post-Foundation Phase pupils in Key Stage 2. It was based on zero tolerance of poor literacy, improvements in the skills of those teaching literacy, targeted catch-up for those between seven and eleven, and better family and community engagement. I was also determined that there would be a greater emphasis on synthetic phonics in the teaching of literacy, which was not always popular in the department in my early days as minister. Cardiff University's Alan Evans, who – I later learned – decades before had been Michael Barber's boss at the NUT, was an expert on what worked in literacy, as well as being chair of governors at the highly effective Kitchener Primary School in Cardiff. I made sure that the department drew on Alan's expertise.

We embarked on the development of an initial National Literacy Plan which led eventually to the Literacy and Numeracy Framework. As I explained to Cabinet in September 2010, the plan required the re-prioritisation of budgets within the department. We organised events to promote the programme and provided additional materials, and the consortia then run by the Association of Directors of Education in Wales had the task of integrating the programme within the School Effectiveness Framework. There was additional funding for catch-up work, aimed at every primary, for activities aimed at boys aged seven to eleven including in libraries, reading volunteers in primary schools, and parent-child engagement programmes. Roger Lewis, chief executive of the Welsh Rugby Union, responded immediately and positively to my text message asking if the WRU would get involved, and Shane Williams and Tom Shanklin took part in our Reading Heroes campaign. Welsh International footballers Gareth Bale, Chris Gunter, Boaz Myhill and Dave Edwards also took part.

I announced in February 2011 the move towards literacy and numeracy tests in my speech, *Teaching Makes a Difference,* a recommendation of the review by the group chaired by Viv Thomas on the Structure of Delivery in education. I had also said I wanted all teachers to be teachers of literacy and numeracy and announced I was tightening up testing of these skills on entry to teacher training and thereafter. We commissioned Professor Rhona Stainthorp of Reading University to provide an objective view of the validity, rigour and practicalities of the reading tests currently used across Wales.

She found that there was a range of Welsh and English commercially produced reading tests being used in schools – with no consistent approach across Wales. There was variation from local authority to local authority. Her advice was clear – whatever test is chosen, all primary schools should administer the same reading test on an annual basis in the early part of the summer term. She recommended that in order to establish a reliable database for monitoring progress for the first five years, annual testing for Years 2, through to Years 7 and 9 would be desirable. We were clear that phonic and graphic knowledge and contextual understanding should be used as strategies to develop reading.

Later in 2011 we widened the ambitions of the National Literacy Plan into the National Literacy Programme, eventually published in May 2012, which set our national expectations, outlined greater support and development, with stronger targeted interventions backed by greater accountability. National Reading and Numeracy Tests would be sat on a statutory basis from May 2013, but on a voluntary basis in May 2012. Other aspects of the programme included support for professional development in literacy and numeracy for teachers from initial teacher training onwards and the continuation of catch-up programmes.

Work on the reading and numeracy tests was already under way and they were being piloted in schools. The new Master's in Educational Practice being launched in September 2012 would include a literacy module and we were shortly due to issue the National Literacy and Numeracy Framework for consultation.

The Framework raised the bar as to what we expected from pupils. It drew on the features of high performing international models, such as that of British Columbia, setting expected annual outcomes in literacy and numeracy. It was aligned with Foundation Phase outcomes and reflected existing curriculum requirements. Planning within the school should enable reinforcement of key literacy and numeracy messages across subjects. Online resources to support the teaching of literacy and numeracy were contained within the Learning Wales website. Professor David Reynolds said 'with this programme, the cavalry has arrived.' The NAHT Cymru and ASCL Cymru, representing primary and secondary head teachers, in a joint submission to the consultation on the Literacy and Numeracy Framework, said it could be 'one of the most stellar developments in devolved education policy-making'. The OECD recognised that education professionals have generally supported it.

The National Literacy and Numeracy Framework (LNF) broke literacy and numeracy down into their core elements. Literacy was broken down into reading, writing and oracy; each element was then broken down into further requirements, for example for writing – writing accurately, which was based on spelling, punctuation and grammar. Numeracy was broken down into key elements of using numeracy skills, measuring, calculating, interpreting and presenting findings. These were then broken down into further aspects, for example, comparing data and recording and interpreting data and presenting findings. Acceptable outcomes for each year were then outlined. The development of the Framework threw up some key issues – for example, the extent to which the existing maths curriculum actually tested numeracy skills, and the extent to which the existing English language curriculum actually tested literacy skills. These issues were addressed in the context of the Qualifications Review with revised GCSEs in numeracy and in the English language and the Welsh language. As the OECD has noted, the LNF was intended principally to be used as a formative assessment to inform the next steps for individuals or groups of learners, rather than as a summative assessment, designed to generate comparable data (between schools or local authorities or to show national progress over time) for accountability purposes. Schools will be able to use the data to identify learners' strengths and areas for development, enabling schools to intervene earlier if they are falling behind, while also stretching those who are more able. By tracking progress from the end of the Foundation Phase right the way through into secondary education, the tests should help teachers gain a clearer insight into a learner's development and progress.

We decided to make the LNF a statutory curriculum requirement from September 2013 and assessment against it would be statutory from September 2014, giving schools a year to embed the LNF into their curriculum planning. Parents would be provided with annual reports on their child's progress in literacy and numeracy from September 2013, including information based on the tests. Governing bodies would report on how the schools had fared in the tests.

The percentage of pupils getting A*-C in maths was consistently lower than those gaining the same grades in English or Welsh first-language. Estyn considered numeracy skills weak in two-fifths of primaries and 50 per cent of secondary schools. Tracking of their skills outside maths lessons was poor. The inspectorate produced a full study of maths performance for the Welsh Government in October 2013 using examples of good practice from schools around Wales, including Eirias in Conwy, Treorchy, Porthcawl, Llanishen, Radyr, Cefn Hengoed and Bishop Gore in Swansea, Duffryn in Newport, and Bro Myrddin and Bryngwyn in Carmarthenshire. Welsh performance in maths GCSE was lagging behind other parts of the UK. Indeed, if we could get maths to the levels of English or Welsh then our overall performance would compare happily with other parts of the UK at GCSE level. We decided to launch a programme for employers to get involved in numeracy initiatives at secondary level, recognising that employer engagement could help pupils understand the importance of numeracy in real-life work situations. The School Standards Unit also published a review of secondary schools which had bucked the trend in terms of underperformance at GCSE so that all could learn from best practice.

I often saw Rhondda schools as a test-bed for our programmes as I knew I would get feedback quickly from them. Schools in the Rhondda were involved in pilots for the literacy and numeracy tests and I was pleased to get comments from head teachers of these schools. Sometimes I asked officials to make direct contact with the heads concerned, and this was done in respect of the literacy and numeracy tests. Some changes were made to the tests after piloting, particularly for the youngest learners. NFER, who carried out the work, found that there seemed to be little awareness generally of test taking techniques. Their assessment also suggested that teacher assessments at all levels may have been overly generous.

We developed a National Support Programme for the Framework. We provided additional material to assist teachers in making assessments. We saw the tests as replacing existing tests run by schools and local authorities so the workload burden should not have been significant, but we did provide some additional funding for the 2012-13 academic year when the tests were first run, as well as a telephone advice line. Disappointingly, there were some problems with some of the presentations at events organised to support the LNF and I made it clear to the organisation that had won the tender for the National Support Programme that I wanted greater senior executive input in its implementation. Huw announced additional support to underpin introduction of the numerical reasoning tests in 2014. Schools that implemented the LNF effectively, as Emma Abraham, Head of Humanities at Cefn Hengoed Community School in Swansea, a comprehensive school with 43 per cent FSM, told a Policy Forum for Wales conference in October 2013, saw standards of teaching rise across the curriculum.

Huw Lewis reported in July 2013 that nearly 700,000 test papers were dispatched to more than 1,650 schools, enabling

300,000 learners to sit the tests during the two week testing window in May. I received feedback from parents whose children had taken the tests, who told me that the information they received was more valuable, and more comprehensible, than any they had received before. Some also said that their own children had a better understanding of the learning targets they were expected to meet.

Huw noted that as expected there were lessons to be learnt from the implementation of the tests in their first year. He said he was very willing to listen to this feedback which will help to inform our review and evaluation of the tests for the future. Though some remain critical of testing, feedback from parents has been strong. As the First Minister himself has said in the Assembly in 2014:

> I am a parent and I welcomed the tests. I know that many others did as well. For the first time, I was able to understand objectively how my children were doing.

From School Effectiveness to School Improvement

The School Effectiveness Framework (SEF), launched by my predecessor Jane Hutt in February 2008, was due to go live in September 2010. It was not without critics and I felt that their arguments needed to be tested. Andy Henderson, head teacher of Ysgol Hen Felin, the special educational needs school in the Rhondda, was on secondment to my department working on the SEF. I knew Andy was a great head running an impressive operation at his school. He made a strong case for the SEF as a vehicle to share best practice and allow teachers to learn from one another.

In principle, the SEF did contain much of what we needed. It had been developed on the basis of international research into what made schools effective and was focused on whole-system reform, based on:

- effective use of data to benchmark performance and identify areas for development and improvement
- strengthening teaching and learning through more coherent continuous professional development
- strengthening school leadership and local authorities
- the establishment of Professional Learning Communities (PLCs) within, between and across schools
- greater clarity on accountability at all levels, including school governors
- the building of capacity at all levels.

However, despite the fact that we asserted that all our education policies should be aligned to it, it was not clear to me that they were. INSET days did not seem to be focused on the SEF; nor did continuing professional development. The point of the framework was to put teachers and head teachers in the driving seat of reform – but that also required effective challenge and leadership from local authorities. The reality was that in most cases they didn't know how their schools were performing. Clearly we had been too optimistic about the capacity within the system.

Introducing the debate on Bill Maxwell's final Estyn report in the National Assembly in March 2010, I warned that there was more to do, saying 'we need to focus on driving up standards further and faster', revealing that I had brought Michael Barber in for a seminar with officials. The report demonstrated the importance of leadership, saying leadership and management skills were improving significantly – but it also demonstrated the importance of spreading best practice across schools, particularly in terms of tackling the link between poverty and poor educational achievement. Estyn's report indicated that in England they had started to tackle this problem of worse outcomes for students on free school meals, but we had not.

The Estyn report also set out expectations of local authorities – 'effective local authorities challenge their schools robustly and intervene where outcomes are not good enough.' They analysed performance data thoroughly to identify underperformance and to take action. The report also included real examples of best practice from across Wales. Effective schools focused on the performance of individual pupils and compared their performance with that of schools in similar socioeconomic circumstances.

In the autumn of 2010 we came under criticism for having abandoned league tables for schools, with a report from Bristol University arguing that their abolition might have cost us a fall of almost two GCSE grades per pupil per year, and the effect was worse in schools in deprived areas.

However, some were critical of the Bristol study, arguing that it did not allow for other policy drivers in England which might have had an impact on standards, separate from the League Table focus. Warwick Mansell, the highly-respected education journalist, who had written extensively on league tables and accountability systems, argued that league tables had been just one element of a system of high-stakes accountability in England, all of which could have driven improvements in results.

PISA's Andreas Schleicher had some observations on high-stakes accountability, as Darren Evans recounted in the *TES*:

> You could say maybe England has had in the past too much high-stakes testing, too little formative assessment, and Wales it's been perhaps the other way round. But clearly you need some benchmark for success and whether abandoning those kinds of assessments altogether was the right thing, that's really up for debate.

Professor Dylan Wiliam, emeritus professor of educational assessment at the Institute of Education, said 'There's probably not enough pressure on teachers and pupils to do well in Wales, and too much in England. Wales in particular has suffered by taking the pressure off teachers and schools.'

I felt we certainly needed more focus on accountability, and in response to the Bristol report I said:

> In Wales, over the decade of devolution, we have implemented most of the changes the profession wanted to see. So we do not have league tables. We will see in December when the international comparisons of school performance are reported in the OECD's PISA survey whether that approach has paid off.

So what had happened in Wales in the first decade of devolution? We had abandoned league tables in 2001, and on a staged basis, ended the key stage tests after the reports on assessment by Professor Richard Daugherty and ACCAC in 2004.

I wasn't in the Assembly when league tables were abandoned, but looking back over the evidence I see that not all Labour Assembly Members had been enthusiasts for their removal. Lynne Neagle, the AM for Torfaen, spoke in the Assembly of her concern 'that parents will find information harder to obtain' and worried particularly that parents from deprived communities might be disadvantaged by the change and might not be able to access the information they needed. The position of the Welsh Assembly Government at the time was that parents could still have access to the information, but that they should consider a wide range of factors when looking at the performance of a school. Rather bravely, a week after my appointment in December 2009, Chris Tweedale told the ASCL conference that 'Wales threw the baby out with the bathwater' when it abandoned league tables.

The decision to end Key Stage tests had wider support, but what has become clear is that the steps recommended by Daugherty for implementation after the ending of the tests were not followed through. In announcing her decisions on the Daugherty report, Education Minister Jane Davidson said 'I am determined not to let up on the drive to raise standards.' Plaid and Liberal Democrat spokespeople welcomed the phasing out of tests. The Conservative spokesperson, David Davies AM, now MP for Monmouth, also backed the move, saying that he had been persuaded by teachers' representatives that tests did not have teachers' confidence and so 'there is not much point in continuing with them'. The NUT welcomed the decision but the NASUWT said it feared that teachers' workload would grow.

In place of Key Stage tests there would instead be statutory teacher assessments backed by moderation and accreditation arrangements. The curriculum and assessment body ACCAC was to design systems and checks and ensure assessments were consistent. There was to be a new form of skills-based diagnostic test in year 5. At the end of Key Stage 3, secondary schools were to be awarded accredited centre status.

However, the moderation process for teacher assessment was never introduced and accredited status was not given to secondary schools. This had clear implications for the accuracy of teacher assessments. The diagnostic test in year 5 was not introduced, meaning there was no national system for measuring literacy or numeracy. As the Viv Thomas report stated in 2011 'The perception is that though some parts including the abolition of formal examination type testing were warmly welcomed and enacted, other recommendations were conveniently placed on the back burner and never firmly put in place.'

I knew we needed deeper cultural change, which required a key to ignite discussion of the need for change across the system. In their study *How the world's most improved school systems keep getting better*, McKinsey's education team identified three common factors: political or economic crisis; a high profile and critical report about performance; new political or strategic leadership. Well, we had not had a political crisis, but we had, following the Labour leadership election, a change of political leadership. We were about to have the high profile report about performance.

Rumours about our performance in the 2009 PISA tests were already in circulation. The tests had been taken just before I became Minister in 2009. PISA, run by the Paris-based OECD, is an international standardised assessment for fifteen-year-olds. Jane Davidson had originally taken us into PISA for the 2006 tests to ensure international comparability following the ending of Key Stage tests. A week before the results were published, the *TES* was headed 'Wales flunks global tests', reporting that the results were far worse than we had expected.

The task of handing me bad news on results was usually given to the bright and always cheerful official Emma Williams, who for several years briefed me on results in the summer GCSE, AS and A level examinations as well as PISA. She delivered bad news with a smile, pulling no punches. Her assessment was stark:

- Wales's results have gone down.
- Reading and Mathematics are significantly below OECD and other UK nations.
- Science was at the OECD average but below the UK average.
- Other UK results were largely stable or improved.
- The results distribution was skewed toward the low end – underperformance at all levels.
- It's not just about socio-economics.

Additionally, it was clear that it was not an issue of investment. Some countries which had done better than Wales spent less than Wales: some countries which had done worse than Wales spent more than Wales. New Zealand, for example was one of the highest performing countries but one that spent below average. Countries like Estonia and Poland performed as well as the United States, Switzerland and Norway, which spent more than double what they did.

When faced with bad news as a politician, there are a number of ways you can react. You can go into denial; you can immediately announce a rash of new initiatives and claim that these will take care of the problem; or you can front up, admit there is a problem and challenge others to join you in facing up to it. I was clear that we should take this last approach, and so was the First Minister when we discussed it. I wanted all in the education system to reflect on the PISA outcomes, not take refuge in debating whether some instant policy response was the correct one. Carwyn agreed that I should attend his press conference on the morning of Tuesday 7th December, and give our response.

I chose my words very carefully, saying 'These results are disappointing. They show an unacceptable fall in our overall performance – everyone involved in the education sector in Wales should be alarmed. There can be no alibis and no excuses.' I said the results 'made it clear that schools in Wales are simply not delivering well enough for students at all levels of ability. This can only be described as a systemic failure; we all share responsibility for this and we must equally share in the difficult task of turning things around.'

I was clear that the young people of Wales had the same potential as young people across the world. We needed to refocus on higher standards, set our ambitions and expectations high and look for improvement in every aspect of our system. This required honesty, leadership and a new approach to accountability.

David Williamson, the *Western Mail*'s perennially effervescent political correspondent, gave an entertaining flavor of my presentation:

> The Senedd's media briefing room is a chilly, dark, concrete cavern which resembles a nuclear bunker. A Hollywood set designer could not have conceived of a better place to deliver bad news, and there are few ministers who can read a riot act with such cold precision as Education Minister Leighton Andrews.

Former First Minister Rhodri Morgan was to refer to this as my 'Sputnik moment'. He said the Sputnik moment was 'when American educators panicked to some degree at the thought that the Russians were ahead of them, and the American press was full of articles that were broadly entitled 'what little Ivan knows that little Johnny doesn't.'

I repeated the messages in my first speech to the ASCL Conference two days later, where there was overwhelmingly positive feedback for what I had to say.

Most people appeared to buy into the need for change, though Estyn chief inspector Ann Keane warned a few months later that 'a minority of people are not taking PISA seriously'. She reinforced the message that 'PISA goes to the core of what a good education is'. She pointed out that you couldn't get through a PISA test having learnt by rote, despite what was said by some Opposition politicians in the Assembly. Professor David Reynolds elaborated on what I had said about 'systemic failure' early in 2011:

> We failed to develop our teachers and build their capacity. We left them on their own to reinvent the wheel in a time-wasting fashion. We left the educational producers – schools, local authorities, higher education – alone also, trusting them to operate without the need for the consumer pressures that are now the hallmark of education policies across the globe.
>
> We created an education system that has all the characteristics of ineffective educational settings: a knowledge deficiency about what to do; a reluctance to embrace change; the use of numerous alibis to explain poor performance; pervading conservatism; and ineffectual leadership.

How reliable is PISA as a test of national performance? Michael Gove came in for criticism from the Office of National Statistics for claims he had made in relation to comparisons between England's 2000 and 2009 results. There are some legitimate reasons for avoiding treating PISA as an international league table. The number of countries taking part is not constant, and it is not necessarily possible to assess whether the pupils involved from each country is a balanced representation of that country's pupils. But there is no question that consistently Wales has shown itself to be behind other UK countries in the test.

I outlined the Welsh Government's response to PISA in a lecture entitled *Teaching makes a difference* on February 2nd 2011 in the Reardon Smith lecture theatre at the National Museum, in front of an audience of teachers, head teachers and other education professionals. The lecture had been long-planned as a state-of-the-nation address, but the PISA results and our response now gave it its cutting edge. This became known as the '20-point plan' speech. Phil Dixon, director of the Association of Teachers and Lecturers in Wales, introduced me.

I told the audience what I had said to Michael Gove the previous year, that one of the advantages of devolution is that it allows England to be a laboratory for experiments. But if we believed in the comprehensive system, then we had to ensure that it delivered for all our children, and PISA suggested it did not. I quoted the words of Estyn Chief Inspector Ann Keane on PISA, that PISA tests the skills that should be at the core of any curriculum.

I made it clear that these results could not be excused on the basis of low socio-economic status or the bilingual nature of our nation and education system. They could not be excused by relative funding levels. PISA, I said, was a wake-up call to a complacent system.

My special adviser, Ian Butler, had rightly warned me not to use PISA as the only example of where we were falling down. We had to face the fact that we were not delivering in performance terms in public examinations overall compared to other parts of the UK. The recent UCAS figures suggested we were not preparing young people well enough for university entry. Estyn's Annual Report for 2009-10, published in January 2011, reviewed the full six years of the previous inspection cycle and noted that while standards had been maintained or improved, improvement in schools overall was slow. Standards were not as good as they should be in over 30 per cent of maintained schools, and standards in very few schools and providers are consistently outstanding. Literacy standards at the end of primary were a particular challenge still. 40 per cent of young people left primary schools with a reading age lower than their actual age. Data was not being used effectively in enough settings.

I explained the work that Michael Barber had done for the department in identifying some clear goals. I also drew on the work of Fenton Whelan and Michael Fullan in identifying what worked best in top-performing systems, and reminded the audience: 'Ultimately, this is about what goes on in the classroom. As McKinsey has said, no education system can perform beyond the level of the teachers within it. Teaching makes a difference.'

There had been a failure of leadership – throughout the system. We had assumed that things were going well, so we had designed systems intended to move us from the good to the great. In fact, ours was not a good system aiming to become great, but a fair system aiming to become good.

I was critical of my department, of local government, and the previous inspection framework. The School Effectiveness Framework needed sharpening. I also sought to establish the moral imperative behind what we were doing:

> Parents and young people have a right to expect the best. They may not know what the best is. Without data they certainly won't. And it is those in the most deprived communities who have the most to lose. I do not accept the socio-economic determinism of those who say that because we have major challenges of deprivation we cannot make progress.

Data empowered people, I said. I also raised issues of leadership, including the role of governors, and of teaching quality.

I made a mistake in that speech. I said we should aim to be in the top twenty of school systems measured in the PISA scores in 2015. The target was too ambitious, and it was naive. With more countries joining PISA, it was actually a target that was unlikely to be hit. It elevated PISA above other challenges our system faced. At the end of the day, I would rather set ambitious targets and have the right policies in place than set unambitious targets and have the wrong policies in place. At a WLGA conference in 2012, the OECD's senior PISA analyst, Michael Davidson, said that a 20-point increase in six years would be a challenge – it was 'a stretching target, but then that's what targets should be'. But, as the OECD itself concluded in its 2014 report, it was not a helpful target – and we also needed a target like Poland had for reducing the number of low performers in reading, maths and science.

The policies I outlined in *Teaching Makes a Difference* were broadly speaking the right ones, as Michael Davidson acknowledged in 2012, saying 'the 20-point action agenda the

Minister's got is really going in the right direction in many of the key things.' In the 2013 Annual ATL lecture in the Spring, *TES* editor at the time, Gerard Kelly, urged people in education 'to accelerate and augment the reforms Mr Andrews has embarked upon', commending in particular our initiatives on literacy and numeracy, reinstatement of public data for parents, moves to force local authorities to work together, and the Master's in Educational Practice. He said 'If there is another agenda out there to raise standards, I have not seen it.' The OECD itself recognised in 2014 that its visit had confirmed 'wide support for the reform journey that the Welsh Government embarked on following the disappointing PISA 2009 results.'

I outlined a five-year programme of twenty clear actions that we would undertake, many of them based on proposals in the Viv Thomas report which I had received, but not yet published. Performance would be driven from my department with the creation of a new School Standards Unit. As part of the National Literacy Plan, we would introduce a new national reading test. We would then move on to numeracy. Key Stage 2 assessments needed to be properly moderated. PISA assessments would be integrated into school assessments at age fifteen. Teachers must have appropriate literacy and numeracy standards. We would look to introduce a two-year Master's course. One inset day would be focused on literacy and numeracy as we wanted all teachers to become teachers of literacy. We would introduce a national system for the grading of schools which would be operated by all local authorities and consortia. Where schools were found by Estyn to be failing, and I regarded the situation as irredeemable, I would close them. I expected to see more federations of schools, operating under single head teachers. We were also introducing statutory training for governors and effective clerking. No school would pass an Estyn inspection unless it could demonstrate that its governing body had discussed the family of schools data and other relevant performance data and had set in place actions to improve its position. We would change the performance management provisions for head teachers and teachers performance to enable closer monitoring of their approach to raising standards.

We would review teacher induction, alongside our review of the General Teaching Council for Wales (GTCW). Development and support for the first three years of teaching would focus on firm foundations for the teaching of literacy and numeracy. All NQTs would have to meet Practising Teacher Standards. CPD would in future be focused on system-wide needs, linked to the three priorities of the School Effectiveness Framework. CPD opportunities would include the opportunity to gain the Master's Qualification. We would produce Statutory Guidance for school improvement, which sets out the best practice currently available in Wales and elsewhere, which we will expect schools to implement through the SEF. This would include kite-marked teaching strategies designed to make 'our best our standard'.

We would expect local authorities to participate in consortia arrangements, including shared consortium services, or suffer financial penalties. The Consortia would identify system leaders, who would support and challenge the Professional Learning Communities, which would have a focus on literacy and numeracy.

Progress on behaviour and attendance, particularly the latter, was not going fast enough. It was not acceptable that Wales had had for years suffered the worst school attendance levels in the UK. If attendance in Wales was at the level of England, our young people would effectively, on average, have an additional eight weeks of learning across their school career.

The speech was largely my own in terms of style, but I had drawn on help from a number of people in respect of the content, including Professors David Hopkins, who had taken over the DfE's Standards and Effectiveness Unit after Michael Barber, and Professors David Reynolds, Alma Harris and Dr Tim Williams. I made it clear that we had world-class teaching practice, but that the best was sadly not our standard.

The reaction to the speech was pretty positive. David Reynolds recorded 'approximately 200 of the nation's educational professionals listened quietly to what was probably the most damning indictment of an educational system ever uttered by a British politician in modern times.' He reckoned the mood music afterwards was positive and the profession seemed up for change.

Behind the scenes, Professor David Hopkins worked with both my department and the Association of Directors of Education in Wales (ADEW), and with Leigh Sandals from the consultancy Isos Partnership, who had worked in the Prime Minister's Delivery Unit under Michael Barber. They prepared work on how we would get the system into shape. David has explained some of this work in his book *Exploding the Myths of School Reform*. As David and Leigh identified, if we were to boost attainment in the short-term then we had to see improvement in the long tail of schools where not enough young people were getting five good GCSEs including English or Welsh and Maths – indeed some schools were falling back; and if we could tackle the geographic areas where failing schools were concentrated, notably the two biggest local authorities of Cardiff and Rhondda Cynon Taff but others as well, then that could make a significant difference.

Under the leadership of Brett Pugh, Chief Education Officer in Newport, who joined us on secondment, the new School Standards Unit (SSU) contained some of the brightest and best within our Department. By collecting and analysing crucial data information and system knowledge, it built a shared understanding of historical performance, trends, patterns, benchmarks and what excellence looks like. It worked to understand exactly what high performing schools and local authorities were doing well.

It was essential, as Michael Barber had told us, that the implementation of good practice became underpinned by clear routines. In the stock-takes undertaken in the autumn of 2011 and spring of 2012, the SSU had set out an improvement trajectory for improving the percentages getting five A*-C inclusive; looked at underperformance in maths and how this was being turned round in some parts of Wales; and worked on the implementation of pupil-tracking systems. They were uncovering some areas of difficulty, notably in capacity building and development of systems leaders; inconsistency in addressing targets, and an absence of systematic routes to disseminating good practice. The SSU had plans in place to address these issues, and knowledge of the detail meant that Brett and his team were providing effective challenge to local authorities' convictions about their own schools.

Professor David Reynolds was also working with the Welsh Local Government Association (WLGA). Their education service director, Chris Llewellyn, was pretty supportive of what we were trying to do. The WLGA told local authorities in spring 2011 that 'expectations of the education system in Wales at national, regional, local and school levels have been raised significantly.'

By the summer of 2011, our system of grading schools, confirmed in our 2011 manifesto, was to be called 'banding'. The new banding system looked at outcomes in context and progress made as well as 'raw results'. The national system for banding was at the very centre of the School Standards Unit's work. The Unit had already made considerable progress, developing the approach for secondary schools which was being used as the basis for pilot stock-takes with consortia. Banding would inform planning and better targeting of differentiated support and challenge to drive continuous improvement across all schools.

I knew my proposals to grade schools would be controversial, so I decided to enlist the help of the media. At a conference on raising School Standards, two weeks after *Teaching Makes a Difference*, I said:

> I do want to say to the teaching unions, that the Freedom of Information Act cannot be un-invented. A vast amount of data is already published on school performance, by us and by local authorities.

I knew that journalists would pick up on this and sure enough the BBC and the *Western Mail* decided to publish their own league tables in May, based on material they obtained from us under the Freedom of Information Act. Their tables looked at the value added by schools, based on predicted performance when pupils were eleven, taking account of socio-demographic factors. As a government we regarded the media approach as simplistic, compared to the banding system that we were working on, but it helped to change the climate on the use of data on schools publicly. In a written statement, I said that we believed there was no role for league tables and 'if league tables were the key to high-performing schools, then England would be at the top of the PISA scores.'

It was clear that educational standards had become a mainstream education story in Wales, which I regarded as key to ensuring that consensus was built behind the reforms we were undertaking. The *Western Mail* ran an education month in September 2011 with contributions from many different practitioners. Both it and the *Daily Post* in north Wales gave increasingly greater focus to education stories.

I had already decided that we had, as a government, to be honest about what had gone wrong in the past. I told the BBC Radio Four *Today* programme presenter John Humphrys in June 2011 that we 'took our eye off the ball' when we dropped end of Key Stage tests in the mid-2000s. I said that the Welsh Government may not have put in place 'sufficient ways of ensuring the judgements that teachers were making were done on a consistent basis, local authority by local authority'. Cabinet endorsed a paper from me in September 2011 which said 'it is clear that we had lost sight of the important role of accountability in our system'. That phrase – 'took our eye off the ball' – came to be the settled consensus of Carwyn Jones's governments about the first decade of educational policy in Wales. Huw Lewis used the term after the 2012 PISA results were published in December 2013, and the First Minister used the same term in early 2014 on the BBC Radio 4 *Any Questions?* programme.

We trialled the banding in the autumn of 2011 before publishing the final banding figures in December 2011. I had promised schools that provisional banding information would be available to them early in the new school year and it was issued on the 15th September. By this stage the BBC had already published its own ranking of schools on a much cruder measure, so I was hopeful that our approach would be seen to be fairer. The *Western Mail* had also commissioned an opinion poll through Beaufort Research, published at the end of October 2011, that suggested parents wanted a form of public accountability scoring for schools. The poll said that 5 per cent of those over sixteen wanted league tables based on GCSE and A level performance, while 32 per cent did not. The percentage was higher amongst those with children.

The banding was based on analyses of four groups of data relating to recent performance, progress and performance taking account of the level of deprivation and other socio economic factors. The four data groups and the indicators used reflected our priorities of literacy, numeracy and reducing the impact of deprivation on educational outcomes. I reiterated that that is banding was NOT about labelling schools, naming and shaming or creating a divisive league table. It was about grouping our schools according to a range of factors to establish priorities for differentiated support and identifying those from whom the sector could learn.

Banding uses the relative performance of schools to group those schools into one of five bands. Band 1 schools are those whose data show strongest overall performance and progress across the measures. Band 5 schools are those where performance and progress are weakest relative to other schools. In a debate in November 2012, I called schools in bands 4 and 5 'keys to the success of our system', borrowing a phrase from the London and Manchester Challenges I had heard Professor Mel Ainscow use.

Parents interviewed by media organisations appeared pleased to have the information, even when their children's schools ranked far lower than they had expected. The advantage of our banding system was that it identified schools which were coasting as well as those which were clearly struggling. When we published the banding information, we had a record number of hits on the Welsh Government's website.

The provisional banding was updated in December 2011 with the summer GCSE grades incorporated. The point of banding was that it should not simply identify those schools which consistently scored well in terms of the percentage of pupils getting five A*-C GCSEs including English or Welsh as a first language and mathematics (five A*-C 'inclusive', in the jargon). The weakness of that approach had been identified in the English system by writers such as Warwick Mansell and the *FT*'s Chris Cook. It essentially privileged those schools in wealthier areas with fewer challenges to overcome; and it led to a focus on the C-/D grade boundary, rather than an approach which looked at the performance of all students. The chair of the Education Select Committee in the House of Commons, Graham Stuart, a Conservative MP, said that this focus on the C-D boundary in the league tables meant schools were not giving sufficient attention to their worst performers. Tristram Hunt, Labour's new education spokesperson, said in 2014 that this had been one of Labour's mistakes: when he was Labour's education spokesperson, Stephen Twigg told me he thought our banding system was better than the league table system operated under the UK Labour Governments's from 1997-2010.

Our approach looked at the challenges facing schools based on the percentage in poverty, represented by the percentage on free school meals; it looked at progress over a three-year time period; it looked at attendance; and it looked at the school's progress not simply in terms of the percentage of pupils getting five A*-C grades (inclusive), but also the 'capped points score', in other words the best eight GCSE grades achieved by each pupil. Improving the performance of all pupils therefore mattered, not just those close to getting a C-grade. Subsequently, the English league table system was amended to include a wider range of data more akin to the system we were using.

Over the first three years of banding the controversy over the nature of the data continued. Some argued that it should be possible to see schools move up the bands with a diminishing number in the lower bands as overall performance improved – an argument I felt had some merit if we saw real system improvements. Others argued that grading a range of factors then expressing them as a single simple score was problematic and reductive. The truth was that there were problems in all kinds of scoring systems. I was ready for the criticism and made it clear that banding was here to stay. It was a manifesto commitment – indeed, our manifesto had called it 'grading' which potentially sounded more judgemental. Some teaching unions tried to claim that lower pupil-teacher ratios in some schools boosted performance in the rankings – in reality, we had examples of schools with higher pupil-teacher ratios doing well, and some with lower pupil-teacher ratios doing badly. Some contrasted Estyn six-year inspection reports out-turns with the banding results – but again, the detail showed consistency in judgements.

The 2012 banding results showed that performance had improved in 61 out of 79 schools in bands 4 and 5 in terms of the numbers getting five good GCSEs including English or Welsh and maths. In band 4 schools, the percentage getting this had gone up from 41.7 per cent to 46.5 per cent and in band 5 the percentage went from 36 per cent to 41.8 per cent. Attention was focused on schools which dropped bands – including Treorchy and Ysgol Bro Morgannwg, but when we analysed the data and discussed it with the heads, it was clear that there were specific reasons in both cases. Both heads identified what they needed to do and made progress again when the 2013 banding was published. Their approach was mature and considered. Both schools improved their outcomes in the 2013 banding. Overall, there was considerable stability, with most schools staying in the same band or moving up or down only one band. When the 2013 bands were published by my successor, Huw Lewis, attention was focused on Ferndale Community School in the Rhondda, which had moved from Band 5 to Band 1 in a year, the first to do so. Some used this to claim it showed that the system was flawed, rather than paying tribute to Ferndale's staff for their achievements. As Heather Nicholas, the head teacher, said, 'People look at the banding and think we have done it in one year. We haven't, but now everything is coming together.' Band 5 schools in general saw a 10 per cent increase in their performance in GCSE L2 inclusive in 2013. 80 per cent of schools stayed in the same band or went up or down one band. Huw is rightly now, after three years, looking at how banding and accountability measurements might develop in the future.

There was extraordinary naivety amongst the teaching unions about data publication and accountability for performance. In other countries, national league tables had been developed by the media. *The Sunday Times* and other newspapers published league tables of schools in England. When I visited Scotland in December 2012, I was greeted by headlines in all of the newspapers. 'How did your school do?' asked the *The Scotsman* front page banner. The *Scottish Daily Mail* banner was 'How did your school do in the exams league?' The *Herald Scotland* was similar. Inside all of them were pages of data on school performance – in a country which was even more explicit that it did not publish league tables. In Wales, our media had effectively colluded in the silence over data. Now there was no going back – the media was part of the process of reform. As I told the *Western Mail* at the end of 2012, after my visit to Scotland 'in the age of freedom of information, you either have banding in the way that we produce – which gives a balanced and rounded view of schools, looking at value-added aspects as well as exam performance – or you get league tables based on journalists' need for copy'.

I decided early on, however, that we would need a different way of grading primary schools, since their size meant that changes in cohorts year-on-year could have significant effects on scores. My written statement on 2nd December 2011 set out the challenges that we faced in developing an objective model for primary schools compared to secondary schools and, in particular, the consistency of teacher assessments and the large number of schools with a small number of pupils. We would not therefore be grading the smaller primary schools – potentially around 30 per cent of primaries – but these were very small schools, and 95 per cent of primary school pupils would be covered by the system.

In September 2013 the *Western Mail* decided to produce its own 'school rankings', *The Real Schools Guide*, using twenty-one different pieces of data. Like the school banding system, it looked at GCSE performance across the board and over time, and also attendance, and percentages on free school meals, but also added behaviour, gender differences in performance, the ratio of teachers to pupils and the state of school finances. The problem was that these latter factors produced further distortions, and moved the debate too far away from attainment and on to a range of other factors.

After the banding was published, I believed it was time to pay tribute to those schools, head teachers and teachers who were doing well, and draw on their experience and their examples of good practice. I decided that the main focus of my speech to the profession, a year on from *Teaching Makes a Difference*, would be 'Learning from the Best'. We had best practice in Wales and we needed to try to spread that good practice throughout the system. As we moved to develop our own Learning Wales website, we needed a strong range of case studies both in subject terms and in terms of best practice in raising standards.

The main thrust of the speech was on the quality of the teaching we had in Wales. I reiterated that we have world-class teachers and head teachers in Wales. We have world-class best practice in Wales. What we need to do better, is share that best practice across the whole of Wales, and enable all teachers to have access to it. It is what happens in the classroom that really matters. Great teachers matter. Great leaders matter. What we are asking of all schools is to replicate in the future what is already happening in the best schools today.

I gave examples of good practice from schools throughout Wales, including Casllwchwr's and Rhos y Medre's work in new technology, Bishop Gore's work on setting aspirational grades,

Eirias High School's work to ensure progress from entry to year 11, and its leadership work on maths teaching locally, St Mary Immaculate's transformation, in part through detailed pupil tracking, Sandfields' work on transition from primary school and pupil tracking, Herbert Thompson Primary's work on parental engagement, Lliswerry Primary's tracking of literacy and numeracy, and Ysgol Emmanual's work on moderating teacher assessments. Estyn subsequently also began to publish examples of best practice.

I said I didn't want a situation where the exciting areas of teaching and learning are going on elsewhere and my department simply focuses on regulation, standard-setting, and budgetary management. I wanted my department to engage systematically with leading teachers and head teachers. But as we did we would go at the pace of the system leaders, not at the pace of the slowest.

The *Western Mail* said that the tone of the speech had been noticed across the sector as a deliberate shift to indicate that we wanted to work with the profession to embed the reform programme, and we were prepared to listen and learn. I had come to the conclusion by the time of the March 2012 speech that we were unlikely to make progress in the PISA tests that autumn as the reforms we were implementing would not have had time to bed down.

The SSU worked with Isos to develop a national school improvement implementation plan in October 2012. Called *Improving schools*, the plan was targeted at leaders throughout the education system in Wales, from schools, local authorities and regional consortia through to government. In the document we clearly set out what needs to be achieved at each level of the education system. The actions set down in this new plan built on my 20-point plan and moved us beyond the School Effectiveness Framework. This translated the PISA goal of being in the top twenty in the world into a GCSE equivalence – that suggested our ambition should be that we hit a figure of 65 per cent of young people getting five A*-C grades inclusive of

English/Welsh and Maths. The figure was there not as a target, but as the document said, 'an ambition'.

This was the most detailed document on school improvement that the department had ever published, identifying across the system in Wales where we stood and what we needed to do to drive change forward. It drew on the stock-takes which the SSU had been undertaking with local authorities and regional consortia across Wales. It showed the performance data for each part of Wales, and set out the challenges specifically in narrowing the gap between those on free school meals and those not on free school meals. The plan set out our expectations of all parts of the system. Effective teaching and learning in schools was at the core, but the strengthening of capacity across the system was key. The plan identified coherently and in one place how we were taking the changes we had agreed forward, gave the timelines for implementation of the actions in train, and the expectations nationally, regionally, locally, within schools, including the responsibility of governors. I had ruled out drawing up a new strategy for education in Wales – I was conscious that writing strategies ties up the best civil servants when you need them focused on delivery. *Improving schools* was clear, intelligible and focused – and deliverable.

I had warned that I would close any school which was failing where I felt that the situation was irredeemable. In 2013, following Estyn's designation of the school as requiring special measures, I closed Llanrumney High School in Cardiff following a consultation and also said I was minded to close John Beddoes School in Powys, a decision which was eventually confirmed by my successor. Standards there had been falling and numbers were in rapid decline. Powers to close schools had been open to ministers since 1998 but had never been used before.

Estyn's Annual Report for 2011-12, published in January 2013, identified failings in school leadership as a key theme, and found particular variability in secondary schools. Ann Keane was particularly concerned about middle and senior leaders below the level of heads, and warned that in some schools mediocre teaching was not being addressed. She also questioned the commitment of staff to raising the achievement of disadvantaged pupils, and said writing standards remained an issue. Over half of all primary and secondary schools needed to achieve better standards in literacy. Local authorities were also criticised – capacity amongst officers was the issue – and a lack of challenge from elected councillors. Estyn also began a consultation on no-notice inspections. In an interview in May 2013 Ann said she was 'frustrated' by the pace of improvement, but she made it clear that she believed that initiatives such as the Literacy and Numeracy Framework would make a difference.

One further action we took to ensure that parents had a good understanding of school performance was the creation of the *My Local School* website. This includes information on pupils' attainment in exams, attendance rates and school budgets. The website also includes links to inspection reports and shows how much money schools spend per pupil. It was another idea from the Viv Thomas report in 2011, based on work which Dr Tim Williams had seen in Australia. It was immensely popular and received a very large number of hits – 200,000 by the time I left my post. The website won the public service award from the Royal Statistical Society in 2013.

In March 2013, just a few days after a reshuffle in which Carwyn Jones had re-appointed me, we held a conference under the theme *Raising our Sights* where I reported back on developments two years after my 20-point plan. I was pleased to be able to report:

> The number of pupils in Wales leaving education without any recognised qualification is at an all time low. In 2011/12 only 152 fifteen-year-olds left full time education without a recognised qualification. We made progress in closing the gap with England in the GCSE results last year.

I was particularly pleased by what we had achieved in terms of attendance. When pupils are in school they are learning – if they are not in school then clearly they are not learning.

2011-12 data showed that attendance rates in both primary and secondary schools were now at their highest levels since the Welsh Government first started collecting the data. Secondary schools saw their biggest single-year improvement in attendance – of 0.8 per cent – following the inclusion of attendance within the banding data. The overall rate of absence in secondary dropped for the seventh year in succession in 2012-13. Every authority bar one had seen secondary attendance improve. Primary school attendance saw its biggest increase in five years at 0.5 per cent. It was clear that many schools were using the School Effectiveness Grant and Pupil Deprivation Grant to assist in raising attendance.

We had worked for some years with Professor Ken Reid on issues of attendance and behaviour, and following discussions with Ken, I resolved to include attendance data within the banding system. Within our department, there had been some excellent forensic analysis on local authority management of attendance and behaviour issues. Ken had rightly complained in early 2011 that while local authority data on attendance was collected, little was done with it. The department's highly detailed work showed how laggardly many local authorities had been in implementing the recommendations of the 2008 National Behaviour and Attendance Report which Ken had led on, particularly in respect of early intervention. However, as Ken kindly recognised,

> It is not my job to say, but I think that the Minister for education, Leighton Andrews, made a very brave and challenging decision, and in my judgement a very correct decision, although I know that it is not liked by the educational community, when he introduced banding for secondary schools and included rates of absenteeism in that.

Local authorities had begun to clamp down after banding, targeting in-term holidays, where thousands of teaching days were lost. Some students were missing as much as a year of their formal education through persistent unauthorised absence. Cardiff and RCT had a particular focus on this, but figures released in 2013 suggested that it was now being taken seriously across the whole of Wales. RCT figures confirmed what we knew – the fewer days children were in school, the less well they did at GCSE.

There had been a 700 per cent increase in prosecutions of parents for their children's truancy between 2008 and 2013, and we decided to move ahead with plans for fixed-penalty fines for truancy, with regulations passing through the Assembly in the autumn of 2013. These were devices of last resort, and we wanted local authorities to intervene earlier, but they could also act to obviate the need for prosecution with the fines, as often merely the threat of a fine could make a difference.

In terms of behaviour, we strengthened the powers available to teachers clarifying when they could intervene physically to restore order in the classroom or on school premises.

Sir Michael Barber returned to Wales to speak at the *Raising Our Sights* conference. He said:

> I think what you're doing in Wales and what's been happening over the last two to three years is really impressive. It's great to see the Welsh education system on the move again.
>
> I know it's sometimes demanding going through these changes but I promise you, all around the world those same demands are being made of other systems because pretty much every political leader, every government and indeed the stakeholders across the whole society can see that unless we get the standards of education higher... the twenty-first century won't be as fulfilling as it might be.

I said that we had to have high aspirations for all, noting that 'if we set our targets too low, then individuals may succeed easily but our nation will fall behind.'

At the event, I announced the appointment of former Secretary of State for Wales, Paul Murphy MP as 'Oxbridge Ambassador'. I didn't go to Oxbridge and I don't believe that Oxbridge is the be-all and end-all of higher education. But I had recently seen evidence which suggested there had been a decline in the number of young people from Wales securing places there. I saw this as potentially down to a lack of aspiration on behalf of some teachers and a lack of confidence amongst some of our young people.

A perennial debate was how well were we doing compared to England? Professor Gareth Rees has said that 'the popular notion of "under-performing" Welsh schools belies a far more nuanced reality.' Professor Rees has made the case that if you compare like for like qualifications, then Welsh performance is on a par with that in England:

> if we look at GCSEs *alone* then, on the basis of the Welsh Government's data, the proportion of young people in Wales achieving the Level 2 Threshold is almost exactly equivalent to that in England. In 2009-10 it was 56 per cent in Wales compared to 56.3 per cent in England. Whilest there is an overall shortfall between Wales and England of some 12 percentage points, this is wholly accounted for by the fact that more young people in England attain the Level 2 Threshold through vocational qualifications.

Professor Rees attributes the gap with England to be principally one of access to vocational qualifications – and historically, Welsh schools have been better at providing academic rather than vocational qualifications. Alternatively, he has said, it could be that English schools are 'playing the game' better.

If one looks at the contribution of non-GCSE qualifications to attaining the Level 2 Inclusive Threshold in England and Wales, there is no question that they do somewhat distort the attainment figures. In 2011, 4.8 per cent of the difference in performance between England and Wales came through permitted vocational qualifications, though even if they were discounted, there would still be a performance gap of 4 per cent. There have subsequently been changes to the equivalence of vocational qualifications, in terms of their GCSE value, in both Wales and England.

None of this undermines the central argument that Welsh schools have been underperforming overall compared to schools in England. To address this, considerable emphasis has been placed in Wales since 2010 in learning from English experience. The most-improved schools in England are in London, following the London Challenge, and individuals and organisations with experience of both the London Challenge and the Manchester Challenge have been working with schools and local authorities in Wales. We have also drawn on the experience of some of the academies in England with most experience of turning round underperformance, such as the Cabot group in Bristol and the Priory CSA school in Somerset (a school that in 2013 achieved 75 per cent GCSE Level 2 Threshold *including English and Maths*) to identify and apply the best teaching techniques. In 2014, the First Minister and Huw Lewis launched the £20 million School Challenge Cymru programme to support school improvement in forty of Wales's most-challenged schools – dubbed the 'Pathways to Success' schools.

2013 results confirmed the closing of the gap with England. Wales had been performing worse than England in respect of the percentage, getting five A*-C grades – in 2011, there were 67.3 per cent of Welsh students achieving this compared to 79.6 per cent in England. But despite this, Wales's threshold pass results in 2011 at GCSE were the best ever. The gap between those in Wales getting A* narrowed compared to England. In 2012 and 2013, Wales began to narrow the gap with England overall. In 2013, the overall attainment gap at GCSE between Wales and England narrowed (77.8 per cent getting A*-C grades in Wales and 81.8 per cent in England, compared to 72.6 per cent versus 81.9 per cent the previous year) as did the gap in terms of the top grades (A*-A) (Wales increased from 19.9 per cent to 20.3 per cent between 2012 and 2013, England decreased from 24 per cent to 22.9 per cent between 2012 and 2013.). In terms of 5 good GCSEs including English or Welsh and maths, the gap with England fell from 8.9 per cent in 2011 to 6.5 per cent in 2013. The gap in the Capped Points Score stood at 25 points in 2011; by 2013 it was 6.7 per cent. Wales had also started to close the gap between those eligible for free school meals and those not eligible at all key stages.

There was a decline in the percentage getting A* and A grades at A level compared to England, with the proportion getting at least an A grade falling for four years from 2010, although in 2013 Wales did not decline at A* level while England did. In 2012, I had seen an overall pass rate increase and a narrowing of the attainment gap with England in 2012. One explanation might have been the numbers now taking the Welsh Bac, which rated at Advanced level the same as an A at A level, and as I said in 2010, was becoming the 'pathway of choice' for many pupils. As the *Western Mail* recognised after the 2011 results 'Leighton Andrews is right – the Welsh Baccalaureate is not always given due consideration, and cannot, by definition, be compared like for like'. But it was hard to tell. My successor, Huw Lewis, pledged to look at this issue in more detail after the 2013 results.

The 2012 PISA results, released in December 2013, brought a further period of soul-searching. I had consistently said that I did not expect them to demonstrate any significant progress. It was too early for our reforms to have been felt. In the end, Wales's score was lower than the OECD average in all three domains of maths, science and reading. There had been a decrease of four points in maths, an increase of four points in Reading and a decrease of five points in Science since 2009. As Huw Lewis said, there was a need to take collective responsibility. He felt there had been 'a mature acceptance that we are too early into our school improvement journey to expect to see a step change in performance.' Huw announced that PISA-based tests for schools would be made available.

The truth is that there are no quick fixes: this is a long haul. We had set out five-year and fifteen-year goals in the initial seminar with Michael Barber in January 2010. By summer 2013, we had started to close the gap with England; attendance was up, and we were tackling literacy and numeracy, based on more reliable data at age eleven. The journey had started.

Local Delivery

Local Government was responsible for the organisation of schools and ensuring the quality of education within them. Until the mid-1990s, education had been the responsibility of the eight county councils, but following John Redwood's changes responsibility fell to the twenty two unitary authorities. It was clear that across Wales, local government was generally failing to deliver the quality of education services we wanted. No local authorities had been graded excellent by Estyn in the previous inspection cycle, and few were regarded as good. Carwyn had given Carl Sargeant, as Local Government Minister, a clear signal that local government had to collaborate better to improve public services, and that if collaboration did not improve, and service delivery did not improve, then local government had to understand that re-organisation of the structure of local government would be likely to follow. He reinforced that message with Ministers.

Carl and I came into the Assembly together in 2003 and have been friends ever since. We were the first two AMs to sit down with Carwyn to plan his leadership campaign. I knew that Carl was passionate about ensuring that local government delivered. He knew that I was concerned about the pace of change and whether local government could deliver for schools. In our early months in Cabinet we began to ramp up the pressure on local government. Carl was seeking to underpin the Outcome Agreements with individual local authorities with a series of stronger targets. He had written a tough letter to the Welsh Local Government Association (WLGA) about these. Carl was impatient with the powers he had inherited in respect of shared services in local government. With the support of his clever and resourceful special adviser Sophie Howe, he was looking for further legislation on collaboration, which subsequently came about with the Local Government Measure. He and the First Minister had signed off on my review of the cost of administering the education system in Wales.

I was very sceptical about the ability of twenty two local education authorities to deliver the scale of improvement necessary in our schools, and made my feelings clear in my first interviews with the *Western Mail* and *TES*. This, coupled with the review of the cost of administering the education system in Wales appeared to un-nerve the WLGA. My first meeting with them in February 2010 was attended by Steve Thomas, the Association's chief executive, as well as its Education Director, Chris Llewellyn, which seemed to us a sign of their anxiety. Officials told me that the WLGA believed I wanted to take education off local authorities.

Fundamental reform, I knew, would depend on whether or not we decided, at some stage in the future, to re-organise local government. That was clearly not going to be on the agenda in the final eighteen months of the Third Assembly. We had to edge forward, continuing to put local government under pressure. By the 2011 Assembly election, we had consensus for action on creating regional consortia, but I felt things slowed down in 2012, in the run-up to the local government elections, in which many authorities changed hands, meaning a new consensus for action had to be built again.

There were also good reasons why we needed the middle tier of local authorities, even if we had too many of them. There are a number of positive factors that schools get from working within a local authority: personnel and legal support in a way they wouldn't otherwise. It is also important that future school plans are shaped at a local level. Services requiring more collective investment – special needs services, school transport and so on – cannot be delivered at a single school level. In England, by June 2010, Michael Gove had written to schools asking them if they wished to leave local authority control – that clearly was not our approach.

During the early months of 2010 I pored over a mound of reading material on education policy and change. One of the reports I studied was the Bain Report in Northern Ireland. Sir George Bain had been commissioned by Peter Hain, then Secretary of State for Northern Ireland as well as for Wales, to examine education funding in Northern Ireland, including strategic planning and school organisation, alongside curriculum and demographic change. One of the members of that review had been Viv Thomas. The report, published in December 2006, gave a comprehensive overview of the Northern Irish school system. I was keen that we did something similar in Wales.

Viv had raised with me during Carwyn Jones's campaign why good practice in some authorities was not being rolled out across Wales. The Welsh Government supplied local government with the bulk of its funding for education, but how did we control the effectiveness of delivery? Structures should be in place, said Viv, for a reason, and not because they had always been there. We had created four regional consortium areas for the delivery of the School Effectiveness Framework, but what was happening in terms of monitoring their delivery? He concluded 'it's not the amount of money that you have that's really important but the effective and efficient use you make of your resources, financial and human.'

The PwC review of the cost of administering the education system in Wales, published in May 2010, added to the pressure on local authorities, revealing that almost £560 million of funding had been retained by local authorities in 2009-10. It also urged more regional collaboration and merged education administrations. The teaching unions used the opportunity of the report's publication to focus on the number of local authorities. Meanwhile, Carl Sargeant continued to keep up the pressure on local government, telling the *Western Mail* in June that while he was concerned about the costs of reorganisation, 'I cannot see why we need 22 of everything – 22 fleets of council vehicles; 22 education services; or even 22 chief executives.' The newspaper endorsed this point of view in its editorial column. Over the summer, I challenged local authorities on their plans for what we called 'transformation' – consolidation of post-16 education services, as well as setting them a challenge over the PwC report to deliver more funding for the front line, telling the *TES* in September that ministers were 'getting tired of some local authorities that are dragging their feet on joint appointments and collaboration'. I said that we would be looking at the strategic capacity of the education system locally to support and challenge performance. At the end of the month Carl announced that he would be commissioning an independent study aimed at providing a clearer framework for the delivery of services currently provided by each of the twenty two local authorities.

Following that announcement, I was free to announce my own review of the organisation of education within local authorities, which I had discussed with Carl. I had recently received further evidence from Estyn highlighting many existing examples of collaboration across local authorities. They suggested that authorities are not reluctant to work together where they can see the benefits of doing so. However, they also stated that there was presently too much variation in the quality of the arrangements for collaborative working and that systems to challenge and evaluate the impact of such arrangements on standards and quality of education for learners were immature.

I announced the establishment of a task and finish group to take a long-term, whole system view on whether education structures enable and support the delivery of best value services to the citizens of Wales. The group would consider the case for change to existing service structures and governance arrangements and, in particular which education services:

- should be provided at national level;
- should be provided at Association of Directors of Education in Wales
- (ADEW) regional consortia level;
- should be provided at local authority level;

- should be devolved to providers, including schools or clusters of schools;
- should be provided on another organisational basis.

The group would also identify the implications for funding, planning and governance of services arising from the above points.

I announced that the group would be chaired by Viv Thomas and would include Wil Edmunds (Former Principal at Deeside College and former Chair of ACCAC); Bethan Guilfoyle (Head Teacher, Treorchy Comprehensive School); Dr Tim Williams, then a London-based public services consultant but a former NUT official and former special adviser to David Miliband; and Dr Brett Pugh, Chief Education Officer of Newport City Council. These were people who understood education in Wales and its challenges and were prepared to think the unthinkable. All had been teachers.

In December, the Education (Wales) Measure started its progress through the Assembly. The measure's driving principle was collaboration, placing a duty on local authorities, schools and FE institutions to consider how collaboration might be the best use of scarce education resources. The Measure utilised the new powers we had secured under the Legislative Competence (Education) Order, finally agreed by Parliament in April, just before the UK General Election.

Viv's group reported to me in early 2011, in time to feed recommendations into the 20-point action-plan I announced in my *'Teaching Makes a Difference'* speech in February. I took their report to Cabinet and then published it in March 2011, the same day as Carl published his independent review into local government service delivery (the Simpson review). While the report noted examples of exceptional achievement and inspiring leadership, looking at which local authorities really added value despite challenging issues of deprivation, it was highly critical of local authority performance, stating that some authorities lacked the capacity to challenge and support the performance of their schools. It recommended that the existing regional education consortia should become more formalised and should focus on school improvement, particularly literacy and numeracy amongst boys and the achievement of pupils on free school meals. There should be regional consortium directors in place by November 2011, with regions underpinned by a firm political mandate. They should identify underperforming schools and set clear targets. The report said that if all schools delivered outcomes that were as good as our best then we would have a world-class system. Our problem was inconsistency, between and within schools. Parents should have clear access to performance information. Too many schools were coasting. The report wanted no school to be rated unsatisfactory by September 2012 and all schools to be rated better than adequate by 2015. The review endorsed my prioritisation of literacy and numeracy.

There were clear failures in local authority support for schools, e.g. human resources. The report also urged the adoption of a national target for surplus places in schools of a maximum of 10 per cent. It reinforced the message about transferring resources to the front-line. It suggested a reform of 16-19 funding and a further reduction in the number of FE colleges. There was, said the report, a lack of clarity as to who was responsible for monitoring performance. The report trailed the possibility of four Regional Education and Skills Authorities, making it clear that local authorities had to shape up if they wanted to keep control of education. There should be a further review in the autumn of 2013.

The report was generally welcomed in the chamber by the opposition parties. Externally, it was also well-received. Professor Ken Reid described it in the *TES* as 'the most thorough and comprehensive report of its kind produced in Wales since devolution in 1999.'

The WLGA produced an internal report the same month entitled *Excellence in Education*, which looked at the prospects for regional collaboration. Buried within it was one very telling sentence: 'The numbers of back office education staff increased following local government reorganization in 1997.' My assumptions about the creation of twenty two local education authorities seemed to be correct. The document revealed that the scope for wide-ranging savings in back-office staff was significant, as PwC had suggested. Estimates provided to us suggested that possibly £20 million could be saved through regional collaboration. I met the WLGA leaders the same month and set out a timescale for regional school improvement services to be in place by September 2012. They told me that education was now their top priority. In April 2012, during the Assembly election campaign, the WLGA chief executive sent out a letter to all local authorities relating to the Simpson review and the Viv Thomas review, noting also the new powers which Carl had secured in his Local Government Measure which the WLGA said added 'legislative weight' to the collaborative agenda. The WLGA said that the 'political imperative' meant that collaboration had to be seen as a 'given'.

Following the election of the Welsh Labour government in May 2011, Carl and I found ourselves back in our jobs, though I had given up responsibility for children and gained the Welsh Language. Carl took his proposals on the Simpson Review to Cabinet in June, and I published my full response to the Viv Thomas review. Carl was concerned at the need to try and ensure consistent regional working across Wales in respect of social services, education and other local authority services on a regularised footprint: I was anxious at that stage not to disrupt work that had already commenced on the regional consortia. Carl produced a further report for Cabinet on promoting regional coherence in service delivery in July, setting out a coherent regional framework, with a footprint of six regions, but his paper accepted that existing collaborations on different footprints did not need to be unpicked. In November he took a paper to Cabinet outlining the scope of a Compact with local government, with a specific implementation contract on education.

Viv's report had urged the new Minister to set out expectations for the new Assembly term in June. I did so in a speech hosted by the Institute of Welsh Affairs at the end of June. Geraint Talfan Davies chaired the lecture. He recalled two years later 'The large lecture theatre was packed to capacity. As I walked in, a leading figure in local government alongside me gaped as he saw the assembled throng and whispered: '"It's just amazing how many people will turn out for a bollocking."' 'Bad luck, I'm back', I said. I reminded people that education had been central to our manifesto. I called for a culture of great expectations. I issued a specific challenge to local government, to ensure that they were on target to delegate more funding to schools, to share services on a regional basis and to raise standards. I gave them a year to deliver on the regional consortia, or to face a reduction in spending. There could be more fundamental change if things didn't improve. I warned if they failed to deliver, then more radical restructuring of education delivery on a regional basis should follow. Local authorities and consortia therefore had two years to demonstrate that they could deliver the improvements in school performance that our system requires.

There were now additional pressures on local authorities. Estyn's Common Inspection Framework was beginning to bite. In July, Blaenau Gwent local education services were put into special measures by Estyn which found systemic failures and lower than expected educational attainment despite the authority being one of the highest spenders per pupil in Wales. I sent in a task force led by Neath Port Talbot County Borough Council, one of our better-performing local education authorities, and in September announced the appointment of commissioners. In August, Pembrokeshire County Council was the subject of a scathing review by Estyn and the social service Inspectorate for Wales, CSSIW, over safeguarding of children. Gwenda Thomas, Deputy Minister for Social Services, and I sent in a ministerial board under Judge Graham Jones to oversee improvements. There were deep-seated cultural problems within the authority. A year on we remained dissatisfied with progress and regarded senior officers at the council as unwilling to get to grips with the problem, and issued a direction to the authority to comply with instructions from the chair of our ministerial board. We made it clear that if the council could not address the fundamental issue of safeguarding then the Welsh Government would. I visited Pembrokeshire in the autumn of 2012 and meet head teachers, to assure them that our concern was with the local authority, not individual schools. Further devastating reports from the Wales Audit Office and Estyn made public in December 2012 confirmed we were right to intervene and provide direction.

Estyn inspection reports into local authorities started to demonstrate more and more flaws and we clearly needed to add to our own capacity to support interventions. We tried commissioners in Blaenau Gwent – Bethan Guilfoyle, former head teacher of Treorchy, and Isobel Garner, former chief executive of Wrexham Council, as lead commissioners, and Nerys Evans and Alan Evans in a supporting role – but subsequently in other places went for Ministerial intervention boards in one form or another. The commissioners in Blaenau Gwent did a good job and when Bethan Guilfoyle followed through as the single commissioner, backed by support from Newport City Council, there continued to be progress, but the reality was that the capacity within the authority was simply too weak to allow it effectively to tackle under-performance effectively and there were problems with specific secondary schools in particular.

Under the leadership of the affable but steely civil servant Steve Vincent, we began to develop a team of experienced educationalists – often former head teachers or former directors of education – who could provide the necessary support or challenge to failing authorities, along with experienced politicians from different political persuasions who could build relationships with local political leaderships and help them strengthen democratic accountability and scrutiny, as the educationalists did with the council officers. Former AMs Jonathan Morgan (Conservative), Helen Mary Jones and Nerys Evans (Plaid Cymru), and experienced Labour councillors Huw David and Paul Hannon all took on recovery roles, alongside leading educationalists.

In October 2012 I published the White Paper explaining our

proposed School Standards and Organisation Bill. The Bill included proposals for intervention in schools causing concern and the development of school improvement guidance. Estyn had found in 2009 that there was significant variability between local authorities. While most had policies for challenging failing schools, they were not intervening early enough, failing to issue warning notices to school governing bodies when problems first arose. They were not using the full range of powers available to them. As I told the Children and Young Person's committee when it examined the Bill, few local authorities even issued warning notices to poorly performing schools. Our view was that they needed to intervene at an early stage, not when things had become irremediable. Their relationships had been too cosy. Former Welsh Assembly Government special adviser turned Rhondda Cynon Taf (RCT) Councillor, Paul Griffiths, said in the *Bevan Foundation Review* that I was to be 'commended' for putting performance management of schools at the heart of local authority endeavours since 'for far too long, school performance was seen as a no-go area for local authorities and civil servants'. We planned to issue new statutory school improvement guidance requiring action from local authorities on school underperformance, which we believed would lead to an increase in interventions in schools causing concern.

The local authority issues intensified during 2012. Launching her annual report, Estyn's Ann Keane reported in February that local authorities needed to raise their game. Too many were failing to understand the performance of their schools. Some schools had been allowed to underperform for too long. The performance of individual learners was not sufficiently well tracked. Out of eight local authorities inspected under the new framework, only two had achieved the category good. Four were 'adequate', a category I had already described as 'not good enough'. None were excellent. By the end of February, Torfaen County Borough Council had been judged unsatisfactory and in need of significant improvement. By the end of March half of Wales's local authorities had been inspected and only four were designated 'good'. In the summer, Anglesey was placed in special measures after a highly damning Estyn report deemed its education services unsatisfactory – again, the authority was producing results lower than expected, with young people not making enough progress at all key stages. As I announced yet another Welsh Government intervention with a recovery board, I sent a warning to all local authorities – 'there's no question that we've had a series of damning reports now from Estyn and we have to ask whether there is sufficient capacity within local authorities to drive the educational improvements that are necessary.' By now, fourteen had been inspected – four unsatisfactory, five good, and five adequate. As we entered 2013 we were awaiting Estyn inspection reports on two further authorities, Merthyr and Monmouthshire, both of which we knew would be poor.

Estyn's reports on Merthyr and Monmouthshire were published in late February 2013. Both were deemed unsatisfactory and Estyn recommended they be placed in special measures. Merthyr Council was criticised for not challenging poor educational outcomes and had failed to respond to past recommendations for action. It was one of the worst Estyn reports we had seen. In the case of Monmouthshire, there were issues on safeguarding, a lack of strategic and operational capacity, and secondary school performance was below what it should be. The leaders of both authorities responded maturely to the reports. Our lead official Steve Vincent and his team were working in overdrive to find experienced teams to give the necessary support to these and other authorities.

In September 2012, the new regional school improvement consortia formally got under way, with different models in each of the four regions. We had been anxious to move the process on swiftly, and had therefore allowed flexibility to ensure buy-in from the local authorities. The four consortia, whatever their models, were meant to be focusing on challenge to schools, the sharing of best practice and the best routes to school improvement. The Education Advisory Service in South-East

Wales came to be the model in which we had the most confidence. As the consortia got under way it was clear that, despite the guidance we had published on the recruitment of system leaders – experienced professionals who could provide direct advice to schools – there were significant gaps in recruiting to a high enough standard. We knew that there was variability – and evidence that some local authorities were maintaining their own school improvement roles and providing direct challenge alongside the consortia. In north Wales, there seemed to be a divide between the Welsh-speaking north-west and largely English-speaking north-east, and it took a long time to recruit an overall director. Service, bluntly, was patchy. We held an independent review of the consortia's readiness to deliver, which made it evident that more pace and urgency were needed.

I was now losing patience with local government over their willingness and ability to deliver at pace. I had met all the new council leaders after the May 2012 elections, and they had re-affirmed their commitment that education remained their top priority. But I couldn't see how this was being followed through in day-to-day practice in many authorities. I discussed the situation with Cabinet colleagues, including Carl Sargeant and the First Minister, and got agreement to bring forward a further review of local delivery of education advocated by the Viv Thomas report. I made a statement in the Assembly on 20th November 2012.

In the statement I confirmed our view that consortium performance so far was patchy. I also reviewed the latest information on Estyn local authority inspections – five good, five adequate, five in an Estyn category of special measures or in need of significant improvement. I noted that local authorities had failed to deliver the expected savings from creating consortia; that they continued to fail to make joint appointments, and rarely used the powers of intervention available to them. I repeated my view that I would not have invented twenty two local education authorities. I said that the fragmentation of education authorities in the mid-1990s was one of the contributing factors in the downturn in educational performance a decade later. The OECD echoed this in their report in 2014, saying 'the decision to divide school improvement functions among twenty two local education authorities appears to have diluted expertise and spread educational expertise too thinly to have impact.'

Effective challenge and support had been lost in many parts of the system and time, energy and resources were dissipated. Local authorities were failing in terms of practical support as well – human resources support was not sufficiently tailored to the needs of schools, many schools did not get the ICT and broadband support they needed as corporate services in local government did not respond to the specific needs of schools. I announced that we were scoping out a more wide-ranging review of the delivery of education services, which would look at what should be done at school, local authority, regional and national levels.

I said that the review would consider whether we should move to forms of regional delivery; whether school improvement responsibilities should be removed from local authorities altogether and vested in a regional service accountable to the Welsh Government; whether we should enforce statutory mergers of local authorities, or whether we should go further and remove all education responsibilities from local government, creating regional school boards accountable to the Welsh Government. The review would also look at whether there should be direct funding of schools, and whether there should be co-operative ownership, management and governance of schools locally, combining primary and secondary. The scoping would be complete by Christmas and the full review group would report by the end of March 2013. I had already set up a group to look at school governance issues and this would work in tandem with the new review.

This was clearly a radical statement and it took place on the eve of my annual meeting with local authority directors of education and cabinet members for education. 'Leighton demands schools revolution' said the front page of the *South*

Wales Echo. Most reports focused on the possibility that local authorities could lose responsibility for education. The WLGA leadership was opposed to this, and it was not an argument that I had taken to Cabinet colleagues. In 2012, the number of local authorities in Wales run or led by Labour had gone from four to roughly half of all authorities. There was strong reaction within the Labour Party in Wales, many of whose councillors would not sanction such a move. However, I felt the debate had to be had, and the WLGA leaders understood the debate was needed. The mood at the WLGA education conference was more subdued than normal – though anger was simmering visibly in some parts of the room. Neath Port Talbot leader Councillor Alun Thomas, who chaired the event, used his customary good humour to soothe matters.

I had deliberately raised radical options in the statement to highlight the seriousness of our intentions, although I wasn't clear that they would find favour with colleagues. I also wanted local authority leaders to think more deeply about their responsibilities to ensure that local education services delivered, asking in an interview with Huw Edwards on *The Wales Report* on the BBC why it was that under-performing education directors were allowed to stay in post. For a few weeks I wondered if I had been allowed to move forward into enemy territory to test the strength of their armoury. But in early December we had the Welsh Labour Policy Forum in Cardiff. The First Minister had decided to use the opportunity to give me full backing. It was clear that the reaction to what I had said had opened up wider possibilities for the discussion of the role of local government in Wales. In our manifesto, we had committed to a commission on public service delivery, and the challenge we were providing in education was opening up space for that to be conducted on our terms.

I told the north Wales dinner of the Institute of Welsh Affairs, a couple of nights before the Policy Forum, that 'when failure happens, heads should roll'. Local authority leaders needed to ensure that education got the relevant focus and political attention that it deserved. Local authority cabinet members for education had to be absolutely focused on performance. Directors of Education needed to be held to account. Local authority-appointed school governors were part of the process of accountability and needed to do the job they were appointed to do. Heads should be able to expect high quality human resources and ICT support.

The First Minister's opening remarks at the Policy Forum made it clear that he regarded the numbers of authorities in special measures as unacceptable. To have only a handful described as good was equally unacceptable. We had been elected on an agenda of improving delivery and we could not do that if local authorities were failing. We should not be precious about the structure of local government – after all, it had been designed by the Conservatives in the 1990s. His remarks were immensely helpful and eased the way for the review we were to develop in the New Year.

In my session, I was able to outline in detail how we had delivered on our manifesto, contrasting what we were doing with what Michael Gove was doing in England. But I made it clear that if we believed in the comprehensive system, then it had to deliver for all in education in Wales. There were around twenty or so contributions from the floor – overwhelmingly in support, including from the GMB trade union, and activists and councillors across Wales. The main contribution from the local authority end came from Cllr Huw David, the likeable and thoughtful young deputy leader of Bridgend County Borough Council, who I was told had been highly critical privately – but very loyal publicly – about my original statement, but who could clearly sense that things were not moving in local government's favour, and there was work to be done together in driving up standards.

At the same time, we were set to announce the appointment of Robert Hill to lead the review of the structure of delivery of education services. Robert, who had served in the Number Ten Policy Unit under Tony Blair, now worked as a consultant on education and public services. I announced Robert's remit in mid-January in the Assembly. The plan was for Robert to provide me with a range of options by the end of March 2013, which would then be taken for consultation. I repeated my concern that there had been plenty of local democracy, but little local accountability until recently. I said that if local government wanted to retain their responsibilities and develop them, then they had to deliver. I repeated my view that changes to the structure of local government in the mid-1990s 'when we went overnight from 8 to 22 local education authorities, dissipated expertise and undermined the quality of support for our schools'.

I was clear that the message we were getting from Estyn reports was that some – not all – small local authorities didn't have the proper strategic capacity to run an education service. This was not an uncontested view – however, the Estyn evidence kept repeating itself – and there was little room for smaller authorities to hide. Anne Keane said that these councils did not have the economies of scale which allowed them to provide the necessary level of support. By late March, Torfaen had been moved into special measures after an Estyn follow-up report showed that the council's attempts to turn things round had not been rigorous enough and it had failed to make use of its powers to improve under-performing schools. The *Western Mail* questioned whether the time for local authority control of education was over.

Robert Hill gave me an informal update on his report as we headed to a major national conference on raising school standards in March 2013. Robert had some quick wins which he thought I could announce at the conference, particularly around the area of improving school leadership across Wales. Robert's view was that we were part-way through a school improvement journey.

I took Robert's report to Cabinet and then published it on 18th June, commencing a three-month consultation on the report the same day. As the *Western Mail's* education correspondent, Gareth Evans, was to comment when the report was published, it was 'radical in the extreme'. I told the Assembly that Robert Hill had presented 85 delivery options for consideration to improve education services. These were categorised as improving classroom teaching and learning, strengthening school leadership, increasing school partnerships within a context of greater autonomy, improving accountability, and organising school improvement functions.

Robert's report contained a telling comment:

> Democratic accountability is a vital principle. In an ideal world, Wales would have local authorities with a passion and vision for young people growing up to be highly educated and skilled. Authorities would ensure that there were enough places at a range of good schools and colleges. They would support parents to make choices on their children's schooling. They would know what was happening in their schools and would help to develop school leadership, build school-to-school capacity and expect heads and governors to be responsible for school performance – though they would intervene where necessary. Authorities would broker federations and hard clusters between schools. As these partnerships took root, they would devolve budgets and services. It is a model based on enabling and empowering schools to support each other in a co-ordinated way. It will take time to achieve and it does not require there to be 22 separate local authority education services.

In terms of organising school improvement functions, the options included cutting the number of local authority education services by a third by April 2014, either by voluntary mergers or by using ministerial intervention powers; local authorities to stop providing school improvement services, with all these functions being provided regionally in partnership with schools; regional consortia and local authorities to have formal agreements regarding the exercise of their respective responsibilities when formal school interventions are deemed necessary; regional consortia to have a standard governance structure involving local authority leaders, school leaders, an education improvement expert and a ministerial nominee; regional consortia to be funded directly by top-slicing the regional support grant; regional consortia arrangements for delivering services and the appointment of their directors to be approved by the Education Minister; and the further strengthening of the school standards and delivery unit. The report proposed that, in the medium term, education should be retained within new slimline elected local authorities, but recognised that this will be a matter for the public service commission to consider.

Following the publication of the review, Robert said that he thought that the most pressing need was sorting out the regional consortia. His view – which echoed that of myself and my officials – was that the consortium in the South-East – the Education Achievement Service – was developing well. I was least happy with north Wales, which had started discussions across the six local authorities back in April 2010, but which still lacked a coherent structure and leadership. Robert said that he had found consensus across Wales – he had been told by 'just about everyone I met that things could not continue as they are'.

The report ran to 130 pages – it was broadly welcomed by all parties in the Assembly, and my successor Huw Lewis was able to take the work of implementation forward. Huw began with the recommendations that local authorities should stop providing school improvement services, and that the regional consortia should be funded by top-slicing the revenue support grant, provided that there was a national agreed framework for the operation of the consortia backed by ministerial consent for their structures and plans. Huw noted that most of local government was against the top-slice, but he said that all the evidence, from Hill, from Estyn, and from the independent review of consortia that I had commissioned, was that pace in some areas had been slow, there was a lack of consistency and some duplication in services across Wales. He said he was not prepared to wait any longer 'for local government to get their act together'. While he was willing to allow local authorities to retain their statutory responsibility for education, he was minded to move ahead on the top-slice and to impose a national model for regional working. I welcomed this statement in the Assembly chamber, saying he almost made me look patient. There was no doubt that this was the right way forward. In our impatience to get the regional consortia up and running, we had allowed the different local authority areas to determine their own structure. Pragmatically, that had seemed right at the time – but two years on it had become clear that local authority leadership was weak in achieving the consensus and structure that was needed.

A week after his statement, local government caved in. The Welsh Local Government Association (WLGA) agreed to voluntarily ring-fence the £19m earmarked for school improvement at regional consortia level. Huw was able to announce that a new national model for regional education consortia would be implemented immediately and a template for a new 'education delivery agreement', formed on the basis of Robert's recommendations, would be signed by all Welsh councils. If local authorities failed to comply with new arrangements, they agreed to forgo money allocated for regional working.

At the end of November, Huw gave his full response to the Hill review. He accepted the bulk of the recommendations made by Robert, aside from the recommendations that educational welfare and the provision of additional learning needs transfer from local authorities to federations of schools or hard clusters of schools; two-tier governance models; and changes to the inspection system. The structural proposals relating to local authorities would have to await the outcome of the Public Services Review, which, by now, most people expected to recommend a reduction in the number of local authorities, with the exception of the proposals on the national model for regional consortia funded by the compromise which Huw had achieved with the WLGA. The national model was announced in February 2014 with the backing of the WLGA, setting out an annual cycle of school improvement.

The reform journey in respect of local delivery of educational services was now well under way. In 2014, Ceredigion became the first Council in Wales to be classed as 'excellent' by Estyn.

In his book on education, Andrew Adonis says that one of the 'blind alleys' he went down in his early days as Schools Minister was the hope that local authorities could be reformed. I have a lot of sympathy with him over that. The OECD has rightly identified that the creation of our Consortia has taken up a lot of energy – and meanwhile, we have had the report of the Commission on Public Service Governance and Delivery, calling for a significant reduction in the number of local authorities. The OECD has said if the regional consortia don't ultimately work, we should look to fold the school improvement responsibilities back in to the new authorities. Time will tell whether our attempt to reform school improvement services by transferring that responsibility to regional consortia, will turn out to have been a blind alley.

A World-Class Workforce

Everyone agrees that 'the quality of an education system cannot exceed the quality of its teachers'. The phrase derives from Michael Barber and Mona Mourshed's 2007 McKinsey report on *How the world's best performing education systems come out on top*. The Sutton Trust has produced research in England suggesting that if the performance of the least effective 10 per cent of teachers could be brought up to the average, then English schools could move into the world's top five education performers within a decade. Wales faces similar challenges.

Dylan Wiliam endorsed the view that the quality of teachers matters, in his *Spectator* lecture in 2010: 'In the classrooms of the best teachers, students learn at twice the rate they do in the classrooms of average teachers.' He makes the case for the development of school-based teacher learning communities – what in Wales we called professional learning communities, recognising that changing teacher practice is difficult, 'because it involves changing long-established habits'. Teachers need to be accountable for continuously improving their practice, and they need to be given support for change.

Leadership, says Dylan Wiliam, matters above all:

> Too many educational leaders, at school, at local authority, and at national level, are content to 'let a thousand flowers bloom' in terms of school improvement. If we had no idea what we wanted to do, then this would be a good Darwinian approach – try out lots of things, and evaluate them to see what works. But when there is clear evidence about what does work, it is frankly self-indulgent.

Michael Barber put it more toughly in *The Guardian* in June 2009, saying 'many still cling to the demonstrably false view that creativity consists of each teacher making it up in the classroom. This is not creativity, it is betrayal.' John Hattie, whose book *Visible Learning* gathers the largest collection of evidence-based research into what makes a difference in classroom teaching, says 'there are things that work and don't work.' He says things like class sizes, homework and choice of school are limited in their effects. Fenton Whelan makes similar points. Hattie argues that tackling difference in performance within schools is key. The Sutton Trust has of course analysed the most effective ways to drive up performance. 'Teaching', says Dylan Wiliam, 'is such a complex craft that one lifetime is not enough to master it, but by rigorously focusing on practice, teachers can continue to improve throughout their career'.

I have a lot of sympathy with these arguments. Who doesn't want to improve? Who doesn't want to learn continually to get better? We know that we have world-class teachers and head teachers in Wales. We have world-class best practice in Wales. What we need to do better is share that best practice across the whole of Wales, enable all teachers to have access to it, and grow the capacity of those within our system. We said in our 2011 manifesto that 'the best teachers can have a lifelong effect on all of us and we have some world-class teachers in Wales. We want to support teachers in their work and to raise the esteem in which they are held'. We said in our manifesto that 'We want our young people to be taught by the brightest and the best'.

As Education Minister, every week I saw the difference that the best teachers make to a child's development. What we wanted from all schools was to replicate in the future what is already happening in the best schools today. The best teachers I saw in schools in Wales were eager and keen to learn about the best practice. They wanted to know about the best practice because they care about learning. They liked learning.

Many teachers who wanted to improve their teaching practice were engaged in professional networks like i-Net and the online community addcym, or taking part in the teachmeets run through the National Grid for Learning Cymru. Many teachers were out there sharing ideas and learning from each other. The reason why we sought to engage the profession through the development of professional learning communities (PLCs) is that used properly, they are a powerful tool for spreading best practice.

In order to strengthen the quality of teaching, we undertook a wide range of initiatives during my period as Education Minister, which are continuing now under my successor, most of which have been welcomed, not least by the OECD in their 2014 report, which acknowledged 'in recent years, Wales has made considerable efforts to strengthen the recruitment, development and retention of its teachers.' These measures included:

- Raising the standard of entry into the teaching profession
- Introducing the Master's in Educational Practice for newly qualified teachers, and refocusing Continuous Professional Development
- Bringing Teach First into Wales
- Developing online resources for teachers through Learning Wales and PLC online
- Replacing the General Teaching Council for Wales with a body representing the needs of all working in education
- Strengthening professional standards requirements and performance management of teachers and head teachers
- Reviewing initial teacher training
- Reviewing the headship qualification
- Creating the new National Education Leadership Council
- Incorporating a responsibility to share best practice to earn the highest Estyn inspection grades
- Developing a Practitioners Panel advising the Minister
- Creating a new Workforce unit within the Education Department

We consulted on plans to make entry to initial teacher training more demanding in 2012, with changes coming into effect from

September 2013. New entrants would have to get a grade B at GCSE English and Maths rather than C. They would also be assessed on standards of literacy and numeracy. All ITT providers would have to demonstrate students were proficient at teaching key skills. I also decided to reduce the number of entrants into the teaching profession, in the light of evidence in 2011 from the GTCW that large numbers of newly qualified teachers were out of work. I was concerned however about whether initial induction of teachers was sufficiently consistent or rigorous across Wales – in 2011 I pointed out that only 8 trainees had failed induction since 2003.

The Master's in Educational Practice (MEP) was launched in September 2012. This was free for every newly qualified teacher (NQT) who took it up. The contract for the work had been won by a consortium including the Institute of Education, Cardiff, Aberystwyth and Bangor Universities. Professor Alma Harris, who had also driven our work on professional learning communities through the school effectiveness framework, had helped to design the programme, based on activities and action research. We had a Task and Finish Group on the Master's led by Emma-Jane Milton of Duffryn Infants School in Newport. Our hope was that it would put Wales at the forefront of professional development in teaching. David Reynolds said, should every NQT eventually take the course, then the hope was that Wales would have characteristics similar to places like Finland where every teacher had a Master's degree. The three-year modular course was designed to be integrated with teachers' own classroom experience. Mentors were recruited from within the profession to support the programme.

Modules ranged from behaviour management to leadership, with a focus on our three priorities of literacy, numeracy and breaking the link between poverty and poor attainment. Training in behaviour management had been a demand of Professor Ken Reid's National Behaviour and Attendance Review and I was pleased to take that forward. The Master's programme replaced the induction and early professional development programme that had previously operated. Professor Amanda Coffey, heading the programme for Cardiff University, said that the MEP programme would open up access to high quality resources and the latest research, benefitting schools as well as the individuals taking the course. The rigorous leadership of the programme and detailed follow-up by its director, Professor Mark Hadfield, meant it had a very low drop-out rate from those who started. We had worked closely with the teaching profession on the development of the Master's. Andrew Adonis told me that he wished the UK government would support something similar – the outgoing Labour government had planned such a move, but Michael Gove dropped it on coming into office. Michael Barber described the Master's in 2013 as a 'great opportunity for Wales to get ahead of England'.

In 2012 I announced that we would be creating a new teacher training programme offering on-the-job training to outstanding graduates to help improve the results of pupils from deprived backgrounds. Recruits to the Additional Training Graduate Programme would teach on a reduced timetable while being fully trained to acquire qualified status. I was delighted when the tender for this was won by Teach First who began their work in Welsh schools from September 2013. The initial programme involved recruiting forty graduates to teach in some of Wales's most disadvantaged communities, focusing on secondary schools in bands four and five. In England, Teach First had been in operation since 2002, developing 4000 teachers in 500 Teach First partner schools. Evidence showed that they'd had had a real impact on raising attainment levels and supporting pupils to believe in their ability to achieve. Participants began training in June 2013. They would follow a two-year leadership development programme, working in partnership with training providers to gain a PGCE leading to Qualified Teacher Status. There was great enthusiasm amongst head teachers for the programme to start in Wales, and it would broaden the range of people considering teaching as a career.

We made it clear early on in 2010 that continuing professional development would in future be focused on system-wide needs, such as literacy and numeracy, linked to the priorities of the School Effectiveness Framework and the Skills Framework. We had become increasingly concerned about the focus of CPD in Wales, not least that delivered through the General Teaching Council for Wales, and my predecessor Jane Hutt had cut the budget for this in 2009. However, I included professional development in the key strategic areas as one of the ways in which the £66.5 million School Effectiveness Grant and Pupil Deprivation Grant funding could be used from the 2012-13 financial year. In June 2014, Huw Lewis announced a national model for workforce development.

In September 2012 we launched the new website *Learning Wales* as a one-stop shop for teaching resources, incorporating best practice examples in key areas, latest news including ministerial announcements and Estyn reports, consultations and events for teachers, and resources from the Master's programme. Professor Reynolds said that this was one of the most comprehensive resources any education system had provided for its teachers. *Learning Wales* incorporated *PLC Online*, which we had trialled in March 2012, using living examples of professional collaborations across Wales to improve teaching practice.

In England, the incoming UK government signalled its intention to abolish its General Teaching Council very early on, though it later decided to retain a form of registration of teachers. I took my time to consider what we should do, initially expecting to take powers to decide the GTCW's future in the UK Education Act 2011, although we did not need to pursue this after the referendum in March 2011. The Act did give us powers to promote teaching as a career and confirmed our powers over teacher training. In 2010, David Puttnam, the first chair of the GTC in England, delivered the GTCW's annual lecture. I knew David reasonably well from my time at the BBC in London in the 1990s, and he congratulated me from the stage for having decided to keep the GTCW in Wales. However, I was starting to have doubts as to whether it should continue in its present form.

I was clear that the GTCW was good at some things, including registration, but I had questions about some aspects of its performance and focus. It seemed to me to duplicate some things which the department should be doing; it seemed highly conservative – its chief executive, for example, made comments to me directly critical of Teach First – and I had concerns about how effective it was in terms of improving professional standards, with doubts about the value of the continuing professional development programme it had run. The new workforce council would register not only the 38,000 teachers in maintained schools, but also the 21,300 school support staff and the 8,810 teaching staff in further education.

I was conscious that as a government we had expanded the range of teaching assistants in schools, recruiting around 5,600 people, often from the childcare sector, to support the new Foundation Phase. In fact, by 2010, school support staff accounted for over 40 per cent of the school workforce, following the roll-out of the Foundation Phase. The numbers had doubled during the period of devolution. We wanted to ensure that their skills were strengthened and that a growing number achieved Higher Level Teaching Assistant status. Unions such as the GMB and Unison, who represented these workers, had campaigned for some time to ensure that their contribution was valued and that they benefitted from training to upgrade their skills, amongst other issues.

Our manifesto in 2011, included a proposal to review the GTCW, and during my time as Minister we consulted on the proposals for the new Education Workforce Council, delivered by my successor Huw Lewis in the 2014 Education (Wales) Act. Meanwhile, in England, the requirement for teachers to be registered was removed in April 2012. Unqualified teachers were free to teach in parts of the English system. Registration continues in Scotland and Northern Ireland as well as Wales.

New professional standards for higher level teaching assistants, teachers and head-teachers were introduced from September 2011. I have sympathy with the OECD view that these need to be reduced in number. The objective was to develop a simple consistent system, including a continuum of professional standards and a framework for professional development, to drive improved standards of teaching. The standards were incorporated in the statutory induction arrangements for NQTs with all NQTs demonstrating they meet the Practising Teacher Standard at the end of their first year of teaching. Literacy and numeracy requirements were embedded within these, as I had stipulated in my 20-point plan for school reform in 2011. We piloted the new National Professional Qualification for Headship in 2011 with the new professional standards underpinning it. Candidates had to show practical evidence that they met the new Learning Standards, drawing on their experience in schools, and were assessed by experienced professional head teachers. By Easter 2013, 400 candidates had applied to undertake the new NPQH. Out of 225 who went forward for assessment, 170 achieved the qualification.

New performance management regulations for head teachers and teachers came into effect from January 2012 with schools required to adopt them by the end of 2012, and guidance was published to underpin these. These had an explicit link to performance data, pupil progress and individual objectives at school and classroom level. Local authorities would have a direct influence over the effective operation of the system through the head teacher performance management process. Statutory guidance was also issued to head teachers and school governing bodies on the implementation of staff disciplinary and dismissal procedures. Estyn's annual report published in January 2013 made it clear that we still had some mediocre teachers and warned that some schools were not addressing this. It also said that in 40 per cent of secondary schools inspected, line management arrangements were not robust and performance management targets lacked focus and challenge. The secondary heads' union ASCL told me regularly that it was difficult to remove poorly performing teachers. I asked them repeatedly what they wanted me to do, but never received any firm proposals.

Some of our more successful head teachers seemed to be able to manage the process of capability reviews and performance management better than others.

We also launched a wide-ranging review of Initial Teacher Training by Professor Ralph Tabberer, former chief executive of the Teacher Training Agency and former Director General of Schools in the UK government's Department for Children, Schools and Families. Estyn inspections of initial teacher training providers in Wales from 2012 demonstrated that we were right to do this, with the South West Wales Centre of Teacher Education only being graded adequate. Professor Dylan Wiliam had told me that our teacher training courses already had a significant amount of classroom time, but he and others wondered whether teachers who were training got a wide enough experience of a range of different teaching styles and practice. Ralph shared his work as it developed with the School Practitioner Panel.

Huw Lewis published the Tabberer Review in October 2013. He said that the report painted a mixed picture – whilst the regulatory framework which governs Initial Teacher Training (ITT) is sound and some good practice has been evidenced, it was also very clear from recent Estyn inspection reports that there is significant room for improvement, particularly at a strategic leadership level across the ITT sector. The report findings issued a stark warning that ITT provision in Wales will need to do better if we want to become a world leader in teacher training. It was necessary to ensure that ITT was aligned to the wider Practising Teacher Standards, that it supported the delivery of the Masters in Educational Practice and reflected the principles of Practice Review and Development, the school improvement and effectiveness measures in place and the wider reform of Education Services planned for Wales. Huw warned that all ITT providers and key stakeholders must 'step up to the mark' to raise standards and improve the quality of provision and leadership in ITT, providing clear direction whether ITT is delivered through university-based provision, employment-based teacher training in schools, or through flexible distance learning.

While Wales was producing some very good teachers, and there were examples of very good practice within the ITT sector, the ITT Centres were not showing clear signs that they were working together effectively, collaboratively, on an all-Wales strategic level to raise the standard and quality of ITT across Wales. Huw planned to move ahead with Ralph's proposal to appoint a senior expert adviser on ITT to lead on these reforms, to help build capacity and ensure that the ITT sector in Wales worked together to meet the challenges ahead. I wondered myself whether this might be an opportunity to review more thoroughly the curriculum for initial teacher training. There is considerable evidence now that the research in cognitive science about learning, such as the work by Daniel Willingham, is not yet finding its way into the classroom. Professor Dylan Wiliam says, in his introduction to Daisy Christodoulou's interesting book about teaching and learning, *Seven Myths About Education*, that many university departments of education do not have a single psychologist. John Stannard and Laura Huxford, in their account of the development of the National Literacy Strategy in England, *The Literacy Game*, note the disconnect between teachers and psychologists over reading practice.

Leadership is obviously key to successful schools. We had already begun to implement additional leadership development with a module within the Master's programme. Pilot programmes had been conducted in each of the consortia to identify aspiring leaders and online materials had been made available on Learning Wales, with an Individual Leadership Review tool also part of this. Robert Hill's recommendations had built on this. Robert said that it was clear that while we had 'some brilliant school leaders' we were not making enough use of them – and nor were there enough of them, as Estyn told us, particularly in primary schools. We should establish leadership development boards, comprised of school leaders, at regional and national levels, to drive up quality, with leadership development pathways agreed. There should be a national curriculum for leadership development with a stepping-stone qualification to headship.

Regional consortia needed to draw on the best schools to provide whole-school improvement programmes. They also needed to invest in recruiting high quality system leaders who could command the respect of head teachers. In the medium-term, the national leadership development board might become a teaching and leadership foundation independent of government. There should be a development framework incorporating the stepping-stone qualification. Our Lead Practitioner Schools Programme enabled us to take this work forward – schools accredited by us for their excellent practice, committed to sharing this with others.

Robert's recommendation for a National Leadership Development Board was key, and this was taken forward by Huw Lewis in November 2013. The NLDB is made up of independent education professionals who will focus on the provision of high quality leadership development in support of the Welsh Government's school improvement agenda. Each of the new members of the board, who were selected following an open recruitment process, has a wide range of expertise and experience in developing leadership capacity within the school system. They will advise and ensure that initiatives from the Welsh Government which relate to leadership development are fit for purpose and meet the needs of the profession in Wales.

Robert identified that in the classroom, we needed to use high quality schemes of work from excellent schools to help weaker schools, in particular with the implementation of the literacy and numeracy framework, based on a nationally approved list of schools authorised to provide such support. There needed to be standardised tracking of all in years 2-9 in the context of the literacy and numeracy framework. Because we were still reliant on teacher assessment, we needed to ensure common tasks were agreed to help teachers assess pupil progress at the end of Key Stages 2 and 3. We needed to roll out the improving teachers and outstanding teacher programme.

Although my department routinely drew on secondments of head teachers and teachers to carry out programmes of work, I wanted more direct engagement with the profession as we developed policies. I conceived of the Practitioners' Panel, which I announced in March 2012, as a forum of leading head teachers, meeting every couple of months, which would have direct engagement with senior policy officials in my department and with me. I had met a wide range of outstanding heads across Wales and this became a really useful forum. The point of the Practitioners' Panel was to advise me and the department on best practice, the exchange of ideas between teachers and head teachers, and the quality of materials and resources that we put are putting out into the system. Members would sit on the panel for two years, allowing us to get a fresh range of input in every two-year cycle. One of the roles of the panel is to offer advice on how the Welsh Government can use best practice which exists in Wales to improve performance and standards in education across the board. The Panel also supports the Welsh Government in developing policies which will make a real difference in schools. The panel acts as a sounding board for Government policies. I also decided to resume investment in the Teaching Awards programme to celebrate excellent teaching. We also took a decision in 2012 to create a new Workforce Unit in the department.

Supply teaching was an area where I thought that the teaching unions had an opportunity to make a real difference. One of my constituents, Clare Jones, an NUT activist, had asked whether it might be possible to establish a social enterprise or teachers' co-operative to coordinate the supply of teachers to cover absences. I thought that Clare's idea was a good one and suggested it in my first meetings with teaching unions. I thought they would be well positioned to undercut the existing for-profit teacher agencies while ensuring that supply teachers got fair pay and conditions. I heard no more.

We undertook a review of supply teaching, commissioning work from the Wales Audit Office and Estyn, who reported back in September 2013. These found that arrangements for covering teachers' absence in Welsh schools do not support learners' progress sufficiently nor provide the best use of resources. The reports highlight an increased involvement of supply teachers and cover staff in the delivery of pupils' education, with just under 10 per cent of lessons now covered by staff who are not the usual class teacher. This has a financial impact for schools and also hampers learners' progress in developing their skills, knowledge and understanding. The pace of lessons can also be slow and expectations too low.

The WAO found that maintained schools in Wales spent an estimated £54 million on classroom supply cover in 2011-12 – an increase of seven per cent since 2008-09 – for reasons such as teachers' sickness, training and attendance at meetings. The WAO estimates that by reducing levels of teacher sickness absence in Welsh schools to the levels in England, 60,000 fewer days cover would be required – potentially saving £9 million a year.

Thanks to the UK Labour governments from 1997 to-2010, teacher salaries rose significantly. From 1999 to 2011, newly qualified teachers (NQTs) saw their salaries increase from £15,080 to £21,830 on average; teachers with five years' experience, from £21,190 to £33,490 on average; those in leadership roles in the primary sector from £29,150 to £49,650 on average, and those in leadership roles in the secondary sector from £38,910 to £59,130 on average (the leadership salaries cover heads, deputies and assistant heads).

Teachers' pay and conditions were not devolved, and we as a government were committed to maintaining the existing position where teachers' salaries and pensions were set on an England and Wales basis. This both reflected our opposition to the introduction of regional pay and the fact that the overwhelming majority of teaching unions were opposed to their devolution, with UCAC, the Welsh-medium teachers' union, the only union arguing for it. The NASUWT made a specific approach in respect of this in the run-up to the devolution referendum in 2011, writing to the First Minister. Carwyn Jones replied that a Yes vote would make no difference to the pay and conditions of teachers. We already had power to seek devolution of pay and conditions through a Transfer of Functions order but decided not to do so. We submitted detailed evidence to the School Teachers Review Body, now chaired by a former BBC colleague of mine, Dame Patricia Hodgson. I welcomed her appointment, though not Michael Gove's failure to consult us on it. We understood the anger amongst teachers and head teachers at the changes being proposed to their pensions. I told the NAHT conference in the autumn of 2011 'we find it unfortunate that, at a time of serious pressure on our public services, we are seeing this kind of pressure being put on public servants. We understand the strength of feeling.'

Pay and conditions also included power over the five statutory INSET days, an issue I found something of an irritant as I wanted to ensure that at least one day was set aside for training in literacy and one in numeracy. I had a telephone discussion with the then Schools Minister, Nick Gibb, about devolving the responsibility for INSET days specifically, and he agreed to reflect on that, but the UK government position, as set out in their submission to the Silk Commission, was that the whole of pay and conditions should be devolved. Silk did, in fact, suggest that pay and conditions should be devolved to Wales, though the Welsh Government did not seek their devolution, and there are serious issues about the transfer of funding to underpin any such move. Both the UK government and the Silk Commission, like the Welsh Government, did not believe that pensions should be devolved, however.

I knew INSET days were not popular with the public, and after the severe weather in early 2010, when many schools had to close, I felt we had to look at the loss of classroom time for students. At the same time, I also moved to ensure that on severely cold days schools were not penalised in respect of absence of pupils in their attendance data. In 2012, I subsequently reduced INSET days to the statutory five. I also took action – now being carried through by Huw Lewis – to standardise term dates across Wales, which was supported by the head teacher unions, and was popular with parents, including those who were teachers.

In early 2011, the *Western Mail* political correspondent Matt Withers wrote: '"What time is Leighton's weekly riling of the unions?" a colleague mischievously asked last week.' Working with some of the teaching unions was certainly different from working with other unions. Most trades unions that I and other ministers dealt with would prioritise issues, identifying potential victories in the context of Welsh Government policy, and securing gains for their members, like the Wales Union Learning Fund. They had strategic vision and tactical sense.

As the OECD has noted, the Welsh Government has a positive relationship with the profession, including the trades unions. I am sure that the Welsh public is largely supportive of the concerns of the two largest teaching unions, the NASUWT and the NUT, on pay and pensions, but they were never likely to win on school reform issues unless they were capable of demonstrating unequivocally that they were on the side of raising standards. The NUT was capable of talking about that while opposing many of the steps we were taking to make it happen. The NUT in January 2013 managed to imply that teachers might go on strike over our Literacy and Numeracy Framework. This was an initiative where we had consulted intensively and the NUT itself had been represented at no fewer than five meetings. The idea of teachers striking against literacy plans was idiotic and would immediately lose public support. I didn't believe for one minute it would happen – and went on the BBC to say so. As the *Daily Post* newspaper said 'teachers will do themselves no favours by threatening to strike over the matter'.

The NASUWT sometimes seemed incapable of talking about anything other than workload, pay and pensions – and then opposing most things we were doing to raise standards. Tactically, they made mistakes frequently. The NASUWT objected to the new performance management arrangements in 2012 and at one stage spoke of likely strike action if these went ahead in autumn 2012. The arrangements went ahead. There was no strike. The NASUWT general secretary managed to issue a statement in the middle of the 2011 Assembly election campaign saying that I had 'frightening similarities to Michael Gove', when we had made raising school standards a key plank of our manifesto. We went on to win half the seats in the Assembly, an increase of four from where we were before, and I was reappointed as Education Minister.

Both the NASUWT and the NUT were in a relentless competition for membership and appeared to think that being seen to express the loudest opposition to our reform agenda was the best way to recruit (indeed, one teaching union leader told me mischievously that the reason he thought the NASUWT was so opposed to the GTCW was that it had been dreamed up by the NUT!) The NASUWT declared a dispute with the Welsh Government in the autumn of 2011. They claimed that local authorities were flouting statutory contracts. Local authorities, of course, were the employers, not the Welsh Government, and we had made it clear that we would look at cases brought to us by the union. We argued back and forth as to whether there was a real dispute. The NASUWT added a range of complaints about our standards agenda to their dispute letter because it was adding to the workload burden. We had what I thought was a constructive meeting with the NASUWT in the summer of 2012 which we felt might lead to a lifting of the dispute but, nominally, they were still in dispute when I left office. One official of a general union said to me in 2012 that he wondered if there would ever be a time when the NASUWT was *not* in dispute.

Despite this, we continued to meet them and I attended NASUWT and NUT meetings when asked. When I spoke to the NASUWT Welsh Conference for the first time, in 2010, I got two rounds of applause and one cry of 'scandalous'. I forget what the applause was for – not being Michael Gove, probably. The shout of 'scandalous' came when I refused to rule out keeping the GTCW. The NASUWT was a curiously conservative union and it appeared to oppose departures from education policy in England, such as changes to qualifications arrangements. The next time I spoke at the NASUWT Conference I got five rounds of applause. I worried afterwards what I had got wrong. In the case of the

NUT, what I found most surprising was the dominant role in its Council meetings not of teachers but of ex-and current head teachers. If I was an NUT member in Wales, I would be wondering about the organisational base of my union.

The truth was that the main dispute of both the NUT and the NASUWT was with the Westminster government over pay and pensions. They wanted us to state our opposition to regional pay and express our concerns about what was being proposed in respect of pensions. We had done those things. They also wanted us to declare that there would be a three-hour limit on classroom observation of teachers within any performance management cycle. Head teachers regarded classroom observation as fundamental to improving the quality of teaching and learning within schools. There never had been any such three-hour limit in Wales under my predecessors and I was not going to introduce one. Apparently this was the price of them lifting their threat to strike in Wales. Huw Lewis, did not accept a three-hour limit either and eventually both unions decided not to hold strikes in Wales in the autumn of 2013. As Gerard Kelly, the editor of the *TES,* wrote in May 2012 'the gravest threat to teaching as we know it appears to be the right of head teachers to wander into a class as and when, observe a lesson and give meaningful feedback to the teacher'. The NASUWT got particularly upset when we wrote to all schools pointing out that there was no set limit on classroom observation.

With the ATL, UCAC and the two head teacher unions, ASCL and the NAHT, it was possible to have an intelligent discussion around standards issues, even where we and they disagreed. For that I was grateful to their union officers in Wales, Phil Dixon, Elaine Edwards, Anna Brychan and Gareth Jones. Margaret Phelan of the University and Colleges Union was also someone with whom we could have a detailed and sensible dialogue even when we disagreed. They were all able to flag up issues that genuinely needed addressing. In the context of the new Education Workforce Council, joined by unions like the GMB, Unison and Unite, anxious to help their members improve their skills and develop, there is a real opportunity for constructive dialogue on how to strengthen the quality of the school workforce in the future, based around the OECD proposal for creating a shared vision of teaching and learning in the future.

Qualifications Reform

Qualifications matter. They matter, obviously, to the students who take them, as a mark of how well they are doing in a particular subject, as an entry qualification for further learning in college or university, or for entry to a specific vocation or apprenticeship. But they also matter to schools – not simply as an indicator of how well teachers or lecturers are developing the students they are responsible for, but also as an indicator of how a particular school is doing compared to others across Wales, particularly those facing similar challenges, and they allow secondary head teachers to see where particular departments are doing well and others not so well. This is particularly important in subjects like English or Welsh and Mathematics, which are seen both as the building blocks for core learning, and are key elements of accountability systems, where the percentage of those achieving five A*-C grades in our schools is one of the measures used to judge performance. So they are key to performance accountability systems in Wales, just as they are in England. Finally, of course, they are important to ministers, as they allow them to look across the system, to see which areas of Wales are doing best and why – and, on occasion, to look across borders where comparisons are possible.

In the first decade of devolution there had been some key developments in the area of qualifications. The Welsh Bacclaureate (The Welsh Bac / WBQ) had been developed and launched, and achieving the full Bac – the advanced diploma – meant getting the equivalent of an A Grade at A level, important for university entry. In developing first the approach to 14-19 Learning Pathways, then legislating through the Learning and

Skills Measure, my predecessors Jane Davidson and Jane Hutt, and their Deputy Ministers Christine Chapman and John Griffiths, had successfully achieved a strategic shift towards making a wider range of vocational qualifications available. The Welsh Bac was widely praised by those in the teaching profession. All five secondary heads in my Rhondda constituency told me in the autumn of 2011 that they could name pupils who had got into university as a result of having achieved the Bac.

This is not to say that there was absolute consensus on the Bac – most summers there would be stories of individual students or their parents complaining about it, but usually in those situations the head teachers of the schools in question defended it. Each summer as the Welsh Bac results were announced I would be armed by my officials with lists of students admitted to strong courses in some of the top universities aided by the Bac. For example, in 2012, at the University of Manchester, for dentistry – either three As or two As and WBQ; Bristol University for Law – three As or two As and WBQ; at Cardiff University for Medical Pharmacology AAB or AA and WBQ; at Nottingham University for Maths three As or two As plus WBQ; at Exeter University, Physics with Astrophysics three As or two As and WBQ; at Southampton for History and Politics AAB or AB and WBQ. But there were still one or two where the Bac was not effectively recognised. Research by Cardiff University's Wales Institute of Social and Economic Research, Data and Methods (WISERD) suggested that the Bac was 'enormously valuable' in helping students enter higher education, including to Russell Group institutions, but the group of students with the Bac were not the highest achievers in terms of degree results.

Meanwhile, Rhodri Morgan's abolition of many Welsh quangoes between 2004 and 2006 had brought the regulatory responsibility for qualifications into government. ACCAC, the Qualifications, Curriculum and Assessment Authority for Wales, merged with the Welsh Assembly Government in April 2006. All parties voted in favour of the relevant resolution when it was debated in the Second Assembly. This meant that Welsh ministers, or more specifically the Minister for Education – whatever their title at the time – acted as the exam regulator in Wales. The exam-awarding body with the largest number of entrants in Wales, the WJEC, had originally been established in 1948 as a consortium of Welsh Local Education Authorities. It was now a registered charity, and a company limited by guarantee, with trustees drawn from the twenty two local authorities in Wales. However, it did not have a monopoly on exam-awarding in Wales, and schools were free to base examinations syllabuses on those offered by a wide range of providers, including OCR, AQA and Edexcel (itself part of Pearson, illustrating how lucrative the examinations business had become). The WJEC had expanded to provide exams to a wide range of schools in England and some in Northern Ireland.

With the exception of the Welsh Bac, general qualifications, such as A levels, AS levels and GCSEs, were shared with England and Northern Ireland. This was known as the 'three-country' system of exam regulation. The exam regulator in England from 2010 had been Ofqual, taking over from the former Qualifications and Curriculum Authority, the QCA, and the exam regulator in Northern Ireland was the Council for the Curriculum, Examinations and Assessment, the CCEA, which was also an exam-awarding body offering exams in England – and theoretically, in Wales. Scotland had its own examinations system, with its own examining and awarding body the Scottish Qualifications Authority, the SQA. Vocational qualifications, of which there were a large number, were supplied across all four nations, regulated in Wales by the Welsh Government, in Scotland by the SQA, and in England and Northern Ireland by Ofqual.

Reforms of qualifications, which have an impact on individual learners as well as on school accountability systems, require careful forward planning over time. They cannot be rushed, and teachers and head teachers, as well as students, and the exam-awarding bodies themselves, need time to plan for change. In a context where qualifications are shared between countries, as with general qualifications, they require co-operation and consultation between different governments and different regulators. Over the period from 2010 to 2013, as we tried to reform our qualifications system in a planned and consultative fashion, we found ourselves having to address constant unplanned policy lurches and sometimes scarcely thought-through proposals launched into debate in the London-based media by the new Secretary of State for Education, Michael Gove, around the future of qualifications which we shared with England. I believe that we came through that period with an approach to qualifications which was widely respected amongst the teaching profession in England as well as in Wales, and trust in our examination system has been enhanced by the approach we took. I also believe that the approach we took will lead to more rigorous qualifications, and a better fit with the needs of learners, further and higher education, and crucially, employers.

Rigour, and the quality of our examination system, was at the heart of our reforms. In my first keynote speech as education minister, to an Institute of Welsh Affairs seminar on Learning Pathways in February 2010, I had specifically raised the question of where the doctrine of learner choice was getting us in our education system. The original consultation document describing the principles of the Learning Pathways stated 'the key to our approach is "choice"'. I quoted the American Psychologist, Barry Schwarz, whose book *The Paradox of Choice* should be required reading for any remaining 'anything goes' libertarians in our education system. Schwarz says:

> When people have no choice, life is almost unbearable. As the number of choices increases, as it has in our consumer culture, the autonomy, control and liberation this variety brings are powerful and positive. But as the number of choices keeps growing, negative aspects of having a multitude of options begin to appear. As the number of choices grows further, the negatives escalate until we become overloaded. At this point, choice no longer liberates, but debilitates. It might even be said, to tyrannize.

Schwarz concludes 'the fact that some choice is good doesn't necessarily mean that more choice is better'. So I said, in February 2010, three months before Michael Gove became Education Secretary in the UK coalition government:

> In terms of the 14-19 agenda, we want to ensure a wider choice between vocational and academic routes. But I do not want that choice to dilute quality. So if we are to be honest with ourselves, we have to recognise that *that* broader strategic choice, to open up vocational options alongside the academic, may require us to limit subject choice if we are to ensure strategic subjects are taught and key skills learned....

I warned that individual choice would always operate within collectively-determined priorities – and that was where democratically-elected governments came in, to provide the framework for choice and quality, balancing a widening of individual opportunities within a context of building a smarter, more sustainable, more prosperous society. The paradox of choice, I said, leads us to 'the language of priorities', which Aneurin Bevan had reminded us was 'the religion of socialism'.

Over the next year, I began to sketch out the case for a review, calling eventually in a speech to the iNet network of teachers in February 2011 for a 'wide national debate' on qualifications. I said then:

> Isn't it time we focused on quality and rigour rather than an apparent choice which simply does not meet the real needs of learners, and that panders to the alphabet soup of qualifications set up by the private examination boards?

That week I told the Assembly that I hoped this would lead to the building of a national consensus on qualifications reform. Just a couple of weeks before my speech, following prompting from the coalition's Higher Education Minister, David Willetts, the Russell Group of universities had published a guide to the subjects that young people should be studying if they wanted to win places at their universities, and subjects that in their views didn't count so highly. To be fair, in opposition, Michael Gove had made similar noises. I suspected this advice had been available to those in public schools for some time. It was not that I felt every student should be applying to a Russell Group university – we had great universities in Wales that were not part of the Russell Group. But this was a symbolic step in allowing more transparency and visibility about qualifications that counted in entry criteria. I didn't want students ending up on courses that would not allow them the right kind of progression. 'Learner choice' was a vapid philosophy. What mattered was informed and meaningful choice based on quality qualifications.

There were 17,000 qualifications listed on the Database of Approved Qualifications in Wales. That surely was too many. Some were dormant, and it was later estimated that there were around 6,500 'live' qualifications.

Professor Alison Wolf's review of vocational education in England found similar issues, suggesting that many young people were trapped in courses that did not necessarily result in employment, and she made recommendations to simplify the system as well as ensuring that young people studied English and Maths as core qualifications. Jeff Cuthbert and I met Alison Wolf to discuss these issues when she was visiting Cardiff. I was not seeking to be prescriptive about particular subject areas. I simply wanted to start a debate on the things that matter for young people. I believed that it was our responsibility as a department to ensure that schools and FE colleges focus on what matters when it comes to skills and qualifications.

Our manifesto for the May 2011 Assembly elections promised to 'simplify the qualifications system in Wales building on the success of the Welsh Bac'. The new Deputy Minister for Skills from May 2011, Jeff Cuthbert, the AM for Caerphilly, took forward the review of Qualifications and did a brilliant job. Having been a Deputy Minister myself, I knew it was important to have a specific project which could engage your interest, and with his background in the WJEC Jeff was absolutely suited to this. Jeff announced the themes of the review at a Business Skills Conference in September 2011:

- Identifying the most relevant qualifications and ensure they are available to learners.
- Ensuring qualifications are trusted and understood.
- Ensuring qualifications remain fit for purpose.

The Qualifications Review

The Qualifications Review in Wales was based on an extensive national consultation led by an independent group. Formally launched on 31st May 2012, following six months of internal debate by the review group, the review asked thought-provoking questions about whether GCSEs should stay, how literacy and numeracy could be at the heart of the curriculum, and whether there was scope for new Wales-only qualifications based around the Welsh Bac. The review group also recognised the need to look at the overall process of regulating qualifications, saying that 'the ability to control qualifications more closely will allow the Welsh Government and partners to work towards ensuring that qualifications are of the highest quality and rigour.'

The review group, chaired by former Coleg Llandrillo chief executive, Huw Evans, included representatives from schools, FE, HE and industry. The final report, published in November 2012 after a widespread public consultation and a year of deliberation, was widely praised, not least for the way in which the Welsh Government engaged with stakeholders in Wales and sought to build a consensus on the way forward. The Review Board heard from an extensive range of interested parties at a variety of meetings and events across Wales. Young people shared their experiences and opinions with the Review team in schools, colleges and at stakeholder events. Many employers, employer representatives, universities, learning providers and parents also put forward their views.

It was important to get this right and to do a rigorous job. During the 2012 GCSE English Language debacle, I watched with interest as some schools in England decided they would opt for the iGCSE in English, which they claimed was more rigorous than the GCSE system, and more consistent. By June 2014, *The Times* was suggesting they had switched to it to 'escape changes introduced to toughen up a core GCSE'. Rigour had to be at the core of what we did, not anecdote or personal preference.

Our Review concluded that the time had come to develop a high-quality, robust and distinctive national qualifications system for 14 to 19-year-olds in Wales, and to support divergence between Wales and other parts of the UK where this was in the interests of learners in Wales. It said the Welsh Government should establish a revised and more rigorous Welsh Baccalaureate model at the heart of the qualifications system for full-time learners at 14 to 19 in the school and further education sectors. The Welsh Baccalaureate should continue to incorporate stand-alone qualifications, a broadly-based core, and the literacy, numeracy and wider skills required for progression in learning, work and life. At 14 to 16, the Welsh Baccalaureate should support a broad and balanced general education. At 16 to 19, it should support coherent programmes of learning. At 14 to 16 all learners should follow the same Welsh Baccalaureate programme of learning, but attainment may be at Level 1 (National Foundation) or Level 2 (National). Post-16 learners should pursue either a National post-16 Welsh Baccalaureate or an Advanced Welsh Baccalaureate.

The Welsh Government should review GCSE English Language and GCSE Welsh First Language in order to introduce revised GCSEs in these subjects for teaching from September 2015. The new qualifications should provide greater assurance of literacy:

- by building explicitly on the levels of literacy that are expected to be developed by the end of Key Stage 3 in response to the new Literacy and Numeracy Framework
- in English Language, by placing significantly more emphasis on the quality and accuracy of writing and on core writing

skills such as spelling, punctuation and grammar than the specifications that were taught from September 2010
- by being assessed predominantly through externally marked assessments that are consistent across Wales and between the two languages.

The Welsh Government should introduce, for teaching from 2015, two new mathematics GCSEs, one covering numeracy and the other covering aspects of mathematics techniques. The Numeracy GCSE should build explicitly on the levels of numeracy that are expected to be developed by the end of Key Stage 3 in response to the Literacy and Numeracy Framework.

Vocational qualifications would be aligned with European frameworks, providing meaningful qualifications that prepared people properly for particular fields.

As Huw Evans said in his introduction to the Qualifications Review 'Qualifications gained in Wales must be recognised and valued across the UK and internationally, equipping youngsters from Wales to work and study worldwide. We have an opportunity to develop a world-class qualifications system for Wales.'

The review did not have an issue about modular GCSE qualifications, though later it was felt that modular GCSE English Language and Welsh Language qualifications should be ended. Huw Evans explained in more detail to the Children and Young Person's Committee in the National Assembly, early in 2013:

> the Baccalaureate provides the wraparound to enable the key skills that employers want to be developed... when employers understood what the Baccalaureate was about... they were overwhelmingly in support of it.... We believe that the Baccalaureate provides us with the model to develop a skills platform while continuing with that underpinning qualification base, using tried and tested qualifications such as GCSEs and A levels.

Responses were generally positive, aside from Conservative MPs in Wales worried about how Welsh qualifications would be seen outside the country – what is known as 'portability' of qualifications. These were legitimate concerns at one level – Welsh qualifications need to have the respect of employers and higher education institutions in England and elsewhere. But at another level, the criticisms were in danger of becoming self-fulfilling, since they rested on an endorsement of the notion that England under Michael Gove was heading in the direction of 'a more rigorous' system of qualifications, and Wales was not. Everything in the Welsh Qualifications Review emphasised the need for rigour and standards.

Huw Evans also dealt with the portability issue at committee, saying universities did not have a problem with a different system in Wales:

> they deal with students coming from over fifty countries, and they have to unpick their students' qualifications base, whether they are from Singapore, China, India or Scotland. Having a different qualifications system in Wales was not something that they were very concerned about.

The review also supported the decision which had been taken by Jeff Cuthbert and me that we should grade the Advanced Diploma of the Welsh Bac to enhance its rigour and value. Huw Evans told the Enterprise and Business committee in February 2013:

> Our qualifications system is very much based on tried and tested qualifications. We are continuing with the A level suite of qualifications, the GCSE suite of qualifications and the vocational range of qualifications. The difference for Wales is that we are wrapping those qualifications into the strengthened Welsh Bac framework, which will hopefully become the skills driver for Wales.

He said that the core of the Welsh Bac was being strengthened with new English- and Welsh-language and new numeracy qualifications. He admitted that the weakness in the old Welsh Bac was the element of duplication with Essential Skills. The National Bac could be taken at sixteen; a Foundation Bac could be gained if an individual doesn't quite make the National Bac, and could then progress to the National Bac at seventeen. The Advanced Bac would be taken at eighteen. With the vocational and academic routes to the Advanced Bac, Professor David Reynolds said that our Qualifications Review stood alongside the Tomlinson Review of 2005 as 'the best attempt to reform qualifications in our education lifetimes'. That was significant praise. The Tomlinson Review in England had recommended what David Miliband, the Minister for Schools who set the review up, had called 'a unified system of academic and vocational study'. Miliband regretted in a speech in Bristol in 2010 that this 'was one area, sadly, where Tony Blair was not the moderniser'.

The Qualifications Review was endorsed by Cabinet and then in his statement on 29th January 29th 2013, Deputy Minister for Skills Jeff Cuthbert confirmed that the Welsh Government would be accepting all of the recommendations from the Qualifications review. He also noted that some equivalence ratings between vocational qualifications and GCSEs lacked credibility, distorting the range of options provided by schools and chosen by learners. We would therefore introduce a maximum equivalence of two GCSEs, from 2016, to encourage a broad and balanced curriculum at fourteen 14 to 16. sixteen. We would also reduce the opportunity for re-sits.

Qualifications Wales and the future of the WJEC

In December 2011, the *Daily Telegraph* had run an exposée of the exam seminar market which made claims about the conduct of examiners in alleging assisting schools to get the inside track on what might come up in examinations. The WJEC was at the centre of the newspaper's allegations. The detail of the issue is described in the next chapter, as it became a core element in the war on Wales unleashed by the Conservative element in the UK coalition government.

As it delivered qualifications in England, the WJEC was subject to regulation there by Ofqual, to whom the *Daily Telegraph* allegations had been referred by Michael Gove. We felt the WJEC was overly petulant in its responses to Ofqual, nit-picking rather than responding to the overall challenge. Further issues arose in the summer and autumn of 2012. After we had to direct the WJEC to issue the correct GCSE certificates following the English Language regrading, we had come to the view that if it had got to the stage that the WJEC had to be told not to do things, then we would direct them on everything. We said publicly that I had made it clear to the chair of the WJEC that I had serious concerns about the organisation and compliance with Welsh Government instructions.

We faced a challenge that the Northern Ireland and Scottish Governments did not, which is that the WJEC's activities in England bring it under the regulatory oversight of Ofqual in England, and means that our qualifications system in Wales can arguably be influenced by regulatory decisions taken in England. Certainly that was true of GCSE English Language in 2012. No elected government can allow the future of its young people and the accountability of its teachers and head teachers to be determined by a regulator elsewhere.

We felt that there was insufficient governance being exercised by the local government representatives on the WJEC's board of trustees. We also believed that the WJEC's remit had become heavily over-extended in recent years – mission creep on a grand scale. It was handling publications, servicing the National Grid for Learning, running the National Youth Orchestra for Wales and a host of other things. My Director General, Emyr Roberts, agreed with me that it needed to be more focused on its core remit. In the immediate aftermath of this, perceptively, the BBC's Welsh Affairs correspondent Vaughan Roderick recognised on his blog that questions about governance, accountability and regulation would raise their heads soon enough.

One thing on which I did agree with the chief executive of Ofqual was that examining bodies had not necessarily been used to such regulation in a particularly meaningful way. We had taken similar powers to Ofqual in the 2011 Education Act to fine the WJEC or other awarding bodies or to withdraw recognition from them. Taking the powers through a Westminster Bill resulted in some complaints in the Assembly in 2011 when I introduced the Legislative Consent Motion to grant Westminster our agreement to their legislating on our behalf, that we should have used the powers we had gained in the 2011 referendum to legislate ourselves. The timing was against us doing that if we wanted to ensure consistent regulatory powers with Ofqual over cross-border awarding bodies.

I suspected that our relationship with the WJEC had been too cosy in the past – in a competitive marketplace, there needed to be a clear distance between the regulator and the bodies it was regulating. That certainly caused me to look carefully at the interrelationships between regulatory officials and the examining bodies. I therefore announced I was setting up a group to look at the structure of the market for qualifications. The review group was made up of two former head teachers, Mike Griffiths OBE and Bethan Guilfoyle CBE, and a former college chief executive, Paul Croke.

When their report came to me in July 2012, it found no clear evidence to indicate that the current market structure had had an adverse effect on standards. Its recommendations were that if Wales-only qualifications emerged from the Review of Qualifications they may be well served by a single awarding organisation structure; in the longer term the Scottish qualifications system based on the work of SQA should be considered as a possible model for Wales; the WJEC should review its mission, structure and governance arrangements, establishing a separate and clear focus on its core awarding functions, possibly splitting its work for England and for Wales; and all awarding organisations should develop guidance regarding the updating and professional development of teachers and examiners. I was not certain the WJEC ever took the commitment to review its governance seriously, until 2013 after local authority leaders realised that things were not going well for the organisation. I wrote to the Chair of the WJEC in the autumn of 2012 to reinforce the importance of this element of the review.

The Qualifications Review then recommended the creation of a body like the Scottish Qualifications Authority, responsible for both regulating and awarding qualifications. I announced that we accepted that early on in December 2012, to give certainty of our intentions for those working in the WJEC. I also announced that Huw Evans would chair a task and finish group to steer the delivery of the organisation, reporting on timing, governance, structures and due diligence. The following week, I met Graham Houston, chair of the SQA, and Janet Brown, its chief executive, in Edinburgh, to learn more of their work.

We were looking at whether it would be possible to dissolve the WJEC into Qualifications Wales. Certainly that would have been my preferred route were it possible, but we suspected that the legal difficulties might be insurmountable. It was more likely, we came to feel in early 2013, that we would look to be setting up Qualifications Wales as a statutory corporation, with the WJEC operating as a separate company and charity, eventually offering qualifications only outside Wales. I told the *Western Mail* in December 2012 that the WJEC had within it skilled and experienced individuals whom we wanted to keep in our system; the WJEC had served Wales very well over the years and had a good reputation for delivering qualifications. But there was 'a tension in their mission' that went back to the time in the 1990s when the WJEC suddenly had to compete for business:

> I think it's inevitable if you are suddenly having to market in a more commercial way and compete with other exam boards, that the overall mission is not simply on the needs of the Welsh education system – but also on activities which further commercial return.

In February 2013 I said we would establish Qualifications Wales by September 2015. The WJEC was critical of this timetable, claiming that there could be 'insurmountable difficulties'. They fought something of a desperate rearguard action to challenge the Welsh Government's conclusions in respect of Qualifications Wales at almost every juncture. There were delays in supplying information on the WJEC's income and expenditure to those carrying out due diligence; the WJEC found it difficult to find time to meet with officials; they objected through letters and articles to the basic policy the Government had determined. We said 'sadly the WJEC appears to be in denial. Qualifications Wales will be established on the model of the Scottish Qualifications Agency. Either the WJEC plays a constructive role in these discussions or the Government may have to take another course of action'.

We were clear that we were moving away from a multi-provider market for general qualifications over time, though there would still be a multi-provider market in relation to vocational qualifications, which was the same situation as Scotland. Qualifications Wales would from September 2015 be responsible for awarding the bulk of general qualifications. The other examining bodies – OCR, AQA and Edexcel – now apparently saw themselves as English awarding bodies, which is how they described themselves to me in a letter in the spring of 2013.

From our perspective, we had taken the decision in principle, and now had to work through the detail in a practical way. The WJEC objected to the decision in principle, and sought to use practical matters to be resolved as reasons to delay or object to the issue of principle.

The WJEC seemed to us unaware of some of the operations of the Scottish Qualifications Agency. As Huw Evans told the Children and Young People's Committee, 'we have looked at the Scottish model; we spent some time in Scotland. The Scottish model has all the characteristics of a world-class system.' He went further 'in Scotland, we also found out how they had managed to separate the awarding function from the regulatory function, which we feel is very important and relevant for Wales as well.'

PwC and Morgan Cole were appointed to conduct the Due Diligence, Organisational Design and Legal Reviews for the development of Qualifications Wales and the proposed incorporation of WJEC's functions, properties and services into the new organisation.

In May 2013, the WJEC clumsily managed to demonstrate precisely why we needed Qualifications Wales to be both a regulatory body and an awarding body. We knew that many teachers disliked the January A level assessments, feeling that they reduced the time available for teaching, and so for new entrants beginning their A level courses in September 2013, we had decided to end the practice. However, I had previously announced in April that A level students who had begun their courses in September 2012 would be allowed to take January assessments in January 2014, as it seemed unfair that students who had started their courses with the expectation of January assessments should not be allowed to have them. However, in England, the same group of students would not be having assessments in January 2014. In Northern Ireland, John O'Dowd was subsequently to announce the same policy as us, that students who had already commenced their course would still get January assessments in 2014.

Two days before I was due to meet the WJEC board, its chief executive wrote to our Head of Qualifications to say that the WJEC did not propose to offer January assessments for A levels and AS levels, entirely contrary to the policy that I had announced. It was clear from the WJEC's letter that they were worried about what Ofqual in England would say. We were aware that Ofqual was not happy with us continuing to offer the January 2014 assessments when they were not, though there had been no consultation with us. They had made their announcement unilaterally.

I was furious with the WJEC. It was clear that its chief executive did not respect the right of the Welsh regulator – the

Welsh Government – to make decisions in the interest of students in Wales, whatever was decided in England. Given the WJEC had roughly an 80 per cent share of the Welsh market, unless dealt with, this meant that the Welsh system was at the mercy of a monopoly supplier.

I did not believe that WJEC board members would be aware personally of the implications for students in their own authorities. At the WJEC board meeting, with individual council Education Cabinet members assembled around the table, I looked them in the eye as I pointed out the implications for students in Bridgend, Ceredigion, Neath Port Talbot, Cardiff, Conwy and other places. The WJEC subsequently backed down. If they hadn't done so, I would have directed them to do so formally. The threat of direction by now was becoming a fact of life with the WJEC.

The WJEC has published the correspondence between myself, officials and the WJEC on its website, so I have no hesitation now in quoting from it. The WJEC tried to dress up its climb-down as being a result of assurances I had given during the meeting with its board. The then chair of the WJEC wrote to me on the 10th May, confirming what had been agreed after my intervention at their 9th May board meeting 'that the WJEC will wish to proceed with the provision of an AS and A level series for January 2014'. This was probably the quickest climb-down in Welsh educational history.

However, the tone of correspondence between the chief executive of the WJEC and our officials made us doubt whether the WJEC had adjusted to more robust regulation or respected it. I wrote to the chair of the WJEC saying that 'the tone and content is unacceptable to the Welsh Government as the regulator and if repeated will have serious consequences for the WJEC as a provider of qualifications in Wales'. I added, 'it is, I regret, typical of how your chief executive behaves towards regulatory officials.' I said that their chief executive 'needs to understand the current regulatory situation and the transparency demanded by the accountability of the Regulator, namely Welsh ministers, to the National Assembly for Wales.' I warned that while we preferred to work with the WJEC on the development of Qualifications Wales our patience was running out, and if necessary we would look to find alternative partners with whom we could work on the development of Qualifications Wales. I had in mind other examinations boards which had greater capacity and international reach than the WJEC, and had the WJEC not subsequently fallen into line, we would certainly have been prepared to move in that direction. I also made it clear in my letter that if necessary, we would take steps 'to direct the WJEC to follow the Regulator's instructions in all matters.'

It was clear to us throughout this period that the WJEC was focused on its market in England and the potential attitude of Ofqual, the regulator in England. Board members of the WJEC, all busy people with onerous responsibilities as policy leads for education in their local authorities, understandably did not have the time to think things through from first principles and focus on the big picture. That changed after the May 9th meeting. Local authority leaders from all parties – and none – understood that things could not continue. Cllr Hag Harris, the witty Education Cabinet Member in Ceredigion, said at the meeting with the WJEC that he was worried about whether board members were sufficiently briefed on the detail to exercise effective governance of the WJEC. That was our concern as a Government. The WJEC chief executive seemed to have a free hand without much intervention by his board or his chair. Over the previous six months we had become increasingly worried that issues of process were being used by the WJEC as a way of undermining key issues of principle. In August 2013 it was finally confirmed that the number of board members of the WJEC would be cut by half, with just six nominees coming from local government, meaning a leaner governance structure.

Huw Lewis took on the challenge of developing Qualifications Wales, launching a consultation in the autumn of 2013. The consultation explicitly stated that Qualifications Wales would be independent of the Welsh Government and would be accountable to the National Assembly. The consultation paper noted:

> Wales, England and Northern Ireland are unusual among European countries in having competing awarding bodies delivering the assessment of the main qualifications taken in schools. Most other nations, such as Scotland and the Republic of Ireland, have a single national body which performs this role.

The paper argued:

- allowing one body to deliver the only qualification in each subject area at each level will guarantee consistency across all centres in Wales.
- stakeholders will be able to make direct comparisons between regions, schools, colleges and candidates without having to take account of varying course content or to rely on complex statistical data.
- a single qualification in each subject area and the removal of competition for qualifications such as GCSEs and A levels will remove any possibility that awarding bodies or qualifications are chosen, or are believed to be chosen, because they are the 'easiest'.

So overall, there was scope to simplify the system, clarify responsibilities, minimise perverse incentives and reduce bureaucracy.

The paper noted that recent developments following the formal establishment of Ofqual in England, and the announcements of changes to GCSEs and A levels in England by the Secretary of State, which were not supported by respondents to our Review in Wales, had made three-country working more difficult. A single qualifications system across three legislatures was no longer possible. In statements in the autumn of 2013, Huw Lewis said that we had an opportunity to ensure that our qualifications were responsive to our needs and 'robust, challenging and free from the undue influence of others'. From the end of 2015, Qualifications Wales would be the regulator – move to become the awarding body over time. Huw said Qualifications Wales would eventually also award the majority of general qualifications offered in Wales. In the short term the Welsh Government would work with awarding organisations, including WJEC, to develop and revise the Welsh Baccalaureate and a single suite of GCSEs and A levels for Wales.

In December 2013 Huw launched the Qualifications Wales website to report on developments. New and revised qualifications to be taught from September 2015 would be developed with WJEC in the short-term. Wales would move towards a single suite of GCSEs, with every learner in Wales taking a subject at GCSE working to the same specification and the same assessments. Huw would bring forward the necessary legislation by the end of the Assembly term. In 2014, the WJEC rebranded itself in England as Eduqas.

Michael Gove and the war on Wales

In March 2014, after a coordinated series of attacks on Welsh public service delivery in London newspapers, the First Minister warned that we were now seeing 'a war on Wales' led by the Conservative Party from London. In Education, the war on Wales began in 2011.

From that year on, Michael Gove sought to use disagreements with education policy in Wales as a way of reinforcing his policy disagreements with UK Labour. I think the British Left sometimes gets Michael Gove wrong. He is a deeply serious, and deeply ideological politician, whose objective is shifting the political agenda strategically. He has a clear grasp of the big picture as it seems to him. It is worth setting out how the Tory right sees him. Fraser Nelson, the editor of the *The Spectator*, had this to say in the *Daily Telegraph* in late 2012:

> He… continually makes his case, in a seemingly endless volley of speeches – an old-fashioned strategy for our soundbite age.... Michael Gove has taught us two things: that in government, impatience is a virtue; and that Conservatism is at its most eloquent when actions speak louder than words.

Matthew D'Ancona wrote in the *Sunday Telegraph* in June the same year, Gove 'is infected with a … determination to get things done by yesterday at the latest.' The impression is of fast-moving reform, and the signals are sent out to the Tory Right that this is a Minister who means business, even if his Lib Dem coalition partners, or the practicalities of implementation, actually prevent the policy coming into reality.

I first met Michael Gove nearly twenty-five years ago when he was a journalist in Scotland. I acted as a public affairs consultant over a number of years on a variety of Scottish-based projects – amongst others, winning public funding for Gaelic language TV; helping the Law Society of Scotland eviscerate the Law Reform Miscellaneous Provisions (Scotland) Bill, with Donald Dewar leading for the opposition and an up and coming young solicitor called Des Browne – later Secretary of State for Defence – teaching his fellow lawyers how to lobby; and helping the steel unions with their doomed campaign to keep Ravenscraig open. I don't remember if Michael ever interviewed me, but he did interview some of my clients, not least Sir Kenneth Alexander, standing for the board of British Steel on behalf of the Scottish local authority pension funds and the steel unions to make a point about the community impact of the closure. I still have a video of the Gove report on that.

I met him again in the mid-1990s when I was the BBC's Head of Public Affairs in London. As the Major government began to crumble, a new Conservative generation started to form. Gove was close to Cameron and his supporters, including Steve Hilton, from the mid-1990s on.

He is, to be fair, often personally engaging, friendly and very polite. He wrote me a charming handwritten letter when I left the Welsh Government, acknowledging our disagreements but saying he knew I was committed to raising standards. But you should never expect the personal charm to displace his ideological mission or the sharpness of his political attack. Nor should anyone be blinded by to the fact that while he is the frontman, he has people who will fight his corner behind the scenes on the basis of unattributable briefings and classic right-wing personal attacks.

He has expressed his admiration for New Labour in government – mainly in respect of the academies agenda. However, the thrust of his argument is that England's schools 'have at worse, declined, and at best, remained stagnant' under Labour, as he argued in the *Daily Telegraph* in December 2013 – and that Labour had deluded itself over rising GCSE results which had been 'propelled upwards by grade inflation'. Indeed, he said in 2013 that the Labour government 'had lied' to students especially over vocational qualifications. Former Ten Downing Street Policy Unit Head Matthew Taylor called this 'the declinist narrative' in an article in *The Guardian* in September 2012, pointing out that 'one of the problems with the assumption of decline is an unwillingness to identify success and also to recognise how the old establishment has, however, grudgingly, adapted.' As Stefan Collini has put it in a different context, in his book on universities, 'There is the mournful idiom of cultural declinism: "standards" are falling, "philistinism" is rampant.... and even the barbarians are going to the dogs.'

The underlying rhetoric of both Michael Gove and of the chief executive of Ofqual, Glenys Stacey, was that standards had not really improved under the UK Labour governments from 1997 to 2010: instead there had been rampant 'grade inflation' and Ofqual's primary focus, under Ms Stacey, was to address that grade inflation. She told the House of Commons Education Select Committee in March 2013 that she faced a range of issues:

> a significant backlog of standards issues: three decades of grade inflation, modularisation, odd proportions of controlled assessment, a very imposing accountability regime and a world that is not used to being regulated.

In early September 2012, Michael Gove said 'for years, under Labour, ministers sat idly by as we endured grade inflation and dumbing down'. Leaving aside evidence from psychologists and educationalists like Dylan Wiliam that standards have been rising over generations, in fact, as Michael Barber revealed in *Instruction to Deliver*, if there had been grade inflation in respect of GCSEs, it began under the Thatcher and Major governments in the late

1980s and early 1990s, 'before the Major government tightened up marking procedures':

> an official who had been there at the beginning of GCSE broke ranks; he sidled up to me, and with a faint smile, began, 'I don't suppose it does any harm to tell the truth now and again'. Then he told me that, in order to ensure the new exam got off to a good start, grade inflation in the early years of the exam had not only occurred, but had been actively encouraged.

The educational war on Wales began, on 8th December 2011, with the exposure by the *Daily Telegraph* of the alleged abuse of examination seminars for teachers provided by the exam boards. The paper carried the headline 'Cheating the system: how examiners tip off teachers', and suggested that exam board officials were revealing the content of future test papers, with one WJEC examiner allegedly telling teachers 'we're cheating. We're telling you the cycle. Probably the regulator will tell us off.' Another appeared to confirm off the record information that certain subjects were unlikely to be the subject of exam questions. Officials from other exam boards were also quoted. The story ran over five pages in the newspaper, and the video footage was made available on their website.

It was a serious issue, and had to be investigated. It was potentially damaging to all exam boards, but particularly, we felt, to the WJEC, which appeared to have been specifically targeted. The front page story said 'in England, three main exam boards offer GCSEs and A-levels – OCR, AQA and Edexcel. However, in recent years the Welsh exam board, WJEC, has become more popular.' The word 'popular' seemed to be deployed here to imply that 'Welsh' meant 'easier' or 'inferior'.

A *Telegraph* article actually said, quoting unnamed teachers and the chair of a Conservative education pressure-group:

Some schools have seen their results soar after dropping one of the three English-based boards in favour of tests set by the Welsh Joint Education Committee.

WJEC – a charity established in 1948 by a consortium of local authorities – has grown much quicker than its competitors in recent years.

According to figures, some 622,500 pupils took GCSEs with the board this summer – up by a fifth in five years.

By comparison, two English exam boards saw entries drop over the same period while a third reported a marginal increase of just 6.3 per cent.

Official documents show how the Welsh board accounted for 18 per cent of GCSE English exams sat by teenagers in 2010, compared with just 7 per cent in 2004.

At the same time, the number of students taking A-levels with WJEC has soared by 80 per cent since 2007, compared with between 10 and 20 per cent at English-based boards.

Teachers approached by The *Daily Telegraph* at revision seminars staged by WJEC told how they chose the board because they believed it offered easier exams – maximising children's results.

One teacher told how the proportion of A* to C grades obtained by pupils had 'doubled' when the school adopted the board's exams.

Chris McGovern, a former head teacher and chairman of the Campaign for Real Education, said: "I know of one school that had a 20 per cent improvement in French straight away after putting weaker candidates through that particular board.

'That was hugely significant and amongst teachers it is pretty widely known that it is the easiest option.'

The *Telegraph* highlighted the potential impact of a competitive market in exam provision – something I had already expressed concerns about – and said that ministers in England had told Ofqual the previous week that they were concerned that a competition between exam boards might be driving a 'race to the bottom' for exam standards. We were not clear to what extent Michael Gove's own advisers might have been working hand-in-glove with the *Daily Telegraph* on the story. Its rhetoric certainly fitted his agenda:

> The disclosures will add to growing fears over the apparent 'dumbing down' of standards in schools which has led to grade inflation in exams over the last decade.

Michael Gove was quoted in the story as having referred the issue to Ofqual and praising the *Daily Telegraph* for its investigative journalism.

I spoke immediately to the chief executive of the WJEC and demanded answers. I told him that the reputation of the WJEC was at stake, and I said so publicly. I referred the individuals – who were practising teachers – to the General Teaching Council for Wales. The WJEC suspended them as examiners pending its investigation. To be fair, both defended themselves at the Education Select Committee subsequently, arguing that they were not breaking rules and that material was available in the public domain.

I reviewed the whole matter with Emyr Roberts, the departmental Director General, and it became clear that it also raised a number of issues for us. First, there was our own relationship with Ofqual. There seemed to be clearly unresolved constitutional issues between us. Our officials seemed overly reliant on Ofqual for support; I felt at that point that some were unable to see the Welsh Government as having a separate jurisdiction and constitutional role; and some seemed uncomfortable at that time – though not subsequently – with our taking on responsibility and going it alone. Additionally there were no agreed protocols to explain how I should operate as a regulator as distinct from as a Minister. Emyr had reviewed the past civil service papers and informed me that no protocols had been put in place following the merger of ACCAC into the Government back in 2006.

Given our concerns about a possible targeting of the WJEC, I decided ultimately, ten days later, that Ofqual's report should be England-only. We believed there were changes of significance in the tone of their report as it was drafted, and we felt they were out 'to get the Welsh'. For example, their preliminary report said that 'any differences between WJEC and the England-based awarding organisations observed in the past have reduced over time', implying that they endorsed the notion that WJEC examinations were easier, basing this on a study by the National Foundation for Educational Research.

Our immediate focus was on the need to make sure that the standards and confidentiality of exams to be taken in January 2012 and the summer were not compromised because some teachers gained privileged information from seminars. At the same time, we wanted to ensure that candidates entered for those examinations were not disadvantaged. After all, it was important that where there is any doubt about the integrity of exams, arising from an actual or potential breach of confidentiality, that urgent action is taken. We took action to instruct the WJEC to postpone a January 2012 ICT GCSE unit.

I subsequently had a perfectly cordial meeting with Ofqual in the Assembly in 2012. I asked Glenys Stacey whether Ofqual were anti-Welsh in their approach early in 2012. She denied it, saying 'Well, my name is Glenys!' Ofqual's eventual report accepted that there was a role for seminars to give accurate advice and information on teaching and assessment to schools and colleges. In July 2013 Ofqual confirmed that there would not be a general ban on such seminars.

The nature of three-country qualifications

GCSEs, A levels and AS levels are owned by the CCEA in Northern Ireland, Ofqual in Wales, and the Welsh Government, in what is ordinarily known as 'three-country' regulation. In

Wales, our independent Qualifications Review team found that GCSE and A level qualifications were highly valued. The Minister for Education in Northern Ireland, John O'Dowd MLA, also said 'GCSEs and A levels have proven to be robust examinations of individual students' abilities.' But in England, from the publication of the White Paper, *The Importance of Teaching,* in November 2010, it was clear that there were to be changes to the structure of GCSEs and A levels, with resits to be reduced, an improved assessment of spelling, punctuation and grammar (this we agreed with), and a move to linear exam-based rather than modular qualifications. Mr Gove confirmed the end of modular GCSEs from September 2012 on *The Andrew Marr Show* on BBC television in June 2011. He made a series of announcements regarding qualifications, with the creation of the English Bac in September 2010 – unlike the Welsh Bac, not a qualification based on additional learning, but a matriculation certificate recognising student achievement in specific designated subject areas which would become a new focus for accountability measurements of schools in England – and in 2011, in response to the Wolf report, a limitation on which vocational qualifications would count in school performance league tables in England. Michael Gove warned in speeches in the autumn of 2011 and in February 2012 that exams would be tougher and 'there will be years when performance will fall'.

In respect of A levels, Michael Gove wrote to me on 31st March 2012 outlining the actions he intended to take. Three days later, coinciding with a letter back to Michael Gove from the chief executive of the English regulator, Ofqual, the front page of the *Daily Telegraph* was headlined 'Dons take charge in A-level shake-up'. The article said 'universities will be given new powers to set A levels for the first time in thirty years because of fears that the gold standard qualification is failing to prepare teenagers for the demands of higher education. Ministers will relinquish control of syllabuses and hand them to exam boards and academic panels made up of senior dons from Russell Group universities'. As the vice chancellor of Aberystwyth rightly said 'the Russell Group universities are important and have a powerful brand – but there are other universities that we know have excellence in student experience and teaching. Why would you not want to include those universities if the option became available?' Mr Gove expected the new A levels to be taught from 2014. The *Daily Telegraph* editorial praised Mr Gove's 'characteristic boldness' and echoed his rhetoric: 'Thanks to decades of grade inflation and an all-must-have-prizes mindset, we have a thoroughly discredited public examination system.'

In fact, the agenda on A levels was a contested one. The chief executive of the university application service, UCAS, Mary Curnock Cook, a former director of Qualifications and Skills at the Qualifications and Curriculum Development Agency in England, challenged some of the simple assumptions surrounding A level standards and comparability. In an article in *Times Higher Education* (*THE*) in August 2012, she said 'does the fact that 34 per cent of candidates who study A-level chemistry achieve grades of A* or A mean that it is easier than psychology, with its mere 18 per cent at A* or A?'

She raised a series of questions about demand, assessment and outcomes, asking:

> just what is it about the assessment of English at A level that means that 7 per cent of candidates achieve A* where 18 per cent achieve purportedly the same standard in mathematics? Is it because the attrition rate between AS and A2 is 50 per cent higher in mathematics than in English, thus upping the concentration of higher performers? What is the correlation with prior GCSE performance? Or is the assessment methodology flawed?

These were complex questions, not helped by the rhetoric of cultural decline, of dumbing down and grade inflation. Mary Curnock Cook pointed out that A levels had been designed as subject qualifications to support progression to mainly academic degree courses. If universities wanted a reliable assessment of higher order cognitive skills as well as deep subject knowledge then they needed a broader curriculum like the International Baccalaureate or other qualifications.

In the end, this was an area where Mr Gove had to back down. Universities did not want to run A levels – they were to be consulted on their content but did not take ownership of them.

It was during 2012 that concerns emerged in both Northern Ireland and Wales about the pace of planned change in these qualifications which were shared on a three country basis, and the lack of consultation with us about the potential impact on our own qualifications. There had been no consultation by Mr Gove with either myself or the Education Minister in Northern Ireland, John O'Dowd MLA, although in Michael's letter to me he had accepted that these were three country qualifications. In March 2012, John O'Dowd said he would not be following Michael Gove in phasing out modular elements in GCSEs. He said that Mr Gove's decision 'did not appear to have been taken on the basis of clear evidence or educational justification'. For our part, we were also sceptical of the reasons for ending modular GCSEs and were clear we would not do anything before the outcome of our qualifications review. Indeed, later in the year, the chief executive of Ofqual was to say that with the exception of GCSE English Language in 2012, 'every other modular GCSE has been awarded without these difficulties'. I wrote back to Michael Gove on the 23rd April, saying 'it is regrettable... that you did not seek to agree the proposals with me and John O'Dowd before they were announced.' Michael Gove responded to my complaint on the 23rd May with a handwritten note at the bottom of his letter saying 'Thank you, as ever, for your forebearance and understanding.' I assume that was tongue in cheek.

In May 2012, the CCEA in Northern Ireland told the heads of all exam centres in England with entries for CCEA qualifications that from a future date it would not be accepting entries from England for CCEA qualifications. The letter said 'this decision has been taken as a result of emerging policy differences between

England and Northern Ireland.' That month, I warned in a lecture in Aberystwyth that 'the reality now, in respect of both A levels and GCSEs, is that we are seeing, without debate, a dismantling of the three-country system for public examinations.'

In June, the *Daily Mail* carried a story that Mr Gove planned a return to O levels, though this was then contradicted by his coalition partners, the Liberal Democrats. I said Wales would not be going back to O levels, whatever happened in England. The same month, the Education Select Committee of the House of Commons said that it thought there was a need for a Ministerial conference between England, Wales and Northern Ireland to look at three-country qualifications and standards comparability.

John O'Dowd came to see me to discuss these issues in July 2012, and we agreed that we would write to Michael Gove asking for a meeting. We wrote in August asking if we could meet to discuss better communication over qualifications policy changes in England which might impact on us given that these were 'jointly owned qualifications'. Michael Gove responded in mid-September, turning down the request for a meeting, instead offering us the opportunity to meet with one of his junior ministers. I decided that was pointless. His newly-appointed junior minister was not the problem.

Following the English GCSE debacle, discussed in the next chapter, in September 2012 Michael Gove promised to replace GCSEs with the new English Baccalaureate Certificates (EBCs) which would end the 'race to the bottom', 'grade inflation' and 'dumbing down' and instead 'raise aspirations and restore rigour'. It would mean only one exam board per subject to prevent competition to offer schools easier tests, rather than 'different exam boards offering easier courses or assistance to teachers, in a corrupt effort to massage up pass rates'. There would be no modular courses, with the main feature being a three-hour exam. More students would be likely to leave school with no qualifications, Mr Gove confirmed, receiving instead simply a detailed record of achievement from their schools for use with FE colleges. GCSEs would survive until at least 2017 in some subjects, with the EBac beginning in core subjects like English and Maths from 2015. The Conservatives were reforming the system 'after years of drift, decline and dumbing down'.

Michael Gove's comments that GCSEs and A levels are not fit for purpose and have been dumbed down come straight from the lexicon of the US new right of the late 1980s and early 1990s. The University of Westminster's Professor Steve Barnett wrote an essay back in the late 1990s which analysed how 'dumbing down' came to be adopted as a phrase in Britain:

> In the five years from the beginning of 1990 to the end of 1994, the entire UK broadsheet press could muster only 11 references to 'dumbing down' between them. The tally rises to 27 in 1995 and 23 in 1996, not enough to suggest that a defining statement about the state of 1990s Britain had arrived. But in 1997, it took off: the British broadsheet press saw over 400 references to 'dumbing down'.

Barnett notes that the discussion is generally pessimistic, seeing a decline in standards from a mythical golden age, when what might be happening is a widening of access to communication. In *Culture and Society* Raymond Williams of course famously dated the conservative concept of a decline in standards to the 1740s, so Michael Gove was reinventing a very old tradition.

Michael's announcement about the EBCs confirmed that three-country collaboration over qualifications was breaking down. We needed to look to collaboration with Scotland and Northern Ireland. The First Minister thought I should also look to the situation in the Republic of Ireland as well. In October, a poll carried out by Beaufort research for the *Western Mail* found that people in Wales wanted to keep GCSEs by 47 per cent to 36 per cent. In every region of Wales there was a majority against the return of an O level style exam.

In Northern Ireland, John O'Dowd said that 'Michael Gove has not proven that the GCSE exams were not rigorous' but warned that his comments might have 'fatally flawed' the GCSE brand. In a statement in the Northern Ireland Assembly he announced a review of GCSEs and A levels, commissioning the CCEA to take it forward. John said he did not rule out sticking with the current system but wanted quantitative and qualitative research into the issues. He had 'no desire for change based on ideological principles alone'. He wanted to ensure comparability 'across these islands' and internationally. He said that it was 'regrettable' that Michael Gove had chosen to break away from a three-country approach to GCSEs. John confirmed in the Northern Ireland Assembly that Michael Gove had refused to meet him and had refused to meet me.

Our own independent Qualifications Review, published at the end of November, said on GCSEs, that it did not 'recognise the analysis in commentary from England that the qualification is "broken" or "devalued".' Wales and Northern Ireland differed from England in our refusal to talk down the very qualifications that young people were actually sitting. We believed in strengthening GCSEs and A levels, not undermining them.

It was clear that opposition had been mounting in England during Mr Gove's consultation on his EBC plans. In October 2012, the chair of the Commons Education Select Committee, Graham Stuart, urged Mr Gove 'to stop taking the urgency pills and recognise the need to slow down'. In December he told Michael Gove that his refusal to share with the committee a letter from Ofqual expressing concerns about the proposals was 'unacceptable'. In January 2013, Mr Stuart's committee stated that it thought the Government was 'trying to do too much, too fast'. They clearly did not accept that GCSEs were discredited and worried about the legacy of GCSEs being discredited once the EBCs started; they were also concerned about the timetable for reform and the link with school performance measures.

In February 2013, Michael Gove backed down on the EBCs and also dropped the idea of ending competition between exam boards. He told the House of Commons that there would, instead, be 'reformed GCSEs'. He also announced reforms to the school accountability system in England not unlike the secondary school banding system we had announced in Wales, with new measures of progress based on average point scores across eight subjects. It was, as Labour spokesperson Stephen Twigg said, 'a humiliating climbdown'. I said I was glad to welcome 'a repentant sinner'. Professor Ken Reid, who advised us on attendance and behaviour issues, sent me an email saying 'You must be a happy man…thank goodness we decided not to follow suit! I wonder if those who criticised me for supporting the Welsh system will now eat their own words!'

When I appeared before the Education Select Committee of the House of Commons in March 2013 to share our experience of the 2012 English Language GCSE results, I made it clear I would be keen still to meet with Mr Gove. Not long after this, John O'Dowd and I received an invitation to meet him on May 13th. John and I met up first for lunch with our officials and advisers in the Welsh Government offices at 25 Victoria Street before walking around the corner to the Department for Education Offices in Great Smith Street. In advance of the meeting, Mr Gove had indicated he was meeting with Ofqual's Glenys Stacey beforehand and might invite her to stay on to join the meeting. Both John and I made it clear in advance that we felt this was inappropriate. We had sought a three-way Ministerial meeting. However, when we arrived, there she was. Since matters from that meeting were subsequently leaked by the Department for Education a week later, John and I subsequently decided there was no longer any point in retaining absolute secrecy on this occasion.

In the meeting, Michael Gove set out his agenda on qualifications reform and invited us to respond. We both made it clear that policy statements made unilaterally by him or his department, often through leaks to the media, were not an appropriate way of handling qualifications whose ownership was shared across three legislatures. It was not helpful to have qualifications being undermined or the approach of different administrations criticised. Michael invited Glenys Stacey to set out what she saw as the difficulty of different approaches to qualifications in the different territories. She made points about the difficulties of qualifications with different specifications being seen to have differing standards.

John and I outlined our approach, which in both cases had been to undertake extensive reviews of qualifications. John suggested that we did not want to see a breakdown of the three-country system – a 'surgical separation' might be something else. One of Gove's special advisers piped up to ask whether a three-country agreement needed to continue. The adviser seized on John's phrase 'surgical separation'. That phrase was subsequently leaked in briefings to *The Guardian* and other newspapers the following week. It could only have come from someone in the meeting. Publicly, John and I agreed that it had been 'a frank but cordial discussion' and that there needed to be better communication between us, and that the concordat would be honoured. Michael Gove apologised to me for breaches of the concordat in respect of some specific announcements.

John said publicly:

> Secretary of State Gove has previously made announcements about the future of examinations in England without any form of consultation with the administrations in Wales or the north of Ireland. I had already expressed my disappointment and concern about the lack of consultation and today's meeting provided an opportunity to reiterate this message and outline the importance of keeping both myself and Minister Andrews informed of any major policy decisions and respecting the concordats that are in place.

A week letter, both of us received a letter from Michael Gove suggesting that three-country regulation was 'no longer an objective to which we should be working' and we should consider whether we should rename the relevant qualifications. He said 'it will not be sufficiently transparent for what will become markedly different qualifications to use the same title, particularly when the students holding those qualifications will be regularly crossing borders.' He said it was clear that reforms were leading to 'very different qualifications', accepting that this was a 'natural and legitimate consequence of devolution'.

Immediately, the content of the letter and the meeting was leaked to *The Guardian* and other outlets. A 'Whitehall source' told *The Guardian*:

> The Welsh are determined to keep dumbing down their exams. Leighton Andrews interfered with exam boards last year. He opposes our attempts to toughen things up and made clear he will continue to interfere to make things easier. It's better that we all go our own way and defend our positions to our electorates. It's been agreed that we will explore what the Northern Irish described as 'surgical separation'.

John O'Dowd was particularly furious at the leaking of the letter and the content of part of the meeting, including his words about 'surgical separation'. We spoke and agreed we would both write to Michael Gove. John said he was disappointed that Michael Gove's letter had been 'leaked within an hour of me receiving it'. He added 'I was also shocked that an almost verbatim report of our meeting last week appeared in the media.' He urged Michael Gove to take 'whatever action necessary to ensure the sanctity of Ministerial meetings and correspondence is upheld.' I wrote in similar terms asking if Michael Gove if he could confirm that the leak had not occurred from anyone who was in attendance at the meeting.

I also wrote to John suggesting we should look at ways of maintaining two-country regulation of GCSEs and A-levels. Michael Gove's letter had suggested we and Northern Ireland might have to re-name our exams. We were not going to change the names of our qualifications and neither Michael Gove nor

Ofqual had the power to make us do so. As John explained 'In my opinion, we can have a common A level name, we can have a common GCSE name. It can be delivered in slightly different ways. It is the robustness of the exam that is important.' I said we would not buckle over the issue. I told the *Western Mail* that I felt 'we've got to lose this inferiority complex and we've got to have confidence in our qualifications.' I said that we were keeping GCSEs and A-levels, and wished Mr Gove well with his plans to re-name these qualifications in England.

The Labour AM Vaughan Gething tabled an urgent question on the leaking of the Gove letter which I answered in plenary on the 21st May. I said:

> Wales is keeping GCSEs, AS levels and A-levels under their existing titles as, we understand, is Northern Ireland. I cannot speak for England.

The *Western Mail* said 'Wales should not be forced into a corner on qualifications not of its own making. Mr Andrews has stayed true to GCSEs and A-levels – it is Mr Gove who has U-turned and turned again. First he was scrapping them, then he wasn't.'

Fast forward two weeks and *The Times* front page on June 4th said 'Gove ready to replace GCSE with new 'I level'. The BBC's Vaughan Roderick said on Twitter it seemed to be 'Game, Set and Match to Leighton Andrews'. The new 'I levels' would have in most cases no coursework, no modular structure and would be graded 1 to 8. *The Times* reported 'England's exams regulator says that a new title is needed because the Labour-led Welsh Assembly (sic) insists on retaining the name GCSE for its unreformed exams, which will retain modules and assessed coursework.'

The Times had clearly been briefed by sources close to Michael Gove. Yet again this was pitched as England doing one thing and Wales another, when of course Wales and Northern Ireland were both heading in a similar direction and England was moving on its own. The suggestion that our exams were unreformed was simply ignorance – we had already made plans through our Qualifications Review to strengthen them. Of course, *The Times* did not check its story with us. We publicly confirmed that we would be keeping GCSEs and A-levels and would work with Northern Ireland and if possible, England, to ensure portability of qualifications. The *Western Mail's* well-informed Education correspondent, Gareth Evans, observed: 'Westminster's decision to re-sharpen the axe on GCSEs is another win for Cardiff Bay. Mr Gove is digging his own grave on exam reform and all Mr Andrews need do is sit, watch and rub his hands.'

After warning John O'Dowd and I that it would not be possible for 'what will become markedly different qualifications to use the same title', it was, said Gareth, Michael Gove who 'had blinked first'.

A week later, and the *TES* was suggesting that I levels were not going to be the answer, and Ofqual was now looking at the title 'GCSE (England)'. Michael Gove then published his plans for the new exams, more or less in line with what *The Times* had said, aside from the title 'I level'.

The Education Select Committee published its report on English-Language GCSEs in June. The committee worried about a rush towards separate systems for England, Wales and Northern Ireland, without sufficient reflection on what might be lost, which it said would be regrettable, and urged Ministers to do everything possible to maintain the three country system. They also called on Ofqual to do all it could 'to improve relations with the Welsh regulator.' I sympathised with that, but it was by now too late, after two years of unilateral actions from Mr Gove. Meanwhile, Michael Gove had now moved on to criticising Scotland. In an interview with the *Daily Telegraph*, he claimed that the Scottish system was moving 'away from rigour'. 'Your turn for a Gove-ing', I joked to my Scottish counterpart, Mike Russell, on Twitter.

I then made our announcement on A levels and AS levels. In November 2012 Ofqual had announced curbs on numbers of resits at A-level, the abolition of January exams, and the expectation that all exams would be taken in the summer at end of year. AS and A levels were to be decoupled. Ofqual had been warned in May by Kevin Brennan, Labour's schools spokesperson and MP for Cardiff West, that Labour believed the evidence for keeping the link between AS and A levels was overwhelming and Labour might therefore reverse Ofqual's plans after the 2015 General Election. Our independent Qualifications Review found no reason for a decoupling.

I said we would keep January assessments for 2014 to allow the current A level cohort to complete their studies, but they would be ended after that. We planned to keep AS levels in their current form, and were confident that we had significant backing for that, including from the vice chancellor of Cambridge University, Professor Sir Leszek Borysiewicz, originally from Llanrumney, whom I had met in March. They would not be decoupled from A levels, unlike in England. He had written to me saying that Cambridge found AS levels to be useful entry performance indicators. Indeed the University of Cambridge publicly criticised plans on AS levels which it said 'would jeopardise over a decade's progress towards fairer access.'

Our proposals mirrored plans in Northern Ireland, we knew. Of course, an unnamed Whitehall source then briefed the *Daily Telegraph* that I was guilty of 'politically motivated dumbing down':

> 'Leighton Andrews has interfered in the marking of exams for political reasons and has made clear that he will carry on interfering in the exam system for political reasons,' the source said.
>
> That's why Ofqual has said that Wales must be cut loose so it does not drag the English system down.
>
> It's sad for Wales but we've got to focus on the credibility of the English system.

In September 2013, John O'Dowd confirmed, following a review by the CCEA, that Northern Ireland would be keeping GCSEs and

A levels. Like Wales, there would be restrictions on the number of resits of modules. Like Wales, AS levels would be retained and John kept the January 2014 resit opportunity as we had done.

The same month, Ofqual decided that it was too ambitious to introduce most of the GCSE and A level reforms in England to Mr Gove's original September 2015 timetable. In October, Ofqual recommended keeping coursework in some A levels, and said that AS levels could be taught alongside the first year of an A level course. As well as Cambridge, Oxford University had been amongst those speaking out with concerns about hasty reform of A levels, saying there was no need to break the link with AS level or to go to a wholly linear model. Private school heads were also critical. In 2014, Ofqual confirmed its plans for GCSEs, which in future would have a numerical grading system and would be accompanied by an annual national reference test to assess performance comparisons between years.

English Language GCSE

I had no knowledge that anything was likely to go wrong with English language GCSEs in 2012 until, at the end of a routine meeting with the chief executive of the WJEC, Gareth Pierce, on 30th July, he made reference to difficulties in the awards and the possibility that Welsh students in particular might lose out. There might be a drop of about 5 per cent in GCSE English Language. I learned that meetings were underway and that some of the issues related to the method of determining grade boundaries, which were linked to expected performance based on results at the end of Key Stage 2, might be a factor.

The 2012 cohort of students awaiting the results were the first to take the new specification. They had begun their courses in the autumn term 2010. The new qualification involved Controlled Assessment – assessments completed in schools under controlled conditions – replacing coursework. The Controlled Assessment amounted to 60 per cent of the marks. In England, a new qualification combining language and literature was taught, which we had not approved in Wales, as regulatory officials felt it did not sufficiently test the whole curriculum.

English language GCSE is one of a number of what are known as 'high-stakes' qualifications. The reason being that they feature heavily in accountability judgements on our schools. In Wales, we look to see how schools are doing in relation to the percentage of young people getting five A*-C GCSEs, including English or Welsh and Mathematics. It is not the only factor we measure in secondary school banding, as I explain elsewhere. But it is one of a number of headline performance indicators.

Ordinarily, Ministers get briefed on GCSE and A level results the day before their publication. Results are supplied in encrypted form to key officials by the Joint Council on Qualifications, made up of the key awarding bodies and regulators. When I was briefed on the GCSE results on Wednesday 22nd August I ended up both cross and depressed. After eighteen months of focusing more sharply on performance than ever before, it seemed our impact had been far less effective than expected. We had particularly been looking for improvements in English, given the additional support and focus that had been brought to it. Instead, the percentage achieving Grades A*-C in English Language had fallen from 61.3 per cent in 2011 to 57.4 per cent in 2012. It was inexplicable.

That evening, as I grumpily scrolled through Twitter, it became obvious that something was happening in relation to GCSE English Language in England as well. (Schools get the results at about the same time as Ministers). Head teachers such as Geoff Barton, a regular columnist in the *TES,* were asking whether others had experienced unexpectedly low grades in English for their students. His school in Suffolk had had 'a disastrous drop' of 15 per cent in English. Overall, Ofqual said, the fall in A*-C grades in English and English language GCSE s in England was 1.5 per cent – from 65.4 per cent in 2011 to 63.9 per cent in 2012.

The next day I was celebrating GCSE results with Sue Davies MBE, head teacher at Cynffig Comprehensive in Bridgend. There, where the students had studied the AQA syllabus in English, one of those most under fire in England that day, there was no evidence of a decline in results – indeed, quite the opposite. Of course, Cynffig was not studying AQA's combined English GCSE, as we hadn't approved it. But its results did not reflect the anger evident elsewhere. So what was going on?

As the day wore on, I became less confident about the security of the results. I decided that we would hold a review, to be carried out by our regulatory officials. I announced the review on the BBC's *Wales Today* programme that evening. I was particularly worried that with the WJEC offering exams in

England as well as in Wales, we might be subject to arbitrary judgements made by Ofqual which had an impact through the three-country system of regulation. I asked whether we could have confidence in the integrity of our system if decisions taken by the English regulator – potentially under pressure from the Secretary of State – were having an impact on our main exam body.

The next day I left on holiday for two weeks, as the media covered stories reflecting anger with the grading of GCSE results overall, and English Language in particular, with exam boards apparently conceding that grade boundaries had shifted between January and June, and head teachers and teachers, including in several of the UK government's favourite academies, reckoning that there had been significant shifts in the number of marks required to get a C-grade. In England, that could have particularly damaging results in respect of schools falling below their floor standards which indicated they were 'failing' and could trigger a requirement that they become academies.

Ofqual had set out an approach called 'comparable outcomes' in a paper in May 2012 explaining how it would set standards for GCSEs and A-levels that summer. The general principle was that:

> a student should get the same grade as they would have done had they entered the old version of the qualification. We call this approach 'comparable outcomes'. It aims to prevent what is sometimes called grade inflation – that is, increases in the numbers of students achieving higher grades when there is not sufficient evidence of real improvements in performance. It also enables us to allow for the dip in performance that can arise when a new qualification is taken.

Little-noticed at the time, Ofqual had written to both the Head of Ofsted (the school inspection service in England) and separately a week later to the Secretary of State for Education,

Michael Gove, explaining that their new approach to grading meant that it was likely that results would decline. In her letter to Michael Gove, the chief executive of Ofqual said: 'It is not credible that the year-on-year rises in top grades over the last 20 years are solely down to real improvements in attainment.'

Her letters explained that Ofqual was using an approach called 'comparable outcomes' which had halted 'grade inflation' at A level in 2011, and was now being applied to GCSEs from 2012: 'it involves getting the exam boards, in setting grade boundaries, to check that the results are in line with what they would expect given the prior attainment of students. If they are out of line, they have to explain that.'

The killer quote in Ms Stacey's letter to Michael Gove was this: 'One consequence of this approach is that it can make it harder for any genuine increases in the performance of students to be fully reflected in the results.'

To my mind, when I finally became aware of the letters in September – Ofqual had not shared them with my department – that sentence indicated that Ofqual was actually driving a process of grade *deflation* in its approach to exam regulation.

In her letter to Sir Michael Wilshaw, Ms Stacey said that 'comparable outcomes is generally regarded as the best approach for now'. She also told him that one consequence would be that it was less likely that schools would be able 'to evidence improvement with better exam results, year after year.' Her letter to Michael Gove admitted that the approach would make it difficult 'to secure system-level improvements in exam results which you have said you want to see.'

Where A levels were concerned, using prior GCSE achievement as an indicator for the overall cohort – not for individual learners – had been found to have value in a review carried out by the National Foundation for Educational Research on behalf of the regulators in Wales, England and Northern Ireland. However, there was no such common prior qualification which could provide an indicator for GCSEs. In England, students took externally marked assessments at the end of Key Stage 2. In

Wales, there were no such assessments. Wales and Northern Ireland relied on a methodology based on predictions for 'common centres' – crudely, exam centres with similar entries in the key subjects year on year. Early in 2012, Ofqual said that they thought KS2 predictors should be used for WJEC candidates too as WJEC had significant numbers of candidates from England. Welsh Government officials would not accept that it was appropriate for results for Welsh candidates to be determined on the basis of prior achievement by candidates in England. However, WJEC was the second largest exam body for GCSE English Language in England, and it became hard to resist use of this methodology in this subject.

In April 2013 the *TES* concluded:

> the balance gradually began to shift: more weight was attached to statistical history and less to current performance. Why? Probably because the certainty of a statistical model was a comforting refuge for regulators buffeted by journalists raging about grade inflation.

The *TES*'s view was that the dip in A level results and GCSEs in 2012 was, as its journalist William Stewart said, 'a direct result of a concerted attempt to get a grip on 'standards' from exams regulator Ofqual, acting partly at the behest of regulators.' The change had huge implications for schools, teachers, students, parents, employers and universities. 'Yet it did not appear in any party manifesto and its introduction was not discussed by Parliament. It was brought in without public debate, with minimal consultation, little publicity and virtually no awareness among the public at large.'

In essence, there is nothing wrong with an approach of ensuring 'comparable outcomes' when an exam specification changes, if the objective was to ensure that no exam cohort was disadvantaged by the introduction of a new exam specification. That had been what our officials had agreed in 2008, when the matter was discussed in meetings between the 'Interim Ofqual' organisation, then part of England's Qualifications and Curriculum Authority, and other regulators. The meeting, under the theme 'Maintaining Standards in Changed Qualifications' discussed a paper from Dennis Opposs of Ofqual entitled *Carrying forward grade standards when qualifications change.* The meeting agreed that the most important factor was a fair outcome for candidates, and regulators and awarding bodies needed to maintain qualification level standards. But with new specifications performance 'invariably drops'. There was 'no reason to believe that outcomes in grade distribution in the first year should be very different from those before the changes', so the comparable outcomes model came into play.

Ofqual subsequently elaborated on the relationship between comparable outcomes and comparable *performance:*

> This means the way that students perform in the exam. We know that performance 'dips' in the first year of a new syllabus. So if we aim for comparable performance in the first year of a new syllabus, it will make it harder for students to get each grade compared with students in the previous year.... Students should not be advantaged or disadvantaged just because they were the first to sit a new set of examinations.

However, Ofqual then went on to argue for prioritising comparable outcomes *after* the first year of a new syllabus, saying:

> If we accept that performance in the first year's exams will be a little lower than in subsequent years, and then we use the performance in those first year's exams as a benchmark for the subsequent years, we will be locking in a lower standard. Over time, this is likely to result in grade inflation with each year, gradually more candidates achieving each grade.

The *TES*'s conclusion was that the approach had become more closely aligned to holding standards down after Ofqual had come into independent existence in 2010, and that its chief executive, Glenys Stacey, had been told by the Department for Education in England that maintaining standards was a top priority. In her first interview with the *TES* in May 2011, she had said that she did not find the term grade inflation 'to be a very helpful expression'. She said 'inflation has a negative import whereas in fact we may be seeing young people being taught well and working hard'. However, in her confirmatory hearing before the Education Select Committee on 1 February 2012 she set two goals for her first year:

> We will contain grade inflation this summer at GCSE and A-level.... we will demonstrate a material difference to schools.

Ofqual produced an interim report on 31st August. This found that the exam standards were comparable with those for previous years; exam boards set standards at the appropriate level; January's exams had been graded generously and that June's exams had been subject to subsequent grade boundary changes. Glenys Stacey said 'the issue is not the June, but the January boundaries.' Ofqual found that the standard set for the 2012 GCSEs was comparable with previous years. Three things caused difficulties – changes to the syllabus; the nature of English as a subject when new qualifications come in; and the structure of exams based on modules with 60 per cent controlled assessment. Students were to be offered the opportunity of November re-sits. Ofqual did not give us 'much advance warning' of their report, their director of regulation, Fiona Pethick, admitted in an internal Ofqual email released to me under the Freedom of Information Act in 2014.

The Ofqual report satisfied no one, particularly after Ms Stacey said that students who took the January assessment had 'got lucky'. John Tomsett, a head teacher in Yorkshire, himself a former English teacher, was scathing:

> OFQUAL's report damages all of us. Two years ago our students attained 68 per cent A*-C grades in English language GCSEs; with a number of hands-on highly effective and sometimes bloody interventions we attained 77 per cent last year and 83 per cent this year. Glenys Stacey now says we were lucky, an individual who has never taught a GCSE student in her life.

The criticisms came from comprehensive heads and academy heads in England, as well as private school heads, with Anthony Seldon, Master of Wellington College, saying 'the raising of the bar between January and June was very unfair.' No one seemed to doubt that the treatment of students who had taken the exam in June was unfair. Even former Ofsted chief inspector Sir Chris Woodhead, scarcely part of the liberal educational establishment, said on BBC Radio Four's *Today Programme*: 'the simplest thing would be to draw a line under it all, and do what the teachers and the teacher unions want, that is to simply give the summer students the grades that they would have got if they'd sat it in January.'

The consequences for individuals who failed to secure a 'C' grade could be significant – entry to certain sixth form or FE courses could be denied. I therefore agreed that we would write to all schools urging head teachers to take candidates' whole range of achievement into account, recognising that their result in English language might be out of step with their wider performance.

As we have seen, the three-country model of regulating GCSEs was already under pressure. Ofqual Director of Regulation Fiona Pethick had written to the Welsh Government's Head of Qualifications on 17th July 2012 following a meeting between Ofqual and our officials, suggesting that Ofqual had the power to regulate qualifications wherever they were taken, including in Wales. Internal Ofqual emails released to me under the Freedom of Information Act in 2014 give Ofqual's summary of this meeting: 'we wrote challenging the Welsh Governments (sic) ability to act as the sole regulator in Wales with no regard for English regulation. The Welsh were so incensed by this letter we withdrew it to redraft'. They never re-issued it. However, Ofqual were essentially suggesting that they could police standards in Wales. Our view, backed by our lawyers, was that if Ofqual were to interpret the Apprenticeships, Skills, Children and Learning Act in that way, then logically it could only mean that we could police standards in England too, and that could not be what Parliament had intended. As our officials tried to work through with Ofqual the implications were a regrading to take place, on the 29th August, Ms Pethick told Glenys Stacey in an internal Ofqual email 'I know that we would all like to put the Welsh regulation issue to one side, but we can't.'

There were some robust exchanges between our officials and Ofqual while I was away. Chris Tweedale, our Director of Schools and Young People Group, said in an email (now released under the Freedom of Information Act by Ofqual)

> You also asked us yesterday if we were exploring re-awarding grades for regulation purposes or due to "political interference" from Welsh Ministers.... Speaking frankly, I reject the implication of this suggestion. Throughout our discussions we have been speaking and acting as regulators. I found your suggestion ill-judged and inappropriate. Should we ask any education professionals or members of the public which of our two respective organisations was being driven by political pressure or political ideology I suggest Ofqual would be at the top of the list.

Chris's email also noted that the Key Stage 2 predictor model was 'untried, untested and it now seems clearer than ever… that it is unreliable for Wales (and possibly for England too).' He said that the 3.9 per cent fall 'in a high entry, high stakes gateway qualification would be unacceptable to regulators in any nation'. He said 'it is morally indefensible to the young people of Wales and plainly unfair.'

The *Western Mail* recognised in early September that the situation challenged the integrity of our system of exam regulation, and if decisions taken in England were to have an impact on students from Wales, then perhaps it was time to 'sever' cross-border links with England.

On my return from holiday officials had prepared their report. I discussed it on the phone with the First Minister at the suggestion of Steve Jones, the special adviser responsible for the media, prior to issuing the report and written statement. Carwyn bought into what we were saying immediately.

The report found that candidates from Wales were issued with lower grades than would normally have been expected under 'agreed regulatory principles of working to maintain comparable outcomes when new specifications are introduced.' The report found that 'a serious distortion to the outcomes of the candidates in Wales had been caused'. It concluded that a 3.9 per cent fall in outcomes for grades C and above between 2011 and 2012 'is unjustifiable and almost certainly unfair to candidates.' I said that I had concluded that the 'apparent injustice' needed to be addressed as a matter of urgency. I was therefore asking the WJEC to re-award its GCSE English Language qualification in line with the report's recommendations to achieve outcomes as similar as possible to the previous year. The report also suggested that WJEC candidates in England should also be re-graded. We would also allow candidates November re-sit opportunities.

95 per cent of Welsh candidates took the exam with the WJEC, and as WJEC had not offered January controlled assessments the issues were different from those being questioned in England. The report raised the issue of 'the extent to which the awarding of qualifications in Wales is currently bound to, and determined by, policies and methodologies designed to be fit for purpose in England – and the challenges this presents to a devolved education system.' It also raised questions about the fitness for purpose of the current English language GCSE qualification. The report considered whether there had been significant differences in the 2011 and 2012 cohorts and concluded that there had not

been. The cohort seemed stable and the slight shift in candidates from different exam centres (maintained schools, FE colleges, sixth form colleges, private schools) was not significant. Data on prior achievement at KS1, KS2 and KS3 suggested that the 2012 cohort might, if anything, have done as well or better than the previous cohort. Our data suggested that significantly fewer WJEC candidates in Wales took exam units early than did WJEC candidates in England (42 per cent compared to 69.2 per cent). Early entry seemed to give pupils an advantage in getting higher grades. This may have been a significant factor. Additionally, the methodology used to predict outcomes – reviewing GCSE outcomes against cohort predictions based on Key Stage 2 outcomes in England. The 60 per cent of controlled assessment was also an important factor.

When provisional results were being assessed towards the end of July 2012 it became clear that the split of candidates in England between GCSE English Language and GCSE English – not available in Wales – was causing difficulties for Ofqual's predictor model, with many centres in England putting their lower ability candidates in for the new GCSE English. An email to Cath Jadhav, Head of Standards in Ofqual, released to the BBC's *Newsnight* programme under the Freedom of Information Act, revealed:

> Centres are placing weaker learner (sic) in GCSE English and stronger learners in GCSE English Language.

Awarding organisations were therefore instructed to bring overall results within a certain percentage point of prior predictions.

It wasn't until the awarding meeting at WJEC on 27th July that it became evident that there were problems and that the predictors had failed to deliver comparable outcomes for Wales. The following Monday, of course, their chief executive had mentioned this to me in our meeting. There had been extensive discussion between Welsh Government, Ofqual, WJEC and other exam boards over the following two weeks before results were finalised. WJEC was having difficulty coming within tolerance and Ofqual would not accept overall WJEC outcomes which produced a 3.4 per cent fall in Welsh outcomes. This, they felt was too generous. Eventually, at a late stage, with a need to reach agreement. Welsh Government officials accepted an outcome which entailed a 3.9 per cent fall for Welsh students compared to the previous year. Emails leaked from other exam boards, notably AQA and Edexcel, later demonstrated the extent of changes they had had to make.

Further evidence showed that if one of the unit grade boundaries had been adjusted downward by one mark then Welsh outcomes would only have been 1.5 per cent down overall compared to the previous year – more in line with England. Following the publication of results and the decision to call a review, Welsh Government officials presented this option to Ofqual on 30th August but Ofqual rejected it on the grounds that it would put WJEC results in England too far out of tolerance (English WJEC results would also have to be adjusted).

Crucially, our report found that there were real tensions in seeking to achieve comparable *outcomes* while maintaining comparable *standards*. If higher numbers in England were taking units early, then the methodology for assessing likely attainment surely ought to reflect the different opportunities available to candidates in England to take the units repeatedly, in judging the eventual outcomes between England and Wales. Not to do so was to disadvantage the Welsh cohort. The work on maintaining standards between the regulators, set in train in 2008, was intended to ensure that outcomes should not be significantly different when specifications changed. This had not happened in this instance. Officials concluded that the standard set in 2012 was not comparable with the standard set in 2011.

Ofqual's chief executive, Glenys Stacey, asked us to delay the publication of our report. I discussed this with Dr Emyr Roberts, Director General of the department, and concluded that nothing was to be served by a delay. We went ahead.

The report was serious, thorough, and detailed. The respected education journalist Warwick Mansell later compared it to Ofqual's reports, in a blog-post on the NAHT website, as 'the more detailed and more revealing Welsh Assembly Government's report'. Internally, in Ofqual, Julie Swan, their Head of Regulatory Development said, in an email to Glenys Stacey and others, 'it reads well and is quite persuasive'. Its publication was news across the UK. Brian Lightman, general secretary of ASCL, said that 'it is heartening to see the Welsh Government recognise that an error has been made and act quickly.' That day I recorded an interview for BBC *Newsnight*. The next evening, after I had issued a Direction to the WJEC to comply with the report, given that they had not given us an undertaking that they would implement it voluntarily, I did a live interview with Jeremy Paxman, as well as interviews with BBC *News 24*, Radio *Five Live*, and all Welsh outlets. The First Minister sent me a text the next morning, saying 'Excellent performance last night!' The Media Wales journalist David James said I had put in 'an impressive performance', dealing 'with Paxman's probing as impassively as a nightclub bouncer faced with a chippy student wearing the wrong kind of trainers'. Our decision even made it on to the BBC Radio 4's *The News Quiz* the following weekend.

In Westminster, the House of Commons Education Select Committee was beginning an enquiry into the issue. The chief executive and chair of Ofqual gave evidence. The chief executive made a number of errors in her evidence which she subsequently had to correct. The chair of Ofqual made an outrageous statement at the Select Committee which infuriated all of us, from the First Minister down. She stated

> there is political difficulty in Wales. In what we are seeing, there is a clear divergence between English and Welsh candidates. If English candidates are where we think they are based on our work, the implication is that Welsh candidate performance is not improving. This is a very difficult conclusion for the Welsh to accept politically, hence what we saw yesterday.

This was just completely untrue. By this time I had been speaking publicly for over eighteen months about the performance gap between Wales and England and our need to address that. In the immediate context, the action which I had taken had been in my role as Regulator, following a detailed and sober report by regulatory officials. In any case, our report had made it clear that we believed that there should have been a regrading of GCSE English Language for WJEC candidates in England as well as in Wales. That would not have reduced the performance gap with England – it would have maintained it.

But the jaw-dropping factor was that this was said by someone who was in a position that was supposed to be politically impartial. The First Minister was incandescent. The chair of Ofqual, Amanda Spielman, was a trustee of the New Schools Network, the body that helped promote the creation of free schools, a body that had contracted one of Michael Gove's Special Advisers as a freelancer for the six months after the 2010 General Election. We agreed that it would not be right for us to call for her resignation – we would not find it acceptable if a Minister in the UK government said the chair of one of our public bodies should resign. However, the First Minister was clear that if any chair of a public body in Wales had made similar comments about a similar situation in relation to the UK government, they would not last long in their job. Following the Joint Ministerial Committee in Downing Street on the 19th September, he said 'For a chair of an arm's length body to criticise another nation's education qualifications is unprecedented'.

The same day Ofqual's Deputy Director, Policy, Jeremy Benson issued a letter which threatened the WJEC's ability to offer exams in England. The letter said Ofqual had been considering whether the WJEC could both fulfill our direction and Ofqual's Conditions of Regulation. There were serious consequences if it could not, he said. We interpreted this to mean that Ofqual would seek to ban the WJEC offering its qualifications in England. We were not about to allow Ofqual to punish the WJEC in this way. We made it clear that 'if Ofqual moves against the WJEC in this way, they need to understand that the Welsh government will see them in court'.

The next day, Michael Gove gave evidence to the Select Committee, and used it as a political platform to mount an attack on my decision and more broadly on Labour education policy. He said my decision was 'irresponsible and mistaken'; it was a political intervention; and I had undermined confidence in Welsh children's GCSEs. English employers would, he said, not consider Welsh results as equivalent to those in England. The truth, of course, was that schools in Wales entered fewer pupils early than schools in England; Welsh pupils attempted fewer re-sits; and we had refused to approve the GCSE combined English qualification because it did not stretch pupils enough. I said that we would stick to the facts which were about fairness to students. Everyone accepted that a cohort of students had been treated unfairly. 'If Mr Gove and Ofqual are prepared to tolerate this unfairness, then that's a matter for them.'

Our reply to Ofqual came in a letter from Chris Tweedale, who had been in attendance at the Select Committee, to Glenys Stacey. He said that the comments by the chair of Ofqual were inappropriate, ill-judged and prejudicial. He also raised the inaccuracies in Glenys Stacey's evidence. We accepted in that letter that significant issues were raised about the future of three country regulation, noting the decision that May by Northern Ireland's regulatory and awarding body, the CCEA, to cease offering its qualifications in England because of the emerging policy differences. Glenys Stacey's reply to Chris parroted what Michael Gove had said in the Select Committee, that our decision to re-grade English language GCSE would cause confusion amongst employers and universities, risking Welsh candidates being seen to have certificates of 'less value' than elsewhere. We hit back, with a Welsh Government source quoted as saying that Ofqual was 'in denial' and 'so intent on slavishly following their minister's line on this issue, that they have abandoned impartiality.'

Officials met Ofqual, and Ms Stacey acknowledged that some of the statements she had made at the Select Committee were inaccurate. In a further letter, she said that her chair 'regrets any offence caused'. That was not enough for us. But she did confirm that she had asked the clerk to the Select Committee to correct her evidence.

But behind the scenes, Ofqual knew that they were sailing close to the edge. Internal Ofqual emails released to me under the Freedom of Information Act and the Data Protection Act, some headed 'The Leighton Andrews dilemma', are revealing. Some of the emails were sent by the Chair and the chief executive of Ofqual. They indicate that Ofqual was aware of the political difficulties. One email from Glenys Stacey makes it clear 'the trouble is with what Amanda actually said' – in other words her comment that the Welsh Government had 'a political difficulty' with what she claimed was evidence that Welsh candidate performance was not improving, 'which was a very difficult conclusion for the Welsh to accept politically'. Glenys Stacey's email recognised that our regrading was based on a thorough report from our regulatory officials, and said 'I do think some sort of apology is in order.' Another email makes it clear that they felt the situation had become more difficult for them after the First Minister had made his statement outside 10 Downing Street, following the JMC: 'the situation is slightly more tricky than it was'. The emails released also reveal significant contact between Ofqual, Michael Gove and his office including around the time of his Select Committee appearance. The Deputy Director of Policy at Ofqual, Jeremy Benson, asked 'how rude' did they want to be 'about Welsh-issued GCSEs'? Ofqual also gave consideration to seeking an injunction to stop the WJEC regrading candidates in Wales, after we had issued the direction to the WJEC. Glenys Stacey said that they should bargain with us about their Chair apologising, to avoid me tweeting 'triumphantly that he's got an apology from Ofqual'. She also suggested they might make a complaint about me to the Welsh Government Permanent Secretary about statements I had made in public. No such complaint arrived.

Ofqual's actions had compromised standards, elevating, in an over-deterministic way, a particular methodology for predicting grades. We regarded Ofqual as having abandoned impartiality and having made a series of incompetent errors at the Select Committee. The editor of the *Times Educational Supplement*, Gerard Kelly, said at the end of that week that 'Ofqual must face the consequences of its cock-up'. He said 'obsessed with maintaining standards between years, Ofqual has failed to maintain them within a single one.'

The legal case against Ofqual was getting underway. Though ultimately unsuccessful, the consortium assembled behind it illustrated the lack of confidence that existed in the regulator. The list included teaching unions, local authorities, some led by Conservatives, and schools including leading academies often praised by Michael Gove. Mike Whiting, the Conservative Cabinet Member for Education in Kent, had said 'Regrading the papers, as they are planning to do in Wales, would avoid asking Kent's young people to go through the stress of another exam'. It was clear that the pressure was mounting on Mr Gove, and not surprisingly, he decided to move the debate forward by making a statement in the House of Commons on Qualifications Reform. The statement was widely trailed in the media in the days beforehand.

I said on the *New Statesman* website that I could see little prospect of the three-country qualifications system holding. The UK government had turned the examination issue into a constitutional issue, which could mean that we ended up with separate systems. I explained that my role was largely 'arms-length' and I only intervened in 'very rare and exceptional circumstances'. I said I didn't think our model was perfect and I was open to suggestions for improvement – but our system had worked and delivered swift results, while in England there appeared to be a crisis of regulation, with a legal challenge under way. In the *Independent*, the veteran political columnist Steve Richards said 'Not Ofqual? Not Gove? Is no one responsible for the exam fiasco?' Steve noted that the 2009 Act defining Ofqual's role said that it 'must have regard to such aspects of government policy as the Secretary of State may direct'. Limited independence, in other words. Steve then said 'in Wales, there is more clarity. The Welsh government is the regulator of exams in Wales.' He said the Welsh system was simpler – 'it's in England that chaos reigns'.

The *Western Mail* said in an editorial on the 20th September that I had 'made the right call' when I directed the WJEC to re-grade the papers. 2386 candidates received revised grades, with 1202 awarded a C grade, 598 went from C to B. The paper said pupils 'will remember the day when a minister in a devolved government stepped in to prevent them being collateral damage in an exams fiasco made in London.'

I made a statement on our actions on GCSE English Language when the Assembly returned on 25th September. I said that the exceptional step of ordering a regrading was possibly only something that an elected representative could do, acting on the evidence and advice from regulatory officials, allowing action to be taken swiftly. I pointed out the inaccurate statements that had been made by the chief executive of Ofqual at the Select Committee, welcoming the corrections that she had subsequently made, while saying that the comments by the chair of Ofqual had been unacceptable.

The Plaid Cymru and Liberal Democrat spokespeople supported my decision to order the regrading; the Conservatives ducked it. All three challenged me as to why officials had accepted the use of the Key Stage 2 predictor, a matter which was to continue as an issue through the subsequent Assembly committee hearing. The *Western Mail* Education Correspondent, Gareth Evans, had also taken this line. I explained that I was not involved in any decision to accept the Key Stage 2 predictor and nor did I accept that my officials had made an error. In the key time-period between the calculation of potential grades and their publication in August, they had argued long and hard with Ofqual and persuaded them to drop two more severe outcomes. But a compromise had had to be agreed if the results were to be published on time.

There was, I said, a degree of 'negotiated consensus' when you are operating within the context of three-country agreement on exams. I explained that my involvement had come after the event, when we had analysed the results and found them to be unfair. I was not going to get involved in the setting of grade boundaries in advance of any such review – Ministers should only get involved when there was an exceptional circumstance and a real injustice.

Ofqual's fuller November report on GCSE English Language raised broader issues of the relationship between the accountability system and GCSE grades, and the tactics used by schools in England to improve their performance in the league tables. Teachers were again offended by conclusions which suggested that there had been over-marking in controlled assessments, perhaps driven by accountability criteria, and Ofqual said that that had been a reason for the raising of grade boundaries. However, exam boards disagreed with this, saying that they had dealt with it through moderation, not through raising boundaries. In the case of the WJEC, it could not have applied anyway as they did not offer controlled assessment in January. Chris Cook, the respected education correspondent of the *Financial Times*, reproduced some of the Ofqual graphs in the report on his blog on Data. He said these seemed to show evidence of bunching of results around the 'C' grade, illustrating this with comparisons between the WJEC's English and Welsh results. He said 'the Welsh performance peaks at around C, but there is not the sudden surge to a peak just to the north of C that you get in England. In fact, it looks pretty normal. Ofqual has found neat evidence that league table measures are implanted in English teachers' brains'.

A considerable amount of the report, however, focused on the role of Controlled Assessment in the exam, and whether 60 per cent was too much. Warwick Mansell said the focus on controlled assessment and the effect on the schools of the accountability system had served as 'a distraction strategy' for Ofqual, and argued:

> Although Ofqual's latest report was better than its very limited first go shortly after the controversy broke, the

public has still not been presented with the whole picture of what happened this year.

On the *FT* blog, Chris Cook said that Ofqual did not really offer 'new evidence about the central question: Did a child in 2012 do as well as a similarly taught child did in 2011?' Cook said he would like to see graphs showing the probability of children of different ability ranges getting a C, say, in 2011 and 2012. In our regulatory report, officials had done just this, analysing the performance of the 2011 and 2012 cohorts at different stages in their educational journey.

Ofqual accepted in the Appendix to this report that Key Stage 2 tests are not taken in Northern Ireland or Wales, 'so the predictions can only ever be used for candidates in England'. That admission, buried in the Appendix, is devastating.

We took steps in October 2012 to prevent a recurrence of the debacle, changing the specification for the GCSE English Language to be completed in the summer of 2014, reducing the element of controlled assessment from 60 per cent to 40 per cent. There would no longer be a requirement to study spoken language. We also said that this would be a unitised (i.e. modular) qualification. We expected only the WJEC to award this qualification as AQA, Edexcel and OCR had said they would not be offering unitised qualifications in future. The qualification would only be offered in Wales therefore and it was clear that we would be able to manage the regulation of the award without interference from Ofqual in respect of its requirements in relation to indications of prior attainment based on Key Stage 2 indicators. The decision we had taken was not wholly popular with English teachers who had already started teaching their courses, but it was the only way in which we could ensure that Welsh students were graded on the basis of Welsh performance, not English performance at Key Stage 2.

We also set out different conditions or recognition for English language GCSE awarding in 2013 in February 2013, designed to ensure that KS2 predictors could no longer have an influence on Welsh qualifications. The Conditions we introduced meant that in 2013 the awarding of WJEC's GCSE English Language qualifications would be separated from the arrangements for the awarding of WJEC GCSE English Language in England. This meant that we would not be agreeing grade boundaries with Ofqual. Our School Standards and Delivery Division also made available recommendations on how outcomes can be improved in the future, looking at the performance of schools that did well in 2012.

In its evidence to the Assembly's Children and Young Ppeople's Committee, the WJEC said that more schools in England had entered students early and if Welsh schools had done the same, 'there would have been far less of a gap between England and Wales results'. England had more of a re-sit culture than Wales; more candidates entering earlier and repeatedly; we had more sitting qualifications in a linear fashion. Only 30 per cent of WJEC's candidates in Wales retook one or more units, but over 55 per cent of their candidates in England did the same.

The WJEC also noted that grade inflation was a bigger issue in England than in Wales: 'in England, between 2007 and 2011, the percentage of A to C grades in GCSEs increased by 7 percentage points. In Wales, where WJEC is the dominant awarding body, it increased by a lot less than that, by about 4 percentage points.'

Questioning at the committee understandably focused on how we had come to accept Key Stage 2 results in England as a basis for predicting GCSE English Language results in Wales. It was clear to us that it was only after the marking of candidates' work that the impact of the KS2 predictor model on Welsh candidates could be seen i.e. at the end of July 2012 when the distribution of marks was known. Even then, we had expected the comparable outcomes model to kick in and ensure that results were not significantly depressed. As I explained to members of the committee, had I intervened earlier to say that KS2 predictors could not be used for Wales, in advance of knowing the results, 'I would probably have been crucified in the media and indeed by Members here because I would have had very little evidence on which to base that judgement'. We only had the evidence after the results. If I had made an earlier decision, I would have been saying that we would have been setting grade boundaries on a different basis from England without evidence to justify the reason.

Ofqual had strayed from the original declared position that the reporting against Key Stage 2 predictors would be 'for reporting purposes only' using them as a device to change results that were already inconsistent with the previous year. We were clear that Ofqual was overly focused on the issue of grade inflation. I regarded them, as I told the committee, as being 'in the grip of an ideological spasm'.

The court case against Ofqual, Edexcel and AQA was lost by the alliance of educational organisations who brought it. The court essentially confirmed in February 2013 that it had been legitimate for Ofqual to use its definition of comparable outcomes to seek to ensure a consistent standard year on year, and to use predicted outcomes to do that. However, the court recognised 'the inconsistent treatment meted out to the students taking assessments in January and June respectively.' The judge concluded 'There is no doubt with hindsight that the former were treated more generously than the latter.' The court said that Ofqual was 'engaged in an exercise of damage limitation'. Whatever it did, there was going to be 'an element of unfairness'. Lord Justice Elias recognised, and Mrs Justice Sharp agreed, that this was a question of judgement, and 'there is no obvious or right answer as to where the balance of unfairness should lie.' Had Ofqual applied January's grade boundaries in June, more could have obtained C grades but that could have created 'an injustice as between those qualifying in June 2012 when compared with students in earlier and subsequent years.' Unfairness might just be shifted.

Of course, the challenge facing us was different – it was not about the difference between January and June grades. Our September 2012 report had noted that the KS2 predictions did not produce comparable outcomes for the 2012 cohort when compared with the 2011 cohort. The court case in England had no bearing on the decision we had taken.

I appeared before the House of Commons Education Select Committee in March 2013. The chair of the Select Committee recognised that the Committee was not there to examine me in respect of the decision that had been taken in Wales – that was a devolved matter, and outside the remit of the House of Commons. I was there to offer my perspective. I took the opportunity to explain that the decision we had taken was not a partisan one – indeed it had been backed by three of the political parties in the Assembly – and we had made the decision on the basis of a 'sober and serious' report from regulatory officials. I pointed out that if, as some claimed, people would be asking what was the difference between a Welsh and an English 'C' grade, then in England they should also be asking what was the difference between a January and a June 'C'. I also took the opportunity to respond to what Michael Gove had said about our decision to re-grade. I said his remarks were 'inconsistent, inflammatory and uncharacteristically ignorant'. I pointed out that Mr Gove had 'made a great play in his evidence of saying that he could not comment on matters that were properly for Ofqual and then sought to denigrate the action that had been taken by the Welsh regulator.'

I welcomed the previous call by the Committee for a ministerial conference on GCSEs and A levels, and said that Northern Ireland and Wales were moving together on these issues. We were taking action to ensure that our students would not in future be subject to a KS2 indicator 'that has clearly failed to provide comparable outcomes in 2012 for learners in Wales' and wasn't ordinarily used in either Wales or Northern Ireland. The changes we were implementing could result in tougher standards being applied in Wales. The *Western Mail* said this was 'a very assured performance on one of the biggest educational stages', and that MPs landed no significant punches.

In September 2013, David Blow, a statistics specialist for the

Association of School and College Leaders (ASCL), said that official figures show that standards in English in 2012 were not "maintained", but were significantly tougher and led to almost 18,000 fewer students gaining crucial A*-C grades. He told the *TES:* 'This shows that Ofqual and the exam boards made a mistake.' The *TES* reported that Mr Blow had looked at Department for Education and Ofsted statistics which compared details of pupils' performance in national primary tests with their GCSE results. They show that 69.5 per cent of these 'matched candidates' achieved an A*-C grade in English or English language in 2012. But Mr Blow said that if standards had remained constant with 2011 then the primary test data showed it should have been 73 per cent of candidates – with another 17,805 pupils achieving an all important A*-C grade. His conclusion was that 'overall the grades were harsher than they should have been.' Even in England the KS2 predictor had not delivered.

Curriculum reform and cultural choices: unfinished business

Any debate about a national curriculum is a debate about national culture. Apart from literacy and numeracy, central to the issue of raising standards, I held back on major areas of curriculum reform until well into my third year as Education Minister, when I began a series of reviews. We are now heading towards the creation of a *Curriculum for Wales*, one of the recommendations of the group I established on Welsh history and the *Cwricwlwm Cymreig*.

I deliberately kicked into the long grass a review of the 8-13 curriculum, undertaken by a group chaired by Professor David Egan. I read the group's work and concluded it would require further and deeper work. There was another reason for not moving forward on it. Wales had been through a series of radical curriculum-based initiatives since devolution in 1999. The Welsh Baccalaureate, the 14-19 Learning Pathways, the 2008 Curriculum, with the introduction – on a non-statutory basis – of the Skills Framework – and the early years Foundation Phase, now being implemented but not due to be rolled out to its final year group until September 2012.

Our own examination of curriculum and assessment, I made clear in October 2012, would be in the context of our objective to raise standards. The Literacy and Numeracy Framework, now a key curriculum planning tool, became a statutory curriculum requirement from September 2013. The LNF rightly raised the bar in terms of what we were expecting from our schools. I therefore said that we would look overall at how the LNF sat within the curriculum and the assessment regimes within schools, looking to streamline assessment. This meant amongst other things reviewing the National Curriculum Subject Orders and the bureaucratic system of 'level descriptors' to see if they were as demanding as the LNF and sat coherently with it.

I myself felt we had an urgent need to embark on a review of the Key Stage 2 curriculum, once the Foundation Phase had completed its roll-out to every year group, and now that we had agreement on the Literacy and Numeracy Framework. We commenced the work on KS2 with a seminar involving practitioners, academics and school governors in February 2013, which I chaired, looking at whether the curriculum was too crowded and whether it built effectively on the Foundation Phase.

I wasn't clear that the previous 2008 curriculum review was intellectually coherent, or that the different curriculum initiatives had been effectively integrated. I felt that the Cwricwlwm Cymreig, designed long ago to add a Welsh dimension to Ken Baker's National Curriculum, needed an overhaul. It was sensible to hold an assessment of the curriculum and assessment in high performing countries, which shows that the Welsh system and immediate plans are well-aligned with the approach of these countries. The task of assimilating that work now falls to the group established by Huw under Professor Graham Donaldson.

The truth is that if you embark on curriculum reform you are immediately faced with a series of issues that need to be analysed carefully and worked through in detail. What should be the core curriculum at each key stage of learning? What is the content of the curriculum that you want to be taught in each area of learning or subject of study? How do you integrate knowledge and skills? Each and every one of these issues provokes more questions, and educationalists – and those outside education, not least in the media – like nothing more than to pontificate about them. Since this is work in progress, in this chapter I simply want to set down a few observations on the future of a Curriculum for Wales.

1. Access to a common culture is a progressive ideal

A few years ago one of Wales's leading historians, Professor Dai Smith, sent me a copy of an article by Professor E.D. Hirsch, reviewing Diane Ravitch's book *The Death and Life of the American School System*, entitled 'How to save the schools'. Dai – chair of the Arts Council of Wales, former Head of English-language broadcasting at BBC Wales, former pro Vice chancellor at the University of Glamorgan, novelist, biographer of the great Welsh cultural theorist Raymond Williams – said 'this wonderful piece is from the current *New York Review of Books*. I thought you'd like to see it – a bit more inspiring than most 'educationalese!'

Dai highlighted Hirsch's words:

> Under the enduring influence of European Romanticism, educational leaders had begun to convert the community-centered school of the nineteenth-century to the child-centered school of the twentieth... the chief tenet of the child-centered school was that no bookish curriculum was to be set out in advance. Rather, learning was to arise naturally out of activities, projects, and daily experience.

Hirsch's article goes on to make the case for context in the teaching of literacy – skills grounded in a base of knowledge. While much of the article is more relevant to an American system without a national curriculum, Hirsch says 'we mustn't surrender the inspiring ideal of the common school, that is, the good, community-centered, neighbourhood school.'

It is perhaps not surprising that the biographer of the early period of Raymond Williams' life – up to the publication of *Culture and Society* and *The Long Revolution* – should endorse an argument for cultural literacy grounded in good community schools. For Raymond Williams' goal of allowing all to profit from an open and expanding 'common culture' should be our priority – and at an intellectual level, it offers us the means to bridge those unnecessary binary divisions of academic and vocational and skills and knowledge.

I determined to read Hirsch's books after Dai's comments. His concepts of cultural literacy and core knowledge accept that society's broad cultural agenda will change as a result of social and political pressures over time, and, contrary to what his critics claim, he accepts that students from diverse backgrounds will bring new perspectives. I found little to suggest that he discounts students' own cultural perspectives. Quite the opposite. In his book *The Schools We Need* he even cites Gramsci as believing that political progressivism required educational conservatism. Another Welsh historian, Dr Tim Williams, had already recommended to me Harold Entwistle's book on Gramsci's educational thinking which made that very point. As Professor Dylan Wiliam, a member of the English National Curriculum expert panel, said in 2010 'I think there is an underestimation about how smart the Hirsch project is. What he did was look at these things with a view to creating a public sphere within which people could debate.'

That does not mean to say, of course, that his views have not been commandeered by some on the Right as a justification for a narrow narrative based on English exceptionalism and ignorance of the four nations of the UK, British Empire and cultural boorishness. But you can't blame Hirsch for Gove.

We don't need to import Hirsch into Wales – we have Raymond Williams' legacy to provide the intellectual grounding. But we must recognise that the ideal of a democratic citizenship requires some endorsement of a common culture alongside a recognition of the power and importance of diversity.

2. Any national curriculum involves a limit to choice – and quite right too.

Kenneth Baker said of the national curriculum 'this will involve a restriction of choice which must be taken up to the age of 16'. I am in favour of a national curriculum in Wales. I am sceptical of the doctrine of learner choice – an adaptation of the language of consumer capitalism for the educational world. What we need to ask is what best equips young people to be full participants in a participatory democracy – active, engaged, enquiring, independent, reasoning citizens who can adapt to or confront the challenges they will face in a world which is unlikely to offer the same career opportunities towards the middle of their lives as it does at the beginning. What matters, and should matter to those of us on the Left, is not the choice of courses but the quality of their teaching.

A national curriculum involves selection. You will always have argument about what should be in it. There always has been. There is nothing wrong with that. In fact, in a democratic society, it should be welcomed. The real danger would be a stilted conformity in which such debate was not allowed.

It is the case that for reasons of student demand (learner choice) or exam board opportunism or whatever, subjects formerly taught only at university have been creeping into post-16 education and even earlier. I once asked why anyone needed to study A level law, for example, only to find that the son of the senior official in the room was taking it, which led to a slightly frosty atmosphere. To my mind – and as far as I can see, to the minds of university admissions tutors too – a grounding in well-taught core subjects matters more. This is not just true of law.

There are ways of short-circuiting curriculum reform which allow you to nudge schools to give a more central place to certain subjects. Michael Gove has achieved this with his original English Baccalaureate introduced in 2010. This of course is not a Baccalaureate at all, but a matriculation certificate – and a way of determining what is taught in schools by being precise about what subjects will count in the accountability system which measures school achievement. The measure recognises where pupils have secured a C grade or better across a core of academic subjects – English, mathematics, history or geography, the sciences and a language. There is no doubt that the English Baccalaureate's introduction was ideological, and it is certainly based around the expectations of Russell Group universities as to which subjects are valuable for entry to their universities.

If your starting point is that you want to halt the decline in the percentage of pupils taking certain subjects at GCSE, it is a clever quick fix. No one can doubt that it has led to an increase in the numbers taking a modern language, history and geography in England. It is simple for parents, pupils and the commentariat to understand, and in setting short-term educational goals that are quickly fulfilled it has achieved its political goals. The DfE may well have a point that some young people had been driven in the direction of lower quality non-academic qualifications for reasons other than the intrinsic value of those qualifications.

It is not the route we would want to pursue in Wales. It would cut across the Learning Pathways for 14-19-year-olds. Instead, we have cut back the number of vocational qualifications that are approved through our qualifications review, and Huw is looking now at the recommendations from the review I established of the curriculum implications of the Learning and Skills Measure, proposing to reduce the number of subjects demanded so that quality can be protected. It may be that if we want to increase the numbers taking modern foreign languages, say, or history, then the quickest way would be to widen the number of core subjects in the curriculum. It would be a debate worth having.

3. All societies expect a grounding in their national history, and rightly so.

I studied history to postgraduate level, so I am biased. But I don't know of any country which does not see the history of its society as core to its understanding of citizenship. History has always been at the heart of debates on the national curriculum. When he was creating the national curriculum in the mid 1980s, Kenneth Baker, then Education Secretary, recalled in 2013 in the *TES* that he knew 'that the new history curriculum was going to be controversial':

> Being a historian myself I very much wanted a linear structure around the main elements of British history. That certainly chimed with Margaret's view. However, the initial

> draft downgraded knowledge and favoured the examination of sources and a very wide, fragmentary range of subjects. We got that changed later.

Nearly twenty-five years ago, as the national curriculum came into effect, the *History Workshop* journal devoted a series of articles to it. The leading Marxist adult educator and historian, the late Raphael Samuel, noted 'the rival claims of the "skills" versus "knowledge" method of teaching, and of the new history and the old, were vigorously debated in the public press, with newspaper editors and columnists taking up positions on either side.' This, he said, was a sign of 'the vitality of the subject'. Samuel worried about the split between university history departments, teaching apprentice historians, and teacher training departments, training graduate teachers in history, and the loss of the cutting edge of radical historiography, 'the broad interpretative narrative or framework'. He warned against locking children up 'in a problematic of pedagogy's own making'.

Dr Alice Prochaska, now Principal of Somerville College, Oxford, was a member of the History Working Group for the national curriculum. She said in the same journal that she 'took it for granted that history teaching involved teaching both content and the specific skills of the discipline, and that remains axiomatic for me, as I believe it always was for all members of the group.' The leading Welsh historian Angela John outlined the difference between that report and that of the History Committee for Wales, which had provided the justification that enabled the National Curriculum to be varied in Wales. It was the Conservative historian Jonathan Clark who correctly observed that the teaching of British history did not by any account have to have an inbuilt bias to the Right, saying 'a national history which takes account of England's chequered relations with Scotland, Ireland and Wales is unlikely to encourage complacency about the neutral wisdom of England's ruling ethic.' Clark warned 'we cannot expect to arrive at an agreed, neutral version of our national past, disinfected, tasteless and unutterably safe, fit to be taught uncontroversially to captive school audiences like a 'dead' language.'

In Wales, we have been accustomed over the past 40 years to the notion that the history – or histories – of our society is – or are – contested. 'When was Wales?' asked Gwyn Alf Williams. 'Wales is a singular noun but a plural experience' said Dai Smith. A popular television history series in the 1980s that gave rise to widespread debate was called *The Dragon has Two Tongues*. In October 2012, therefore, I asked Dr Elin Jones to chair a task and finish group to look specifically at the teaching of Welsh history, the story of Wales and the Cwricwlwm Cymreig.

4. Try to build a consensus, and give space for debate.

It was an underlying principle of the National Curriculum that learners aged 7-14 should be given opportunities to develop and apply knowledge and understanding of the cultural, economic, environmental, historical and linguistic characteristics of Wales. However, there had been significant changes in the curriculum in Wales since the introduction of the Cwricwlwm Cymreig, including the Welsh Bac and the Foundation Phase. At the same time, there had been a significant growth in interest in the history of Wales over the last decade. Meanwhile, online resources to support the study of Welsh history have also continued to grow.

The Welsh Government had made significant investment in digitisation of resources through the National Library of Wales, Cymal, and the National Museums & Galleries of Wales's (NMGW) 'People's Collection'. There was a renewed interest in Welsh history evidenced in the Green Bay/BBC Wales series *The Story of Wales*, narrated by Huw Edwards, alongside an Open University course. We had invested in some additional material narrated by Huw in both Welsh and English which is available on the Department's Hwb website and also on its iTunes U sites. Not only the BBC but also the *Western Mail* had developed resources on Welsh history.

Our review group, made up of key stakeholders with experience and expertise in Welsh history and its teaching in primary and secondary schools, examined: whether there was sufficient emphasis on Welsh history and the stories of Wales in the teaching of history and the current programme of study; and, whether the teaching of history sufficiently took account of the latest research and the new resources available about the historical development of Wales to the present day.

Members of the group were carefully selected for their experience and expertise across heritage, local and national history, black and minority ethnic history, and the range of academic, school and work-based expertise. I had come across history teachers in secondary who were making great use of local archive resources, like Dr Hugh Griffiths at Ysgol Bro Myrddin in Carmarthenshire, and others putting new technology to great effect, like Dave Stacey at Olchfa Comprehensive School. They joined other teachers and historians in Dr Jones's group, which reported initially in May 2013.

I was anxious that we should see the Welsh experience as not a narrow, provincial one, but as the experience of a modern country grappling with the challenges of the world and actively engaged in shaping its own future in that context. In their report, the group recognised that the programmes of study for history in the different key stages had always given appropriate consideration to local and Welsh history, but experience suggested that in too many places there was an over-reliance on teaching versions of British history with England at their core. There was a danger that Welsh history, instead of being part of history as a whole, came to be regarded as a sideshow or an appendage. An element of Welsh history should therefore be integrated into the GCSE history curriculum. We should also be thinking not about the Story of Wales but about the different *stories* of Wales. They felt there was also an overly narrow range of topics in relation to European and global history.

Our approach can be contrasted with England's. Michael Gove's draft history curriculum launched in early 2013 drew serious criticism from historians and teachers, including the Royal Historical Society, the Historical Association and the

British Academy. There were suggestions from some that the eventual draft had come from inside the Department for Education because Ministers did not like the proposed global sweep which failed to produce a necessary focus on supposed key individuals and events of the British past. Even Conservative historians were critical. In part this was about the subject content, and whether it was possible actually to teach what was demanded to any depth at each key stage. It was also a debate about the wisdom of essentially expecting certain areas largely to be taught in a chronological fashion from primary through to secondary, which might mean no examination of pre-1700 history at secondary, for example. But it was also a debate about the notion of the 'Great Figures' of history who had to be covered within the curriculum. Richard J. Evans, Regius professor of history at Cambridge University said 'this is a curriculum that will produce a generation of young Britons with no knowledge of the history of any part of the world beyond the shores of the British Isles.' It was, he said 'a political narrative that might have been lifted straight from a textbook written in the 1930s.'

Michael Gove acknowledged the attacks on his history curriculum in 2013, saying that he wasn't surprised by the intensity of the criticism because after all 'there may, for all I know, be rival Whig and Marxist schools fighting a war of interpretation in chemistry or food technology but their partisans don't tend to command much column space in the broadsheets or get onto *Start the Week*'. In an act of rhetorical sleight of hand, he then switched his attack to teaching practice 'which infantilises children, teachers and our culture'.

5. You can't separate skills from knowledge

Wales has a proud history of creativity, discovery and innovation. A Welsh mathematician conceived the use of the pi symbol; a Welsh mathematician devised the equals sign; a Welshman invented the microphone, teleprint and crystal radio; a Welsh physicist conceived the first fuel cell.

You could, of course, Google all that. I have sometimes seen it argued that in the age of Google what matters is skill, not knowledge. In my year as a tutor at Cardiff University before being elected to the National Assembly, I found some students who seemed to have based their essays on a few facts from Google stuffed together without context. Not persuasive and not for me. I got a reputation as a bit of a tough marker, apparently. These were postgraduates. I imagine it can be worse in secondary schools.

There is considerable research evidence to suggest that understanding context is key to understanding texts, and that that requires a base of knowledge. Google doesn't give you knowledge, it gives you information. Even Google findings have to be interpreted. As David Cannadine, Jenny Keating and Nicola Sheldon say

> Now that it is possible to look up the names and dates of all the country's kings and queens on Google or Wikipedia the need to provide boys and girls with some sort of broad framework and long perspective on the past is more urgent than ever.

Sometimes it seems as though parts of the British left simply want to drown Michael Gove's demands for a knowledge-based curriculum in a shower of warm spit about skills. We would do better to engage with his intellectual argument rather than with the pyrotechnics of his polemics. Thankfully the discipline of history combines both the teaching of knowledge and skills. Indeed, so do most subject-disciplines. As the quotations above from Raphael Samuel in the *History Workshop* journal reveal, the debate has been around for a long time. The words of Raymond Williams fifty years ago still apply today: 'We cannot in our kind of society call an education system adequate if it leaves any large number of people at a level of general knowledge and culture below that required by a participatory democracy'.

This debate has taken a more interesting turn recently with work by the American cognitive scientist Daniel T. Willingham who argues that building memory through memorising scales or times tables frees up our working memory, allowing us to perform more advanced functions and display greater mental creativity. Willingham says that the underlying science is that knowledge is crucial to support cognitive processes, and children who grow up in disadvantaged circumstances have fewer opportunities to learn important background knowledge at home. Because he has been quoted by Michael Gove, and others have used him to attack Ofsted, some seem to think he must be an agent of the right. In fact, he works with the American Federation of Teachers and has valuable things to say, just as Raymond Williams worked with the National Union of Teachers to analyse the development of communications.

Personally, I was grateful when I launched the Literacy and Numeracy Framework in Swansea that Barry Island School had given me a good grounding in multiplication tables, when the BBC and ITV tried to wrong-foot me with some basic arithmetical questions! Knowledge matters; skills matter. You can't teach skills in the abstract. As Dai Smith said, in his report on Arts and Education which Huw Lewis and I commissioned, 'we seek to reconcile the base camp of "Knowledge" with the "Skills" required to reach out for a summit for all to reach'.

6. We need a new language that bridges the vocational and the academic.

One of the main reasons why I think reaction on the Left to Michael Gove has been inadequate is that in England Labour lost sight of the moral imperative for school improvement driven by David Blunkett in the early years of the New Labour government, once structural reform became more important after 2001. Blunkett's early focus on ensuring that all had access to the basics of literacy and numeracy – something that the Wolf Review re-emphasised subsequently, and something which we have enshrined at the core of our curriculum in Wales with the Literacy and Numeracy Framework – seemed to get lost.

A second reason is that Labour in England failed to find an

adequate intellectual framework for ensuring a balance between vocational and academic education – and allowed Conservatives such as Michael Gove to equate vocational education with 'progressive education' and 'dumbing down', an argument in which he was assisted by the spectacularly mistaken GCSE equivalence given to certain vocational qualifications. The rapid growth in take-up of vocational qualifications in England sometimes also made it look like the left thought students from deprived backgrounds should be channeled into vocational areas away from what are, like it or not, seen as academic subjects. In that situation, Michael Gove's rhetoric of 'Enemies of Promise' scores some easy hits. Language and context – and bluntly, intellectual grounding – are important to the way these issues are handled. Labour has also failed to recall certain traditions of its own which would have allowed a better engagement on these issues.

As Professor Sir Adrian Webb wrote in his report for us on post-16 education, the earliest universities were founded as vocational institutions. Medicine is a vocational subject, but it requires detailed academic understanding. Surgery requires practical skills. In my early weeks as Education Minister I was encouraged when I heard about a consultant surgeon at the Royal Glamorgan Hospital who sent his trainee orthopaedic surgeons to spend a week working with chisels and saws on a timber roof with a team of carpenters in South Wales. I visited GE Aviation in Nantgarw with Jeff Cuthbert, Deputy Minister for Skills, where we met GE apprentices who were studying the Welsh Bac alongside their engineering qualifications. They said that it gave them a broader understanding of the world – the company and their instructors were wholly positive about the experience. Quality apprenticeships have always been highly desirable in Wales, from the days of the National Coal Board to those offered today by companies like BT, Tata Steel and Airbus. Founding our new qualifications system on a more rigorous and all-embracing Welsh Baccalaureate, with different routes, vocational and academic, will be an advantage to us.

Raymond Williams wrote in *Culture and Society*, published over fifty years ago

> Many highly educated people have, in fact, been so driven on in their reading... that they fail to notice that there are other forms of skilled, intelligent, creative activity: not only the cognate forms of theatre, concert and picture-gallery; but a whole range of general skills, from gardening, metalwork and carpentry, to active politics. The contempt for so many of these activities, which is always latent in the highly literate, is a mark of the observers' limits, not those of the activities themselves.

This illustrates that the vocational-academic divide has been there for quite some time.

7. Stay sceptical and ask fundamental questions.

Too many politicians indulge in casual half-considered ideas about the curriculum – and more nonsense is probably talked about the teaching of modern foreign languages than on almost any curriculum issue. No question, there has been a drastic drop in the numbers taking modern foreign languages. I studied French to A level – and I have German, (and indeed Latin) O levels. I certainly want more young people to take up foreign languages. It may, or it may not, have an impact on our ability to do business in the world. Most commentary on this is anecdotal, not research-based. I think the case for learning foreign languages should be made on its own terms.

The EU Commissioner for Education attacked the UK on this issue in the autumn of 2013, saying that the UK was at the bottom of the EU table for the number of 15-year-olds learning a foreign language, with the Netherlands and Sweden at the top with 80 per cent.

Let's look more closely. In 2012 the European Commission said:

> English is the most taught foreign language in nearly all of the 32 countries covered in the survey (27 Member States, Croatia, Iceland, Liechtenstein, Norway and Turkey) – a trend that has significantly increased since 2004/05. In lower secondary and general upper secondary education, the percentage of students learning English exceeds 90 per cent.

In Wales, of course, we were teaching English and Welsh from an early age (not very well, in the case of Welsh as a second language, as I say elsewhere). We invested in CILT, the national centre for modern languages, to support the languages strategy *Making Languages Count*.

Proposals for turning this situation round were usually unworkable. The Welsh Conservatives wanted a range of different languages to be taught in primary schools, without specifying how we would recruit sufficiently qualified teachers or how long this would take – the exact problem they are now facing in England.

Plaid Cymru pointed to Luxembourg where three languages were taught, arguing 'Luxembourg, a country with a population roughly the same and Cardiff and Vale together, successfully introduces three languages – Lëtzebuergesch, French and German – one after the other by immersion methods, by the time pupils reach secondary school.'

Great. Which three languages would you like to focus on in Wales? On the Luxembourg model, it would probably be English and Welsh, plus one other. So, do you choose French as the key European administrative language? Spanish, as a leading global language, or Mandarin for the same reason? What about the languages of the Indian sub-continent spoken in so many of our ethnic minority communities? Or Arabic? If you want three languages taught, assuming you are going to have the two indigenous languages as a starting point, you have to decide which is your third priority. You will never have enough qualified teachers to teach a very wide range of languages on a mass basis.

If you actually want to turn this situation round in a meaningful way, you have to decide there will be certain core modern foreign languages taught in schools and concentrate recruitment in those areas. Only after you have decided on some key questions, and assessed your recruitment needs for these subjects, can you meaningfully answer some of these issues. If you are not prepared to do these things, then you are not serious.

8. You cannot develop the national curriculum beyond the skills of your teaching staff.

It is not just foreign languages which require investment in specialist teachers – the same is true of the STEM (Science, Technology, Engineering and Maths) subjects, which is why we have incentives for graduates in certain disciplines to enter teacher training. We have in fact invested significantly in these areas over the years, and there was a little growth in the numbers taking A level examinations in these subjects in 2013. We have had businesses like EADS developing initiatives around the teaching of maths in Newport schools, and Corus – now Tata Steel – in Port Talbot, Airbus in Deeside, for example, and many other businesses have invested time and energy in this area.

We should add Computing. The proposals to develop computing, set out in the next chapter, will require considerable industry/education collaboration. I would myself like to see us integrating computing into maths, if possible. Culturally, we also need to find ways of enabling these to be seen as the creative disciplines they are if we are to widen the field of entrants, particularly girls.

9. No phase should be out of bounds in a curriculum review – even the Foundation Phase.

Extra money had been found year-on-year to implement the Foundation Phase (FP), with around £170 million spent between 2008 and 2011. It was a flagship policy for the first decade of devolution, but it wasn't perfect, nor was it perfectly implemented. As Ann Keane, chief inspector of Estyn, said, on its own it was not enough to raise standards. She said that in some settings there was not enough direction to children and the balance between teacher-led and children-led activities was not right.

Sometimes I worried that our commitment to the rights of the child meant that some saw the concept of child-centred learning not as ensuring learning was focused around the needs of each child, but instead as simply allowing the child to determine the pace of their own learning, rather than being challenged always to grow and develop. That would lead to the abandoning of ambition and the institutionalisation of inequality. The FP was never, as I said many times, meant to mean 'anything goes'. It was never intended to be some kind of hippy libertarianism, though the inability at the outset to formulate a simple way of summarising the FP may sometimes have given that impression – 'learn through play', 'learning through doing' were two of the phrases which were often used to summarise the FP, though as Iram Siraj says in her 2014 stock-take, it was intended that play-based pedagogy should be underpinned by a strongly developmental approach, and the importance of language development, literacy and numeracy 'are well recognised within the Foundation Phase framework'.

The Institute of Welsh Affairs characterised the FP in 2006 as a 'liberal' or 'progressive' outcome of what it identified as 'the new producerism' underpinning education policy in the first two Assembly terms. I had received feedback from some head teachers that they were concerned that they saw less focus on core literacy and numeracy in some schools, and this was confirmed by Estyn in relation to a minority of primary schools. It had not been intended that the FP should lead to a diminution of standards and I made it clear that that was not acceptable. The Viv Thomas review warned that the assessment model for the FP 'must ensure that experiential learning is linked in an enjoyable and meaningful way for children to effective reading, writing and the use of mathematics.'

We needed to draw on the best research. How early years

programmes are organised is crucial, as the longitudinal EPPSE studies, carried out for the Department for Education in England, have shown. EPPSE, the Effective Provision of Pre-School, Primary and Secondary Education, EPPSE 3-16 project carried out by Professor Iram Siraj, amongst others, is a key research study. It examines why and when certain children succeed against the odds while others fall behind.

They found that young people whose academic progress defies the odds of disadvantage were:

- helped by parents
- encouraged and nurtured in pre-school
- had positive self-image
- had good – quality teaching at school
- had support from school if there were problems
- had support from their peers

The official evaluation of the FP by the Welsh Institute of Social and Economic Research, Data and Methods at Cardiff University, published in July 2013, shortly after I left the government, said that practitioners had varying interpretations and attitudes towards it. It said so far there was no evidence to suggest that it had made a difference to attendance, to tackling inequality in terms of gender or ethnicity or socio-economic background, or to literacy achievement. There was some evidence that performance in some of the pilot schools had improved compared to earlier cohorts. But implementation had been inconsistent between local authorities. Part of the problem may have been what the researchers called 'the relatively decentralised' approach to implementation and support. The attitudes of leaders such as head teachers was critical, as were the skills of newly qualified teachers and teaching and learning assistants.

Following the evaluation, Huw appointed Professor Iram Siraj to look at whether changes needed to be made to the FP. Her stock-take, published in 2014, found that there needed to be greater guidance on how best to support language, literacy and numeracy development, and, like Estyn, that implementation of the FP was inconsistent and that there were issues with some practitioners and teachers understanding the nature of disadvantage, particularly in the context of the home environment. The stock-take found that the assessments introduced under the Literacy and Numeracy Framework (LNF) 'would not unduly interfere with the pedagogy and practice within the Foundation Phase'. The Review of Curriculum and Assessment will rightly look at the reconciliation of outcome measures in the FP and the LNF. The stock-take also emphasises the importance of the quality of practitioners supporting children in the Foundation Phase, rather than the quantity, suggesting that the ratios of adults to children could be modified in reception classes. The quality of teaching is as important in the FP as in any other phase of learning.

10. Avoid unnecessarily narrowing the curriculum.
When Huw Lewis was Minister for Heritage, Regeneration and Housing, he and I commissioned reviews into the Arts and Education and Sport and Education.

As far as the Arts went, I was concerned that we had a range of initiatives, worthwhile in themselves, but I wondered whether we were approaching creativity and the arts in a systematic enough way. I had formally decided to fund Filmclub in Wales, an excellent initiative begun by television director Beeban Kidron, which was backed in Wales by the actor Michael Sheen. Carwyn and I had dinner with Michael and Beeban and their team in Cardiff in the autumn of 2010, but I was already sold on the project which had been piloted in Treorchy Comprehensive amongst other places. Filmclub UK were quick to understand how they could contribute to our agenda on literacy, with the significant emphasis that they gave to film-reviewing by pupils. It was a great success. They also played a lead role in establishing the Children's Cultural Poverty Forum in Wales. There had also been a review of music in schools, and we funded CânSing, an initiative which took professional singing coaches into Welsh schools, amongst other activities. I saw great initiatives on the arts and education across Wales, including for example at Hafod Primary School in Swansea, which had a full scale reproduction of Da Vinci's *The Last Supper* in one of its learning areas, a school with philosophy on the curriculum thanks to its creative head teacher Rachael Webb, herself an artist.

Dai Smith's review of the Arts and Education reported after I had left the government. Dai met schools, practitioners, students and others before producing a blockbuster of a report. In his passionate report he says bluntly 'arts in education is the best instrument we (potentially) possess for a small nation's (confident) future to be played out on a global stage.'

Huw and I had also established the Schools and Physical Activity Task and Finish group chaired by Baroness Tanni Grey-Thompson. This included teachers and head teachers, and Professor Laura McAllister, chair of the Sports Council for Wales (now Sport Wales).

We already had a range of sports activity underway in schools designed to increase the number of hours of sports activity undertaken by young people – in both competitive and non-competitive activities. The group's report made one clear recommendation, that physical education should be made a core subject in school, based on a National Physical Literacy Framework. I launched the report with Tanni and with Huw's successor, John Griffiths, in June 2013 at what turned out to be my last public appearance as Minister for Education and Skills. Tanni said: 'Evidence shows that we are facing a ticking obesity time-bomb and, unless we make sport and physical education and school sport a core subject, we will still be here in 20 years' time having made little or no progress.'

Everyone has a view on what should be taught in schools, which are seen as platforms for social engineering and behaviour management of all kinds. In thinking about curriculum reform, above all, a Minister needs to learn to say no. Throughout my time as Education Minister, I had plenty of people wanting to add things to the curriculum, but precious few wanting to remove things from it. In 2011 the British Heart Foundation and other charities ran quite an effective lobbying campaign of Assembly Members arguing that emergency life-support skills should be made statutory within the PSE curriculum. I told the Assembly that June I had received fifteen letters from Members on the issue. I was forever signing letters explaining that we would not be moving forward on this, however.

In revising the curriculum, we will need the widest possible consensus on all of these issues – and a teaching workforce with the skills and knowledge to support it.

Learning in a digital world

Teachers I met who understood the potential of new technologies were creative, energetic and can-do in their approach. They were often natural leaders, flexible and adaptive, keen to learn new skills and pass on their learning to others, impatient of bureaucracy and ready and willing to work across boundaries.

I was determined that we took advantage of the opportunities which I knew digital technology was opening up. We had to get several things right. The most modern technology needed to be available in our schools; teachers needed to be empowered and enabled to use that technology; they needed a range of resources to support their teaching; we needed to develop not only young people who could use the technology, but who could also be the developers of the future; and our schools needed a strong broadband infrastructure to support their use of data and particularly bandwidth-devouring media. In other words, we needed to think about skills, content, the national digital learning infrastructure and the underlying telecommunications support.

When I came into post, I quickly had to launch the One Wales government laptop pilot at a school in Newport in March 2010. This was an initiative which derived from a commitment in the Plaid Cymru manifesto at the 2007 election. The pilot supported 1200 laptops for children aged 10-11 in some Communities First and Flying Start areas. While the idea was interesting, it was essentially a hardware solution to a multi-faceted problem that depended on skills, software, culture, teaching practice and connectivity. It was a policy designed before the explosion in usage of smartphones and tablets. Indeed, it was designed before iPhones and Android smartphones came into use. I scrapped the pilot after the 2011 Assembly election. This didn't mean, however, that there hadn't been good work done through it: I had seen excellent work at Rhos y Medre primary school in Wrexham, for example, where they had invested in thirty MacBooks and used the technology to address parents' digital literacy skills as well. Meanwhile, Ysgol Golwg y Cwm in Ystradgynlais used the project to improve reading ability.

Work by Nesta, the UK's innovation foundation, has established that the massive investment in education technology since the millennium has barely shown an improvement in educational performance. In July 2013, Michael Fullan and Katelyn Donnelly developed an Index for Nesta to be used 'as an evaluative tool to predict the transformative power of the emerging digital environment'. I am pleased – and not a little relieved – that the innovations we undertook from 2011-13 in technology would, I think, score quite well against their index. The reason, I think, was that we were able to find the right leader for our work.

I found the right person, funnily enough, at my old primary school in Barry Island. I hadn't been back inside the school since 1967. In 2010, Janet Hayward was head teacher at Barry Island, and is now head teacher at Cadoxton in Barry.

Unusually, she has a degree in computer science, and technology therefore holds no fears for her. I visited her school early on in my time as education minister to launch the new Apple Regional Training Centre at the school. Her pupils were digitally literate and able to demonstrate competence in a wide variety of applications. Some in her junior school were even taking their GCSE in ICT. Her school had also recently been awarded the ICT Quality Mark by the British Educational Communications and Technology Agency (Becta), and in 2010 was named joint UK winner of the Becta primary school award. Her school was also highly-ranked by our inspectorate Estyn.

After the 2011 Assembly election I asked Janet to chair a Task and Finish group to look at the issues involved. I felt that if we got the technology issues right, we would simultaneously be creating a platform which would encourage teachers to share teaching resources and best practice. Networks such as the online Twitter forum #addcym were already linking teachers together. Why should teachers have to learn by trial and error when there were proven teaching practices already for successfully working with technology? I was convinced teachers could benefit from sharing what they know with others who develop content need a means of sharing it with other professionals, so that they can adapt and use it in their own classrooms.

Children, parents, learners and teachers increasingly expected to be able to find their teaching and organisational materials online. Since 2002, Wales had had a website which gave us a function along those lines, namely the National Grid for Learning (NGfL) Cymru, but I felt that it looked dated and was barely user-friendly compared to the powerful web-based applications and resources that people were now routinely accustomed to using in their personal lives. Meanwhile, the OU had been pioneering online learning materials. Web-based material proliferates on YouTube and through the iTunes University. The Khan Academy had brought lessons in fifteen-minute bite-sized chunks to children and young people across the world.

I was mindful of issues around digital inclusion and online safety. We knew we had a significant number of young people with no access to technology at home. We also were well aware of the dangers to young people online, which is why I asked Sangeet Bhullar of WISEKIDS to join the group. Her charity works to empower young people's use of technology while ensuring that they know how to keep safe online. Our own guidance on bullying dealt with cyber-bullying issues and we had taken early steps to enshrine e-Safety in schools in Wales. In 2008, we were the first nation in the UK to introduce the teaching of safe and responsible use of the internet into both the primary and secondary school curriculum.

I was also well aware of the frustrations of teachers in Welsh-medium schools who often had to wait for English-medium resources to be translated. Digital production could shorten the timeline between commissioning and publication and reduce cost at the same time. I was clear that we should move to digital-only production in future.

I wanted the group to be led by practitioners who could say confidently what works in the classroom, but also to be challenged where appropriate by ICT professionals at the cutting edge, not least in leading high-tech companies, who could look at the full range of applications available. I deliberately added Bruce Steele, a lively Australian software developer who had done some great work in the Heads of the Valleys, to bring some challenge to the group, and Sioned Wyn Roberts, then working for the digital television production company Magic Lantern, and now S4C's Content Commissioner for Children's, Learning and Digital. Former Editor of BBC Radio Wales, Julie Barton, Alan Morgans of Tinopolis and Stuart Ball from Microsoft were also members, along with National Librarian Andrew Green, Ysgol Bro Morgannwg Head teacher Dr Dylan Jones, who brought a Welsh-medium school dimension, and Janet's former deputy, now Barry Island head teacher, Ty Golding.

Janet began with teaching practice or pedagogy. I wanted the group to concentrate on what digital materials worked in the classroom and how we could get to a situation where all Welsh schools are able to deliver digitally to improve performance. They produced a compelling report on how we should take forward the use of digital technologies in schools.

The group started with the view that teachers and learners now lived in a world where communication and knowledge were routinely digital, ubiquitous and interactive. They said that the use of digital technologies and resources needed to change from being sporadic and patchy to being ubiquitous and everyday. They felt that there was a need for national action in two areas – encouraging and supporting teachers to operate in a digital environment and to share best practice, and also to establish a system and a national collection for creating, storing and sharing digital resources. Their operating name for this was 'Hwb' – in Welsh, 'hwb' means 'push' or 'spur', and it would act as a hHub for sharing and using digital resources.

Key recommendations therefore included establishing a powerful organisation to oversee the developments, supported by a group of practitioners; ensuring that educators' digital competencies and skills were upgraded; creating a national digital collection in both English and Welsh; giving all users an individual log-in for the lifetime of their learning and the ability to access the materials form anywhere; commissioning new resources and national licences for key resources; managing intellectual property rights; using existing tried and tested web-based products and services; encouraging a culture of digital citizenship.

This was a compelling report and following its launch in March 2012 we got on with its implementation. I announced in June that we would be establishing a National Digital Learning Council to provide expert guidance on the use of technology in teaching and learning, which launched that September. We launched Hwb as the new bilingual learning platform for Wales in December 2012, acting not only as a platform for educators and learners but also offering a personal e-portfolio for learners. The platform would be accessible from any device anywhere. It would provide the online home for a national digital repository of teaching and learning resources. Resources already on NGfL Cymru would be migrated to Hwb, which would also provided a range of licensed educational tools and content negotiated nationally, and teachers would be able to upload their resources to Hwb.

There was significant investment in this programme, with £4.5 million for the development of Hwb, £3 million for improving the teaching of digital literacy and £1.5 million for new original content to be hosted on Hwb.

We were fortunate throughout that in this field there were enthusiastic practitioners keen to share their experiences with other teachers. Experts working as Field Development Officers for NGfL like Melanie Blount were incredibly well-informed and full of advice. It was clear we needed a national team of digital leaders.

One of the schools leading the way in Wales on use of technology was Casllwchwr Primary School in Swansea where the head teacher Simon Pridham and deputy head teacher Sarah Reece were enthusiastic proponents. Simon warned that there was no place anymore for the traditional teacher who did not get technology. Teachers could not stand still. The new technology was disruptive – and often pupils knew more than teachers and were bringing them along on a lifelong learning journey. As Simon explained to the *TES* 'With the iPad, pupils have the internet, a camera, a notebook, a sound recorder and a range of other tools at their fingertips, instantly.' By the 2012-13 academic year every Key Stage 2 pupil in Caslllwchwr had their own iPad and were confident users of technology. They had their own email addresses and were encouraged to interact with each other and with teachers. When I visited Casllwchwr for the first time in early 2012, they had iPads, iPod Touches, Apple TV and other devices and had policies in place to allow 'Bring your own Device' (BYOD) to operate. They were able to demonstrate how use of technology was helping to address the literacy gender gap between girls and boys. The use of technology encouraged young people to learn from one another. They were using apps to create word collages, for presentations, for animation supported by scripts, screen casting and in many other ways, such as the production of booklets with sports stars and local authors. They also had processes to engage parents with these new approaches to learning. The school was recognised across the UK for excellence in ICT, winning a UK NAACE 'Highly commended' award. In June 2012 it became the first school in Wales given the Lighthouse status by Apple, meaning it was a beacon school for the use of Apple technology. By 2011-12, the school had closed the gender gap to 0 per cent in Level 5 in English. There was a 25 per cent improvement in boys achieving Level 4. They had moved to one iPad per pupil in Key Stage 2 and had banks of iPads for use in the Foundation Phase, and moved to one iPad per pupil subsequently. They were awarded the Third Millennium Learning Award in 2012 – one of only eight in the entire UK and the only one in Wales. They partnered with Cedars School of Excellence in Greenock in Scotland, where the school has rolled out an iPad for every pupil under its inspirational Technology Development officer, Fraser Speirs. Pupils from both schools interviewed me via Skype in 2012.

Casllwchwr's work spread elsewhere in Swansea, through the Lifelong Intergenerational Furthering Education (Life) programme, designed to tackle educational underperformance across generations using new technology to open up opportunities. Through this in 2012-13, they partnered with Sea View Community Primary school in Townhill, Swansea, one of the most deprived communities in Wales. The project introduced one iPad per pupil in Year 6. There was peer-mentoring between teachers, pupils and parents at both schools. By the end of the year, there were significant uplifts in reading ages across the class, with many young people achieving reading ages in their teens, well above their chronological age, with scores objectively marked on the NFER scales, well above their predicted levels and improving significantly on their levels in Year 5. Attendance also went up. In recent years, Seaview had been in the fourth quartile for everything, but after working with Casllwchwr they ended in 2012-13 in the second quartile overall and for literacy.

Estyn reported in July 2013 that the impact of ICT on standards in literacy was good or better in the majority of primary schools – and in these schools, boys who were reluctant readers and writers were motivated by ICT to improve their literacy skills. In some schools oracy, presentations, research and writing skills, as well as collaborative and thinking skills, also improved. Throughout most primary schools, use of ICT had a positive impact on teaching and learning, though teaching overall is better in the Foundation Phase than in Key Stage 2. However, assessment and tracking of pupils' skills was poor. Half of the schools visited were successful in raising standards in and through the use of ICT and these schools tended to have heads with a clear vision to improve use of ICT. The Estyn report gives some fantastic case studies of primaries that are leading the way. Aside from Casllwchwr, these include Ysgol Llanrug in Gwynedd, in the Welsh-speaking heartland, whose work has helped to drive digital take-up and delivery throughout the community, with 92 per cent of families with children at school now subscribing to a tablet-purchase scheme to enable work at home by pupils and parents.

Estyn also warned that the level of filtering or blocking of sites by local authorities hindered classwork 'unnecessarily' in the majority of schools. I had changed policy on the use of social networks in schools in March 2013. In 2006, following a tabloid storm over internet safety of children, a decision had been taken to block school access to such sites. My view was that young people needed to become confident digital citizens, learning to use the web safely under supervision and independently, and I was pleased that the Children's Commissioner for Wales, Keith Towler, backed me in this.

I was also aware that in many places local authority support for schools' ICT needs was poor. In my own constituency, there had been a time when the Wi-Fi platform available to schools went down in bad weather. In another part of Wales, one local authority had had a fibre network installed, paid for by the Cymru Ar-lein programme, then dropped it because of the running costs. Corporate ICT departments in local authorities had little understanding, in many cases, of the unique needs of schools, which were more akin to small or medium-sized enterprises in their technology needs. I decided that we would use some of the capital money we had available to upgrade broadband links to schools. We planned a £39 million investment, which was announced in January 2013 by the First Minister. This new Learning in Digital Wales grant was designed to improve school broadband connectivity infrastructure significantly, as well as in-school connectivity, ensuring that all learners in Wales had access to secure Wi-Fi systems. The intention was that by 2020 all primary schools would have 100 Mb capability and all secondary schools 1GB capability. The immediate upgrades have gone well, with Cwmclydach Primary School in the Rhondda reporting its download speed had increased from 0.9 MB to 9 MB. Glyn Derw comprehensive in

Ely in Cardiff, which had an old run-down school site, found its educational practice transformed because of better broadband links and an innovative cloud-based education technology programme called Seren, which it demonstrated to great effect on YouTube in March 2014. Technology could take young people beyond the confines of their schools, ahead of the roll-out of our 21st Century school building programme.

Using technology was one thing. But we also wanted to develop the coding skills of young people so that they could become the software and application developers of the future. In Wales, the sector included blue-chip corporate companies through to dynamic and innovative small and medium-sized enterprises. The innovative Raspberry Pi was now being manufactured at Sony in Pencoed and I went to see their operations. We had seen a decline in the numbers taking GCSE ICT, and I felt it was right to consider the future of computer science and ICT in schools in Wales. We had had discussions with the team behind the Next Gen report, written by Ian Livingstone, founder of Games Workshop and president of Eidos, and Alex Hope, and many other professionals. I chaired a seminar on these issues in November 2012, which brought together educators and people from industry. Several key themes emerged as a result of this:

- ICT in schools needed to be re-branded, re-engineered and made relevant
- Digital literacy was the start and not the end-point – learners needed to be taught to create as well as consume
- Computer science should be introduced at primary school and developed over the course of the curriculum, alongside the skills of creative problem-solving
- Revised qualifications needed to be developed

I set up a steering group to take these issues forward. Its co-chairs were Stuart Arthur, Managing Director of Box UK, a leading UK digital development company headquartered in Cardiff, which developed its own coding masterclasses for education; Dr Tom

Crick who coordinated the Computing@School and Technocamps initiatives and Janet Hayward. The steering group included a wide range of educators with digital expertise including Simon Pridham, Lucy Bunce, Glyn Rogers, Hannah Matthias, Chris Britten, Gareth Edmondson from Ysgol Gyfyn Gwyr, and industry representatives from the Wales-based company Monitise, Fujitsu, and Vision Thing communications, and academics like Professor Khalid Al-Begain, Professor Faron Moller, and Magi Gould.

We already had some primary schools who were leading the way in the development of coding schools. One amongst them was Cwmclydach Primary School in my own Rhondda constituency, thanks to the innovative ideas of the head, Gareth Dacey and teacher Alison Howells, who had the computing skills. They had run a collaborative digital learning project with Bryn Primary School in Carmarthenshire, engaging pupils from Years 2-6 in a range of problem solving and collaborative activities. The activities in which they were involved went well beyond the existing National Curriculum, using code such as Scratch, Python, Robot Friend and Augmented Reality. Children in Year 2 were being taught to code through Scratch. They used a range of other music, animation, artistic and other apps. The schools won the first Welsh National Digital Learning Award for their work, and Rhondda Cynon Taff council now wants them to run this out across other schools in the county. Cwmclydach created a state of the art digital learning room – called 'hwb@cwm' – replacing their previous ICT suite. Designed and built with the aid of the school caretaker, the digital learning room looked like something out of Google's headquarters when it was launched by Huw Lewis in October 2013. It housed a variety of mobile technologies including iPads, laptops and touchscreen computers housed in a series of 'pods' focused on particular areas of learning such as coding, robotics and animation. The pupils were also able to work with the Raspberry Pi. The school had integrated its digital learning into the delivery of the whole curriculum, including the Literacy and Numeracy Framework.

The ICT curriculum steering group reported back to Huw Lewis in October 2013. It contained some radical and far-reaching recommendations. A new subject called Computing should be created to replace ICT from Foundation Phase onwards. This new subject would disaggregate into two areas – Computer Science and Information Technology. Computing should be integrated into the curriculum as the fourth science, served by a mandatory but adaptable Programme of Study, with the same status as the other three sciences, encouraging creativity, thematic working and real-world problem-solving with industry interaction. There should be a statutory Digital Literacy framework alongside the Literacy and Numeracy Framework running through to sixteen. The key role of computing and technology in society needed to be understood, and the importance and diversity of careers in IT should be disseminated. New qualifications should be developed. The best talent needed to be recruited into teacher training and there should be continuing professional development to support the roll-out of the new curriculum.

The week before I left the government, I spoke at the first National Digital Learning Conference. I was pleased with what I was able to report. Hwb had been officially launched in beta mode in December 2012. One of the initial tasks was the migration of tens of thousands of digital resources from NGfL Cymru into the publically accessible Hwb website. Another challenge was establishing the data management protocols which will allow all learners aged 3 to 19, and their teachers and parents, to have secure Hwb Plus accounts which they can use throughout their school lives. We had thirty-three early adopter schools piloting Hwb Plus across Wales. They were being intensively supported by the eight Digital Leaders we had recruited at the start of the year – experienced and successful practitioners who now act as mentors to schools and promote digital learning online.

At the same time as we launched Hwb, we started publishing resources on the Welsh Government's first iTunes U channel, Addysg Cymru Education Wales.

iTunes U is the largest online repository of free Open Education Resources in the world. We had worked with Welsh company Green Bay Media and with BBC News presenter Huw Edwards to create high quality iTunes U resources which promoted and explained Welsh culture and history, drawing on the BBC's television series, *The Story of Wales*, which Huw had narrated. More content was planned for iTunes and Hwb as part of a new content acquisition programme, for which we had allocated £500,000 per year for three years. We also had examples of schools making their own use of iTunes U, with Welsh teachers creating their own iBooks and courses to use with their students and share with professional colleagues.

I genuinely believe that this is an area where Wales can be world leaders, and we must take advantage of these opportunities. Having invested in the digital infrastructure within our schools, the next task is the implementation of the curriculum recommendations on computing. Huw Lewis announced in March 2014 that the recommendations would be taken forward in the overall curriculum review by Professor Graham Donaldson, designed to create a Curriculum for Wales. I believe that the steering group's proposals are fundamental to the future of Wales. The curriculum proposals have been better received by industry than the more prescriptive suggestions in England. Coding and creativity can go hand in hand.

A Living Language

As a Welsh-learner, and step-parent to two children who had been through the Welsh-medium school system, I was adamant that we would support and develop Welsh-medium education. That meant responding to the growing demand for Welsh-medium education from nursery through to higher education. After the May 2011 Assembly election, Carwyn gave me responsibility for Welsh Language policy as well. This meant we could bring together the previously under-powered Welsh Language Unit alongside the stronger Welsh-medium education team, and there were clearly synergies that we gained from this. The decision was welcomed by Ieuan Wyn Jones, as leader of Plaid Cymru.

The Welsh-medium education sector had grown rapidly across Wales in the years since the establishment of the first state Welsh-medium primary school in 1947. By 2009, 438 primary schools (29 per cent) were Welsh-medium. The first Welsh-medium state secondary school had opened in 1956 – by 2009, there were fifty-five providing Welsh-medium lessons in more than half the curriculum subjects (25 per cent of all secondary schools).

In April 2010, I published the Welsh-Medium Education Strategy. This was a One Wales commitment. Jane Hutt had published a strategy in draft form. I would have preferred a bit longer to go through all of the targets, but time was pressing. I ensured that alongside the strategy we published a clear implementation programme setting out the expectations we had of our partners.

I was determined to make the announcement in Welsh, and worked hard on the oral statement I outlined in the Assembly. I had been taking Welsh lessons since before entering the Assembly in 2003 with tutor Elaine Senior, who subsequently coached me through a number of statements and major policy announcements and speeches. My command of Welsh certainly improved over time as an Assembly Member. Working in a bi-lingual environment helped. With Elaine's assistance, I steadily became more proficient, and I was happy to conduct recorded media interviews – and by 2011, meetings – through the medium of Welsh.

The strategy would not be delivered in a short period – it required long-term commitment and so contained five-year and ten-year targets, we would publish annual reports that would enable people to assess progress towards these. We would be increasing the budget for Welsh-medium education to underpin the strategy. There had been considerable successes over the previous fifty years, but much had developed in a piecemeal fashion and now we needed a proper strategic planning on a national basis. This required effective local planning. It also required increased numbers of qualified Welsh-medium teachers. There was cross-party support for the Strategy. It was a historic moment for the language.

A key focus of the Strategy is to improve the process of planning Welsh-medium education on the basis of measuring demand from parents. Welsh in Education Strategic Plans and a Welsh in Education Grant would be crucial in achieving this aim. The new plans were to come into force from April 2012 and would replace the Welsh Education plans being monitored by the Welsh Language Board. The plans would be a means for the Welsh Government to monitor the way local authorities are responding and contributing to the implementation of the strategy by:

- expecting Welsh-medium education to be central to policy development;
- expecting Welsh-medium provision to be designed and extended according to demand;

- working towards a Welsh-medium support service based on consortia in the near future;
- improving standards and expanding children and young people's use of the Welsh language; and
- showing progress against the Welsh-Medium Education Strategy's specific targets.

I expected local authorities to conduct a thorough assessment of the demand by parents for Welsh-medium education. We wanted to know how authorities were increasing the number of Welsh learners who receive Welsh-medium education; working towards increasing post-14 Welsh-medium provision; improving follow-up rates; training the workforce; and improving support for learners with additional educational needs. My officials would look closely at performance data and challenge local authorities where improvement was needed. I also announced more funding for training of Welsh-medium teachers and classroom assistants in the summer of 2010 to support early years education in particular.

As a result of the strategy, the Welsh Government published 160 new titles to expand the range of teaching and learning resources available to schools and colleges who teach through the medium of Welsh or teach Welsh second language. The Sabbatical Scheme has become the main national programme for providing Welsh-language and methodology training for practitioners. All further education (FE) colleges have Bilingual Champions and a Bilingual Champion was appointed to support the work-based learning sector. Since 2009 we had invested around £135 million to deliver seventeen major projects for Welsh-medium school buildings.

It was fine having a strategy, but if local authorities were not responding to parental demand by expanding the number of places, then we would have a long-term problem. Meri Huws, then chair of the Welsh Language Board, suggested to me that we should look at making the Welsh in Education Strategic Plans statutory, and I secured a commitment to that in the Labour manifesto for the 2011 election. As well as this, the manifesto promised the effective measurement of parental demand for Welsh-medium education.

I believe in a Welsh Labour party comfortable with its Welshness; and that means, comfortable with the language. In my experience most Labour Party members are supportive of the language and a high proportion of members who do not speak Welsh send their children to Welsh-medium schools. Welsh-medium schools across Wales reflect the social context of their communities.

We legislated in 2012-13 for the most radical set of proposals on Welsh-medium education that had ever been considered in Wales. I had explained our intention at the Annual Conference of RhAG (parents for Welsh-Medium Education) in October 2011. There was enthusiastic support for our plans. The School Standards and Organisation Bill implemented our manifesto commitment to put Welsh in Education Strategic Plans on a statutory basis, and this came into effect from April 2014. Local authorities had to satisfy the Welsh Government of their intent. The bill also ensured that Ministers could require local authorities to undertake a survey of parental demand for Welsh-medium education in their area when they prepared their plans, which in turn had to explain how they would satisfy that demand. This was an area where we had cross-party support and I tightened some of the provisions during the passage of the Bill following representations from Opposition politicians.

The UK government did not always honour its obligations in respect of the Welsh language. In the autumn of 2010, the Schools Minister Nick Gibb managed to write to all teachers in Wales urging them not to strike over pensions in English-only, contrary to the 1973 Welsh Language Act. A formal complaint over this was made to the Welsh Language Board. The minister later apologised and separately Michael Gove promised me they would take the issue more seriously and told me he was sorry for the mistake after I wrote to him. In 2014, the then Conservative Party vice-chairman, Michael Fabricant, blundered into the debate on *Any Questions*, when he appeared to lay the blame for failings in Welsh education on the Welsh language, stating that it was hard to recruit teachers to teach Physics in English let alone Welsh. He said:

> The Welsh for neutron is neutron. It's difficult enough to find in England people who are good maths, physics and chemistry teachers. To ask them to be bilingual as well is nonsense.... The problem is there are not enough maths and physics teachers who can just speak English, let alone English and Welsh, and that's the problem.

In taking on responsibility for Welsh language policy after the 2011 Assembly election, I was eager to ensure that we widened the range of voices commenting on language policy. I was very taken with a comment by Colin Nosworthy, of Cymdeithas yr Iaith Gymraeg, at an early meeting of the Welsh Language Strategy Advisory Group which I had inherited from the previous Heritage Minister, Alun Ffred Jones, that he was virtually the only person around the table not funded by the Welsh Government in some shape or form. Given our budgets were under pressure, I also warned groups that we would be expecting results from the money we were spending. How were they contributing to strengthening the language? I spelt this out at the 2011 Eisteddfod in Wrexham, saying that every organisation receiving money from the Welsh Government should be able to demonstrate what they were doing with that money to help people use the language in the community. I was also clear, as I said in a Cymdeithas Cledwyn speech at the Eisteddfod, that legislation like the Welsh Language Measure may provide a framework, but it would not be what saved and developed the language. Increasing *usage* of the language had to be at the heart of our new Welsh Language Strategy, something I stressed to the members of the new Welsh Language Partnership Council after their appointment.

I took the regulations on the appointment of the Welsh

Language Commissioner through the Assembly in June 2011 and we moved straight into the appointment process, with Plaid Cymru AM and former Culture Minister Rhodri Glyn Thomas representing the Assembly (ministers do not sit on such appointment panels.) The First Minister was able to announce Meri Huws' appointment in October.

We launched the consultation on our proposals to make Welsh in Education Strategic Plans statutory, and to ensure effective measurement of parental demand for Welsh-medium education, as part of the consultation on the School Standards and Organisation Bill in October 2011.

Cabinet discussed the draft Welsh Language Strategy in January 2012. My objective was to maintain the consensus on the language that had previously been reached and subsequently developed by the One Wales Government. The broad strategy was generally consistent with the draft on which Alun Ffred Jones, as Minister for Heritage, had consulted between December 2010 and February 2011. However, I had added a new section on technology and new media, which I regarded as key to the language being seen as part of a living, modern Wales where Welsh-speakers of all ages could confidently expect online Welsh-medium services enabling them to participate fully as digital citizens. I had also commissioned a review of population trends, with a statistical analysis which suggested that the country was losing between 1,200 and 2,200 Welsh-speakers per year. What our review showed also was that there was little evidence about the projects which really worked to drive up the use of Welsh, hence the emphasis subsequently on accountability for the investment we made in organisations across Wales under our Welsh language responsibilities.

The Strategy contained key strategic areas for language development, focusing on families, children and young people, the community, the workplace, services to citizens and strengthening the Welsh Language infrastructure, which included broadcasting, technology and new media. This was also intended to be a cross-government strategy, recognising that all Government Departments had a responsibility for mainstreaming Welsh language policy.

We launched the strategy, *Iaith Fyw, Iaith Byw (A living language: a language for living)* on St David's Day with Welsh-speaking members of the Wales Rugby team and coaches taking part in a coaching session with Welsh-medium pupils at the Welsh team's training ground in the Vale of Glamorgan. The strategy was welcomed by all parties, with Plaid Cymru's then spokesperson for the language keen to establish their party's role in shaping it under the One Wales Government, which had published the original draft.

I used my foreword to the document to set out a manifesto for our objectives for the language. I said that over the decades, the Welsh language had been sustained by dedicated individuals and communities working together locally and nationally, often under great pressure, in a wide variety of organisations and activities. The preservation of the Welsh language in the twentieth and early twenty-first century had also been a positive demonstration of how politics can deliver policy objectives. The promotion and protection of the language has always depended on political support and grass-roots campaigning.

However, the future development and survival of the language depended on the commitment of the people of Wales, and must be owned by all of us. Its protection could not depend on those who are professionally employed in its development or promotion. We must also ensure that we are encouraging people to use the language skills that they have – and not to contribute to a climate in which they feel that less than perfect Welsh language skills are a barrier to participation. In developing language policy in the future, we needed to invite in new voices. I wanted a coalition of the unconventional to develop the new strategy.

The strategy was launched in the thirtieth anniversary year of S4C's first broadcast. The most damaging thing to happen to the Welsh language since 2010 had been the decision by the UK government to abandon the funding formula for S4C, set down in statute, without any effective public debate. The budgetary loss to the Welsh language in the five years to 2014-15 will be at least £60 million. I had been staggered at the failure of the then S4C Authority to maximise the cross-party public pressure that existed in Wales in defence of what was a statutory obligation on the UK government demonstrated an institution whose pre-devolution mentality failed to understand the realities of post-devolution Wales.

I also mentioned the new emphasis on new media and technology. Throughout the twentieth century, the broadcast media played an important role in the development and preservation of the Welsh language through both radio and television. In the twenty-first century, the existence of Welsh-language digital media content and applications not only allows the Welsh language to flourish, but it also enables Welsh speakers to participate fully as digital citizens and demonstrates to all that the Welsh language is a creative, powerful, adaptive and modern medium. Our ambition and our expectation should be that Welsh speakers should be able to conduct their lives electronically through the medium of Welsh, should they so desire, whether that be for cultural, informational, entertainment, leisure, retail, transactional, community, or social networking purposes.

The pace of change had been significant and striking. In December 2011 alone, the first Welsh-language e-books became available on Kindle, the Welsh-language magazine *Golwg* became available via an iPad app, and the Welsh Language Board consulted on Welsh language terminology for use on Twitter.

I said that some of the most exciting developments in the digital supply of Welsh materials online had come from user-generated content and applications created by Welsh speakers themselves. How did we harness that energy and commitment? We needed to think big, have ambition, and aim high. We could not leave the future of the Welsh language to the established institutions who have built an industry around their own small-scale needs over recent years.

The strategy set out a clear responsibility for the whole of the

Welsh Government to lead on the future of the Welsh language, and develop ideas which have implications for the whole of Wales. The strategy was endorsed by the Cabinet of the Welsh Government, and we now sought popular support for its implementation.

I followed through in the commitment to bringing in new voices to the debate on the language in the groups we established to look at specific issues, whether they be the teaching of Welsh as a second language, Welsh for adults or the future of the Eisteddfod, appointing active Welsh-learners such as film-maker and Cardiff City announcer, Ali Yassine, a Welsh-learner turned Welsh-language tutor, and former BBC Head of Politics Ashok Ahir, runner-up as Welsh Learner of the Year in 2012, amongst others. My specialist adviser Aled Eirug, former head of news at BBC Wales, worked quietly behind the scenes building support for what we were seeking to achieve.

We opened up conversations with leading technology companies including Apple, Microsoft, Google and others to discuss how they could do more to improve the range of Welsh-medium services. We also set up the new language and technology fund. The Welsh Language Unit was now headed by Dr Caroline Turner, a hard-working and effective civil servant with whom I had worked on the Communities First programme when I was Deputy Minister for Regeneration who also led across the Welsh medium education section. Jeremy Evas, who had left the Welsh Language Board for Cardiff University, brought valuable experience of helping Microsoft deliver its Welsh language interface. We also supported campaigns by publishers in Wales, such as Y Lolfa, and the Welsh Books Council, to ensure that their publications could be available through Amazon, which had taken a decision to end their availability. Amazon relented in 2013 after a great deal of hostile publicity. We wrote to Amazon and kept pressure on them.

I was particularly pleased with the work on new technology. We produced a Welsh language technology and digital media action plan, as well as convening a very valuable group on the

Welsh language and technology involving a wide range of organisations including S4C, Golwg360, the BBC, Haciaith and experts from higher education. It is important that Welsh speakers can access technology which supports and facilitates the use of Welsh in every aspect of life. The action plan set out our commitment to drive developments in the field of Welsh-language technology and digital media.

I also launched a Welsh-language Technology and Digital Media Fund to support the implementation of the action plan. The Fund – £250,000 a year over three years – included a grant scheme to award grants on an annual basis, intended to fund new Welsh-medium software applications, infrastructure projects to support the development of Welsh language digital services – and initiatives to raise awareness of Welsh language technology and digital content. The first six grants were awarded in November 2013. We also provided support to the *papurau bro* – Welsh language community newspapers – to go online, holding a session at the 2012 Eisteddfod where we promoted this.

Strengthening the infrastructure for the language also involved strengthening the support on the ground, and here the Mentrau Iaith were key. Mentrau Iaith were community-based organisations which work to raise the profile of the language in a specific area. Each local Menter Iaith received a basic grant from the Welsh Government, as well as financial support from a number of other sources, to work with individuals, organisations, and local business to promote the use of Welsh in its area. We funded Mentrau Iaith Cymru as a national body for the first time in 2012-13, as an umbrella body to provide support to Mentrau Iaith locally. We decided to see whether we could get more even work across the Mentrau Iaith and held a review whose results were published after I left the government. The government agreed with the review's suggestions

- for a longer funding cycle based on linguistic outcomes;
- to improve the planning of activities to promote the Welsh language;

- to provide clarity with regard to the role and responsibilities of organisations funded by the Welsh Government to promote the Welsh language.

Some Mentrau Iaith were excellent. In Cardiff, under the creative leadership of Sian Lewis, its chief executive, Menter Iaith Caerdydd ran an exceptionally successful annual festival called Tafwyl, drawing in a wide range of organisations, including the Welsh Rugby Union and the Football Association of Wales, to celebrate the use of the Welsh Language in Wales, with a range of activities for young people in particular. There was a danger that the event could be lost in 2013 after cuts in spending but I stepped in to ensure that the event could go ahead with a grant from the Welsh Government. Maintaining an annual festival of this kind in our capital city should rightly be a priority, and 2013's event attracted record numbers, with the Hollywood actor, Matthew Rhys, in attendance.

One issue which I inherited from the One Wales Government was what to do about the Welsh Language Scheme of Ofcom, the communications regulator. The Welsh Language Board had referred this issue to Alun Ffred Jones as Heritage Minister in May 2010. I do not know what happened between May 2010 and the Assembly election in May 2011, but the issue was brought up with me again in June 2011 by Meri Huws on behalf of the Welsh Language Board. The issue essentially was that the Welsh Language Board had wanted Ofcom to include within its Welsh Language scheme a commitment to give appropriate consideration to the use of the Welsh language in carrying out its licensing functions, particularly for local radio services, in Wales. Welsh Language Board lawyers said one thing; Ofcom lawyers said another. I was not a lawyer, and decided that the only way to resolve this was to refer it to the Counsel-General for his view.

Following the legal advice that I received, I took further evidence from both Ofcom and the Welsh Language Board and warned Ofcom in February 2012 that I was minded 'to impose a scheme which included an appropriately worded measure about

Ofcom considering the Welsh language when carrying out its services to the public', including in its approach to its services. Following further representations and further consideration, I imposed the conditions in Ofcom's Welsh Language scheme in May 2012. In my letter to Ed Richards, chief executive of Ofcom – and a former BBC colleague of mine in the 1990s – I said that 'Ofcom has the power to influence the linguistic character of programme content' and that programme content through the medium of Welsh may constitute local material as defined in the Communications Act. In my view, this decision could have been taken by the One Wales Government when Plaid Cymru held responsibility for the Welsh language. Had that course of action been taken, it would have had an earlier impact on some radio services licensed by Ofcom.

In July 2012 I decided to take forward reviews of Welsh for Adults and Welsh as a second language. In 2006, six Welsh for Adults centres had been established. There were just over 18,000 adults learning Welsh through the centres. Questions were being raised about their effectiveness: and some suggested that the emphasis appeared to be on the achievement of qualifications rather than spoken ability. I asked Haydn Edwards, former principal of Coleg Menai, to review the work and make recommendations, supported by a group representing a wide range of interests within the community. Their report was published shortly after I left the government. Its recommendations included calls for a national body to provide leadership for the sector, a reduction in the number of providers to ensure quality, better use of data to target those who did not take up the opportunity to learn Welsh, coupled with better marketing, a focus on Welsh in the workplace and Welsh in the family, revisions to the curriculum and greater online provision, less focus on exams and more on raising attainment levels, and better opportunities for learners to meet together and share experiences.

In terms of Welsh as a second language, we knew that standards of attainment were worse than in other subjects and too few pupils were making good progress at GCSE. Estyn reports had shown that outcomes were poor. The short-course GCSE was particularly weak. We also seemed to be seeing something of a decline in the numbers studying Welsh at A-level. Despite a commitment to ensuring that young people studied Welsh to sixteen we were far from producing a cadre of confident Welsh-speaking sixteen-year-olds. Again, I appointed a strong group of people, chaired by Professor Sioned Davies of Cardiff University, to take this work forward. Their report called for fundamental changes in the delivery of Welsh as a second language. Recommendations included raising its status within the National Curriculum, ensuring the quality of teaching Welsh second language counted more highly in Estyn assessments, using the National Literacy and Numeracy Framework to establish a continuum of learning in Welsh, which would include expectations for pupils learning Welsh in Welsh-medium, bilingual and English-medium schools, ensuring availability of A level Welsh, abandoning the short-course GCSE, creating a revised GCSE based on new course requirements, a revision of A level to ensure an emphasis on oral language skills suitable for the workplace, compulsory modules within the Welsh Bac, the development centrally of online learning materials delivered through Hwb, and a stronger focus on training of teachers. This work will be taken forward in the review of Curriculum and Assessment being pursued by my successor, Huw Lewis, who has already announced that the GCSE short course will be put out of its misery.

In October 2012 I appointed a Task and Finish Group to look at the future of the Eisteddfod, bringing together people with a commitment to opening up the language from a wider range of backgrounds alongside individuals with experience of running festivals, business and artistic activities and others with mass media experience, particularly in appealing to young audiences. The broadcaster Roy Noble, a Welsh-speaker and former head teacher with considerable popular appeal, agreed to chair the group, which included broadcasters like Bethan Elfyn, Nia Parry,

Ali Yassine, Sioned Wyn Roberts and Sian Eirian, artistic directors like Peter Florence and Daniel Evans, educational figures like Eirlys Pritchard Jones and Aran Jones, and business adviser John Pritchard.

There had been a long-standing debate about whether the Eisteddfod should focus on one site, like the Royal Welsh Show, with strongly-held views on either side. I wondered whether, rather than one site, we could conceive of a four-year cycle, based around two permanent sites with the Eisteddfod continuing to travel in the other two years. I thought there might be scope for reinforcing the language in its heartland areas in the west and north-west, building a strong network of cultural industries around modern sites properly plumbed for broadcast and new media transmission – sites which promoted public art and local cultural initiatives. But I was entirely relaxed about the outcome. I felt the debate needed to be resolved one way or the other. I knew, however, that the Eisteddfod hierarchy were opposed to a permanent site or sites, something they made clear publicly. Inevitably, some people assumed the worst, thinking I wanted to do away with the Eisteddfod's Welsh-only rule, even though the terms of reference specifically ruled out such a move. I certainly believed that the Eisteddfod could provide a better visitor experience, with clearer sign-posting of events. The journalist Gwilym Owen said in *Golwg* that by setting up the group I had forced the Eisteddfod to be more democratic in its approach. Certainly, following the appointment of the group, the Eisteddfod organisers sought to place a greater emphasis on the visitor experience, with a more welcoming arrival area.

The Task and Finish group report, with an elegantly-written introduction by Roy Noble, was published after I left the Government. It recommended that the Eisteddfod should continue to tour, that it should appoint an artistic director, develop a proper marketing strategy to deliver stronger visitor numbers, work more closely with the Urdd Eisteddfod to encourage more young volunteers, and develop a proper digital strategy. The group asked the Government to provide more funding to support these aims, and to encourage public bodies to plan their presence at the Eisteddfod in partnership with the Eisteddfod. The Government accepted all of the recommendations in full or in principle, noting that most were for the Eisteddfod to implement.

As part of the move to ensure that the Welsh Government as a whole delivered on the strategy, my department worked with Edwina Hart's Economy department to set up a group looking at the Welsh Language and Economic Development which she established in December 2012, chaired by Elin Rhys, managing director of the independent TV production company Telesgop. Edwina announced in February 2014 that work on their recommendations was being taken forward across Government. Following a resolution of the Assembly in 2012, I also established a group to look at the future of the language in rural areas, chaired by Rhodri Llwyd Morgan, Assistant Director for Education and Community Services in Ceredigion, a member of the new Welsh Language Partnership Council. The latter group produced a hefty report with some clear recommendations, including the development of Bangor, Aberystwyth and Carmarthen as City Regions, Language Impact Assessments in planning, more consistent 3-14 education provision across Anglesey, Gwynedd, Ceredigion and Carmarthenshire 'so that all pupils become fluent and confident in both Welsh and English', building on the education practice of Gwynedd in particular, and supporting leisure and workforce initiatives through the medium of Welsh. The Government's response in March 2014 was broadly supportive, though it stopped short of designating Bangor, Aberystwyth and Carmarthen as City Regions. In the same month, S4C took the decision to move its headquarters from Cardiff to Carmarthen.

With the publication of the disappointing Census results in 2013, I felt that Plaid Cymru were moving away from a position of consensus on the language. The Census results should not have been unexpected. Our own analysis had established in 2011 that there was a year-on-year reduction in the numbers speaking

Welsh. Crudely summarised, we were not replacing and adding to the numbers of Welsh-speakers. Those leaving Wales and deaths of older Welsh-speakers outnumbered those learning the language, although the census figures did demonstrate that in the under-3s there was positive news, the percentage of 3-15 year-olds speaking Welsh held steady, and those aged 20-44 showed a growth in numbers. Some communities seemed to be growing, even in the heartland areas such as Gwynedd; there was a significant growth in Cardiff; but there was a serious decline in Carmarthen. The truth was that the encouraging results of the 2001 Census had probably masked some of the longer-term issues, and, as Meri Huws said, perhaps lulled people into a false sense of security. The Iaith Pawb strategy, drawn up in the first Assembly, was naïve and over-optimistic. To my mind, it is questionable whether sufficient analytical work was done by the Welsh Language Board on the question – and I would also question whether the success or otherwise of schemes designed to promote the use of Welsh was actually measured effectively.

The leader of Plaid Cymru said in a debate in January 2013 that the Census results showed that we needed 'to change our Welsh language strategy completely'. I did not agree. The strategy, adopted only in 2012, was far more realistic than the Iaith Pawb strategy adopted in 2001, and demanded more of our partners, setting clear expectations on the use of Welsh Government money, and opening up new areas for development. It had been drawn up in the context of our knowledge of what was happening year on year in terms of the declining numbers of Welsh-speakers, thrown up by our own analysis in advance of the Census results. Further, as I pointed out in the Assembly, responsibility for the language between 2007 and 2011 had been in the hands of Plaid Cymru ministers. Indeed, I had inherited responsibility for the language after the Census had been carried out. The strategy which we had published in 2012 was essentially the draft strategy drawn up by Plaid's Alun Ffred Jones as Heritage Minister in the One Wales Government, with the addition of sections on technology and new media. This was not a time for playing the blame-game – it was a time for building consensus on the new strategy which in fact had been welcomed on publication by Plaid Cymru.

At the end of February 2013, I announced that we would not be adopting the proposed Welsh Language Commissioner's standards, following a meeting with the Commissioner, explaining my reasons in a long and detailed letter and a Written Statement. We did not believe that the proposed standards would allow us to lay a Regulatory Impact Assessment before the Assembly, nor would they establish clear linguistic rights for Welsh speakers. The following day, in the Assembly, Plaid Cymru sought an urgent debate on the issue that afternoon. We resisted, offering instead a debate in Government time the following week, and the request was defeated, with Plaid Cymru's Dafydd Elis-Thomas abstaining on the request.

In the Government debate on 5 March 2013, I explained our reasons for rejecting the standards and what we would now do. Legally, standards had to be made by the Welsh Ministers. I explained that the language commissioner had chosen to carry out a non-statutory consultation on her draft standards. I explained that, during the passage of the Welsh Language Measure, the then Minister for Heritage, who had responsibility for the Welsh Language, Alun Ffred Jones, had outlined the process he expected to see adopted, beginning with a statutory standards investigation. My officials had reiterated this process in a document presented to the commissioner in January 2012. The Director General of the Department for Education and Skills, Emyr Roberts, re-stated that expectation in a letter to the Commissioner in August 2012, and officials wrote again in December 2012.

We had concerns about what the Commissioner had proposed. We did not want the standards to be subject to court proceedings and legal challenge, and we felt that this was a real danger in what the Commissioner was proposing. We would now as a Government act to deliver the policy aims of the Welsh Language Measure. I made it clear that I wanted to see clear rights for

Welsh speakers in respect of Welsh language services. We envisaged being able to deliver those standards in early 2014, whereas, if we followed the Commissioner's process, we did not believe that the standards could be delivered until mid 2015.

Many people had wanted, during the process of appointment of the Commissioner, assurances that she would be independent. Some seemed to confuse that status of independence with an expectation that if she decided something, the Government would automatically implement it. In fact, the status of independence includes the possibility of being independent – and wrong. My decision not to adopt the Commissioner's draft standards for submission to the Assembly's approval, confirmed the independence of the Commissioner from Government, but confirmed also the responsibility of the Government, under the measure, to bring before the Assembly standards which we regarded as legally watertight.

The first set of Standards in relation to the Welsh language were announced on 6th January 2014 by the First Minister. The Welsh Language Commissioner will use the proposed standards as a foundation for their implementation with Councils in Wales, National Park Authorities, and Welsh Ministers.

It was inevitable that my decision not to confirm the Welsh Language Standards put forward by the Welsh Language Commissioner would be controversial. Cymdeithas yr Iaith Gymraeg made me a specific target of their campaigns. In March, I was on visits in west Wales, where I was also scheduled to deliver a speech on the language in Welsh, when I got a message that the First Minister wanted to see me back in Cardiff later that afternoon. It became clear that a re-shuffle was starting. On my way into the Ammanford venue where I was to make my speech, I was picketed by Cymdeithas members. After the speech, my Private Secretary, Matthew Mithan, a Welsh speaker from Bethesda who supported me on Welsh language policy and events, warned me that the Ministerial car had been occupied by Cymdeithas activists. I thought this was pretty silly. I had just agreed to meet Cymdeithas a couple of weeks further on to discuss a range of issues. I spoke to Colin Nosworthy, Cymdeithas's Assembly Liaison Officer, who was at the event, to suggest that if they wanted that meeting to go ahead, then their activists should leave my car immediately. They promptly did so.

Carwyn felt that, following the Census, we needed a new public initiative to engage with people on the future of the language, and so the Big Conversation – Y *Gynhadledd Fawr* – was born. This was designed to bring together all kinds of voices to debate the way forward for the language. I left the Government the week before, and the First Minister took on responsibility for the language himself and led the discussions at that event. Amongst the initiatives which I had started to boost the language were plans for an advertising campaign through English-language media to encourage more parents from English-speaking homes to send their children to Welsh-speaking schools. This was duly launched in the autumn under the slogan 'Live in Wales: Learn in Welsh?' supported by a Facebook page and other publicity.

One of the organisations which played a major role in taking forward the work on digital media was the Urdd – the young people's organisation which ran activities through the medium of Welsh. The Urdd, under its dynamic chief executive Efa Gruffydd-Jones, rightly awarded an MBE in the 2014 New Year's Honours list, was key to ensuring leisure, sports and entertainment for young people provided through the medium of Welsh outside school. We supported the Urdd with a large £800,000 grant. We also invested in its facilities in Wales. It had risen to the challenge of modernising its activities well ahead of the National Eisteddfod. The Urdd carried out research for us on how best to develop activities to support the use of Welsh amongst young people outside the classroom. Like the National Eisteddfod it developed an app explaining its Eisteddfod site. It also joined S4C in running coding lessons for children through the medium of Welsh.

I was also delighted that we were able to launch the Coleg Cymraeg Cenedlaethol in 2011. Having been involved as a student in Bangor in the 1970s in campaigns to strengthen the use of the Welsh language in higher education, this was the fulfilment of longstanding ambitions and a key commitment of the One Wales Government. Geraint Talfan Davies brought the project to fruition, chairing the implementation board for the Coleg. Subsequently, Professor Merfyn Jones took this work forward as Chair of the board of the Coleg. Dr Ioan Matthews, the chief executive, assembled a strong team of executives to take the college's development forward.

One of the main reasons for establishing the Coleg was to provide a single independent body responsible for supporting, developing and overseeing Welsh medium provision in higher education institutions in Wales. The Coleg's main aim is to increase, develop and broaden the range of Welsh medium study opportunities at universities in Wales. The Coleg, through its agreements with institutions will ensure that all funds allocated through the Coleg for Welsh medium education are used appropriately, and will ensure that this funding is additional to current institutional spending from their own budgets.

There will be firm targets for increasing the numbers of students studying through the medium of Welsh. However, the Coleg will also act as an advocate for the principle of studying through the medium of Welsh, arguing that the Welsh language cannot take its rightful place in academic life and in university education until the provision and choice for students is substantially broadened to correspond to the patterns already established in other educational sectors, including primary and secondary schools. In its first years the Coleg has registered 1,600 students as members of its academic community, along with 600 university staff; funded forty doctoral students through its research scholarships scheme; developed a Digital Resources Library for students, with e-books, video clips and podcasts and other materials, with materials available on its Porth e-learning platform; funded collaborative provision in a range of academic subject areas and supported several publications. I was particularly pleased that they were taking Welsh-language teaching to the world, making materials available on iTunes U.

Adapt or Die

A week before the Welsh Labour leadership ballot result was declared, Jane Hutt delivered an oral statement in the National Assembly outlining the Welsh Assembly Government's strategy and action plan for 21st-century higher education. She told the Assembly that the strategy, *For our Future*, built on two fundamental pillars of 'One Wales', social justice and building a stronger economy. It was, she said, 'the start of radical change in our higher education system in Wales'. She said that the funding of higher education in future would be targeted at specific strategic outcomes 'to enrich the economic and cultural life of Wales, and to drive our economy forward'. In her foreword to *For our Future*, she had said 'higher education in Wales needs to change, and change fast'.

The strategy aimed to eliminate 'wasteful local competition' and improve access to and participation in higher education. It recognised that HE providers had different strengths and missions, and the Government wanted to work in partnership with the higher education institutions to deliver the overall strategy. Higher education in Wales needed to compete internationally, deliver domestic goals such as increasing Welsh-medium HE provision through the Coleg Ffederal to be launched in 2010, prioritise research of relevance to Wales's economic and social goals, and contribute to creating a modern skilled economy. *For our Future* recognised the strengths of Welsh higher education, in particular the quality of teaching and learning, the positive experiences of students, the successes in employability, the strong record in access, and a good record in respect of knowledge exploitation with staff and graduate start-ups and spin-out companies. But more needed to be done in terms of raising participation rates from less advantaged communities, there needed to be greater diversity in the design of provision, more collaboration with FE with a regional dimension to the planning and delivery of higher education, and a stronger effort to win research council funding.

More radically, the document made it clear that public funding would follow the strategy. 'Only institutions that can deliver these priorities can expect to be the beneficiaries.' HEFCW would have to put in place a regional planning and delivery structure to ensure that this happened. The document made it clear that there would need to be a change in the relationship between government and the higher education sector. Academic freedom and institutional autonomy was protected, but there needed to be a re-consideration of the relationship between autonomy and accountability. The document said 'a national higher education system for Wales will be created' and funding would underpin the planning and delivery of this, and there would be a need to ensure an infrastructure which demonstrates coherence and better responsiveness. Institutional governance needed to be reviewed to ensure that effective challenge was being brought into play at institutional level.

I had no problem with *For our Future* and fully endorsed it. Carwyn's manifesto had contained an explicit commitment to ensuring that HE institutions in Wales worked with the large anchor companies of the Welsh economy to strengthen research capacity – and for Wales to win a larger proportion of Research Council funding.

However, I was less convinced about the capacity of the higher education sector – either the institutions themselves or the Higher Education Funding Council for Wales (HEFCW) – to deliver the *For our Future* goals. I felt it would require a clear steer from the government about priorities and our commitment to delivering on them. In particular, I felt that the higher education reconfiguration agenda, the policy of successive Welsh Assembly Governments since the 2002 policy document,

Reaching Higher, designed to strengthen the sector by reducing overhead costs and attract research investment, would need a specific push. I was prepared to give the reconfiguration strategy up to three years – by then, we would be more than a decade on from *Reaching Higher,* and if things could not be achieved in that time-scale then they never would.

More recently, the Audit Committee of the National Assembly had produced a scathing report on the higher education sector's commitment to Wales and to the reconfiguration agenda in April 2009. The committee was chaired by the thoughtful Conservative Assembly Member David Melding, now the Deputy Presiding Officer of the National Assembly. Its report, *Collaboration between Higher Education Institutions,* was unanimous. It stated that barriers to collaboration stemmed from the autonomy of institutions, and the Government might need levers other than the existing Reconfiguration and Collaboration Fund operated by HEFCW to drive change. The committee felt that 'unlike the position in Scotland, there is little of a community HE culture amongst institutions in Wales'. The committee endorsed the idea that the Government should use core funding to drive reform. Damningly, the committee said this:

> We were struck by the difficulty that the Assembly Government and HEFCW had in terms of bending institutions' minds to the Assembly Government's ways of thinking; we likened it to herding cats. It is also of some concern that most institutions seem to consider that there is no such thing as a Welsh HE sector.

The committee said there was a need for 'a sea change in the relationship between the Assembly Government and HE institutions'. It concluded:

> We think that the Assembly Government and HEFCW between them need to be much more robust in this area. There seems to us to be some complacency here.

> Institutions appear not to recognise that the world has moved on since devolution in 1999, and that, to all intents and purposes, they are very much part of a Welsh HE sector and a wider Welsh public sector.

The committee said that the Assembly Government and HEFCW should use the core grant to institutions, as appropriate, to drive forward their goals. I agreed with the committee. Failure to see themselves as part of a Welsh HE sector had cost institutions dearly. They were failing to win a high enough share of Research Council funding, not least through a failure to collaborate. The absence of a veterinary school in Wales meant that they could not claim to offer a full prospectus to students from Wales for every subject. That was something that could and should have been resolved collectively. It is now under active discussion. But national leadership through HEFCW also needed galvanising.

The reconfiguration agenda not only pre-dated my time as Education Minister, and had been the policy of my predecessors, it had also commanded all-party support in the Assembly since its earliest days. It even pre-dated devolution. At the request of the Secretary of State for Wales, prior to the Assembly coming into existence, HEFCW had written a paper called *The Scope for Institutional Mergers at the Higher Education Level* in September 1999. The paper noted that a Welsh higher education sector, as such, had been created by the 1992 Further and Higher Education Act, and concerns about the relative size of Welsh institutions had been a focus of HEFCW's attention since its creation. Indeed, in 1994 HEFCW had established a merger and integration fund. HEFCW's paper said that it saw a case for five or six 'multi-mission' higher education institutions in Wales.

The Assembly Education and Lifelong Learning Committee, chaired in 2000 by the Plaid Cymru AM Cynog Dafis, produced a wide-ranging report, noting HEFCW's observation that five or six institutions might be the optimum. This was subsequently taken forward through the Welsh Assembly Government's strategy for higher education, published in March 2002 by

Education Minister Jane Davidson, *Reaching Higher*, which explicitly said that 're-configuration and collaboration must be at the heart of the strategy for HE in Wales'. However, as Geraint Talfan Davies recounts in his autobiography *At Arm's Length*, 'localism constantly trumped the still novel concept of national objectives... higher education provided a salutary example of where the proper defence of the arm's length principle was not followed through with a reciprocal obligation to autonomous reform'.

My officials were already working on HEFCW's remit letter for 2010-11, and I was determined that it should send some clear signals that funding in future would follow strategic priorities. Universities rightly wish to protect their autonomy, and I understood that that autonomy was important in respecting academic freedom. Section 68 (3) of the FE and HE Act 1992 was designed to stop ministers determining what subjects HE institutions could teach or research. But I was concerned that academic freedom was increasingly used as a rationale for 'whatever the vice chancellor wants to do'. I decided that if we could, we would ensure tighter control over higher education capital spending. Officials' early draft of the remit letter was in my view too weak, and I sent some lines of my own through to them. I warned HEFCW's chair, Roger Thomas, and chief executive, Phil Gummett, at our first meeting in February 2010, that their remit letter would be the most 'dirigiste' ever sent by an Education Minister, and it would test the law.

I decided that I would make an early start on the HE governance review referred to in *For our Future*. With lawyers, we considered whether we should have a legislative competence order – the process under the 2006 Government of Wales Act to bring powers to the National Assembly/Welsh Ministers on a case-by-case basis – to allow ministers to fund higher education directly. We also discussed with lawyers whether we could control all higher education capital spending directly.

Carwyn authorised me to take on the well-respected outgoing Bangor University vice chancellor Merfyn Jones as a specialist adviser on higher education, for two days a week. Merfyn had also carried out an important review of the funding of higher education for Jane Hutt and knew the key arguments well. I was now also starting the search for someone to lead the HE governance review.

One organisation that took governance seriously – at least, it had done in the past – was the BBC. The BBC had to address similar issues of managing creative individuals as did higher education, also operated independently of government and protected that independence just as fiercely as did universities. John McCormick, former Controller of BBC Scotland, and the former Secretary to the BBC Board of Governors, an even more relevant role, was an obvious choice. John had been chair of the Scottish Qualifications Authority and had come into broadcasting from education. He had direct experience of governance of several higher education institutions in Scotland. He ticked all the boxes. Alongside John, I appointed a group of senior people who knew higher education but who did not work in the higher education system in Wales.

Higher Education Wales (HEW), the body that represents vice chancellors in Wales, had organised a 'Governor Development Day' for the 3rd March and I was due to speak. I announced the review of governance there. I said that the review would consider whether support independent of HE management should be given to members of HE institution governing bodies to enable to carry out their task of holding HE management to account.

I made it clear that I did not expect governors simply to be cheerleaders for their institutions. It was not that we feared that there was a crisis in governance of higher education institutions in Wales, or that there was corruption or maladministration or an issue with quality. The real issue was whether the governing bodies of institutions were thinking widely about the focus of their institution, the interests of both existing and future learners at a time of considerable change in the higher education sector, and whether they as individuals had an understanding of the wider context of Welsh Assembly Government ambitions for the sector.

At the conference, I took a number of questions from governors about what we were looking for. I waited for a while, then asked the fifth questioner how she had been appointed as a university governor. 'I got a phone-call', she said. One university administrator later told me 'at that point, we could have killed her.' For me, that illustrated the cosiness of higher education governance in Wales. It seemed that the vice chancellors essentially picked the people to whom they were accountable. Professor Dylan Jones-Evans – a Conservative and not a natural supporter of mine – said that the announcement of the governance review 'certainly set the cat amongst the pigeons and has let the university sector know who is actually paying the bills at a time when there is clear inevitability about future cuts in expenditure.'

We also wanted to be clear about the national governance of higher education, and that brought me to HEFCW. By now I had issued my remit letter. I said that I expected there to be a step-change in their approach to funding, and referred to the Wales Audit Office and Audit Committee concerns about the need to use core funding to drive forward strategic goals. I told the Council I wanted them to create a Strategic Implementation Fund which would ultimately include the majority of revenue funding. Capital funding should be focused on *For our Future* goals and all existing plans should be re-assessed against these. Capital spending should not be allowed to drive unnecessary competition between institutions. From 2011-12 I expected there to be a single HE capital pool and HEFCW would have to submit an annual capital plan to the government for approval. HEFCW was asked to take forward the regional planning agenda and reminded of its responsibility to protect strategic subjects on an all-Wales basis. The letter introduced a 'soft cap' on student numbers for the first time – caps on numbers were operating in other parts of the UK already. The letter reinforced messages on access and the need to increase the share of Research Council funding. I also referred to the forthcoming governance review, saying that I expected this to look at the University of Wales. I explained the philosophy behind this at a meeting with the HEFCW Council members on the 10th March, saying HEFCW needed to decide whether it was part of the solution or part of the problem. I was concerned that higher education governance in Wales was the last resting place of the crachach. I said that we needed to see from HEFCW an implementation plan for *For our Future* in May and that HEFCW's plans needed to be more radical.

It was clear that HEFCW had got the message, when two weeks later it announced forthcoming HE allocations with the Strategic Implementation Fund accounting for 20 per cent of the grant. *Times Higher Education* (*THE*) described this as 'the biggest overhaul in funding policy for over a decade.' I was clear that the message was getting through when I read one vice-chancellor telling the *Times Higher* that 'with a minister like this there is no room for anyone to hide.' Some in HE were hostile. Sir Emyr Jones Parry, recently appointed chair of Aberystwyth University, criticised *For our Future* and warned me at a meeting that he wouldn't tolerate Aberystwyth being turned into Ceredigion Community College. We had no such plan.

During May I received the PwC report on the cost of administering the education system in Wales. The higher education sector did not like its conclusion that only 48 per cent of HE spending went on teaching, research and knowledge transfer, and 52 per cent on support services, though some academics wrote to me to ask why we needed more managers in higher education, and why economies of scale had not been achieved following a merger, and why there were so many internal committees. PwC said there was urgency in respect of reconfiguration given the likely budget cuts. Fewer than half of higher education staff were on the academic and research side.

At the end of May I delivered a lecture at Cardiff University entitled 'Leadership in Higher Education – in difficult times'. I said in the new context of austerity we needed real leadership, but speaking bluntly, in my first six months in post I had begun to wonder whether the higher education sector wanted the Welsh Assembly Government to have a higher education strategy, or whether it believed that there was such a thing as a Welsh HE sector, or whether it welcomed devolution or democratic accountability. I said we had an agenda of democratisation in education, moving to the next stage of what Raymond Williams had called 'the long revolution'. In HE our agenda of democratisation included our ambition to widen participation in HE, and I announced additional funding for the University of the Heads of the Valleys Initiative; the need to refocus the relationship between HE and government; the governance of HE institutions, and the role of HE institutions within their regions and communities. I noted that there was a significant number of academic collaborations under way and suggested that the academics were rather ahead of institutional leaders.

I set out the real scale of issues facing the Welsh higher education sector. In terms of turnover, the picture given by 2007-8 figures was stark:

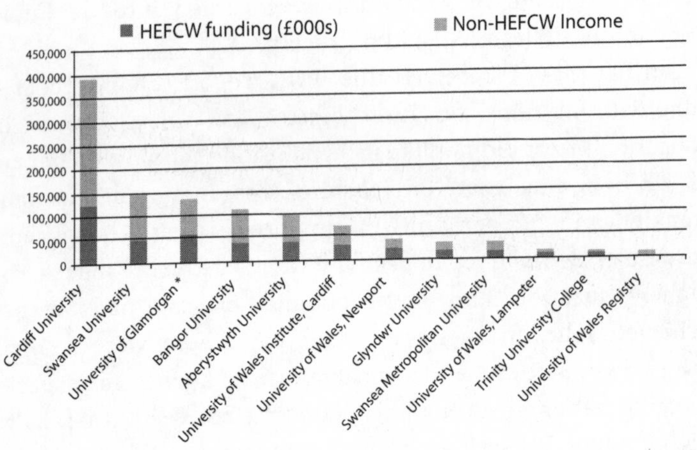

Figure 1

Welsh universities were in general not of the same scale as universities elsewhere in the UK:

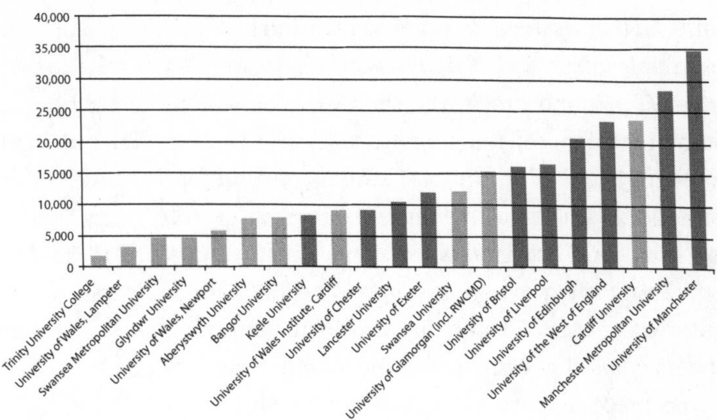

Figure 2

I pointed out that political intervention had been behind the merger in 1987 of the then University College Cardiff and the University of Wales Institute of Science and Technology. Cardiff was in danger of closing on the eve of the 1987 General Election. The then Secretary of State for Wales, Nicholas Edwards, recalled in his autobiography that Mrs Thatcher was against the bail-out of a university, and thought that Cardiff should be made an example. Edwards responded by doing a deal with the then University Grants Committee. He said in his autobiography:

> At that time, the Welsh Office had no direct responsibility, financial or otherwise, for higher education in Wales, but in order to obtain an agreement I offered to find £1 million towards the required package and the deal was done.

The speech was seen as setting a new direction for the HE sector, and introducing a new sense of urgency. I had a wide range of supportive messages in the days afterwards, particularly from serving academics. The director of the Institute of Welsh Affairs, John Osmond, called it 'remarkable', 'highly prescriptive and radical in its demands' and 'a wake-up call to vice chancellors across Wales'. The vice chancellor of Swansea University told *Times Higher Education* I had 'energised the sector'.

As requested, HEFCW delivered their action plan to take forward *For our Future* and I took it to the One Wales Cabinet on 21st June. The action plan set out a series of items to take forward in the context of HEFCW's corporate strategy, including the development of a national system of higher education, more coherently planned provision, and 'substantially fewer institutions'. The HEFCW corporate strategy which accompanied the Cabinet paper set the target that at least 75 per cent of the higher education institutions in Wales would have an annual income in excess of the UK median, with no institution to be in the lower quartile by 2013-13. The Cabinet minutes approving the paper explicitly noted the 'need for substantially fewer institutions'.

A week later, I made a statement on this to the Assembly in plenary. I explained how HEFCW's plan built on *For our Future* and was a response to the remit letter. I explained HEFCW's target and said:

> This target does not mean fewer students, but it is likely to mean fewer vice chancellors. We will have significantly fewer HE institutions in Wales, but they will be larger and stronger.

I stated that our agenda was the democratisation of higher education in Wales. David Melding, the Conservative who had chaired the Audit Committee when it reported on collaboration in higher education, said

> I have no doubt that we have heard this afternoon one of the more significant statements that we will hear in this Assembly. I am not quite sure whether I am in shock or in awe.

A week later I met Higher Education Wales (HEW), the organisation representing the vice chancellors. These were regular meetings but were weirdly unfocused and inconclusive. The impression one took away from them was that the vice chancellors could barely agree on a collective position and probably didn't like each other very much. However, at this particular meeting one of the vice chancellors said that there had been more discussion on merger and collaboration in the previous six weeks than there had been in the previous six years.

The nature of these meetings barely changed over the first eighteen months I was Minister. Indeed, in that period, the most coherent critique of our HE policies came from the National Union of Students in Wales, then under the intelligent leadership of the persuasive Katie Dalton, always ready with a well-crafted quote, often delivered just after 6.00 a.m. on the BBC's *Good Morning Wales* programme, or via the industrious *Western Mail* journalist, Gareth Evans.

In June 2011 my new special adviser, Matt Greenough, accompanied me to one of the HEW meetings and came away shell-shocked at how directionless it was. Thankfully, Bangor's vice chancellor, John Hughes, then took a grip of the situation and turned them into far more business-like occasions. Meetings with the chairs of higher education institutions, known as CHEW, could be even more pointless, although they did give me the opportunity to tease Aberystwyth's chair, Sir Emyr Jones Parry, who recounted at one meeting how he had turned up to his first university council meeting to find that he was expected to sit in a kind of throne on the stage. 'You must be used to that, Emyr', I said.

By the summer of 2010, the policy direction was set. I was questioned on the higher education situation when I gave evidence to the Assembly Finance Committee in July on the PwC Report on the Cost of Administering the Education System. I told them 'I think that the message for higher education is "'adapt or die", to be blunt.'

In December that year, shortly after setting out the distinctive Welsh response to the implications of the Browne review, I told Welsh higher education leaders at a conference in Carmarthen that it was better to use core funding to drive change in a time of rising budgets – 'but the HE sector in Wales has had a decade of rising budgets and I am afraid that overall, with some worthy exceptions, HE managements have failed to respond adequately to our agenda.' Failing to respond, I said, was costing the sector money. We now looked to the sector to address the inefficiencies in HE on lower budgets. In the Assembly budget for 2011-12, developed in the context of the UK coalition government's comprehensive spending review published in October 2010, higher education spending in Wales was set to fall over the next three years. The message was therefore clear, and I repeated it: 'adapt or die'. I also warned vice chancellors that there would be no automatic access to the new fees regime. I said that would depend on the willingness of vice chancellors to sign up to the reconfiguration agenda – much to the fury of NUS Wales, whose President Katie Dalton, said 'it is entirely unacceptable to use this tactic to deliver the merger agenda.' Later that month, Swansea Metropolitan University and Trinity St David's announced their plans to merge, and just before Christmas, HEFCW stated that it wanted no more than six institutions in Wales by March 2013 – down from eleven.

On 17th February 2011 John McCormick submitted to me his group's report on the governance of higher education in Wales, *Achievement and Accountability*. I took the report to Cabinet on the eve of the Assembly's dissolution for the 2011 elections.

The group identified that there was a continued collective lack of commitment in the sector to address Welsh strategic priorities, with an obvious unwillingness to embrace real change and real systemic reconfiguration with any sense of urgency. Institutional self-interest too often preceded national need and interest. There was scope for greater dynamism both from the sector and HEFCW, a new system which embedded a real energy for change and created a sustainable model for addressing the challenges of the future. The Review therefore proposed:

- a new arm's length body, provisionally called Universities Wales, with increased powers of direction and intervention and more clearly defined accountability to the Assembly Government for the performance of the sector; and

- a defined role for sector representatives on the new body to ensure 'a mutual responsibility to deliver'.

The new body should have more input in assessing quality of governance and leadership in higher education.

At an institutional level, the group suggested that, overall, institutional governors failed to inject any sense of dynamism or innovation into the system; offered no real monitoring of the executive or institutional direction; and did little to ensure alignment between the strategic direction of the institution and national strategic imperatives. The group said *'one interviewee went so far as to refer to the governing body involvement in strategic planning as limited to 'improving the punctuation'.'* They argued that 'It is entirely proper that institutional governors should take account of the needs of the future student body, the longer-term interests of research and the interests of the wider society in which they operate.' Boards should be smaller and more business-like; there should continue to be staff and student representation on boards; there should be a rigorous, nationally consistent and regular self evaluation programme overseen by the national body; a more professional and transparent approach to appointments of governors; and stakeholder forums within institutions.

In the chamber the next day I made it clear that at that stage we had made no decision about the need for an arm's length funding and planning body. I knew from my conversations with John McCormick that his group had debated this issue long and hard before making their recommendation. I did not want the sector, however, to think that we were a soft touch.

If higher education institutions had any remaining doubts about the competence of the Assembly in regulating the sector, those would have been ended by the result of the March 2011 referendum on law-making powers, ending the need for legislative competence orders to widen the scope of the powers of the

Assembly and the Welsh Assembly Government. In the manifesto for the May 2011 Assembly elections, Welsh Labour stated its policy on higher education, with commitments to create a strategic planning and funding body, using the full range of powers including legislative powers to re-shape the sector, driving transformation and rationalisation to ensure a smaller number of stronger universities, strengthening governance and ensuring there were properly funded student unions in all higher education institutions.

In my 2011-12 remit letter to HEFCW I had made it clear that I was ready to use powers under the Education Reform Act to force mergers in higher education if necessary. I asked HEFCW to provide me with advice on the future structure of the higher education system in Wales. Shortly after the Assembly election, HEFCW presented me with its plans for the further stages of reconfiguration and I published these for consultation on July 13. Their report recommended:

> Cardiff University should remain committed to securing a position as a world class research-intensive university, while collaborating particularly with Swansea in areas where together they would be more effective;
>
> Swansea University should maintain its aim of developing as a research-intensive university, and strengthen key research and teaching partnerships with Cardiff.
>
> Aberystwyth and Bangor Universities should substantially widen and deepen their strategic partnership, and should develop a longer-term plan for merger;
>
> Glyndŵr University should develop strong structural relationships with a range of FE colleges within a group structure led by Aberystwyth and Bangor Universities in order to expand the range of HE provision available in NE Wales;
>
> The University of Glamorgan, University of Wales Institute, Cardiff and University of Wales, Newport should merge to create a true 'metropolitan' university in SE Wales;

> University of Wales Trinity Saint David and Swansea Metropolitan University should merge as already planned, potentially but not necessarily also with the University of Wales.

Of these, I was well aware that the two most controversial proposals affected Glyndwr in North-East Wales and South-East Wales. Civic pride was always likely to be an issue. As Professor Sir Deian Hopkin had said back in 2001, 'the truth is that staff, students, even governors, continue to believe that their universities are unique institutions with separate cultures and ploughing a separate furrow'. In respect of Glyndwr, its formation had been specifically referenced in the One Wales Government document, and its role was underpinned by civic pride in the Wrexham area. In the South-East, there were issues of civic pride in Newport in relation to the University of Wales, Newport, but we were well aware that the vice chancellor of UWIC, shortly to be renamed Cardiff Metropolitan University, was deeply hostile to merger. We had our manifesto commitment and I took the precaution of ensuring Cabinet backing for the proposals.

As the Cabinet minutes record 'The paper contained the key components of the Welsh Government's response to the report, including its proposals for the reform of higher education governance.' Our plan was for HEFCW to be reformed with increased responsibility to regulate, monitor and intervene in higher education institutional governance in Wales. We would have a national code of governance, which all governing bodies would be expected to comply with. The plan was to hold a consultation in autumn 2011 leading to legislation. The Cabinet paper noted how the proposals would effectively implement two of Welsh Labour's manifesto commitments in respect of HE. However, the paper differed from McCormick in one crucial respect. The McCormick review had envisaged a new regulatory body with an equal number of institutional representatives and independent representatives. The Cabinet paper argued that this did not allow the independent representatives to dominate; did not allow full stakeholder representation (e.g. of FE institutions delivering HE, or of the Open University (OU). I subsequently outlined the plans for the new national body in a speech to the Leadership Foundation for Higher Education in December, warning the HE sector that 'there is nothing in the manifesto that says that that planning and funding body could not be chaired by the Minister.'

The Cabinet also discussed the plans to merge several of Wales's smaller higher education institutions and supported the case for the reform of higher education. One of the issues to which I had been alerted early on was the situation of the University of Wales. Following the decision by most of its former constituent colleges to take on their own degree-awarding responsibilities, this had been an institution in search of a role for the best part of a decade. Its 2005 assessment by the Quality Assurance Agency (QAA) had declared it had 'limited confidence' in the institution, and senior people in several universities had concerns about its management and focus. During 2010 these concerns exploded into the public eye following a report by the BBC which raised concerns about its international associations. Many higher education institutions validate courses overseas, but there were clearly problems here. BBC Wales continued its enquiries and the *THE* was later to describe the University of Wales as 'a validation machine'. I felt increasingly that the adverse publicity around the university was having an impact on the brand of Wales internationally and on the reputation of higher education in Wales. It mattered personally to many of us in the Assembly, and our constituents, whose degrees, in the days when Bangor, Aberystwyth, Cardiff and Swansea were constituent colleges of a federal university, were actually University of Wales degrees. It was clear that the governing body of the University of Wales was not going to get a grip of the issue without external pressure from the media and the government. I had asked the McCormick review to look at this: it reached a number of conclusions about the University of Wales. It rightly recognised the historic role of the University, saying 'For its first 100 years the UoW represented a symbol of nationhood for many', but said that the current role of the University of Wales was ambiguous and posed reputational risk, and that it had to reform radically if it was to add any value to Wales. The status quo was not sustainable, so three realistic options were identified: the absorption of the university into one or more of the higher education institutions to create a single unified institution; the transformation of the university into a service organisation for the whole of the sector in Wales, involving the absorption of Higher Education Wales, the chairs of Higher Education Wales and the Wales International Consortium; or the winding down and eventual closure of the organisation.

In June 2011, the QAA had made it clear that weaknesses in the University of Wales external validation arrangements had to be addressed as a 'matter of urgency'. The QAA said that the university had failed to carry out thorough checks in relation to institutions in Singapore and Thailand in particular. HEFCW said that the QAA had identified 'a considerable range of serious shortcomings' and 'a failure to establish proper control' by the university. The university accepted that its arrangements were 'no longer fit for purpose'. I said that the University had let Wales down.

Sadly, the University of Wales had become a case study in how not to manage relationships with overseas institutions and was regularly featured in the pages of the *THE* between 2010 and 2012, as well as the Welsh media, for the wrong reasons. Claims of alleged 'visa scams' in a further BBC Wales programme titled *Cash for Qualifications* didn't help; nor did problems with what had been a high-profile scheme known as the Prince of Wales Innovation Scholarships, funded with European monies which was suspended in October 2011 following information supplied by a whistle-blower and a subsequent Welsh Government internal audit investigation which found that the business model was significantly different from that originally approved by the Wales European Funding Office (WEFO). The scheme was closed down.

I was also made aware by a different whistle-blower of relationships which the University of Wales had with some fundamentalist Christian colleges that were allegedly homophobic or taught Creationism.

In October 2011, the new vice chancellor of the University, Medwin Hughes, who as vice chancellor of Trinity St Davids, one of the remaining constituent colleges of the university, had played a blinder behind the scenes in sorting out the situation, said that the university would in future only award degrees on courses designed and fully controlled by the university itself. In a statement, I recognised the historic role of the University of Wales:

> The University of Wales has a long and illustrious history. As an institution, it has helped to create and define the modern character of Wales. Many Assembly Members and many thousands of people all over the world are proud holders of University of Wales degrees.

I reminded members that:

> McCormick considered that the University of Wales, because it receives so little public funding, '…is the nearest thing Wales has to a private institution in higher education. However, it is an institution that is deploying a national asset – the all-Wales brand – and yet has no national accountability.'

I said that the chair of the Council of the University of Wales should consider his position in the interest of the institution and of Wales, a position which was supported in the Assembly Chamber by representatives of other parties, including Dafydd Elis-Thomas of Plaid Cymru and the Conservative Leader of the Opposition, Andrew R.T. Davies. In an interview with the BBC I said that I felt it should be given a decent burial.

Indeed, five of Wales's leading vice chancellors were also

concerned that the University of Wales was damaging the reputation of Welsh higher education internationally and called for it to be wound up. The same month it was effectively abolished after agreeing to subsume itself under the 190-year-old charter of the Trinity St David, one of the oldest university charters outside Oxbridge and Scotland, when Trinity merged with Swansea Metropolitan University. Its chairman announced his resignation 'in the best interests of the transformed university'.

There was understandable concern as to what might happen to some of the services associated with the University of Wales, including the University of Wales Press, the University of Wales Dictionary, the Centre for Advanced Welsh and Celtic Studies and the historic Gregynog Hall. In December 2012, I was able to confirm that Medwin Hughes had said these would all be assured under a 'Wales pledge'. For contractual reasons, the University of Wales will have to continue to validate some courses until 2017-18.

HEFCW's proposal to merge Glyndwr with Bangor and Aberystwyth provoked a strong reaction, with newspapers in north and north-east Wales and local politicians expressing their concern at the proposals. I had some sympathy with their position, as it was not clear to me that the geography of north Wales would lend itself to a sustainable position, though I had less sympathy with some of the arguments being used privately about the proposal, which seemed to be based on a fear of Welsh-speaking north-west Wales dominating the strategy for higher education in north-east Wales. NUS Wales President Katie Dalton, herself a graduate of a post-'92 institution, made the case that retaining a post-'92 institution in north-east Wales was vital in order to maintain a commitment to local recruitment and widening access in north Wales, which was very different to the mission of pre-'92 universities such as Aberystwyth and Bangor.

However, I was concerned about the long-term sustainability of Glyndwr – particularly after its decision to opt for a lower fees model in 2011- its ability to support the research and skills needs of industry in north-east Wales, and its generally opportunistic strategy. HEFCW felt that its position looked 'challenging in the long-term, and is sub-optimal in terms of provision for NE Wales'. My private view was that Glyndwr's future lay in a closer relationship with the very strong FE institutions in its region.

In the case of south-east Wales, I was under no illusions about the likely reaction from UWIC, now re-named Cardiff Metropolitan University, though I had little sympathy with them. As the *Western Mail* noted in February 2011:

> UWIC has regularly dug its heels in and a reluctance to engage in collaboration has been all too apparent.

UWIC had theoretically explored merging with Swansea Met and Trinity St David's during 2011, but had pulled out in July when its other partners were already becoming sceptical of its commitment to the process. During my entire time as Education Minister, the only occasion when I was lobbied by students about the quality of their university courses was by students from Cardiff Met who had lost lecturers in the middle of their course. However, the students' union at Cardiff Met was ineffectual in representing their interests. It was the only university students' union in Wales not affiliated to the National Union of Students in Wales, and lacked the independence from administration control that NUS-affiliated unions enjoyed. It was clear from the beginning that we would get little encouragement in our plans from Cardiff Met's vice chancellor and governing body, though we had support from the University and College Union representing the academic staff, and there were plenty of insiders happy to share information with me. There was, I felt, a general lack of understanding of the position of higher education in Cardiff. Cardiff University was well-known, but too many in the capital seemed unaware that the University of Glamorgan, which now included the Royal Welsh College of Music and Drama, as well as its own splendid Atrium campus, had 5000 students in the city. Glamorgan also had a significantly stronger research base than Newport or UWIC.

However, the most important factor for us was making progress, and we were not going to be held back on the reconfiguration agenda by UWIC, or Cardiff Met, as it was now known. We wanted to ensure that their foot-dragging could not hold back the evident progress that was being made by Newport and Glamorgan. Although I was prepared to use the powers under the Education Reform Act, I did not myself believe I could do so unless we had the support of another political party. It was a fundamental step and really required greater political consensus than a simple majority vote. But it was necessary to keep the pressure on Cardiff Met to see what could be achieved. In the case of Newport, where I had expected the civic pride issue to emerge, the leadership shown by the governing body and its chairman, Andrew Wilkinson, was very important. The institution called for a 'genuinely new' entrepreneurial university for South-East Wales. The University of Glamorgan meanwhile expressed its support for a new institution which would be 'of a size and scale to compete with its cross-border neighbours'.

Cardiff Met's approach was different. Its new chair said Glamorgan had always had a predatory attitude towards it, a view that was majestically rebutted by former University of Glamorgan Chair of Governors, the respected businessman Rudi Plaut, in a letter to the *Western Mail* on 17th October 2011:

> Our offer to merge the two boards of governors, so as to ensure that any merger would not be seen to be a 'take over' was never reported to the board of what is now UWIC.
>
> We learnt that instead the board was told that Glamorgan wished to take it over to sell all its valuable property, which was totally untrue.

Opposition from Cardiff Met to the proposal appeared to focus on a feared loss of identity, without any evaluation of the strength a new institution could bring. Current and past students of Cardiff Met's former incarnation, UWIC, canvassed by their institution, were opposed, but UCU, representing the academic staff, was in favour.

We received 400 responses to the consultation, and I took a paper to Cabinet on the 22nd November. The paper broadly accepted HEFCW's recommendations, but rejected the proposal that Glyndwr should move to a group structure managed by Aberystwyth and Bangor. Instead I would commission a review of HE provision in north east Wales and of Glyndwr's role in both this and in building stronger links with FE provision in the region, which Professor Sir Adrian Webb was to chair.

We saw no need for Aberystwyth and Bangor to head to merger, but agreed the recommendation to merge the University of Glamorgan, Cardiff Metropolitan and University of Wales, Newport, which would be subject to a detailed consultation with the bodies concerned. The merger proposal for Swansea Metropolitan, Trinity St David and the University of Wales was already progressing well. The proposals would result in seven institutions remaining in place compared with the originally envisaged six. Cabinet approved the paper, and I made a statement explaining what we proposed to do in the Assembly Chamber on 29th November.

It was clear from the responses of Opposition spokespeople that they would not – at that stage – support a forced dissolution of an institution, but we could not afford to lose momentum if we were to hit our own deadlines for reconfiguration, and I was determined not to back off at that point. During a debate a week later I said we preferred voluntary collaboration to forced mergers, and that is what we would be seeking to encourage. However, we also believed in planning our HE provision, as the One Wales Government said, and not leaving it to the market as they did in England. That means that if we had to use the powers of dissolution set out in the Education Reform Act 1988 as a last resort, we would be prepared to do so. It would be bizarre if, having campaigned in a referendum for additional powers, including powers over higher education, politicians in Wales said that they would be afraid to use the powers that they already have. Plaid Cymru, unfortunately, were clearly going to bottle it. I also used the opportunity to set out our ambition for a new merged institution in south-east Wales, which, I said, 'could be the most powerful post-'92 institution in the whole of the United Kingdom.'

During 2012, the debate intensified. Previous reports for and against university mergers in south-east Wales were pulled off library shelves, dusted down and scrutinised for helpful sentences. I appointed the vice chancellor of the University of Exeter, Professor Sir Steve Smith, possibly the most successful vice chancellor in the UK in terms of the progress he had led in his own institution, as an independent advisor on the situation in south-east Wales. Since Steve became vice chancellor in 2002, Exeter rose from 34th in the university rankings to 10th – 12th in *The Guardian* and 7th in the *Sunday Times* – has joined the Russell Group and expanded its student intake and campus facilities. I held meetings with each of the three universities in the south-east. I put forward three routes – creating a new institution, dissolving all three; dissolving two into a third lead institution; or voluntary merger of two with the third being dissolved.

In July 2012, the University of Glamorgan and the University of Wales, Newport, revealed they had begun positive discussions on a merger, with a joint working group consisting of managers and governors taking the plans forward. They said that their plan would be sufficiently flexible to welcome other partners if required. I welcomed their news as 'the first major step in strengthening higher education provision in south-east Wales'. Steve Smith's report was published later that month and argued for the merger. Steve had held more than fifty meetings and phone conversations with key stakeholders. He said that the current structure was 'sub-optimal' and said south-east Wales needs one successful Russell Group university and one successful post-'92 university. Steve said he thought it would be increasingly difficult for Cardiff Met to prosper and would face 'fiscal attrition on a year-by-year basis'. Along with Steve's report, officials had developed a Strategic Outline Case for the merger using the Treasury's 'Five Case Model'.

Student dissatisfaction with courses at Cardiff Metropolitan University, expressed in the National Student Survey, was leaked to the *Western Mail* in October 2012, which showed that many students were concerned that their final degree and grading was undermined by a lack of teaching continuity and staffing after the university had made lecturers redundant. Students felt they had been poorly informed about these changes. Staff turnover was also high on some courses; some lecturers were felt not to have the specialist experience necessary to teach the courses and there were absences by lecturers at short notice. As well as performing poorly in the National Student Survey, Cardiff Met dropped seventeen places to 109 in the *Sunday Times University Guide*.

We published proposals for the dissolution of Cardiff Met and Newport and went to consultation. Discussions between Glamorgan and Newport were progressing fast and there were strong prospects of the merger taking place. Cardiff Met, by contrast, continued to demonstrate that it was not interested. Much as I had expected from the beginning, they seemed to have little intention of being a willing partner. The institution was not important enough to our strategy to continue to waste energy on it, when this might obstruct a positive and voluntary merger between Glamorgan and Newport.

The University of Glamorgan was understandably sceptical about Cardiff Met's willingness to work with others and its chair, Professor John Andrews, as a former chief executive of HEFCW during the abortive Glamorgan/UWIC merger talks in 2004, had been here before. When I was convinced that Glamorgan's merger with Newport was unstoppable, I decided to scrap the consultation on the dissolution of Cardiff Met. That meant that Glamorgan and Newport would be free to merge. The new University of South Wales launched in April 2013 was headed by the dynamic Glamorgan vice chancellor Julie Lydon. In the summer Trinity St David's and Swansea Met formally merged. We could now safely say that the reconfiguration agenda had been completed.

In July 2012 I published a white paper on the proposed FE and HE Bill. We had already imposed conditions on HEFCW to ensure regional coherence in its 2012-13 remit letter. The white paper noted that from the 2012-13 academic year onwards, the majority of HE teaching funding would move from teaching grant to student fee grants and fee loans. It was possible that by 2014-15 some institutions would no longer receive teaching grant from HEFCW. This would have implications for HEFCW's role in fee planning, ensuring quality and controlling student numbers. The White Paper therefore sought provision for HEFCW to have regulatory oversight of all HE provision delivered in Wales by HEIs, and also of that delivered by other providers with courses designated for statutory student support specifically. These powers would allow us to control the operations of private providers being introduced in England should they seek to operate in Wales. The consultation on the bill also included the suggestion that there should be a provision in the Bill to enable HE provision to be funded directly by Welsh Ministers in instances where it is strategically appropriate to do so (the SNP Scottish Government subsequently proposed more interventionist powers than we were considering).

Following the strong representations by NUS Wales during the drafting of fees plan regulations in 2011, we had made it clear that we expected to see Welsh institutions setting the agenda on student representation and student voice. We believed that students should have a real say in the governance arrangements of their institutions, underpinned by well-funded students' unions. Following our regulations, in 2011 HEFCW published guidance on Student Charters, and we looked to all our higher education institutions to have a Student Charter in place by August 2012. We also said that students' unions should also be properly resourced so that they can represent their members effectively, and warned higher education institutions against reducing student union funding. Now the white paper included commitments to fair funding of students' unions to be monitored by HEFCW.

The consultation response resulted in a fair amount of agreement except around the issue of whether the Welsh Government should be able to fund higher education provision directly. With the completion of the reconfiguration agenda, it was less certain that we would want that power – and there was a danger that the Office of National Statistics might reclassify higher education institutions as part of government, meaning their borrowing would count as our borrowing. The new proposals meant that any provider offering courses to students from Wales if it were to benefit from Welsh Government support through fee grants or fee loans would have to have charitable status, as universities did, and fee plans in place, with a strong role for HEFCW's role to take action where necessary to guarantee the quality of provision. HEFCW would be able to ensure compliance across the sector with a Financial and Governance Code of Practice with which each institution would comply. The Code would be laid before the National Assembly by Welsh Ministers. In 2014, Huw Lewis published the FE and HE Bill designed to address the regulation of higher education in the new fees era. The McCormick proposals are for future legislation.

In the autumn of 2013, Sir Adrian Webb's report on the future of higher education in north-east Wales was published. Sir Adrian's report stated clearly that the status quo is not an option; and north-east Wales needs a HE presence which it can feel it owns and which is focused on the needs of the region. Glyndŵr University was perceived as acting opportunistically rather than having a strategic approach. While current HE provision in the region was highly focused on the economic needs of the region, and is an undoubted strength, many stakeholders strongly argued for expanded provision – particularly at undergraduate first degree and postgraduate level – and for a rebalancing of provision across FE and HE.

Sir Adrian's group recommended a federal model to be formally inaugurated between Glyndŵr University and the new Coleg Cambria. In the interim the two institutions, with the active involvement of the OU and the support of HEFCW, should begin to work informally but systematically and collaboratively to deliver the strategic objectives. Relevant Welsh Government departments should also examine the merits of developing an Advanced Manufacturing Centre or similar entity in the Deeside Enterprise Zone as a base for an R&D (and advanced skills) partnership comprising Bangor, Glyndŵr (and possibly other universities), that would directly provide R&D support to the advanced manufacturing sector.

The New Higher Education Policy

In his valuable book about higher education, *What Are Universities For?*, Stefan Collini, Professor of English Literature and Intellectual History at Cambridge University, says 'every politician is a closet historian', to which the only reply is that some politicians have studied more history than others. Collini's book is both a careful corrective to some of the dumber market-orientated policies underlying higher education in England – what he calls 'a mercantilisim of the intellect, a fear that the stock of national treasure will be diminished rather than augmented by the success of enterprises elsewhere' – and at the same time a warning against a defence of some imagined golden age of independent intellectual inquiry without accountability to governments, recognising that if universities 'want reasonably generous support from the government of the day, then they have to accept becoming answerable to that government and its conception of what the electorate will bear.'

Collini's historical analysis points to a mix of models for universities from at least the beginning of the twentieth century. He also reminds us that it was only after 1945 that the state provided 'even half' of the income of any university. He suggests that there is no decade which can be seen as a golden age for higher education, as the pace of change has been so significant, with two-thirds of degree-awarding HE institutions not existing as universities until 1992. He also identifies how the language of consumer choice has overtaken political decisions around higher education. The Browne review epitomised this, 'contending that we should no longer think of higher education as the provision of a public good, articulated through educational judgement and largely financed by public funds.... Instead, we should think of it as a lightly regulated market in which consumer demand, in the form of student choices, is sovereign in determining what is offered by the service providers (i.e. the universities). Browne's 'frequently repeated mantra is 'Student choice will drive up quality', and the measure of quality is 'student satisfaction'. Fundamentally, Collini recognises that the UK coalition government is 'using the whipped-up frenzy about the deficit in the public finances as a cover for a recognisably ideological assault on all forms of public provision'.

Collini is right to identify the long-term cultural role of our universities in disseminating knowledge and understanding for current and future generations. The philosophy of the Welsh Government was precisely that higher education institutions were cultural institutions operating in a national system, and public funding was there to influence priorities, through the intermediary body that was HEFCW, with a guarantee that the system would ensure certain national priority subjects were safeguarded and not left to the whims of consumer choice – the STEM subjects, say, or modern foreign languages, or Welsh-medium provision, or subjects which spoke to the culture, history and politics of Wales. The advent of a system more dependent on fees inevitably threatened to reduce the influence of national planning, something which we sought to influence through revamping the role of HEFCW, a process which is still under way and which will require legislation later to complete it.

Our philosophy in relation to universities was different from a market philosophy based on consumer sovereignty. Our approach recognised that the development of higher education in any society will be influenced by public priorities, and that choices are and always will be limited by resources. No institution had always taught and researched in every subject. But governments will make strategic choices about the range of subjects that need to be maintained across a higher education system for economic and social well-being. While the UK government emphasised the role of students as consumers exercising sovereignty, we preferred to focus on the collective voice of students in influencing course, institutional and national policy development through their students' unions. We believed that the student voice had never been more important in helping to shape the whole higher education experience.

One of the difficulties of the constant clamour of market-orientated philosophy from the UK coalition government was that it was sometimes difficult to explain that what we were doing in Wales would have been seen as entirely normal in other European countries. Instead, the situation in England was too often treated as the normative default position, including by institutions such as the Higher Education Policy Institute (HEPI). In 2012 HEPI published a report on *Universities and constitutional change in the UK*, looking at the impact of devolution on the higher education sector. The report recognised that 'the social democratic governments in the devolved countries have shown little appetite for the market-based reforms adopted in England and while acknowledging the need to maintain the autonomy of universities they seem to be moving in some respects in the direction of a more traditional European model of higher education'. In Wales, I said repeatedly that we preferred to plan the development of our higher education sector, not leave it to the market.

But because it saw England as the default position, HEPI argued that 'the autonomy of universities is in danger of being eroded and there is a possibility that their relationship to government may soon be similar to that of the further education colleges or to the polytechnics in England and Wales before incorporation'. On the contrary. I don't think that the evidence of the HEPI study bore out such a conclusion. In any case, I think our proposals for institutional governance, drawn up by John McCormick and his team, would strengthen university autonomy and ensure more sustainable institutions. Autonomy without sustainability is of course meaningless. The problem with the HEPI study, as with so much writing about university autonomy, is that it counterposes a supposedly ideal state of university autonomy with an environment in which democratically-elected governments expect some degree of acknowledgement of the investment they make in the higher education sector, and their overall goals for it. University autonomy and its partner academic freedom are not the same thing as the freedom of vice chancellors to do whatever they wish. You can have an ideal state of autonomy if you wish: Simon Jenkins makes the case for this in *The Guardian* at regular intervals, arguing for universities essentially to operate as private institutions in a choice-driven market. I don't agree with his vision – but it's a perfectly logical one.

I am not sure universities ever were so autonomous. In Wales, they weren't. The Aberdare committee in the 1880s recognised that 'higher education in Wales could not survive without assistance from the state'. As Professor J. Gwynn Williams, who taught me Welsh history at Bangor, recorded in his study of the development of the University of Wales, *The University Movement in Wales*: 'The £2,500 granted to Aberystwyth in 1884 was the first instance of government aid for university education in England and Wales.' The creation of the University of Wales had been a determined political act, resulting from the campaigning of a political movement, with two new colleges sanctioned by the Aberdare report, in 1881, a result of political campaigning and political compromise. Historians such as the late Gwyn Alf Williams, Dai Smith and Ken Morgan have all made links between the creation of the University of Wales and the development of a nineteenth century Welsh political consciousness. The history of the establishment of a University in Wales in the nineteenth century is a story of public campaigning and political manoeuvring fought, as J. Gwynn Williams says, 'in the offices of Whitehall and, above all, on the floor of the House of Commons.'

HEPI's study rightly recognised that our 'policy autonomy is constrained by the impact of changes in the financing of higher education in England, and the need to maintain funding at competitive levels.' HEPI was also right to say that 'reforms in

England have been made without adequate consideration of their impact outside England'.

Our higher education institutions didn't suddenly spring up as private enterprises or as creations of the higher education funding councils or as works of art sketched out by the refined imaginations of their vice chancellors. They have a history. They are the product of a particular set of economic, social and cultural circumstances and the political struggles which shaped them. They have both been shaped by, and subsequently helped to shape, the popular history and culture and indeed national identity of Wales – and they have always, in Wales, required substantial state largesse to support them. They exist in a public sphere, and they always have done. Those involved in the creation of the University of Wales had public goals and national aspirations. Public policy shaped them at the outset. Public policy shapes them now. So public interest in our higher education institutions and their development is not something alien to the traditions of higher education development in Wales, but is something that has always been central to it.

The UK coalition government, as evidenced by its implementation of Browne, and its June 2011 White Paper on Higher Education, 'Students at the heart of the system' was enshrining the philosophy of consumer sovereignty, determining that in England it is the market that will dictate the development of higher education:

- new low-cost private providers able to cherry pick certain subjects
- the core and margin proposals designed to drive fees down for some institutions
- allowing elite institutions to hoover up students with the highest grades without penalty

Arguably, this was the deviant pattern and the devolved administrations in Wales, Scotland and Northern Ireland were closer to European norms for higher education development. Our approach to mergers wasn't so different to that of other EU countries.

We had a distinctly Welsh tradition of which we must all be proud, of adult learning – with institutions which have held a unique historical place in the opening up and emergence of Wales in the last century – the WEA, the institutes, the involvement of trade unions in learning. All of them looking to the potential for the ordinary person to engage in and thrive through learning. Such establishments opened doors for people for whom university was out of reach. Also enabling people who had not come from a traditional academic background to discover their own talents and potential, with benefits for their esteem, careers and with wider benefits for the community as a whole.

I believed that developments in technology also offered the opportunity to reunite the principles of adult education with those of our higher education agenda. I had been particularly concerned that the Welsh sector should think beyond the immediate local challenges and be fully aware of the opportunities to a generation of students raised to be familiar and comfortable with digital technology. I was particularly conscious at how easy it was to access high quality material online. I had many conversations with academics and with vice chancellors over this subject from 2011 onwards. There was widespread discussion in higher education circles about the opportunities for Mass Open Online Courses (MOOC) and the 'flipped classroom'. The idea was that anyone could sign up to a MOOC and work their way through it; and that in the flipped classroom, students would watch lectures in their own time and have interactive time with their 'lecturers'. There was, of course, a considerable amount of technological utopianism, not to say, determinism, about some of these ideas.

I raised some of these issues in a lecture at Aberystwyth University in May 2012, asking where were Welsh HEIs in the digital world? It was disappointing that only the University of Glamorgan and the OU appeared to be taking online learning seriously, utilising platforms such as iTunes U, though the Coleg

Cymraeg Cenedlaethol is now looking at this as well and is looking at what it can do to produce more resources online which can be used by learners within FE and schools as well as HE. The success of the Khan Academy in school-level online learning had inspired developments in HE as well, such as the Artificial Intelligence course run by Sebastian Thrun, whose free online course that he taught with Peter Norvig, attracted 160,000 students from 190 countries, 23,000 of whom completed. Thrun had now quit teaching full-time at Stanford to set up his own online university, Udacity. Then there is MIT's own MITX. There were significant moves by venture capitalists to invest in new ventures like Udacity and Coursera, and EDx, launched by MIT, Harvard, and others. In December 2012, the OU launched Futurelearn along with a number of other universities including Cardiff University, with ambitious plans and some initial online courses.

Some authors argue that digital learning is the kind of disruptive innovation that is likely to be truly transformative in its impact. They argue that online technology disrupts traditional teaching; that there are now two kinds of students, those for whom the traditional campus-based experience is essential, and those who want to learn while they earn. There was a very active debate around these issues. Sir Michael Barber and his colleagues from Pearson had published a report on higher education for the Institute for Public Policy Research which hinted at some of the same issues, suggesting an 'avalanche' was coming. They said traditional universities were 'being unbundled'.

Barber's work suggested that governments would need to rethink their regulatory systems which were geared for an age when university systems were national rather than global. How should they fund part-time students? Should a student taking courses from a range of providers, including online, be funded like any other? How do governments ensure that universities in their own country thrive? How can they promote employability of their students? How can the equation of cost and quality be broken when students can get excellent quality online based on costs already sunk by a host institution providing mass courses?

How to engage with new providers while ensuring quality? Their analysis echoed those which said that there was a danger of the Napsterising of higher education. Their analysis also pointed to the falling value of a degree as the cost of tuition rose well above inflation. In the US, there had been a 72 per cent growth in the cost of tuition between 2000 and 2010, while graduate earnings fell by 14.7 per cent over the same period.

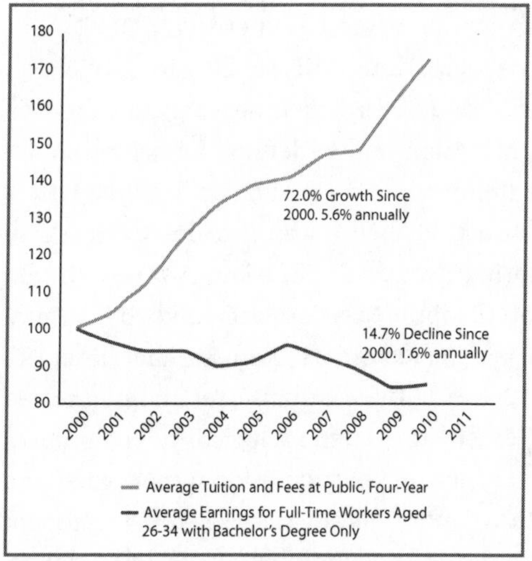

Figure 3

Source: College Board, U.S. Department of Education, Census Bureau, and Citi Research. Tuition and earnings were weighted in 2010 dollars; tuition fees were enrolment-weighted.

The Bill and Melinda Gates Foundation has funded work on accreditation for MOOCs. But there were doubts as to the completion rates amongst people taking online courses; systems for accreditation and validation and quality assurance were barely developed; financial models were not developed; and the consensus was that higher learning required some level of campus-based interaction. Professor Andrew Ng, co-founder of Coursera, has said that certification offered for MOOCs will never be as valuable as degrees from their partner institutions.

While I think that digital learning does have the potential to be a disruptive innovation, I recall that, in the context of broadcasting, in the BBC we were told for many years in the 1990s that the Internet would take over. While some new brands emerge powerfully, strong old brands survive as citizens seek trusted pathways. The unique selling point of institutions and academics across the globe has always been content. Arguably, the real threat of initiatives like MOOCs is to the managers in HE. The evidence at the moment as to whether MOOCs will contribute to widening participation is mixed. One to one tuition is highly valued by mature and younger learners, and is likely to remain key to ensuring retention and widening participation.

I dislike technological determinism as much as I dislike socio-economic determinism. I established a group to look into these issues, chaired by the former National Librarian, Andrew Green, to look at the potential opportunities afforded by digital developments for the Welsh sector, as well as the potential competitive threat posed by global technology-based developments, to what extent these technological developments may provide a platform to increase participation in part-time and full-time higher education, and whether the Welsh Government should stimulate investment in a new model of delivery of part-time higher education, working with the OU, HEIs, FEIs, broadcasters and employers, drawing on new digital delivery models. The group included Dr Bela Arora of Newport University, Dr Dafydd Trystan of the Coleg Cenedlaethol, former Bangor University student union President Jo Caulfield, Sarah Porter from JISC, and Professor Patricia Price, pro vice chancellor at Cardiff University, Rob Humphreys of the OU, Professor Dylan Jones-Evans and Coleg Cambria chief executive David Jones. Their report was published in March 2014 and recommended a series of practical actions to develop open and online resources for schools and colleges on our Hwb platform; for skills development at work; for developing Welsh language skills, to extend the reach of higher education institutions and their teaching, as well as improving the skills of HE staff.

As the reconfiguration agenda moved towards a conclusion in 2012, and we consulted on the legislative proposals on governance, I felt it was time to move towards a new higher education policy. Clearly, widening access, building research strength and winning more research council money would remain key elements, but I wanted to signal to the sector that we were now focused on promoting the quality of Welsh higher education rather than trying to address issues of structure. I said in a speech to the Leadership Foundation for Higher Education in December 2012 that the new policy would look 'outward, not inward'. There should be a real role for government in promoting the quality and strength of the sector in Wales internationally, aiming for continuous improvement of teaching and learning, research and innovation, access and participation.

While reconfiguration and governance issues took up many of the higher education headlines, behind the scenes we had continued to work in partnership with universities to develop the sector. More than £110m of Welsh Assembly Government funding was set aside to transform the opportunities and prospects for young people, local residents and businesses in the Heads of the Valleys region, to go toward three major projects – – UHOVI, a partnership between the University of Glamorgan and the University of Wales, Newport, the Merthyr Tydfil Learning Quarter and the Blaenau Gwent Learning Works.

The development of Swansea University's Science and Innovation Park, backed with a £60 million investment from the European Investment Bank along with Welsh Government money, had taken a long time to get agreement but will be a major contributor not just to academic excellence, technological innovation and industrial collaboration, but will make a major contribution to the Welsh economy in the future. As others pointed out, Wales performed above its collaborative weighting in areas such as collaborative research, regeneration income and development programmes, and granted software licences, as well as spinout companies and staff start-ups that have survived three years, and graduate start-ups. New patent applications from Welsh universities were increasing though still had further to go, as did commercialisation of intellectual property. Other major capital development programmes continued, with Bangor's Pontio building and other developments also gaining EIB funding, and we launched Cardiff's Maindy Park campus to house its European Cancer Stem Cell Research Institute and its Neuroscience and Mental Health Research Institute.

The HE sector in Wales under John Hughes's leadership as chair of Higher Education Wales was now getting its act together. The sector was strengthened with the arrival of the new vice chancellor of Cardiff University, Colin Riordan, highly experienced and widely-respected, who brought new ambition and an understanding of how to work alongside a supportive government to promote Welsh higher education, internationally and with new sources of investment. Shortly before he arrived, Cardiff had regained its place in the *Sunday Times* list of the top twenty HEIs in the UK. As vice chancellor of Essex, Colin had spoken out against the UK government's inclusion of students in its immigration targets, and chaired Universities UK's international committee, and early on began strengthening his institution's relationships with China and India. As a Government, we had opposed the UK government's immigration plans with their destructive impact on higher education and the economy.

With Colin's support, a more optimistic and realistic approach to examining the research contribution of Welsh universities began to be developed in 2012, led by Professor Peter Halligan, Dean of Strategic Futures at Cardiff University, who recognised the need for the sector in Wales to market its research contribution better. He demonstrated that Wales was winning more than its notional share of social science research council funding, and although Wales certainly needed to win more research grant funding overall, it was performing as well as most English regions, with the exception of Oxbridge and some of the major London institutions. He pointed out in *THE* that citations per paper of research from Wales were growing faster than other parts of the UK, and on some measures Wales could be shown to be in the top twenty countries in the world in terms of research. He said:

> It is likely that this is due in part to strategic improvements in institutional research management, as well as to Welsh funding council initiatives that have forced research-intensive institutions to pay closer attention to research productivity and quality, inter-disciplinary collaboration and competitive funding schemes.

Professor Halligan developed the marketing of Welsh research further on behalf of Higher Education Wales with an important article in the academic journal *Science*. He said 'reputation is based on the idea of awareness and universities in Wales haven't done well in getting recognition for the work they do.' He also acknowledged the importance of the Welsh Government's *Science for Wales* strategy. The *Science for Wales* document, developed by Chief Scientific Adviser Professor John Harries, was technically the responsibility of the First Minister and the Minister for Business, Economy Science and Technology, Edwina Hart. However, there was considerable input from my department, and we helped to find the funding necessary to attract scientific 'stars' to Wales, to set up the National Research Networks in the three 'Grand Challenge' areas identified by the strategy – Life Sciences and Health, Low Carbon, Energy and Environment, and Advanced Engineering and Materials – and to recruit high-profile directors to lead them. Under the scheme, Cardiff University, for example, recruited the acclaimed neurobiologist, Professor Yves Barde, from Switzerland.

We had been disappointed that Welsh universities did not work together to submit a single joint bid for a Doctoral Training Centre in Engineering and the Physical Sciences. A collaborative bid in the Social Sciences had paid off. *Science for Wales* was a very honest assessment, which recognised that there were too few UK or international facilities in Wales. Most politicians tend to have backgrounds in the arts or the social sciences. In the sciences, we needed someone who could tell us precisely what was best in class. John Harries knew just what was world-class and what was, bluntly, average. The Natural Environment Research Council's Centre for

Ecology and Hydrology in Bangor was the only standalone Research Council centre in Wales, but there were Research Council units or centres embedded in Welsh Universities, with 'two excellent examples' being the Medical Research Council Centre for Neuropsychiatric Genetics and Genomes at Cardiff University and IBERS at Aberystwyth, formerly a Biotechnology and Biological Sciences Research Council Institute. The document, subtitled 'a strategic agenda for science and innovation in Wales', set a series of challenges for strengthening university science research, which included the need to improve practice in winning competitively funded research, raise research quality and getting better use of EU structural funds to build capacity and skills to underpin future EU research and development funding programmes under Horizon 2020. The document set specific research targets to increase the Welsh share of UK Research Council funding to 5 per cent (from 3.3 per cent) and for Welsh scientific research achieving 3* and 4* quality and impact levels to reach the highest UK percentage.

We wanted the Welsh research base to realise its potential and make the most of its strengths. The Chief Scientific Adviser and I had met the Research Councils who had told us there were not enough Welsh-based researchers represented within the committee structures – we needed a new generation of research leaders. We said we should never be afraid of learning from what works elsewhere, and the Scottish research pooling model inspired the National Research Networks, created as part of the Sêr Cymru initiative. We can only compete against the biggest and best in UK science by playing to our strengths, and by getting our researchers, and our universities, to work together. This is especially important as the Research Councils are funding fewer, larger projects, and concentrating their funding on excellence – which means that our relatively small universities and research departments could be at a serious disadvantage.

We also developed a new focus on higher education and business working with the Council for Industry and Higher Education, whose chief executive, David Docherty, was another former colleague from the BBC in London. Industry and university collaboration was moving at pace across institutions in Wales with the key anchor companies. The then University of Glamorgan signed an agreement with British Airways, backed by the Civil Aviation Authority, to train students in Aircraft Maintenance Engineering. Swansea's new Innovation campus involved link-ups with Tata, IBM, Airbus and BAE systems. Welsh universities were leading on initiatives such as climate change, food security, health research including neuroscience, behaviour management and many others.

Before we had published the new policy statement I sought to ensure that Welsh Universities were involved in Welsh Government international marketing. The annual St David's Day reception organised by the Foreign and Commonwealth Office for the Welsh Government, provided an early opportunity. The First Minister asked me to host this. The invitation list drawn up by the Foreign Office included ambassadors and consuls from all over the world. It was a good opportunity to ensure the engagement of universities from Wales, as well as industry and people in London with Welsh connections. Many of the vice chancellors came to reinforce the message about the strength of Welsh HE.

The new policy statement, when we published it, asserted from the outset that Welsh higher education is a success story. It noted that the changes we had put in place through the new student finance regime would put the Welsh higher education system in a much stronger financial situation.

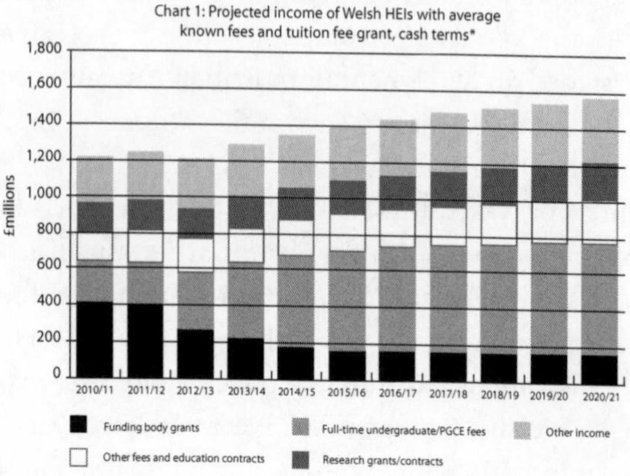

Figure 4

In terms of structural change, the document noted that by the end of 2013, following the Glamorgan/Newport and the UoW/Trinity St David and Swansea Met mergers, 'Wales will have a smaller number of stronger universities – institutions better placed to compete on the global stage and to contribute strongly to the economic, educational, cultural and social well-being of Wales.' The manifesto commitment had been delivered. The statement's purpose was to set out a new vision for higher education in Wales with close cooperation between Government and the sector.

The statement emphasised the role of universities in stimulating innovation and economic growth, noting the growth in graduate start-ups in Wales, and a higher rate of engagement with SMEs than other regions of the UK. Universities accounted for around half of all research and development expenditure in Wales, and that as a nation we were more dependent on university investment in research and development than other parts of the UK, given the relatively low level of industrial research and development in the country. There were areas where the sector needed to grow, including in consultancy, patent registration and intellectual property development. In terms of employability, Welsh institutions were overall achieving higher than average graduate employment levels than other regions of the UK.

Internationally, Wales was an attractive place for people to come and study, and the Welsh Government would support them in developing their international links, not only in terms of student and staff recruitment, but also in terms of research collaboration with institutions overseas, such as the Cardiff University/Beijing University Medical collaboration. Aberystwyth University had been selected as one of the top universities in the Science without Borders scholarship programme developed by the Brazilian Government, for example.

Widening access of course remained a key Welsh Government priority. The Universities of the Heads of the Valleys Initiative (UHOVI) had won the 'Commitment to widening participation' prize in the 2013 *Guardian* HE awards. The tuition fee plans agreed by Welsh HEIs with HEFCW underpinned this work on widening access, and placed an important focus on retention. HEIs were engaged in outreach programmes to communities with lower than average participation rates. New technology was opening up new models of delivery and HEIs were planning more flexible provision in bite-size chunks and through part-time opportunities. Our part-time support was envied across the UK, as the Master of Birkbeck, University of London, told me in May 2013, and we had not suffered the catastrophic fall in part-time numbers seen in England. Closer relationships between HEIs and FE colleges were being developed as well, notably in south-west and south-east Wales, and this was to be a strong recommendation of Professor Sir Adrian Webb's review of provision in north-east Wales. Our universities continued to have higher proportions of students from the most underrepresented groups compared to the UK as a whole.

We had also taken forward Welsh-medium teaching and research with the launch of the Coleg Cymraeg Cenedlaethol in 2011. Its Academic Plan set out a three-year focus for the Coleg from September 2012, and it had been an early convert to new digital learning, taking this forward internationally.

The context for all HE institutions was changing rapidly. Although UK government proposals in England privileged admission for A level entrants, there had been a growth of entrants over recent years in all HEIs in the UK from non-traditional backgrounds, who didn't necessarily come via the three A level route. For new entrants forced to pay higher fees, the quality of the student experience would become more important, and this would be a factor for Welsh universities attracting students from beyond the Welsh border. The democratisation of higher education internationally, with more potential entrants from the BRICs countries and also from Africa presented opportunities, though also challenges as these countries developed their own HEIs. Public accountability for the remaining public money being injected into the system would inevitably sharpen in an age of austerity.

We also needed to look at future funding of higher education in Wales. I had discussed this in outline with a number of people. David Grant, then vice chancellor of Cardiff University, had presented me and my then HE adviser Professor Merfyn Jones with charts illustrating the comparative indebtedness of English institutions compared to Welsh. Lord Davies of Abersoch – Mervyn Davies, formerly the Chairman of Standard Chartered Bank, one of the banks which had NOT run into trouble during the global financial crisis – was Chair of the Council of Bangor University, and he explained to me how he had found that Bangor was managing its funds too conservatively, sitting on cash that was earning no interest, when he was clear that this was the time to invest to enrich the student experience. I discussed the options with former City fund manager Gerry Holtham, specialist adviser to Finance Minister Jane Hutt, and he explored the opportunities for an investment vehicle for Welsh higher education with the Treasury, who were positive.

On June 11th 2013 I was able to launch the new strategy. I told the Assembly that the higher education sector had undergone a period of significant change, with changes to funding and student finance arrangements that have put the sector in a much stronger financial position. I said we had made substantial progress against our manifesto commitment to fewer, stronger universities, which are more sustainable and better equipped to meet the needs of both learners and the Welsh economy. It was now time to set a new direction for higher education policy in Wales, building on its strength and quality.

The new policy statement recognised that the sector makes an enormous contribution to the economic prosperity of Wales, to research and innovation, and has an excellent track record of widening access to higher education. Universities in Wales contribute more than £3 billion a year in gross expenditure to the Welsh economy. They employ more than 24,000 people. They have an annual turnover of £1.3 billion. They contribute to sustainable economic growth through knowledge creation, the development of a highly skilled workforce, and through engagement with local communities.

The Welsh Government remains committed to opening up higher education to all those with the potential to benefit from it. We have had success here, too. The number of Welsh-domiciled students enrolled in higher education in the UK has risen from around 93,000 in 2000-01 to over 102,000 in 2011-12. Our universities generally score highly in surveys of student satisfaction and they have been more successful in achieving participation by students from non-traditional backgrounds than other areas of Britain. They have considerable strengths in research and teaching and we are proud that Wales is a net importer of students. Our higher education system is held in high regard around the world and attracts students from across the globe.

We should aspire to a higher education system that demonstrates excellence at every level, not only in the quality of research or teaching within our institutions but also in terms of how well higher education providers in Wales work with business and employers to enhance skills and employability; how effectively the constituent parts of the higher education system in Wales work together to provide smooth pathways and progression for learners and to ensure maximum value for public funds invested in higher education; how collectively the higher education system in Wales contributes to regional and national goals; and in terms of the impact that the Welsh higher education sector has on the international stage.

Possible other areas of focus might include the move to more specialised universities, having a smaller number of research-intensive institutions in Wales, with others focusing on provision of world-class teaching and learning experiences; developing new ways of delivering part-time higher education; finding new ways to support postgraduate study, for instance through trialling a small number of two-year condensed undergraduate degree programmes with a third-year paid Master's degree funded through the statutory student support system; and creating a more self-sufficient higher education sector in Wales, capable of providing the broadest range of subject content available elsewhere in the UK, for example offering the opportunity to study veterinary medicine in Wales, which I knew was under discussion in two institutions in Wales.

The statement reflected the very positive developments I had seen taking place in higher education in Wales in the previous few years. We were able to focus on how the sector can take advantage of the opportunities to work with the Welsh Government for mutual benefit. The new policy for HE had been developed in close collaboration with the sector. I now had good reason to believe that we had a Welsh HE sector that saw itself contributing to national goals.

Tuition Fees and Funding

One of the biggest challenges heading our way when I became Minister was the question of tuition fees for university students. The Browne Review, established by the outgoing UK Labour government, was due to report in 2010. There was considerable evidence of lobbying already by vice chancellors across England for a significant hike in fees. I wrote to Lord Browne in March 2010, setting out the Welsh Government's concerns. In my first telephone conversation with the new Minister for Higher Education, David Willetts, I asked him whether he really wanted to have the highest tuition fees in Europe.

Tuition fees had already proved controversial in the Assembly. Back in 2005, a compromise had had to be brokered between all the party leaders as Labour had no majority in the Assembly. Personally, I had no objection to graduates paying a contribution to the cost of their higher education, as I had said in the chamber in 2005, given the inequitable distribution of the intake into higher education, dominated by middle-class families. But what was now being talked about in 2010 was, for me and many others, a step too far.

Responsibility for tuition fees was devolved to the National Assembly from 1 April 2006 through the UK Parliament's 2004 Higher Education Act. Under the 2005 compromise:

- Welsh HEIs could charge maximum flexible deferred fees of £1,800, in addition to the existing fee of £1,200. The existing fee element would no longer be charged upfront – a key element in removing barriers to entry.
- Welsh-domiciled students would receive fee remission

grants if they attended Welsh HEIs. This benefit would also have to apply to EU students studying at Welsh HEIs.
- Welsh domiciled students would not get that benefit if they studied in England, but a scheme would be created to assist Welsh domiciled students pursuing courses not available in Welsh HEIs (veterinary science was the most-quoted example)
- A National Bursary Scheme would be created to help improve access for the least well-off students

Evidence showed that less well-off students tended to study at home, so the decision to restrict the fee remission grant to those studying at Welsh HEIs should have had a redistributive effect. Based on written questions I had tabled to Jane Davidson at the time, I knew that around 85 per cent of students from the Rhondda, for example, studied at Welsh-based institutions. Over half of these got a full public contribution to the cost of their fees, and 19 per cent got partial help towards them. The Welsh Government had already introduced the Assembly Learning Grant to assist students from the least well-off backgrounds with day-to-day living costs. The Graham Review subsequently recommended what was called a 'combined' model of direct support for part-time students through Student Finance Wales and additional resources for institutions taking significant numbers of part-time students.

The backdrop to the debate in 2005 was concern about the comparative funding gap between Welsh and English HEIs, and an associated fear that if Welsh HEIs charged lower fees than England, then there would be a flood of what in June 2005 First Minister Rhodri Morgan called 'fee refugees' from England. Professor Teresa Rees's review had put forward a number of different options to address these issues, and the 2005 compromise essentially implemented several of her recommendations. The additional pledge to find ways of supporting Welsh students studying subjects outside Wales that were not being delivered in Welsh institutions was harder. Legal advice revealed in the Assembly by Jane Davidson during 2006 indicated that were such support to be provided, then

EU students studying the same subjects in institutions outside Wales would also have to be supported. EU case law moves on, and in 2010 we were able to adopt a different approach.

My immediate predecessor, Jane Hutt, had agreed a new policy in May 2009 with Plaid Cymru which revised the 2005 compromise. In 2008, she had appointed a review team chaired by Bangor vice chancellor, Professor Merfyn Jones, which recommended the ending of the fee remission grant (known by now as the tuition fee grant), instead creating a new, more substantial, means-tested grant towards living costs, which would also assist the least well off Welsh students studying outside Wales. Some of the money – assessed at around £31 million by 2015-16 – would be released for investment in the higher education sector. Loans would be increased to ensure that students did not have to pay the fees up front. More bursaries and scholarships should be offered to encourage students to study at Welsh HEIs. The plan involved phasing out the tuition fee grant from the 2010-11 academic year. £44 million would instead be invested over time in the student finance system to enhance the Assembly Learning Grant (ALG), raising the maximum amount from £2,906 in 2009-10 to £5,000 in 2010-11. Household income thresholds for access to partial ALGs would go up by £10,000. A graduate recruitment grant would be introduced as well as a national bursary framework. Additionally, Welsh-domiciled students would have up to £1,500 written off their loan debt regardless of where they had studied, as the One Wales Agreement demanded. Officials succeeded in negotiating additional Annual Managed Expenditure cover (AME) from the Treasury to support the scheme.

In 2010, I was concerned about the impact the issue could have on the One Wales Government as a coalition, just as we were heading towards a referendum on the powers of the Assembly. It was clearly an issue which mattered hugely to both parties. The One Wales Agreement was quite explicit. It had anticipated that the issue of higher fees would have to be addressed in 2009. The agreement stated that the One Wales Government would do:

> Whatever is possible to mitigate the effects on Welsh-domiciled students if the Westminster Government lifts the cap on fees in 2009.

There was therefore room for manoeuvre – but it was not yet clear what might be done. Balancing the political, economic, legal and social justice issues would be difficult – and potentially very costly.

Clearly, we had to wait for Browne. Substantial numbers of Welsh students travel to England for their higher education, and substantial numbers of English students travel to Wales. Internal UK cross-border flows of students mattered more to us than they did to Scotland or Northern Ireland, as the chart below shows. We had the autonomy, in policy terms, to determine our own course of action – but decisions taken in London for English universities would inevitably have an impact on our budget and what we could do. This was also an issue which I knew would excite attention from Members of Parliament, not least on the Labour side, some of whom had been critical that the 2005 compromise did not provide assistance to Welsh-domiciled students attending universities outside Wales.

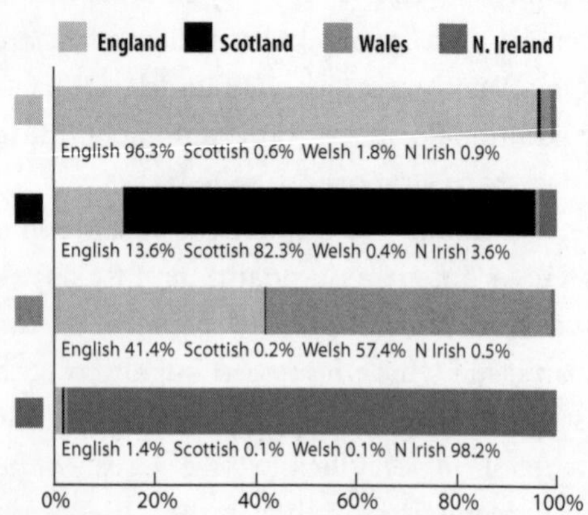

Figure 5

From Times Higher Education, 25 August 2011, 'Toll barriers' by David Matthews.

In 2008-9, there were 125,000 students in Welsh HEIs, with more than 40 per cent coming from outside Wales. We were a net importer of full-time students.

The policy on tuition fees obviously had a direct impact on university income. The review by Merfyn Jones had pointed to HEFCW comparisons of funding between Welsh and English universities which amounted to a gap of £61 million in 2005-6. But, as Jane Hutt had explained to the House of Commons Welsh Affairs Select Committee, when it was taking evidence on cross-border issues in 2009, if you took the funding we provided for HEIs and our more generous support for student finance, our overall spend was comparable. Vice chancellors and others continued however to argue about the level of spending given to their institutions by the Welsh Assembly Government. One academic specialising in constitutional issues, Alan Trench, however, told the *THE* 'it's not a surprise that Welsh higher education is poorly funded. Wales, generally, is underfunded.'

I'd had the benefit of an informal off-the-record briefing from Lord Browne in September, and I had also had a number of conversations with the UK Higher Education Minister, David Willetts. It was clear that fees were going to at least double in England. Because of the political sensitivities, I talked the issues through initially with Carwyn. He wondered whether we could reinstate the tuition fee grant, which was due to be phased out under the proposals Jane Hutt had announced. That opened up some possibilities. When Browne reported, with its proposals to transfer the bulk of the funding responsibility from the state to graduates, it became evident to me that we should draw together the budgets for student support and higher education, and see if it was feasible to create a single funding stream for higher education. Lynne Hamilton, the lead official in charge of student finance, who had understandably been worried about the cost to our budgets, immediately set to work with policy officials on the higher education side, principally Neil Surman and his team, to work out what might be done. Could we create a win-win situation, in which support for our students remained in place, while universities in Wales benefitted from a better funding stream – underpinned in part by a surplus of students from other parts of the UK coming to Wales?

We decided to get people thinking about the likely cost of the Browne Review to the Welsh budget if all we did was cover the increased cost of tuition for Welsh-domiciled students going to English universities. We were not prepared to see a one-way transfer from the Welsh Assembly Government budget into the English higher education system. I made a statement on 12th October in the Assembly on the implications of the Browne Review. I explained that if fees were levied at £7,000 on the 16,000 or so Welsh students annually attending English universities, then we could face a cost of an additional £70 million by 2015-16, £55 million of which would be a transfer into the English higher education system from the Welsh Government's budget. I said that the proposals would result in a largely market-based system where institutions competed on cost not quality. I questioned the long-term sustainability of the Browne proposals when European institutions were offering courses through the medium of English at low or no cost, saying we did not wish to see the development of a market in higher education where institutions competed on price and students chose their courses or institutions on the basis of relative cost. Media outlets largely led with our estimates of the likely cost to the Welsh budget and the potential transfer of funding to English HEIs. Later that week, the cartoonist Mumph provided ITV's *Sharp End* programme with a cartoon of UK Business Secretary Vince Cable picking my pocket for the money.

In order to ensure the full support of Cabinet, we took our proposals to them in stages. At the same time steps were taken informally to brief Plaid's Education spokesperson, Nerys Evans, who, like other influential AMs, was being heavily lobbied by NUS Wales. I reported to Cabinet colleagues on the Browne Review proposals in September 2010. I warned that it was possible that English HEIs might be able to charge up to £10,000 fees per annum. I also informed them that we were undertaking statistical modeling on the potential financial consequences for Wales.

The Browne report cannot be read outside the context of the UK coalition government's first Comprehensive Spending Review, published two weeks later on 26th October 2010. The UK government's Comprehensive Spending Review slashed £860 million from the Welsh Government budget for 2011-12 in real terms compared to the 2010-11 budget. This had serious implications for the Education budget, and it was inevitable that higher education would have to take a significant hit if we were to protect spending on schools in line with Carwyn's commitment. We also subsequently determined to protect spending on skills in the FE and workplace learning budgets. It also confirmed the plan foreshadowed in Browne to slash the teaching budget for higher education in England by 80 per cent from £3.5 billion to £750 million. As I said in the Assembly during questions on my statement on the Browne Review on 12th October:

> The campaigning by some of the universities to obtain higher fees to get more income has resulted in their charging higher fees for the same level of income.

Vice chancellors had got their higher fees – but at an enormous cost. This decision made it clear that in England, at least, the funding of universities was to all extent and purposes being privatised, with the bulk of funding in future coming from the fees of individual students, rather than the state. The political fall-out for the coalition, particularly for the Liberal Democrats, whose election manifesto had promised to abolish tuition fees without cutting university income, was immense, with student protests dominating the main network news in ways not seen for decades.

A paper went to Cabinet on 15th November, a fortnight after the UK government had announced its conclusions on the Browne Review. Outline discussions took place about how we might respond, based on the work being done by my officials, with a discussion around four options:

- Additional loan support to Welsh students studying in England
- A means-tested tuition fee grant to Welsh students wherever they studied
- A non-means-tested tuition fee grant to Welsh students wherever they studied
- A means-tested tuition fee grant for Welsh domiciled students studying in England, and a non means-tested tuition fee grant for those studying in Wales

Tuition fee levels would be capped at the same level in Wales as in England. I did not regard Option 1 as viable, and said so, and Cabinet agreed to rule it out.

The following week's Cabinet had just one paper on the agenda as it approved the proposals I was to take to the Assembly. The Cabinet paper presented more detailed financial analysis and risk assessments. I proposed that we adopt the third option of a non means-tested fee grant wherever Welsh-domiciled students studied. The paper confirmed that higher education institutions in Wales would 'be able to charge tuition fees up to £9,000 per annum, providing they could demonstrate a commitment to widening access and other strategic objectives' through fee plans scrutinised by HEFCW. Amongst the risks the paper identified was the possibility that average fee levels might rise to £9,000, above the £7,000 assumed in the figures I presented to Cabinet. Affordability depended on the cap on publicly-funded student places, which I had introduced in July, remaining. The paper also noted that there was a risk arising from the UK government's policy to promote private HEI providers in England. The paper also included a summary of Counsel's opinion on the risk of discrimination on grounds of nationality if Welsh Ministers were to pay a tuition fee grant to students ordinarily resident in Wales and studying in other UK administrations. Cabinet was advised that this was an affordable and sustainable solution, which protected all Welsh students from higher levels of debt, while discharging the One Wales commitment to mitigate the impact on Welsh students of any increase in tuition fees. Furthermore, Welsh students wishing to study subjects not currently available in Wales would not be disadvantaged.

I was being lobbied on our statement by NUS Wales President Katie Dalton right up until it was delivered, through meetings, letters, print, broadcast and social media. We had had one meeting, where the decision had been taken in Cabinet but not yet announced, where I was largely unable to tell her anything. That was unfortunate, as one of the decisions I'd had to make was to scrap the national bursary scheme I had only announced six months before as part of our student support system, one of the outstanding elements of the Merfyn Jones review, and an issue on which NUS Wales had pressed harder and more persuasively than the vice chancellors' lobby. Our new proposals returned elements of the national bursary scheme to individual institutions.

I delivered our policy statement in the Assembly Chamber on 30th November, a week before Parliament was due to vote on the UK government's policy for England. In the statement, I confirmed our opposition to full-cost fees and markets in higher education. I explained the overall proposals, then said

> I am pleased to say that Welsh-domiciled students will pay no more in 2012-13 than they would have done if fees were not being increased to those levels. From 2012-13, Welsh-domiciled students will continue to be eligible for subsidised loans to meet the cost of fees up to the current level. However, the Welsh Assembly Government will also provide a non-means-tested tuition fee waiver or grant for the balance over and above current fee levels. This grant will be payable through HEFCW on behalf of Welsh-domiciled students wherever they study.
>
> In other words, the increase in fees for Welsh-domiciled students, whether they study in England or Wales or Scotland or Northern Ireland, will be paid by the Welsh Assembly Government. Welsh-domiciled students will not have to find either £6,000 or £9,000 to study. The public

> purse will continue to subsidise higher education for Welsh-domiciled students. Welsh students who go to university in 2012-13 will be paying the same in real terms as students going to university in this academic year.

I explained that we would pay for the policy by top-slicing the grant for Welsh universities by 35 per cent, but we expected the income for Welsh universities would be at least the same in real terms by 2016-17 as it was in 2012-13.

Parliament, of course, had not yet approved the UK government's proposals for England, and we were conscious that what we were saying would play straight into the wider UK debate. I said that if Parliament refused to endorse the UK government's proposals, then we would 'rejoice and develop an alternative approach'.

I summed up what we were doing:

> Students domiciled in England will have to find the full cost of the new fees. Students domiciled in Wales will not. We have made it clear that, in Wales, we believe in planning the future of higher education, rather than letting the market rule. We have delivered on our 'One Wales' commitments, and Wales is leading the way.

Jocelyn Davies, Plaid Cymru's likeable and experienced Business Manager, had suggested to Cabinet that all Cabinet Members should be in the chamber for my statement. Unusually, as the Assembly's Record of Proceedings records, there was a round of applause when I had finished. That week Mumph produced a further cartoon for ITV about tuition fees, this time dressing me up as Father Christmas presenting a Christmas present to the Yes for Wales campaign for more powers to the Assembly. I received emails of support from parents of potential students.

Of course, there was a backlash. The right-wing national newspapers, the *Daily Mail* and *Daily Telegraph*, both offensively branded our policy educational 'apartheid'. The *Daily Mail* front-page headline the following day was 'Punished for being English'; the *Daily Telegraph*'s 'Higher tuition fees, but only if you are English'.

Some were simply hilarious. Writing in the *The Sun*, the paper's former editor, Kelvin MacKenzie, said 'I suspect they (the Welsh) would still like to burn down our cottages, but we can't afford them any more as we are having to subsidise their children's education.' In the *The Spectator*'s Christmas edition, Susannah Herbert predicted that 2011 would be:

> The year when wise parents will consider renting a cottage on the other side of Offa's Dyke, declaring it their primary residence.

However, others saw this as demonstrating, once and for all, the power of devolution as a policy. Professor Sir Deian Hopkin noted that the policy would 'cause consternation in England… it will be said, there is an alternative to the English model after all.' The *Western Mail's* Political Correspondent, David Williamson, called it 'one of the boldest decisions ever taken since the dawn of devolution' in the *Wales on Sunday* newspaper. He said we hadn't 'just pulled a rabbit out of a hat – it's more of a live-and-kicking kangaroo.' From the BBC newsroom in London came the message:

> Leighton – wish you'd seen the response in the newsroom… think the penny dropped at last about the reality of devolved powers. Da iawn.

One issue which the right-wing papers particularly didn't like was the fact that our subsidy would have to be extended to students from other EU member-states. We were clear on the law. I remember explaining to a *Daily Telegraph* journalist on the telephone, on the afternoon that I made the statement, that he should remember that students from the UK taking courses in other EU countries were entitled to the same level of support as students from those countries. But the *Daily Mail* went ballistic:

'Even EU students will pay less in fees than the English' roared its headline page lead on December 2nd. An editorial in the *Mail* saw our policy as a 'Threat to the Union':

> Today, bitterness and division are spreading ever further, as Wales joins Scotland in exempting its nationals from Whitehall's increases in tuition fees.

Policies unique to Scotland and Wales were 'affronts to fairness' likely to incite the English 'to break away from the union'. The *Daily Mail* columnist Stephen Glover fulminated that 'sooner or later the English will refuse to go on subsidising Scotland and Wales, and start insisting on their rights.' He caricatured the policy:

> Free for Jock. No increases for Taffy. A rise of 200 per cent for John Bull.

What was absurd about these arguments was that it was the government which the *Daily Telegraph* and *Daily Mail* supported which was making the English pay more. I replied on *The Guardian* 'Comment is Free' website:

> I am responsible for the student support arrangements for students domiciled in Wales. The Scottish government is responsible for students domiciled in Scotland. Northern Ireland ministers in their assembly for students domiciled in Northern Ireland. And – wait for it – Vince Cable and David Willetts in the UK coalition government for students domiciled in England. They are welcome to follow our example in Wales. We are making a policy choice. So are they.

Some thought there might be legal issues with our policy – a group called Public Interest Lawyers was planning a challenge to the Scottish policy, but our policy was different – our institutions were not charging differential fees depending on the country of origin within the UK. We were simply providing student support in the form of tuition fee grants to those for whom we had responsibility – students domiciled in Wales. A makeshift think tank suddenly emerged in November 2011 claiming that it was going to campaign to get more EU students to come to the UK, arguing that the Welsh Government would have to pay EU students' fees wherever they studied in the UK. The 'think tank' was never heard from again, but the Welsh Conservatives absurdly claimed that our policy 'could now see millions of pounds spent encouraging EU students to come to Wales'. There has been no legal challenge to the Welsh Government's policy, and no great influx of EU students.

Indeed, by 2013, the broadsheets, including the *Daily Telegraph*, were routinely running articles on the cheaper cost of studying in other EU countries who were teaching through the medium of English, including the Netherlands and the Scandinavian countries, and increasingly Germany. Even France, so strong in defence of its language, debated and agreed a law in May 2013 which would allow for courses in foreign languages, principally English, to be taught in its universities. Tuition fees were abandoned in Germany – Bavaria and Lower Saxony being the final states in Germany to jettison their fees for university students.

While the modeling was complex, we estimated the cost of the tuition fee grant to be £125 million at 2013-14, and that it would cost £200 million a year to operate by 2016-17. Our statisticians and policy officials had worked hard on the detailed modeling of the policy which we took to Cabinet. Our initial calculations for Cabinet were based on assumed fees of £7,000 per annum, which were the same initial assumptions as in England. We had, however, run similar modeling based on average fees of £9,000. In the autumn of 2013 the Wales Audit Office issued a report on our tuition fees policy. The Welsh Conservatives suggested that the WAO report meant that this modeling was known only to me and a few other ministers. Under the Ministerial Code, I cannot go into the detail of the Cabinet discussions, but the First Minister was sufficiently annoyed by what the WAO said to put the Cabinet papers of our tuition fee discussions into the public domain. The paper received by Cabinet on 23 November clearly said that 'Higher education institutions (HEIs) will be able to charge tuition fees up to £9,000 per annum' provided they met strategic objectives including widening access. We planned our policy on tuition fees carefully over the three months from early September to late November 2010. No Cabinet Minister was unaware that we had modeled an average fee regime of £9,000 per annum. In December 2010 I published a written statement setting out our estimates of how the income to Welsh HEIs would rise over the years to the end of the next Assembly, based on fees of £7,000.

						£Million
	2011-12	2012-13	2013-14	2014-15	2015-16	2016-17
Funding body grants	395	354	325	307	300	301
Full-time undergraduate / PGCE fees	224	254	308	357	391	411
current level of fees	*224*	*229*	*234*	*239*	*245*	*252*
net additional fee income	*0*	*25*	*74*	*118*	*146*	*159*
Other fees and education contracts	158	162	167	171	176	181
Research grants/contracts	161	163	167	172	176	181
Other income	243	246	253	260	267	274
Total	1,180	1,179	1,219	1,267	1,311	1,348

Table 1: Projected income of Welsh HEIs, with average £7,000 fees and tuition fee grant, cash term

Source: WAG forecasts, HESA finance record and student numbers projected forward

A Freedom of Information request on the detailed modeling of the costs of our fees policy was answered in January 2011 based on estimated fees of £7,000. The estimates were that the policy would cost £653 million by 2016-17 and £1.522 billion to 2020-21. The BBC Wales education correspondent had inspired the FoI request and claimed we had not modeled costs based on £9,000 fees. I told him live on Radio Wales that we had. He hadn't asked for them. We provided estimates based on £9,000 in March 2011, during the last days of the One Wales Government, following a further FoI request from the BBC. Overall costs were estimated to run at £1.023 billion to 2016-17 and £2.384 billion to 2020-21.

During 2011, it became clear that universities in England were likely to push fees right to £9,000, the maximum allowed by the cap. We consulted on the likely basic rate – suggested initially at £6,000, but following the consultation, we settled on £4,000 unless institutions could persuade HEFCW that they had a clear plan for widening access and participation in higher education. As I told the Assembly in March 2011, this was a result of 'the representations from student unions, led by the president of NUS Wales, Katie Dalton, who made a convincing and persuasive case that contributed to the decision to set a lower basic fee', on the grounds that no institution should be allowed to automatically double their fees. We expected them to show that they were devoting about 30 per cent of their fee income to equality of opportunity and promoting higher education. We needed to get the legislation in place before the May 2011 Assembly elections to allow institutions to plan in good time. Katie also lobbied hard on the nature of the Fee Plan regulations demanding that universities be required to strengthen the student voice and deliver improvements in widening access, retention and the student experience. We ensured that HEIs would consult their students' unions and HEFCW would consult with NUS Wales. Our guidance to HEFCW set out the centrality of the student experience and the importance of ensuring opportunities for the views of students' unions to be taken into account in the preparation and approval of fee plans. Further guidance on bolstering the voice of student unions was also be set out in the HEFCW remit letter for 2011-12, which contained the expectation that HEFCW would 'establish best practice in the funding of effective, democratic students' unions, and student representation on decision-making bodies, and to ensure that best practice in respect of student union representation becomes the norm in the Higher Education sector in Wales'. HEFCW worked with NUS Wales to develop guidance published its Circular which provided guidance – for implementation by August 2012 – on the funding of effective, democratic students' unions (SUs), and student representation.

The Welsh Labour manifesto for the 2011 Assembly election campaign committed the party to ensuring that the fees policy would remain in place for the lifetime of the Fourth Assembly, i.e. until 2016-17. As I explained to the Enterprise and Business Committee of the Assembly in July 2011:

> The commitment is sustainable but expensive. More institutions have opted to charge £9,000 than we expected – certainly in the autumn. That is true for us and the UK government overall. However, we carried out our modeling both on the basis of fees being at an average of £7,000 and on the basis of fees being at an average of £9,000.

I always assumed that Welsh Government estimates for the cost of the tuition fee policy would have to be revised continually. As I put it in an answer at the Enterprise and Business Committee of the Assembly, in October 2011, giving evidence on the draft Welsh Government budget for 2012-13:

> We have been through this with our statisticians. We have shared figures with Government departments in the other countries. We have the best estimates that we can make at this stage. However, these are clearly things that we will have to review. I suspect that, if I am honest, Chair, the

> one thing that I can say about all of our calculations is that they will be wrong.

In June 2011, HEFCW sent back every fee plan submitted by universities in Wales. I told HEIs that they needed to 'get real' on issues of widening access and improving the student experience – in 'typically brutal fashion', according to the *Western Mail*'s editorial, which backed HEFCW's decision and my statement. In July, it became clear that they had managed to extract firm and clear proposals from Welsh universities. Most went for fees of £9,000, though Swansea Metropolitan University sets its fees at £8,500 and £8,750. The University of Wales, Newport and University of Wales, Trinity St David, had some courses lower than £9,000. Glyndwr went for a lower average fee of £6,643.

It was inevitable that the Welsh Conservatives, who did not support the policy and would make Welsh-domiciled students pay the higher tuition fees wherever they studied, would question the policy repeatedly. It has been clear for some time that the Welsh Conservatives recognise that their own policies are unpopular in Wales, and the best that they can do is seek to undermine the credibility of Welsh Labour Government policies by trying to sow doubt about their sustainability. They have repeatedly questioned the durability of the policy since December 2010, jumping on every announcement about student application data to suggest that the policy is unaffordable, even when applicant numbers are going up.

In the case of Plaid Cymru, it has been harder to understand their desire to undermine a policy in which they should be able to share the credit, since it derived from the One Wales Government, and their ministers applauded me after I delivered the statement announcing it. But then, they went into the 2011 Assembly elections attacking Labour, rather than speaking up for the achievements of the government of which they had once been part. If they wish to leave the credit for this policy to Welsh Labour, then we will have no worries about owning it. As early as July 2011, their new education spokesperson said of the policy his colleagues had agreed less than a year before 'we have to question whether it is financially affordable', and by March 2012, six months before the policy came into operation, he said 'the cracks are beginning to appear in the facade that this is a sustainable policy for the life of the Assembly' and claimed the Welsh Government 'cannot afford its own tuition fee policy'.

In May 2013, as we approached the end of the first year of the policy in operation, we had better data on which to draw, and I supplied a highly detailed paper to the Assembly's Enterprise and Business Committee explaining how figures were being modeled monthly. Our latest estimates were that the likely cost of the policy, based on £9,000 fees, had fallen from a March 2011 estimate of £1.023 billion to £809 million (the cost of the Tuition Fee Loan was marginally lower, the average tuition fee being paid was actually lower than £9,000, and the take-up of tuition fee grant was 98 per cent not 100 per cent). In fact, it looked far more affordable than we had initially feared. Additionally, HEIs in Wales would receive real terms increases in income as a result of the policy, rising from £1.217 billion to £1.444 billion in cash terms or £1.209 billion to £1.277 billion in real terms between 2012-13 and 2016-17.

Bizarrely, the University of Oxford excluded Welsh students from its fee reduction scheme for lower income students, because the Welsh Government covered the higher fees. The University of Cambridge did not discriminate against Welsh students. I took this up with Lord Patten, Chancellor of Oxford University, when I was a guest of the BBC at the Wales versus England rugby international in 2013. He was already depressed about the English performance before I began my complaint. I followed up with a letter and on my last day in office, Oxford University agreed to amend its approach, as my successor confirmed a week later.

Part-time higher education remained a major concern for us. In England, their Higher Education Funding Council (HEFCE) reported on the 1st March 2013 that part-time numbers in

England had fallen 26.6 per cent. We postponed any increases for part-time students until 2014-15 so that we could observe what was happening over the border. I announced our new policy in March 2013, saying we would make funding available to the Higher Education Funding Council for Wales (HEFCW) to continue to subsidise the delivery costs of part-time courses.

We were aware that some students may need access to support to cover the up front costs of tuition fees for part-time courses. In order to ensure that undergraduate students had sufficient funds to cover the full fee, from 2014/15 eligible students studying at an intensity of over 25 per cent of a full-time course will be able to access a non-means tested loan from Student Finance Wales. This policy was widely welcomed by NUS Wales and the Open University. Katie Dalton had argued that it would help us meet our *For our Future* objectives on widening participation. In May 2013 the vice chancellor of Birkbeck College, the leading provider of part-time HE in London, told me he wanted to see something similar being developed in England.

It is entirely possible that in 2015 a new UK government could be elected which determines to introduce a more rational system for student fees in England. The UK Labour Party has talked about reducing fees significantly. Even reducing them to £6,000 in England might free up resources for the Welsh system. The current Welsh policy is one designed for a period while a UK government insists on fees based on a £9,000 cap. As a policy, it has the benefit of simplicity and clarity, and can be explained in a single sentence: Welsh students will not pay higher fees wherever they choose to study. It illustrates a position where the Welsh Government may have policy autonomy through devolution, but that policy autonomy is limited by the cross-border nature of university recruitment in which young people choose to travel to England to study, incurring whatever fee costs are demanded there. The Higher Education Policy Institute, and before it the Select Committee on Welsh Affairs, have both observed that decisions taken in Whitehall without effective engagement with the devolved administrations create a distorting impact.

I always planned to announce a review of the policy to commence before the 2016 Assembly election and report after it, bearing in mind the potential for a new UK government to change the English policy. My successor as Education Minister, Huw Lewis, has now announced that he plans to do just this, with a review to be chaired by Professor Sir Ian Diamond, vice chancellor of Aberdeen University. That review will need to consider how successful the current policy has been in delivering for both students and Welsh HEIs. Though I announced the policy in November 2010, the first students to benefit did not start their courses until autumn 2012 and will not be graduating until the summer of 2015. It would be hard to judge the success of the policy on outcomes for just one cohort, and UK policy changes could also have an impact on the future position, so it makes sense for the review not to complete its work until after the 2016 Assembly election.

Meanwhile, the UK government's policy is coming under increasing pressure, both from those who would like to have no cap on fees and raise them even higher, and others who take the view that the fees policy is destabilising to the economy. As early as February 2011, the University of Glamorgan Business School lecturer Hywel Williams estimated that when inflation was taken into account, £75 billion a year might have to be written off by the Treasury to pay for those students who did not pay back their loans. Sir Peter Lampl, chair of the Sutton Trust, warned in July 2011 that their research suggested that graduate debts would delay home purchase, and argued study in the US was becoming more attractive. In 2014, the Sutton Trust estimated that teachers in England would still be paying off their tuition fee loans into their fifties. In the autumn of 2012, the Higher Education Policy Institute (HEPI) said that the UK government had underestimated the costs of the tuition fee policy, particularly the cost to the Treasury, of funding student loans. HEPI estimated that the increased cost could wipe out the savings claimed from replacing direct public funding with higher tuition fees.

There is no question, for example, that the increase in tuition fees in the autumn of 2012 has had an impact on inflation, as the academic Andrew McGettigan, author of *The Great University Gamble*, has demonstrated, which feeds through into higher public spending in other parts of government where benefits are linked to inflation increases. As Will Hutton pointed out in the *The Observer* in October 2013, in England, though not in Wales, Scotland or Northern Ireland, graduates' spending will be depressed by the weight of debt they carry.

> Only the US has the same cavalier approach, but the average graduate debt there is a mere £15,700, with much lower interest rates, and a good third of American students leave with no debt. The English combination of high interest rates and sky-high debt is a unique double whammy.

In 2014, it became clear that the English policy was under pressure. Higher Education Minister David Willetts admitted that 45 per cent of student loans would never be repaid. Original estimates had been that 28 per cent would not be repaid. In Treasury terms, this is known as the Resource and Accounting Budget (RAB) charge, which covers the subsidy for maintenance and fee loans. When this RAB charge reaches 48.6 per cent, according to London Economics, the £9,000 tuition fee policy will cost as much as the previous policy in which the bulk of higher education funding came straightforwardly from the government and students only paid just over £3,000. Work by the Institute of Fiscal Studies for Universities UK, published in April 2014, suggested that the UK government would make no overall public spending savings from its policy. Student recruitment to Welsh universities from England in 2013-14 was reported in the same month to be up 9.4 per cent on the previous year. Research for the Economic and Social Research Council published in 2014 also said that taking our fee and student support together, the Welsh system would mean that Welsh students would carry less debt than students from any other part of the UK. Clearly Wales took the right course in 2010.

Skills for Employment

The development of skills was where the work of the department interacted most closely with employers and the wider economy. Our objective was to create a properly skilled workforce with high quality opportunities for all. Broadly speaking, we had four priorities: helping young people to develop to their maximum potential, encouraging investment in skills as a driver of growth, creating routes into employment for those with lower skills than the economy could support, including those with disabilities or other disadvantages, and ensuring the infrastructure was there to deliver the framework for skills development.

This was also one of the areas which drew us most into conflict with the UK coalition government after 2010. Employment policy, of course, is not devolved. The UK government's programme of welfare reform, including their plans for Remploy, was developed on an English template which did not take into account different policies, models of delivery or financial support arrangements in Wales.

A great deal had been achieved. Year on year, we saw a smaller proportion of young people leaving full-time education without a qualification. The Learning and Skills Measure, piloted through the Assembly by John Griffiths as Deputy Minister for Skills in 2009, created a wider range of vocational opportunities for young people both in Key Stage 4 (14-16) and in post-16 education, whether delivered through sixth forms or FE colleges, based around a local curriculum which providers were expected to collaborate in delivery. It was one of the first Assembly Measures to be passed by the National Assembly for Wales following the Government of Wales Act 2006. By 2012 all learners were able to access a local curriculum comprising a minimum of thirty course choices, with a minimum of five vocational course options. I had some concerns about the quality of the offer, however, and commissioned a review of this, which subsequently reported to Huw Lewis suggesting a reduction in the number of available courses.

Following the global financial crisis, Rhodri Morgan as First Minister began a series of economic summits from the autumn of 2008. John, together with Jane Hutt as Minister, had developed the innovative ProAct scheme, worked up by Grenville Jackson in the department. ProAct was launched by John in January 2009, with an initial budget of just under £50 million. ProAct, initially piloted within the automotive sector which had been particularly badly hit, was designed to be a short-term scheme operating during the economic crisis. Both the Wales TUC and the CBI in Wales had called for such a scheme.

The aim was to provide training assistance to businesses, providing financial support for employees to undertake training and receive wage subsidies while training. The measure was designed to avoid fundamental lay-offs of workers. It ran until 2010 when Lesley Griffiths, who became Deputy Minister for Science, Innovation and Skills following Carwyn's election, launched the Skills Growth Wales programme, which continued the support for training though without a wage subsidy element. ProAct sat alongside the ReAct scheme which supported training for individuals facing redundancy. We were also able to announce an additional £49 million to support our skills programmes, including the continuation of Pathways to Apprenticeships, and the Young Recruits programme, and for Skill Build and ReAct.

John and Jane, along with Ieuan Wyn Jones, had launched the *Skills That Work for Wales* strategy and action plan in the summer of 2008, drawing on the work of Professor Sir Adrian Webb's review of the mission and purpose of further education in Wales, *Promise and Performance*, published in December 2007, and the 2006 Leitch review of future UK skills needs. Adrian's work was intended to address the issue of young people becoming disengaged in school and ending up what was termed 'NEET' – not in education, employment or training. The report emphatically stated 'both opportunity and social justice suffer' when too many young people fail to get five good GCSEs including English or Welsh and maths. The report identified that Further Education Institutions had improved quality and exceeded Welsh Assembly Government targets for learner achievement and the quality of teaching. However, the review group's data suggested that the size of an FE institution mattered and they recommended further consolidation within the sector, suggesting that ten was about the right number of FEIs. They also recommended that the Careers Wales companies should be restructured to create a single organisation, and there were recommendations related to the interface between devolved and non-devolved areas, where the Department for Work and Pensions was in the lead, with a Labour Market Framework agreement which I was to sign with Yvette Cooper, then Secretary of State for Work and Pensions, in February 2010, and the Joint Employment Delivery Board between our department and DWP, a board of senior officials from both the Assembly Government and DWP and key stakeholders, both announced by John on his last day as Deputy Minister for Skills before becoming Counsel General after Carwyn's election, in 2009.

The lead role on most skills programmes, particularly work-based learning, apprenticeships, and programmes to tackle economic inactivity and unemployment, was taken during my time as Education Minister first by Lesley Griffiths, as Deputy Minister for Science, Innovation and Skills, working to Ieuan Wyn Jones, and then by Jeff Cuthbert as Deputy Minister for Skills. Both took the skills area significantly forward with new programmes, Lesley developing Skills Growth Wales and Jeff launching Jobs Growth Wales. Ken Skates took over Jeff's responsibilities in 2013. Work in these areas was significantly strengthened with Owen Evans's arrival as Director of Skills, HE and Lifelong Learning, bringing with him experience of HE, the private sector and business-community links.

Informed choice of course depended on the advice being offered to young people, and we had concerns about the effectiveness of the Careers Service. It had been a Labour manifesto commitment in 2007 that the Careers Wales companies should become a single national organisation, and Adrian Webb had recommended this. John had commissioned a review of Careers Wales by Professor Tony Watts, which had made recommendations on the need for a strategy to be developed as to whether the careers companies were able to offer an all-age service. Watts concluded that 'the current structure of six independent Careers Wales companies, plus a seventh jointly-owned company which is a servant of the six, is problematic'.

Estyn had also reviewed the service, noting differences in quality between the different careers companies. John had announced an external review of Careers Wales, and appointed a review group in November 2009 to consider whether there was a case for a reduction in the number of careers companies. It was due to hold its first meeting a week after I was appointed. I decided to change the remit for the group and spoke to officials, then to the review group chair, former Coleg Menai Chief Executive Haydn Edwards, to warn him. I asked the group to work on the basis that a unitary structure would be established for Careers Wales, announcing this in a statement in January 2010.

The detailed review by Haydn, Professor Danny Saunders and Dr Deirdre Hughes, was subsequently published as *Future Ambitions*. There was considerable scepticism about the performance of the Careers Wales companies amongst Assembly Members and others. Their budget had doubled during the period of devolution from £20 million to £40 million. In budget negotiations in 2010, when we had to find additional savings following the UK coalition government's budget cuts, we decided to reduce the Careers Wales budget by stages to £30 million by 2013-14, as we protected frontline spending on schools and skills.

There was also considerable confusion about the status of the Careers Wales companies. Originally part of the public sector, they had been privatised following local government reorganisation in the mid-1990s. These private companies were essentially awarded rolling contracts with the department, but legal advice suggested that under EU procurement rules it would be impossible to continue this arrangement year on year. The decision to create one company, and the impact of the funding situation, concentrated the minds of the leadership of the Careers companies, and helped to drive things forward. We debated the best model for the new service, and decided ultimately that it made most sense to take the service back into the public sector, as a subsidiary company of the Welsh Government. Following the May 2011 Assembly election, Jeff Cuthbert took over the responsibility for Careers Wales. By 2012-13 the companies became a single entity, Career Choices Dewis Gyrfa, offering a more personalised service. Jeff then secured its transfer back into the public sector – after months of Herculean work by our official, Andrew Clark, who had to work his way through complex meetings on legal structures and intricate discussions with local authority pension funds. Within the department, we also established work on labour market intelligence to inform better careers planning, with new links established between BITC and Careers Wales to ensure more long-term engagement by businesses in schools.

One area where I felt that the department did not have a clear story to tell, or a coherent policy, was in the area of young people not in education, employment or training. Although we had the Skill Build programme, effectively, as Lord (Ted) Rowlands, described it, 'a safety net to support young people', we needed a more coherent approach. Early in 2010, I had to make my first speech on this subject. Often as a Minister it is in the process of reading the department's draft of a speech for a public engagement that you start to question the direction, focus and detail of policy. If a speech is not one that would convince you, then you know you have a problem. I asked for the speech, for a WCVA conference on economic inactivity, to be rewritten. I still wasn't happy with the finished draft, and resolved there and then to set up a quick external review of our policies on youth unemployment chaired by Martin Mansfield of the Wales TUC, Marcella Maxwell of Working Links, and Rachel Moxey, who had headed the successful JobMatch programme in the Heads of the Valleys when I was Deputy Minister for Regeneration. I also decided to carry out a full internal policy review of what triggers children and young people to disengage from learning in the first place, to ensure that our approach to identifying the problem of young people becoming disengaged was coherent and holistic, working across the whole department, with an early presentation on options at my monthly Policy Board.

Both reviews led to action. Alongside important work from the Wales Employment and Skills Board in the same area, they fed into the new Youth Employment and Engagement Action Plan, the first version of which was published in January 2011. We had evidence to the Assembly's Enterprise and Learning committee in 2010 from third sector organisations that the issue we faced was not the money going into the system – they admitted they were often competing for the same young people for the programmes that they were running. The issue was coordination of services and early identification.

I reckoned that we had some £100 million in the system potentially chasing the same young people through a variety of different agencies. I wanted a single person to act as a 'lead broker' for every young person identified as being at risk of being outside education, employment or training. In some areas, Careers Wales took the main role, in other areas, it was the learning coach in a school, or it could be people in the Youth Service. Tracking young people through the system was key. I felt the evidence suggested that the only thing that had made a real difference to the numbers of young people who were not in education, employment or training was the state of the economy and the availability of reasonably-paid but low skilled employment. Some local authorities had effective work in place to improve things – Swansea had made good progress on coordinating services more effectively, and Wrexham had some good work on the early identification of young people who would likely turn out later to be in danger of falling outside education, employment or training, illustrating the need to begin addressing these issues at a younger age. Internally, this became a good issue for getting the department to engage across its different sections as to how we could create a holistic approach, from early years to post-16, a task Owen Evans took forward with relish. Internally, we created a new team with responsibility for youth engagement and employment.

Our manifesto for the 2011 Assembly election included a commitment to the creation of a new programme to support young people into employment, promising 4,000 job, training or apprenticeship opportunities a year for the first three years of the new Assembly term, based on a £75 million investment. I took the paper explaining the new programme, Jobs Growth Wales, to Cabinet in September 2011 and announced the detail of the new programme in October 2011. Jeff Cuthbert carried it through to launch, piloting and then full roll-out and implementation. Built on the best practices of the former Labour UK government's Future Jobs Fund, scrapped by the UK coalition government, it targetted unemployed young people aged 16 to 24 and providing them with work experience for a six-month period. Participants would be paid at or above the national minimum wage for a minimum of twenty-five hours per week.

The significant difference was that Jobs Growth Wales would target far more job opportunities in the private sector, significantly improving the potential for individuals to progress into sustained employment with those employers that have identified opportunities for business growth. We would avoid duplication with DWP schemes. We said we would target growth businesses being supported through the Skills Growth Wales programme, working closely with anchor and regionally important companies to identify their recruitment needs and match those employment opportunities with young people seeking work.

The third sector would continue to play a key role in assisting those young people requiring a more supported environment as they enter the labour market for the first time. We would deliver specific strands of support to help graduates find work opportunities, to support young people to enter self-employment and to assist microbusinesses to recruit their first employee.

In April 2014, the new Deputy Minister for Skills, Ken Skates AM, was able to report over 80 per cent of young people continuing their employment after 6 months on Jobs Growth Wales. This compared favourably with the UK government Work Programme which had a success rate of around 11 per cent. Additionally, the drop-out rate from Jobs Growth Wales was around 10 per cent compared to a Work Programme drop-out rate of 50 per cent. Over 11,000 job opportunities had been created. The Labour Party was considering rolling it out across the whole UK if it won power at the 2015 General Election.

Our partnership with the trades unions made lifelong learning at work a possibility through the Wales Union Learning Fund. In all, 166 projects had been approved between 1999 and 2012. There was direct involvement of employers along with the Wales TUC in assessing projects, with a wide range of schemes approved across different sectors.

Over the ten years from 1999 to 2009, we had doubled the numbers of apprenticeships in Wales from 13,000 to 25,000. The economic recession hit these hard, however, particularly for those under twenty five, which was why we had introduced our *Young Recruits* and *Pathways to Apprenticeships* schemes. Apprenticeships recovered to a record high of 28,000 by 2012-13. By April 2014, Ken Skates reported that apprenticeship completions had risen to 86 per cent from 54 per cent in 2006-7, ahead of the equivalent English rate of 74 per cent. As part of the agreement on the 2013-14 Budget an additional £20 million a year for two years was put into apprenticeships, which was intended to lead to a further 5,650 apprenticeship places, including Welsh-medium places.

Welfare Reform was one area where our policies as a Government in Wales clearly diverged from the policies of the UK government. The UK government's plans for welfare reform were published in the White Paper *Twenty-first Century Welfare* at the end of July 2010. Their plans were for a new system underpinned by Universal Credit to commence in 2013. Notwithstanding our opposition to the broad thrust of policies such as the bedroom tax, to the policies on mandation and sanctioning, to the UK government's proposals to close Remploy factories in Wales, and their decisions on the Social Fund, on the Independent Living Fund, on Council Tax benefit which transferred responsibilities to us while cutting budgets, there were also serious practical issues which the UK government had failed to think through in designing its policies. We were also of the view that we should not be forced to use Assembly budgets to make up for cuts coming through from Westminster in DWP provided benefits. Iain Duncan Smith's ignorant and ridiculous comments that the people of Merthyr were too 'static' and needed to get on a bus to find work in October 2010 illustrated for most of Wales how out-of-touch the UK coalition government was. They didn't learn. In May 2013, Lord Freud told the House of Commons Welsh Affairs Select Committee that those hit by the bedroom tax should 'use the sofa bed'.

During the period of the One Wales Government, welfare reform issues were discussed in Cabinet and in Cabinet sub-committees on Economic Renewal and Children and Young People. We discuss issues such as the impact on Assembly Government-funded services in relation to childcare, substance misuse, housing, training, social services and primary care, as well as looking at the cost implications overall. After the 2011 Assembly election, we established a Ministerial Task and Finish Group, which consisted of myself, Carl Sargeant as Minister for Local Government and Communities, Gwenda Thomas as Deputy Minister for Social Services, and Huw Lewis as Minister for Housing, Regeneration and Heritage. After the March 2013 re-shuffle, responsibility transferred to Huw Lewis, then to Jeff Cuthbert after I left the government.

As a government, we were not opposed to welfare reform. Indeed, we made it clear that we would welcome a simpler, more transparent system that made work pay and provided genuine support to individuals to help them find and keep work. However, we had serious concerns about many aspects of the UK government's programme. Our programme for government committed us to doing what we could to mitigate the negative impact of the changes to welfare benefits. We published a detailed analysis of the impact of the UK government's programme and held public meetings with a wide range of organisations representing groups who were likely to be affected.

Our first stage analysis, published in February 2012, drew largely on work from the Institute for Fiscal Studies. The latest statistics showed that 18.4 per cent of the working age population in Wales was claiming welfare benefits, compared to 14.5 per cent across Great Britain as a whole. This meant that changes would have a disproportionate impact on Wales, where higher numbers were claiming sickness or disability benefits, not surprising given our history of heavy industry. The South Wales valleys, and inner city areas of Cardiff, Newport and Swansea were the areas most likely to suffer. The poorest households with children were estimated to lose the largest proportion of their income, and non-working single parents and workless couples with children would also be badly hit. Our estimates were that the changes would increase relative child poverty by around 6,000 in 2012-13.

Our second-stage analysis found that the likely income lost to Wales would be £90 million in 2011-12 increasing to around £600 million per annum in 2015-16. Further losses of over £100 million per annum each were likely to accrue from decisions to increase benefits by 1 per cent rather than by inflation (by 2015-16), by those losing entitlement to Disabled Living Allowance (by 2018-19), and the time-limiting of Employment and Support Allowance (by 2015-16). These cuts would also have an impact of course on health, including mental health, on local authority services, and on the economy.

One area where we had particular concerns, and which the UK government had clearly not thought through, was in the area of benefit sanctioning and conditionality. In essence, this meant that people would lose their benefits unless they took up training or other opportunities. Initially, the UK government wanted to mandate people on to schemes run by the Welsh Government. The DWP had clearly assumed that they could mandate people on to work-based learning or FE programmes in Wales as they planned to do in England, and had not thought through the implications of devolution.

In February 2011, I wrote to Chris Grayling, UK government Minister for Employment about the potential impact of the DWP's skills conditionality policy in relation to Welsh Government funded provision. In subsequent correspondence over an extended period, most recently in April 2012, I continued to express concern about DWP's policy of trying to enforce unemployed people to learn through the threat of benefit sanctions. The Welsh Government was not convinced by this approach and I consistently requested that the UK government provide evaluation of their activity in England before deciding whether to support the implementation of the policy in Wales.

Despite making our position clear, the DWP confirmed its intention to push ahead regardless and tried to put arrangements in place to make attendance at Welsh Government funded provision mandatory for customers perceived as needing to address a skills gap.

I was resolute in my commitment to oppose this apparent disregard for our position. By June 2012, I was able to advise Cabinet, and then the Assembly in a written statement, that in a sudden reversal of their decision, DWP had confirmed that it would respect the Welsh Government position of continuing to deliver learning and skills programmes on a voluntary engagement basis until such time that it was able to provide evaluation of activity for us to review our position again. It would therefore only mandate skills conditionality through programmes that the DWP itself funds.

In May 2012, the First Minister and I had taken our concerns about welfare reform to the Joint Ministerial Committee in London. This is the committee designed to allow UK wide issues to be discussed by the devolved administrations and the UK Government, and for issues to be resolved where there are conflicts, if possible. It was chaired by Nick Clegg and Lord Freud attended on behalf of the Department for Work and Pensions. The Scottish Government also had concerns about welfare reform. The Scottish Government raised its concerns and then I raised a long list of questions that we had. We were still unclear on many detailed elements of universal credit. These were issues we had been raising in ministerial meetings since the summer of 2010. In particular, there were issues which again we felt had not been fully thought through by DWP. For example, we were keeping the educational maintenance allowance in Wales though it was being abolished in England. How would that be allowed for in assessing family income in respect of Universal Credit? We had had no answer. We were also concerned about the implications for passported benefits. I finished my list of questions and Nick Clegg, in bringing in Lord Freud, said that he had been asking many of the same questions that I had!

In June 2012 I took a paper to Cabinet which highlighted the lack of information forthcoming from the Department of Work and Pensions, including the lack of detailed data on Universal Credit in particular, which would have implications for our modeling of 15 passported benefits. This would have implications for our own services, such as eligibility for Free Schools Meals. It was apparent to us that the UK government was pushing ahead on its reforms without being able to quantify the implications.

On 7th March 2012, I was telephoned by Maria Miller, the UK Minister for Disabled People, who told me that she would be making a written statement at 12.30 accepting the recommendations of the Sayce Review, radically reducing the UK government subsidy to Remploy, resulting in the closure of Remploy factories in England, Scotland and Wales. Seven factories were to close in Wales, with only the factories at Baglan making furniture, and at Porth in my own Rhondda constituency, which cleans data from computers and prepares them for recycling, regarded as 'potentially viable' and intended to stay open for the time being. The seven due for closure were in Aberdare, Abertillery, Bridgend, Croespenmaen, Merthyr, Swansea and Wrexham. I decided to make an immediate statement on this to the Assembly that afternoon which was granted by the Presiding Officer. In Westminster, MPs, led by my Rhondda colleague Chris Bryant, demanded that Maria Miller follow my example and come to the Commons and make a statement.

In responding to the UK government's proposals for Remploy, we were able to develop a Welsh response which genuinely helped to mitigate the impact of the UK government's proposals. We were opposed to the closure of Remploy factories. We believed that there was considerable scope to improve the way Remploy factories operated. We believed that they were top-heavy in management terms and often poor at marketing.

The next week, I told Cabinet that I would be meeting Maria Miller after the Cabinet meeting, pressing her to devolve the budget for Remploy factories in Wales to the Welsh Government for a three-year period, so that we could put in place measures that would provide a lasting solution. We also asked for the timeline for closure to be extended. I also met the chief executive of Remploy. I had conversations with the Scottish and Northern Irish governments about their arrangements (Northern Ireland was outside the Remploy arrangements but had their own similar operation). My request for the Remploy budget to be devolved was turned down. I visited all of the Remploy factories in Wales by the end of April, speaking to the workforces and examining with officials what we might do. We discussed how to take things forward with the leaders of local government in the relevant areas, and established a group with trade unions, including Unite and the GMB, and social enterprise organisations, as well as some private sector bodies, including the Wales Co-op Centre and Social Firms Wales, to coordinate activities.

Our emphasis was not on saving factories per se, but on preserving jobs for those affected. On 17th July 2012, I was able to announce that we were creating a support grant for public and private sector businesses and organisations who were able to offer suitable sustainable employment to disabled former Remploy workers. This involved a package of tapered support for up to four years for each eligible Remploy worker. Our employer support grant (ESG) was popular and the trades unions saw it as a model for the rest of Great Britain. By April 2014, Jeff Cuthbert, as Minister for Communities and Tackling Poverty, was able to announce that 221 former Remploy workers had found work under the ESG in eighty different businesses. A further 177 posts had also been approved for support. At the same time, I was pleased that the Remploy factory in Porth transferred under a management buy-out into a new social enterprise, E-Cycle Ltd, with ESG support. The ESG also supported the creation of businesses by former Remploy workers, including a new co-operative in Swansea.

FE colleges had been delivering for Wales, as Estyn and the Adrian Webb review had recognised. David Jones, the personable chief executive of Deeside College, and subsequently, Coleg Cambria following the merger with Yale College, was rightly able to claim in 2011 that FE was 'the most efficient, high performing and socio-economically engaged part of our education system.' But we had too much over-supply in post-16 education. Too many unviable classes, too many small sixth-forms below 150 students, and FE colleges that were also not organised in the most efficient way. The First Minister's manifesto had included a commitment to eliminating unnecessary competition between providers and this was carried through in our 2011 election manifesto.

To be fair to the FE sector, they were taking the Welsh Government's commitments on Transformation of post-16 education seriously. Under the leadership of David Jones, who chaired Colegau Cymru for much of this period, supported by its sensible chief executive John Graystone, they anticipated our objectives and responded well to what we were suggesting. By 2012, the number of FE Corporations had reduced from twenty five in 2008 to fourteen. A further three mergers took place in

2013, taking the sector almost to the point that Adrian Webb had suggested it should be back in his 2007 report. Efficiency gains were being obtained and more funds focused on learning authority led as against back-room operations. Major investments had taken place in many institutions, including the Ebbw Vale campus of Blaenau Gwent, in Merthyr, the Nantgarw campus of Coleg Morgannwg, at Coleg Llandrillo and many other centres, with exciting plans for a new city centre campus for Cardiff and Vale College. The merger of Coleg Harlech with the Workers Educational Association in South Wales was also finally accomplished in January 2014, after years of pressure from the Welsh Government, culminating in my threat to suspend funding to the college after its unsatisfactory financial arrangements came to light, again with Stakhanovite work by Andrew Clark and his team. However, as I told Cabinet in April 2012, local authority-led secondary school reorganisation was moving at a slower pace. This was partly a result of foot-dragging and local opposition, coupled with a belief in some quarters that FE colleges could not offer high quality academic programmes and adequate pastoral care. The announcements of the twenty-first century schools funding in 2012, coupled with additional future investment announced through the local government borrowing initiative in 2013, meant that the transformation agenda was on its way to being completed.

We had an outstanding commitment to trying to secure a common lecturers' contract across Wales in further education. In 2003, the Assembly Government had made funding available to achieve pay parity between schools and colleges. The First Minister's manifesto had committed us, and we had repeated this in our 2011 election manifesto, to trying to seek a common contract for FE lecturers across Wales. Several years of negotiation were still continuing when I left office in June 2013.

We had a commitment to address issues of governance in further education. We were seeking to change the corporate status of FE colleges, following the First Minister's leadership manifesto commitment, again followed up in our 2011 election manifesto. John Griffiths had announced plans to address the governance of FE institutions in June 2009, and had established a stakeholder group to look at these. This made recommendations on accountability for use of public funds, effective governance and scrutiny of senior management, representation of staff and students, and the ways in which the 14-19 networks were governed. I also said I would develop a remit letter for the post-16 sector. I saw these as a model for effective governance under current arrangements, but resolved to take forward the incorporation issue in a paper to Cabinet in early 2010. In May 2010, I announced a further review, looking at a social enterprise model for FE, to be chaired by Rob Humphreys, director of the Open University in Wales, and confirmed the other members in July.

The Humphreys review was submitted to me in February 2011 and I took it to Cabinet in March, which agreed to a consultation being held on its proposals. This proposed a new model of governance for FE inspired by the model for Dwr Cyru (Welsh Water), one of the largest social enterprises in Wales, with a policy-making Board accountable to a Membership Body. I took the outcome of the three-month consultation to the Cabinet of the newly-elected Welsh Government in November 2011. I overturned one proposal of the Humphreys Review, to ensure that learners, through their students' unions, did have a place on the Board, following last-minute lobbying by Katie Dalton and NUS Wales. I had hoped to legislate to ensure that at least 40 per cent of Board Members were women, as I told Cabinet in the paper, but discrimination and equality issues were not devolved.

However, the Humphreys proposal fell foul of EU rules following a decision by the Office of National Statistics in response to EU legislation to declassify FE colleges as public sector bodies rather than its former, rather bureaucratic title, of not-for-profit institutions serving households (NPISH). For the first and only time, in June 2012, I had to ask Cabinet to reverse a decision it had previously taken. The reason was that the ONS change would have a very significant impact on Welsh Government budgets. All

FE income and expenditure would count against Welsh Government budgets. Capital budgets would be affected, which would be likely to mean a reduction of £20 million capital each year. FEIs would be inhibited from carrying forward budget surpluses and building reserves for future projects. We therefore legislated in the Further and Higher Education (Governance and Information Wales) Bill to return the status of FE Colleges to NPISH. As I told the Assembly, the new legislation was not my preferred route, but I felt that we had no alternative as we could not carry the financial costs at a time of severe cuts to our budgets.

Devolution, Difference – and Delivery

'What's the deal on Wales?', the US chat show host David Letterman asked the UK Prime Minister in 2012. It was a good question. I sometimes think that the Letterman question should replace the West Lothian question as the touchstone of post-devolution politics and commentary in the UK.

Indeed, I would like to propose to news editors in London that from now on they adopt the Letterman question whenever they are analysing a new policy initiative from the UK government. I would also like to propose to UK government ministers – whatever party they may be drawn from in the future – that they consider the Letterman question whenever they are thinking of a new policy initiative.

Too often England, because of the size of its population, is treated as the default model by the media, when arguably the devolved administrations are often more in line with mainstream European practice. Too often also, England is taken as the default model when UK government ministers and their officials are constructing schemes to be rolled out on a UK or Great Britain basis. Too often, there is simply ignorance of a key fact, that cabinet ministers in the UK government are often merely ministers for England.

We have a highly-centralised set of national newspapers in the UK. If Michael Gove says that A levels or GCSEs are too weak and need to be strengthened – in the process, for example, radically simplifying the debate over modular and linear forms of assessment – then that is what the so-called national newspapers will report. A perspective on those exams is given, largely unchallenged. Given their reach into Wales there is potential for serious confusion amongst Welsh parents and pupils over what is actually happening. While the reality of devolution is that decisions are for us to take, and our policy autonomy is unchallenged, if the validity of the exams has been publicly questioned, then it has an impact on the confidence that people place on exams taken here too, particularly when cap-doffing Conservative MPs from Wales, anxious for ministerial preferment at a UK level, ignorantly claim that English qualifications will be more rigorous than those in Wales. The *Mail on Sunday* in 2013 reported that Michael Gove would be rolling out a new maths qualification to all UK schools. His powers, of course, were limited to England. The BBC, normally the most attentive to these issues, reported on its website in September 2012 that Michael Gove would be announcing new exams for England and Wales, until the Welsh Government corrected them.

It was occasionally suggested that I spent too much time focusing on the media. With the potential for mis-reporting I have just indicated, I would argue that a major part of the role of a minister in a Welsh government is advocacy.

There are many issues relevant to the study of the media and politics post-devolution that are thrown up by the examples in this book:

- to what extent, for example, is the policy autonomy of devolved institutions constrained by a centralised media?
- What is the right way to manage intra-government relationships over common interests at a time of policy divergence?
- Has the UK system yet evolved to a mature state post-devolution?
- Is it feasible to envisage UK-wide editorial judgements being made by any media organisation, able to analyse policy forensically and explain it intelligently to the overall audience?

These are not just issues for the constitutional anoraks. They have meaning in all our lives.

In Wales, we are now used to alternative centres of power in the UK. I am not sure that UK ministers are. There are now three kinds of UK ministers, it seems to me.

- Those, like the Foreign Secretary, or the Defence Secretary, who operate on a genuinely UK-wide basis.
- Those, like the Secretary of State for Education, who are largely ministers for England – except on teacher's pay and pensions.
- Those, like the Secretary of State for Work and Pensions, who work principally on a UK or GB basis, but have to deliver some of their functions through the devolved administrations. They design systems which treat England as the default model – then have to revise them when they discover, to give but one example, that we have kept education maintenance allowances in Wales unlike England and we need to know if this will affect the income of families on Universal Credit.

In Wales, our policy autonomy is constrained of course not just by the interpretation of issues through the public sphere of the UK media, but by decisions taken in England which have an impact on us, because of strong cross-border flows, such as the decision to allow tuition fees to rise to £9,000. It is also limited, as a result of our membership of the EU, by EU laws, as we saw over FE Governance. Nothing wrong with that – sovereignty has been pooled in return for greater and very tangible benefits.

I am writing some months before Scotland votes on independence. If Scotland were to vote yes, then that of course changes everything. But whatever the outcome of that vote, we need a new culture at the centre of political discourse in these islands, one informed enough to understand the differences between the different nations in our multi-national state, and one sophisticated enough to recognise that England is not the default model, and the other nation-states interesting only for their exoticism in diverging from it. Could it be that Wales, Scotland

and Northern Ireland are more in step with each other, and under the coalition England is the eccentric? Could it be that Wales, Scotland and Northern Ireland are more in tune with mainstream European thinking, and the UK coalition government's English administration is the loner howling in the attic?

If we were to conceive of the UK in this way, with a more balanced sense of the four nations emanating from London newsrooms, how would the media report Michael Gove launching a unilateral attack on GCSE and A level exams, when Wales and Northern Ireland continue to support them? Like this, perhaps:

> 'Constitutional crisis over English Education Secretary's unilateral threat to qualifications'

Or perhaps not. So, what's the deal on Wales? How would it be if Wales were treated as normative, as the default system, rather than England? We have suffered a UK coalition government practising a policy of what I called in 2012 'English exceptionalism', with a Westminster political and media class, mired in what both Lord Morgan of Aberdyfi (Kenneth O. Morgan the historian), and Raymond Williams separately called 'metropolitan provincialism'. That English exceptionalism today threatens the unity of the United Kingdom itself.

When Seymour Martin Lipset's *American Exceptionalism* book came out in 1996 I recall a frisson of excitement amongst the Conservative Party policy wonks who used to attend the receptions and dinners and visits to the Proms that – as the then BBC Head of Public Affairs – I used to have to organise. Was there not, I heard some of them say, a kind of English exceptionalism that underpinned the conservatism of England – the kind of individualist, mercantile philosophy which differentiated English from continental history? Many of those people, of course, subsequently went on to hold positions under the Conservative party of David Cameron.

What they meant then by that label of 'English exceptionalism' is different from what I mean by it. Under the coalition, it is English policy that is moving away from the other constituent nations of the UK, particularly, as the TUC pointed out in its 2014 publication, *Education for Sale*, in education policy. English exceptionalism is the political practice of this Conservative-led coalition, unperturbed by the difference of Wales, or Scotland or indeed Northern Ireland. There is no effective UK public sphere of policy discussion. The UK has a dysfunctional political and media culture which no longer reflects the state we live in.

Michael D. Higgins, then the Irish Culture Minister, now the Irish President, idealised the public sphere as 'a free space of public discussion among citizens' in his Green Paper on Broadcasting, published in 1995 (this is, by the way, the only government consultation document I have ever read which refers directly to the German sociologist Jürgen Habermas, the main theorist of the evolution of the public sphere.) I am not convinced, more than fifteen years after devolution, that we have evolved an effective UK public sphere, but that is a subject for another essay or another book. In this book I have simply tried to sketch some of the contours of complexity that underpin the making of policy on education by a devolved government in a stateless nation within a multi-national state with a centralised media at a time of radical policy divergence.

Professor Philip Schlesinger, probably the leading analyst of the relationships between media and the political spaces to which they relate, suggests that the formation of Habermas's 'classic' public sphere coincided with the growth of nationalism and nation-state formation. But Schlesinger argues powerfully that it is no longer adequate, if it ever was, to conceive of a simple 'functional fit' between a nation and a national media. Schlesinger identifies three political levels where the concept of a communications space is elaborated: the supranational, the nation-state level and below the nation-state. Our new Welsh democracy operates in a complex world in which spaces of identity, to borrow the title of an important book by David Morley and Kevin Robins, are changing and contested. As they say, 'Our senses of space and place are all being significantly reconfigured.'

Of course, in terms of daily papers, most people in Wales read papers produced in London, but these rarely cover Wales at all. What is regarded in south Wales as our national newspaper, the *Western Mail,* sells to a small percentage of the population. In north Wales, the *Daily Post* does similarly. The local and regional papers add another layer, but with a focus that is not itself national. The public broadcasters reach the most, through the evening news bulletins particularly, and provide, principally through the medium of English, the nearest thing we have to an idealised public sphere. Meanwhile, through the medium of Welsh, we have S4C and Radio Cymru, *Y Cymro* and *Golwg* in either its physical, online or app versions.

In other words, in Wales we have a fractured and fragmented public sphere, in which a minority of our citizens engage. Our Wales is not a hermetically-closed space but a permeable one. In the digital world, borders and boundaries are more complex.

We have no perfect Welsh public sphere and no perfect singular Welsh political space. In Wales, we may determine our education policy in a recognised political space physically constructed as the Senedd, but our policy-making is part of a fluid and messy process that sometimes looks confusing not only to our citizens and our media but also to ourselves as a political class. Democracy is messy. Democracy in a stateless nation with a largely coterminous national media such as Scotland is messier still. Democracy in a stateless nation *without* a coterminous national media like Wales is the messiest of all.

I think sadly there remains a culture of deference within the Welsh media. Deference to London and London-based editors, deference to a centralised culture which is assumed to be normative, the default mechanism, or just too often assumed to be right because it has been around longer. So for example, when the Attorney-General referred the Welsh Government's Bye-laws Bill to the Supreme Court, too many commentators in the media here told us that this, to quote BBC Wales, was 'an embarrassment for the Welsh Government'. In the end of course, the Welsh Government won five-nil. On all counts.

That alone suggests to me that it is time to say to our own media here in Wales – stop looking over your shoulder. Stop tugging your forelock. It's time to abandon the Cymric cringe.

At the peak of the English language GCSE regrading row, the former Plaid Cymru MP, Adam Price, said in *The Guardian* that I had been prepared to flex my 'devolutionary muscles'. I make no apology for believing that we need to have the confidence, a decade and a half after devolution, that we can build our own capacity, not separate from the UK but learning alongside our co-residents of these islands, and develop our own education system to a level of expertise and excellence. There are lessons to learn from England, from Scotland, from Northern Ireland and elsewhere. There are things that we have brought to the table, like Jobs Growth Wales, like our Qualifications Review that created a revised qualification in the Welsh Bac genuinely aspiring to offer both vocational and academic pathways, like our support system for Welsh students, full and part-time, from which others may wish to learn.

In their report on Welsh education, the OECD said:

> Due to its close cultural, historical and political ties, Wales has a natural tendency to compare itself and look towards England for inspiration when it comes to educational best practices. This comparison is becoming less relevant as the two education systems have taken different paths since devolution in 1999.

After the UK General Election in 2015, Academies will stay in England whoever is in power, and the challenges facing that system will be significantly different to the challenges facing our own. In Wales, as in Scotland, there will be non-selective community based schools, operating within a framework of local authority responsibility. We need to develop our own capacity for the future. As the Finnish educator, Pasi Sahlberg, says 'it is better to have a dream of your own than rent one from others.'

To do this, however, we need to confront our challenges honestly, admit mistakes when made, commit to high standards, abandon excuses, and be prepared constantly to seek to get better at what we do. Professor Dylan Wiliam says, seriously but light-heartedly (and you can find it on Youtube here: https://www.youtube.com/watch?v=eqRcpA5rYTE#t=20-):

> every teacher needs to get better... every teacher fails on a daily basis. If you're not failing on a daily basis, you're just not paying attention.... As teachers we fail all the time... our daily experience as teachers is of failure. Which makes it the best job in the world. Because you never get any good at it.... This job is so hard that one lifetime isn't long enough to master it.

He argues what is needed is a culture of continuous improvement. A strong focus on the quality of teaching and learning should drive the next phase of educational development in Wales – and we should remember that quality trumps choice every time and in every setting.

Dylan Wiliam's words on continuous learning of course are as valid for ministers and other politicians as they are for teachers. Honesty and openness about past mistakes and a commitment to improve make for better policy and implementation in the future. I said at the outset of this book that the media is largely interested in the fractures in policy-making between successive ministers, rather than the continuities, but no one would I think consider Carwyn Jones's governments to be prisoners of 'the new producerism' identified by the Institute of Welsh Affairs in 2006 as the educational narrative of the first two Assembly terms.

Since Carwyn Jones's election as First Minister, we have seen standards improve in Wales. Our GCSE performance is closing the gap with our neighbours. The number of young people leaving schools without a qualification is at an all-time low. Attendance is better all round. We have got better at using data in schools to assist performance. We provide better data on schools and better quality information on students' performance to parents. We have developed a high quality literacy and numeracy framework supported by the profession. We have embedded the Foundation phase. We have strengthened pre-school with a doubling of the spending on Flying Start.

We have strengthened our qualifications system. We have invested more in our schools, including on their buildings and the technological infrastructure to support teaching and learning. We have taken steps to promote teaching as a high-quality job, bringing in the new Master's qualification and Teach First, raising standards of entry to teacher training and setting out an action plan for the training of support staff, backed by an Education Workforce Council supportive of all who work in schools. We have established a new system to back educational leadership in schools. We have taken steps to strengthen school improvement and support services on a regional basis. We have started on the journey towards a Curriculum for Wales. We have given parents the right to have their demand for Welsh-medium education properly measured by local authorities.

We have protected Welsh students from higher tuition fees. We have re-shaped higher education so it is stronger for the future. We have invested in skills, ensuring more apprenticeships with higher completion rates than England, maintaining support for the most needy students after sixteen with the education maintenance allowance, and we have created the successful Jobs Growth Wales programme for young people and the Employer Support Programme for former Remploy workers, and re-fashioned our careers services for the modern age. Our Further Education colleges are stronger and better.

Much has been done. There is always more to do. The point of devolution was not to be different for the sake of it, but to deliver better for the people of Wales. We have to have the confidence that we can continue to improve, and the willingness, all of us, to try and do even better in the future.

Politician of the Year Leighton Andrews AM 2012

With kind permission of Mumph
www.mumph.co.uk

Acknowledgements

No Minister can deliver without the support of their civil servants and Private Office. There is a convention in the civil service that books by ministers can only mention senior civil servants, with the exception of positive references to the Ministerial Private Office team, so I am unable to name all of those who played a fundamental role in our education work in this period, including the legal teams and the press office. They know who they are – and many thanks.

In HE, Neil Surman led a great team who sorted out tuition fee policy and the vice chancellors. Andrew Clark did a formidable job on further education, sorting out the detail of the passage of Careers Wales into the public sector, and gave Coleg Harlech the last rites. Sonya Reynolds successfully delivered the Transformation agenda. From 2011, Dr Caroline Turner began to re-position our work on the Welsh language, successfully integrating staff from the Welsh Language Board into Government, delivering our new Welsh Language Strategy and the Language Commissioner's appointment and office. For a statistician, Glyn Jones had a good sense of humour and knew just how far any minister was allowed to go.

Teresa Holdsworth joined together policy on young people and skills. Carla Lyne held together the financial strategy of the department, keeping a close eye on pressures and managing relations with central finance with great skill, as well as leading on key reviews such as the Viv Thomas review. Emma Williams brilliantly managed the analysis of qualification results and PISA, before escaping to handle assessment. Lindsay Harvey took a grip of our ICT programme, and did an outstanding job developing the Hwb and Learning Wales websites and then the roll-out of Learning in Digital Wales. Steve Vincent was our local authority enforcer and no one could pull the wool over his eyes.

In the most senior roles, Chris Tweedale did a great job leading on schools and young people. As I said at his leaving party, continuing our banter over three and a half years, 'hasn't he done well – for a geography teacher!' Jo-Anne Daniels had great assurance and calmness in taking literacy, numeracy and the curriculum forward. Lynne Hamilton did an immense job on the finances and in overseeing the twentieth-century schools programme and the development of our tuition fee policy. Brett Pugh brought new depth and intelligence to our analysis of data and the development of school standards. I enjoyed the brief time I worked with Dennis Gunning and Grenville Jackson, who had great insight into the sector. Owen Evans not only oversaw the execution of our higher education and skills policies, but led the groundwork on Jobs Growth Wales, the Qualifications Review and the Employer Support Grant for former Remploy workers.

At the head of the department, Emyr Roberts and then Owen both calmly delivered, anticipated trouble and found solutions without fuss and drama, while building alliances inside and outside the Government.

Helen Childs was outstanding as head of my Ministerial Private Office and assembled an extraordinarily effective team around her, including at different times Helen Palmer, Rhian Atkinson, Matthew Mithan, Penny Watkins, Mike Weatherhead, Gareth Chard, Matthew King, Gemma Bright, Karen Morris and Shona O'Shea. They worked immensely hard and no one could have asked for more.

My special advisers, Professor Ian Butler and then Matt Greenough, provided thoughtful insight, analysis and counsel, and held me back when they needed to do so. As specialist advisers, Professor Merfyn Jones and Aled Eirug knew their areas well and were able to anticipate new policy needs.

My Ministerial Advisory Board (MAB) was a great source of intelligent commentary. This included the Chair of the Higher

Education Funding Council for Wales, Roger Thomas; the Estyn Chief Inspector, Ann Keane; the Welsh representative on the UK Council for Employment and Skills, first Professor Sir Adrian Webb and subsequently Scott Waddington of Brain's; and a number of public appointees, including former Treorchy Head Bethan Guilfoyle, Professor Danny Saunders of the University of Glamorgan, Huw Evans, initially chief executive of Coleg Llandrillo, then Chair of our Qualifications Review, Liz Kidd, former Head of Estyn's post-16 section, special needs expert Cliff Warwick, with an international reputation in the early years of childhood development. Professor Iram Siraj, and with shrewd insights into English policy, Fiona Millar.

The Practitioners Panel of head teachers was a great asset from 2012. Dr Dylan Jones, head teacher of Ysgol Bro Morgannwg, proved an outstanding chair, and the group also included former head teacher Bethan Guilfoyle and serving head teachers Simon Pridham, Emma Laing, Marc Belli, the late Sue Jenkins, inspiring head teacher in Newport, Phil McTague, Janet Hayward, Liz Edwards, Rhys Angell-Jones, Andy Henderson, Martin Grimes, Dewi Lake and Rachael Webb. Thanks to all of them.

Any mistakes, of course, were mine.

Glossary

ACCAC	Qualifications, Curriculum and Assessment Authority for Wales
AQA	Examining body
ASCL	Association of School and College Leaders (principally the secondary head teachers union)
ATL	Association of Teachers and Lecturers (most moderate teaching union)
CCEA	Council for Curriculum, Examination and Assessment in Northern Ireland
CSR	Comprehensive Spending Review
DWP	Department for Work and Pensions
EBCs	English Baccalaureate Certificates Edexcel Examining body
ESG	Employer Support Grant for disabled former Remploy workers
Estyn	Education inspectorate in Wales
FE	Further Education
GCSE	General Certificate of Secondary Education
GTCW	General Teaching Council for Wales
HE	Higher Education
HEFCE	Higher Education Funding Council for England
HEFCW	Higher Education Funding Council for Wales
HEW	Higher Education Wales – vice chancellors' lobby
ICT	Information Communications Technology
iNET	International Networking for Educational Transformation
INSET	In-Service Training days
ITT	Initial Teacher Training

LCO	Legislative Competence Order
LNF	Literacy and Numeracy Framework
MAB	Ministerial Advisory Board
NASUWT	National Association of Schoolmasters/Union of Women Teachers
NGfL	National Grid for Learning
NUS	National Union of Students
NUT	National Union of Teachers
OECD	Organisation for Economic Co-operation and Development – runs PISA, amongst other things
OFQUAL	Exam regulator in England
OFSTED	Education inspectorate in England
ONS	Office of National Statistics
NQT	Newly Qualified Teacher
PDG	Pupil Deprivation Grant
PISA	Programme for International Student Assessment
PLCs	Professional Learning Communities
PwC	PricewaterhouseCoopers
RSG	Revenue Support Grant
SEF	School Effectiveness Framework
SQA	Scottish Qualifications Authority – examining body and regulator in Scotland
SSU	School Standards Unit
TES	*Times Educational Supplement*
THE	*Times Higher Education*
UCAC	Union for Welsh-medium Teachers
UCAS	University application clearing house
UCU	University and College Union (lecturers' union)
WJEC	Welsh-based examining body
WLGA	Welsh Local Government Association

Bibliographical Essay

The primary sources used in this book are the published Cabinet Minutes and Cabinet Papers of the Welsh Government, the Record of Proceedings of the National Assembly for Wales, and the reviews and publications undertaken by and for the Welsh Government's Department for Education and Skills, all of which are available online. The 2011 Welsh Labour Assembly Manifesto, *Standing up for Wales,* puts our education policies in context. The One Wales Government agreement, which covered the period 2007-11, is also available online. Carwyn Jones's manifesto was called *Time to Lead* and set out some of the policies we took forward after his election in 2009. Links are available to many of the documents and reports, and my key lectures and speeches, from the blog I established while writing this book, www.ministeringtoeducation.com. The websites of educational organisations in Wales such as Estyn and HEFCW are a further source of material for researchers, as are the Welsh Government's Hwb, Learning Wales and My Local School websites. The 2014 OECD report, *Improving Schools in Wales,* is obviously important. The *TES* and *THE* covered many of the stories and are quoted in various places, as is the *Western Mail.* Gerald Kaufman's book *How to be a Minister* (Faber edition, 1997) is entertaining on ministerial life and not yet bettered.

In terms of the political literature on educational change, for the New Labour governments from 1997-2010, I have drawn on Michael Barber's *Instruction to Deliver* (Politico's, 2007), and *Deliverology 101* (Corwin, 2011) and his essay in Andy Hargreaves and Michael Fullan's *Change Wars* (Solution Tree Press, 2009). John Stannard and Laura Huxford's *The Literacy*

Game (Routledge, 2007) is also useful. As Michael Barber and Conor Ryan, David Blunkett's former special adviser, have confirmed to me, there is no single coherent volume on David Blunkett's time as Education Secretary. There is valuable material in a couple of chapters of Stephen Pollard's biography, *David Blunkett* (Hodder & Stoughton, 2004); the story is told episodically in *The Blunkett Tapes* (Bloomsbury, 2006); David's earlier autobiography, *On a Clear Day,* (Michael O'Mara Books, 2002) covers the story of those years in education in a breathless couple of pages which conclude 'this is not the place to describe in detail how we achieved what we did'.

Andrew's Adonis's book *Education, Education, Education* (Biteback Publishing, 2012) is a compelling story, well-told, of how in government he set out 'to reinvent the comprehensive school.' But it is also a story of how to get things done in government, and rightly it has drawn praise for that. If you want to read how the Academies programme developed and the successes that it had, then immerse yourself in Andrew's account. Peter Hyman's *1 out of 10* (Vintage, 2005) is a terrific read. Tony Blair's autobiography, *A Journey*, (Arrow, 2011) gives his views of the Academies programme, and Alastair Campbell's diaries (Arrow, various dates) are fascinating, of course, on the internal dynamics of policy-making on education, as well as everything else. You will find effective challenges in Melissa Benn's *School Wars* (Verso, 2011) and John Bangs, John MacBeath and Maurice Galton's *Reinventing Schools, Reforming Teaching* (Routledge, 2010). Sally Tomlinson's *Education in a Post-Welfare Society* (Open University, 2005) combines both detail and critique. The Tower Hamlets story of achievement without academies is well-captured in the November 2013 paper by Institute of Education director Professor Chris Husbands, Professor David Woods, and Dr Chris Brown *Transforming Education for All: the Tower Hamlets Story*. There has been a series of papers on the performance of academies from the LSE's Centre for the Economics of Education. Professor David Reynolds and Professor Tony Kelly of the University of Southampton wrote a useful RSA paper on 'Accountability and the meaning of "success" in education systems' which reviewed the New Labour period, and Professor Ruth Lupton and Polina Obolenskaya's paper 'Labour's record on education: policy, spending and outcomes 1997-2010' from the LSE's Centre for Analysis of Social Exclusion is also useful. I also found her 2012 paper with Amelia Hempel-Jorgensen 'The importance of teaching: pedagogical constraints and possibilities in working class schools' in the *Journal of Educational Policy* (27:5) useful. Peter Mortimore's *Education Under Siege* (Policy Press, 2013) is worth reading and reflecting on as a counter to some of the educational initiatives of the last twenty years. In 2014, the TUC produced a report on English education, *Education Not for Sale*, written by Martin Johnson and Warwick Mansell, which said that England, compared to the devolved nations, was now 'the odd man out' in terms of education policies.

For Conservative education developments, the chapter on Michael Gove in Matthew D'Ancona's *In it Together* (Viking, 2013) is very interesting. Kenneth Baker's autobiography *The Turbulent Years* (Faber and Faber, 1993) is worth reading on the development of the National Curriculum and the 1988 Act, and the spring and autumn 1990 editions of the *History Workshop* journal have the essays by Raphael Samuel, Alice Prokaschka, Angela John and Jonathan Clark that I mention in the text. *The Right Kind of History* by David Cannadine, Jenny Keating and Nicola Sheldon (Palgrave Macmillan, 2011) carefully fillets the debates on history-teaching in the twentieth-century. Professor Steve Barnett's article on the concept of 'dumbing down' is in the Political Quarterly, vol. 69, issue B, in 1998.

More unreadable books on school improvement have been published than should ever have been written. It's a shame they don't have the clarity and directness of John Kotter's book on change management *Leading Change* (Harvard Business Review Press, 1996). Readable ones I recommend include most things by Michael Fullan, particularly his *All Systems Go* (Corwin, 2010) and *Leading in a Culture of Change* (Jossey Bass, 2007);

David Hopkins' books *Every School a Great School* (Open University Press, 2007) and *Exploding the Myths of School Reform* (Open University Press, 2013) and Kenneth Leithwood, Alma Harris and Tiiu Strauss's *Leading School Turnaround* (Jossey Bass, 2010*);* and Pasi Sahlberg's *Finnish Lessons* (Teachers' College Press, 2011) is also worth reading, not least to remind us that reform takes time and it is easy to focus on the wrong drivers.

In terms of teaching, key texts are Professor Dylan Wiliam's *Spectator* lecture from 2010 and his website and John Hattie's *Visible Learning* (Routledge, 2008). Daniel Willingham's *Why Don't Students Like School?* (Jossey Bass, 2010), and Daisy Christodoulou's *Seven Myths About Education* (Routledge, 2014), are thought-provoking. I thoroughly recommend Fenton Whelan's *Lessons Learned* (Fenton Whelan, 2009), and Philip Adey and Justin Dillon's *Bad Education* for myth- challenging (Open University Press, 2012). Barry Schwarz's *The Paradox of Choice* (Harper Perennial, 2005) gives good arguments as to why we should be wary of apparently unbounded choices.

The marketisation of higher education is now virtually a subject in itself, which may be why critics of the government have been so unsuccessful in challenging UK government policy – they have been too busy foot-noting. Roger Brown's collection of essays *Higher Education and the Market* (Routledge, 2010) is a good starting point; Mike Molesworth, Richard Scullion and Elizabeth Nixon add to the mix in *The Marketisation of Higher Education and the Student as Consumer* (Routledge, 2010); Rosemary Deem, Sam Hillyard and Mike Reed's *Knowledge, Higher Education and the New Managerialism* focuses on the 1998-2000 period; Thomas Docherty's *For the University* is, as Stefan Collini wrote in his *New Statesman* review 'more critical than practical in character.' Andrew McGettigan's *The Great University Gamble* (Pluto, 2013) is excellent on the tuition fees mess and he has been exceptional in taking his arguments into the political field with fluency and focus. I also recommend the 1998 post-Dearing essay on managerialism in HE by my brother,

Dr Geoff Andrews, in the *New Statesman*. Meanwhile, Stefan Collini's *What are Universities For?* (Penguin, 2012) should be read for pleasure as well as enlightenment. Clayton M. Christensen and Henry J. Eyring's *The Innovative University* (Jossey-Bass, 2011), along with Saad Rivzi, Katelyn Donnelly and Michael Barber's IPPR paper *An Avalanche is Coming*, are thought-provoking on the storms which may lie ahead, although I am slightly more sceptical about the potential napsterisation of HE, as I explain in this book. HEPI's pamphlets are also valuable.

The history of Welsh education debates is well-captured in Gareth Elwyn Jones and Gordon Wyn Roderick's *A History of Education in Wales* (University of Wales Press, 2003) and Richard Daugherty, Robert Phillips and Gareth Rees did an excellent job of dissecting administrative evolution over education in the decades before the National Assembly in their *Education Policy-Making in Wales* (University of Wales Press, 2000); Robert Smith's *Schools, Politics and Society* (UWP, 1999) is valuable on the 1870-1902 period; Richard Lewis's *Leaders and Teachers* (UWP, 1993) is excellent on the adult education leaders in Wales in the early twentieth century, including the ideological battles between the WEA and the Plebs League and the Labour colleges, and since he places Rhondda figures at the heart of the battles, I think everyone should read it; Joe England's edited collection *Changing Lives* (Llafur, 2007) delivers a fascinating focus on the WEA from 1907-2007; Professor J. Gwynn Williams *The University Movement in Wales* (UWP, 1993) demonstrates that public policy has always influenced Welsh higher education. Dai Smith's and Meic Stephens' collection *A Community and Its University* (UWP, 2003) illustrates, through the story of the development of what is now the University of South Wales, the twists and turns of education policy post-18 over time. Lord Crickhowell's autobiography *Westminster, Wales and Water* (UWP, 1999) reminds us that universities in Wales have always needed bailing out by politicians. Sir Deian Hopkin's and Richard Wyn Jones's IWA lectures, respectively *The Role of Universities in the Modern Economy* and *The Failure of the*

Universities in Wales are both valuable though now outdated. Anyone who wants to understand modern Wales needs at least a passing acquaintance with our history and our historians, in particular, but not exclusively, Gwyn Alf Williams's *When was Wales?* (Pelican, 1985), Dai Smith's *Wales, A Question for History*, (Seren, 1999) K.O. Morgan's *Rebirth of a Nation* (OUP, 1982) and John Davies's *A History of Wales* (Penguin, 2007). Geraint Talfan Davies's memoir *At Arm's Length* has a good account of the early years of devolution and the recalcitrance of the HE sector is mentioned (Seren, 2008). The Institute of Welsh Affairs book, *Time to Deliver*, (2006) has a useful commentary on education policy in the first two Assembly terms.

The cultural politics of education are debated in historical terms in Raymond Williams' *Culture & Society* (Pelican edition, 1961) and *The Long Revolution* (Pelican edition, 1965) and his earlier *Reading and Criticism* (Muller, 1950), as well as his essay 'Culture is Ordinary'; most of my understanding of technological determinism comes from his essay on 'Culture and Technology' in *Towards 2000* (Pelican, 1985). John McIlroy and Sallie Westwood's *Border Country: Raymond Williams in Adult Education* (NIACE, 1993) pulls together most of his essays on educational theory and practice. Dai Smith's biography *Raymond Williams: A Warrior's Tale* (Parthian, 2008) gives great insight into his intellectual development up to 1961 (Stefan Collini's July 2008 review of this in *The London Review of Books* is a valuable commentary.) Daniel Williams' useful collection of Raymond Williams' essays about Wales – *Who speaks for Wales?* (UWP, 2008) – includes his important essays on the Welsh historians.

In terms of the literature on poverty and education, particularly in the early years, EPPSE, the Effective Provision of Pre-School, Primary and Secondary Education, EPPSE 3-16 project carried out by the Institute of Education's Professor Iram Siraj, a member of my own Ministerial Advisory Board, Professor Edward Melhuish, Professor Pam Sammons, Professor Kathy Sylva, Dr Aziza Mayo, and Brenda Taggart, is a key research study. There is a complex debate as to what extent educational reform itself will address issues of social mobility. Professor John Goldthorpe, of the Oxford Institute of Social Policy, for example, has argued (in a 2012 paper entitled *Understanding – and misunderstanding – social mobility in Britain: the entry of the economists, the confusion of politicians and the limits of educational policy*) that the biggest impact on social mobility is likely to be changes in occupational and class structure, and therefore policy shaping economic development will be more important than educational policy. Professor Chris Taylor and the gang at WISERD in Cardiff University are producing valuable and detailed work on the early years, poverty and attainment.

I think the debates in the US around E.D. Hirsch's core curriculum are interesting and more complex than many allow. I read with great interest his *Cultural Literacy (Random House, 1988)*, *The Knowledge Deficit (Houghton Mifflin 2007)* and *The Schools We Need (Anchor, 1999)*. I didn't need persuading that knowledge matters as much as skills. Hirsch cites Gramsci in his support – Dr Tim Williams had already recommended Harold Entwistle's book on Gramsci *Antonio Gramsci: Conservative Schooling for Radical Politics* (Routledge, 2009) though I should point out authors in Carmel Borg, Joseph Buttigieg and Peter Mayo's *Gramsci and Education* (Rowman & Littlefield, 2002) would probably disagree with most of this; maybe, at the end of the day, we should simply acknowledge what Gwyn Alf Williams said about Gramsci in *Proletarian Order* (Pluto, 1975), that after his death 'he became an altogether congenial fellow who could be put to all manner of useful work.' You can make up your own mind by reading Gramsci's thoughts on education in *Selections from Prison Notebooks* (Lawrence & Wishart, 1971).

Anyone who wants to read more about the anxiety of 11-plus results day should read *Modernity Britain: Opening the Box 1957-1959* (Bloomsbury, 2013), one of the volumes in the remarkable series on post-war Britain by the social historian David Kynaston, who records memories of those waiting for the verdict, demonstrating why the middle class – not left wing zealots – decided Grammar Schools should be abolished. Selina Todd's *The*

People – The Rise and Fall of the Working Class 1910-2010 (John Murray, 2014) contains an entire chapter on the subject which provides a thorough examination of the issues, including the persistence of class divisions even within grammar schools.

In the final chapter I move into discussion of the role of the media within our multinational state. My article in the March 2006 edition of *Media, Culture and Society* (vol. 28 No. 2), 'The National Assembly for Wales and broadcasting policy, 1999-2003' lists some of the relevant sources for discussions on the media, the nation and the British state after devolution, of which the most useful tend to be the essays by Professor Philip Schlesinger, including 'Scottish devolution and the media' in Jean Seaton's collection, *Politics and the Media* (Blackwell, 1998) and 'The new communications agenda in Scotland', in *Scottish Affairs, 47* (Spring 2004). David Morley and Kevin Robins, *Spaces of Identity* (Routledge, 1995) is a very engaging account of the interactions between global media, nations and cultural spaces. Habermas's sociological classic *The Structural Transformation of the Public Sphere* (Polity, 1992) provides an important underpinning for these debates.

Aside from books, there is a very active community of bloggers in England, ranging from individual head teachers like Geoff Barton and John Tomsett, whom I found very engaging during the English language GCSE saga, to organisations like the NAHT, the Local Schools Network, Head Teachers' Roundtable, and others. Others such as Dylan Wiliam, Conor Ryan, Fiona Millar, Warwick Mansell, Chris Cook, Laura McInerney, Andrew Olds, Tom Sherrington, Daisy Christodoulou and many others too numerous to mention are often thought-provoking and challenging. We could do with more like them in Wales, as well as Olchfa's ubiquitous Dave Stacey. Diane Ravitch and Daniel Willingham's blogs in the USA are also valuable. In higher education, Andrew McGettigan has up-to-date and important commentary on the fees debate. There are a number of bloggers, mainly in the US, whose arguments for and against Mass Online Open Courses (MOOCs) demonstrate that we don't yet know what might develop.

Further Reading

Andrew Adonis, *Education, Education, Education*, Biteback Publishing, 2012.

John Bangs, John MacBeath and Maurice Galton, *Reinventing Schools, Reforming Teaching*, Routledge, 2010.

Michael Barber, *Instruction to Deliver*, Politico's, 2007.

Michael Barber, *Deliverology 101*, Corwin, 2011.

Tony Blair, *A Journey*, Arrow, 2011.

David Cannadine, Jenny Keating and Nicola Sheldon, *The Right Kind of History*, Palgrave Macmillan, 2011.

Stefan Collini, *What are Universities for?*, Penguin, 2012.

David Hopkins, *Every School a Great School*, Open University Press, 2007.

Peter Hyman, *1 out of 10*, Vintage, 2005.

Gerald Kaufman, *How to be a Minister*, Faber edition, 2007.

Pasi Sahlberg, *Finnish Lessons*, Teachers' College Press, 2011.

Barry Schwartz, *The Paradox of Choice*, Harper Perennial, 2005.

Dai Smith, *Wales, A Question for History*, Seren, 1999.

Fenton Whelan, *Lessons Learned*, Fenton Whelan, 2009.

Professor J. Gwynn Williams, *The University Movement in Wales*, UWP, 1993.

Raymond Williams, *Culture & Society*, Pelican edition, 1961.

Raymond Williams, *The Long Revolution*, Pelican edition, 1965.

Chronology

2009

December	Appointed Minister for Children, Education and Lifelong Learning

2010

January	Michael Barber seminar
	Announcement of review of cost of administering education
	First Policy Board meeting
February	Speech on *The Paradox of Choice*
March	Announcement of HE Governance Review HEFCW Remit Letter
April	Welsh-Medium Education Strategy
May	Publication of PwC Review of cost of administering education
	Lecture on *Leadership in HE in difficult times*
	UK coalition government formed
June	School closures Statement
	HE Corporate Strategy published with Assembly Statement First meetings with Michael Gove and David Willetts
July	Tell Finance Committee HEIs must 'adapt or die'
September	School Effectiveness Framework goes live
	Estyn Common Inspection Framework starts
	Viv Thomas review announced
October	Browne Review published UK government Comprehensive Spending Review
November	Welsh Labour Policy Conference
	Welsh Government Tuition Fee Policy Announced
December	HE 'Adapt or Die' speech PISA 2009 results published
	Publication of estimates of tuition fee costs

2011

January	FoI of £7,000 fee modelling published
February	*Teaching Makes a Difference* speech with 20-point plan
	Call for 'wide national debate' on qualifications
March	Referendum on Assembly powers
	Publication of McCormick HE Governance Review
	Publication of Humphreys FE review
	Publication of £9,000 fee modeling under FoI
	Publication of Viv Thomas Review
	Education (Wales) Measure approved
May	Assembly election
	Formation of Welsh Labour Government – appointed Minister for Education and Skills
	School Standards Unit formed
June	IWA lecture setting out plans for consortia HEFCW rejects fee plans
	Say in Radio 4 interview 'we took our eye off the ball'.
July	HEFCW Reconfiguration Advice published Blaenau Gwent in Special Measures
August	Pembrokeshire in Special Measures
September	Provisional Secondary banding published October
	White Paper on Schools Standards Bill
	Coleg Cenedlaethol launched
	Announcement of Jobs Growth Wales
November	HE Reconfiguration statement
December	Final Secondary Banding published
	Daily Telegraph Exam seminar scoop

2012

February	Torfaen Council 'in need of significant improvement'
March	Learning from the Best lecture.
	Practitioners' Panel announced
	Learning in Digital Wales report launched Welsh

	Language Strategy published
	Remploy closures announced
April	Welsh Language Commissioner formally starts
	Pupil Deprivation Grant comes into effect
May	Local Government elections
	National Literacy Programme published
	Education and the Public Sphere lecture
	CCEA in Northern Ireland says it will no longer accept entries from England for its qualifications
	Formal launch of Qualifications Review
	Welsh language conditions imposed on OFCOM
	JMC on Welfare Reform
June	*Daily Mail* says Michael Gove will bring back O levels
July	Meet NI Education Minister John O'Dowd
	Anglesey Council in special measures
	Review of Welsh for Adults and Welsh Second Language launched
	University of Glamorgan and Newport University announce September merger talks
	Employer Support Grant for former Remploy workers announced
August	GCSE results published and review of English language GCSE announced
September	Report of English language GCSE published, followed by re- grading
	New university tuition fee system takes effect
	Learning Wales website launched
	Master's in Educational Practice programme starts
	Regional Consortia formally launched
	Michael Gove announces new EBC qualifications
October	Literacy and Numeracy Framework consultation
	Improving Schools Plan published
	Review of Welsh History and the Cwricwlwm Cymreig commences
	Review of Eisteddfod launched

November	Qualifications Review published Further review of structure of education delivery announced
December	Qualifications Wales announcement Speech to Leadership Foundation in HE signals new HE policy to be drawn up Visit to OECD and commissioning of report Visit to Scotland Hwb learning resources website launched alongside iTunes U site Education Wales

2013

January	Qualifications Review recommendations accepted Robert Hill appointed to carry out review of structure of delivery
February	Welsh Language Standards rejected Merthyr Council in special measures Monmouthshire Council in special measures Michael Gove backs down on EBCs
March	School Standards and Organisation Act becomes law *Raising our Sights* conference and speech Appearance before House of Commons Education Select Committee Reshuffle – stay in post *What's the Deal on Wales* lecture
April	Careers Wales returns to public sector Glamorgan and Newport Universities merge to form University of South Wales
May	National Reading and Numeracy tests start Meet Michael Gove with John O'Dowd Teach First Launched in Wales
June	National Digital Learning Conference New HE policy launched Robert Hill Review published Resignation from Government

Index

Aaronovitch, David 17
Ablett, Noah 1
Abraham, Emma 98
Adamson, Stephen 78
Adonis, Andrew 30, 37, 65, 75, 148, 153, 386, 393
Ahir, Ashok 272
Ainscow, Professor Mel 51, 115
Al-Begain, Professor Khalid 261
Alexander, Sir Kenneth 188
Andrews, Geoff 16, 389
Andrews, Professor John 308
Andrews, Peggy 16
Antoniw, Mick 7, 17
Armitstead, Claire 11, 86
Arora, Dr Bella 320
Arthur, Stuart 260
Atkinson, Rhian 21, 380

Baker, Kenneth, (Lord Baker of) 232, 234, 236, 387
Bale, Gareth 94
Ball, Stuart 255
Balls, Ed 79
Bangs, John 65, 386, 393
Barber, Sir Michael ix, 24, 25, 29, 31, 32, 40, 44, 55, 71, 73, 81, 94, 101, 108, 111, 112, 124, 128, 149, 150, 153, 189, 318, 385, 386, 389, 393, 394
Barde, Professor Yves 323
Barnett, Professor Steve 198, 387
Barton, Geoff 208, 392
Barton, Julie 255
Belli, Marc 11, 78, 381
Benn, Melissa 65, 67, 386
Benson, Jeremy 220, 222
Bevan, Aneurin 1, 5, 80, 138, 171
Beynon, Ann 17
Birt, John (Lord Birt of Liverpool) 32
Blair, Tony 29, 31, 65, 74, 75, 143, 177, 386, 393
Blount, Melanie 256
Blow, David 229, 230
Blunkett, David 29, 31, 64, 71, 72, 242, 386
Borysiewicz, Professor Sir Leszek 205
Boston, Dave 80
Brennan, Kevin 205
Britten, Chris 261
Brown, Gordon 7
Brown, Janet 180
Browne, Des (Lord Browne of Ladyton) 188, 295, 312, 313, 316, 331, 334, 335, 336, 337, 394
Brychan, Anna 47, 49, 165
Bunce, Lucy 261
Burden, Richard 17, 27, 98, 164
Butler, Professor Ian, 21, 41, 42, 45, 108
Butler, Rosemary 9, 19, 380

Cable, Vince 336, 342
Cameron, David 13, 188, 372
Cannadine, Professor David 241, 387, 393
Chamberlain, Kate 61
Chapman, Christine 10, 168
Childs, Helen 20, 380
Christodoulou, Daisy 158, 388, 392
Clancy, Claire 25
Clancy, Mike 25
Clark, Andrew 237, 356, 366, 379
Clark, Dr Jonathan 387
Clegg, Nick 363
Coffey, Professor Amanda 153
Collini, Professor Stefan 189, 312, 313, 388, 389, 390, 393

Cook, Chris 116, 225, 226, 392
Cook, Mary 195
Crick, Dr Tom, 261
Croke, Paul 179
Cuthbert, Jeff 50, 172, 176, 177, 243, 354, 356, 358, 360, 365

D'Ancona, Matthew 187, 387
Dacey, Gareth 261
Dafis, Cynog 287
Dalton, Katie 295, 296, 303, 339, 345, 349, 367
Daniels, Jo-Anne 48, 380
Daugherty, Professor Richard 103, 389
David, Cllr Huw 137, 143
Davidson, Jane 8-10, 19, 64, 103, 104, 168, 288, 332
Davidson, Michael Davies 50, 109
Davies, Geraint Talfan 136, 283, 288, 390
Davies, Jocelyn 340
Davies, Mervyn (Lord Davies of Abersoch) 328
Davies, Professor Sioned 276
Davies, Sue 208
Davies, Professor Sue 51
Dewar, Donald 188
Diamond, Professor Sir Ian 350
Dixon, Dr Phil 47, 107, 165
Docherty, Dr David 324, 388
Donaldson, Professor Graham 51, 232, 263
Donnelly, Katelyn 253, 389
Drakeford, Mark 54

Edmondson, Gareth 261
Edmunds, Wil 133
Edwards, Dave 94
Edwards, Elaine 165
Edwards, Dr Haydn 275, 355
Edwards, Huw 142, 238, 263
Edwards, Liz 11, 381
Edwards, Nicholas 293
Egan, Professor David 231
Eirian, Sian 277
Eirug, Aled 272, 380
Elfyn, Bethan 276
Elias, Lord Justice 228
Elis-Thomas, Dr Dafydd (Lord Elis-Thomas of) 280, 302
Entwistle, Harold 234, 391
Evans, Alan 87, 94, 137
Evans, Daniel 277
Evans, Darren 102
Evans, Eifion 51
Evans, Gareth 144, 204, 224, 295
Evans, Huw 173, 175, 176, 180, 181, 381
Evans, Nerys 4, 137, 336
Evans, Owen 38, 48, 49, 354, 358, 380
Evans, Professor Richard J. 240
Evas, Jeremy 272

Fabricant, Michael 267
Farrell, Professor Catherine 78
Florence, Peter 277
Francis, Hywel 10
Freud, David (Lord Freud) 360, 363
Fullan, Michael 38, 108, 253, 385, 387

Galton, Maurice 65, 386, 393
Garner, Isobel 137
Gething, Vaughan 203
Gibb, Nick 162, 267
Gibbons, Brian 8
Glover, Stephen 342
Golding, Ty 255
Gorard, Professor Stephen 88
Gould, Magi 261
Gove, Michael vii, 44, 61, 66, 67, 71, 72, 79, 107, 130, 143, 153, 162, 164, 170-172, 176, 178, 187-206, 210, 220, 221, 222, 223, 229, 234, 235, 239, 240-

243, 267, 369, 370, 372, 387, 394, 396, 397
Gow, Bill 17
Graham, Professor Karen 51
Gramsci, Antonio 234, 391
Grayling, Chris 362
Graystone, John 365
Green, Andrew 255, 320
Greenough, Matt 42, 295, 380
Grey-Thompson, Tanni (Baroness Grey-Thompson of Eaglescliffe) 250
Griffiths, Dr Hugh 239
Griffiths, John 10, 19, 21, 168, 250, 352, 367
Griffiths, Lesley 20, 27, 353, 354
Griffiths, Mike 179
Griffiths, Cllr Paul 138
Gruffydd-Jones, Efa 282
Guilfoyle, Bethan 11, 51, 87, 133, 137, 179, 381
Gummett, Dr Phil 288
Gunning, Dennis 25, 26, 380
Gunter, Chris 94

Habermas, Jürgen 373, 392
Hadfield, Professor Mark 153
Halligan, Professor Peter 322, 323
Hamilton, Lynne 25, 26, 335, 380
Hannon, Cllr Paul 137
Harries, Professor John 323
Harris, Professor Alma 47, 111, 152, 388
Harris, Hag 184
Hart, Edwina 81, 278, 323
Hattie, Professor John 150, 388
Hawker, David 23, 39, 48
Hayward, Janet 11, 253, 261, 381
Henderson, Andy 100, 381
Higgins, Michael D. 373
Hill, Christopher 18
Hill, Robert xi, 78, 143-145, 158, 397
Hilton, Steve 20, 188
Hirsch, Professor E.D. 233, 234, 391
Hodgson, Dame Patricia 162
Holtham, Gerry 328
Hope, Alex 260
Hopkin, Professor Sir Deian 299, 341, 389
Hopkins 111, 112, 388, 393
Houston 180
Howe, Sophie 130
Howells, Alison 261
Hughes, Dr Deirdre 355
Hughes, Professor John 295, 322
Hughes, Professor Medwin 302, 303
Hume, Colette 55
Humphreys, Rob 10, 320, 367, 395
Hunt, Tristram 116
Hutt, Jane 9, 19, 20, 21, 60, 61, 76, 100, 154, 168, 264, 284, 289, 328, 333, 335, 353
Hutton, Will 351
Huws, Meri 266, 269, 274, 279
Huxford, Laura 158, 385
Hyman, Peter 65, 386, 393

Jadhav, Cath 217
James, David 219
Jarman, Nick 50
Jenkins, Peter 7, 11
Jenkins, Simon 72, 315
John, Angela 237, 238
Jones, Alun Ffred 268, 269, 274, 279, 280
Jones, Carwyn ii, ix, 2, 7, 21, 27, 52, 114, 122, 131, 161, 376, 385
Jones, Clare 160
Jones, David 320, 365
Jones, Sir Derek 39
Jones, Dr Dylan 47, 255, 381
Jones, Eirlys Pritchard 277

Jones, Dr Elin 238, 239
Jones, Helen Mary 137
Jones, Ieuan Wyn 4, 8, 27, 264, 353
Jones, Merfyn 44, 283, 288, 328, 333, 335, 339, 354, 380
Jones, Rhys 11
Jones, Steve 8, 216
Jones-Evans, Professor Dylan 290, 320

Kaufman, Gerald 21, 385, 393
Keane, Ann 43, 45, 76, 93, 106, 108, 121, 138, 144, 246, 381
Keating, Jenny 241, 387, 393
Kelly, Gerard 110, 165, 223
Kelly, Professor Tony 74, 386
Kidron, Beeban 249
Kotter, John 32, 387

Lampl, Sir Peter 350
Letterman, David 369
Lewis, Huw xi, 5, 11, 20, 23, 32, 51, 62, 92, 98, 114, 126, 127, 146, 154, 155, 157, 159, 162, 165, 184, 185, 242, 249, 261-263, 276, 310, 350, 353, 260, 360
Lewis, Roger, 94, 117
Lewis, Sian 274
Lightman, Brian 219
Lipset, Seymour Martin 372
Livingstone, Ian 260
Llewellyn, Dr Chris 113, 130
Lupton, Professor Ruth 89, 387
Lydon, Professor Julie 309

MacBeath, John 65, 386, 393
Mackay, Professor Tony 94
MacKenzie, Kelvin 341
MacTaggart, Fiona 17
Mainwaring, W.H. 1
Mansell, Warwick 65, 102, 116, 219, 225, 387, 392
Mansfield, Martin 357
Marr, Andrew 194
Masters, Adrian 15, 157
Mathias, Glyn 78
Matthews, Dr Ioan 283, 334
Matthias, Hannah 261
Maxwell, Bill 45, 101
Maxwell, Marcella 357
McAllister, Professor Laura 250
McConnell, Jack (Lord McConnell of Glenscorrodale) 17
McCormick 289, 296, 297, 299, 300, 302, 310, 314, 395
McGettigan, Andrew 351, 388, 392
Melding, David 286, 294
Miliband, David 3, 25, 66, 133, 177
Millar, Fiona 44, 65, 67, 69, 71, 381, 392
Miller, Maria 363, 364
Millman, Mick 11
Milton, Emma-Jane 152
Mithan, Matthew 281, 380
Moller, Professor Faron 261
Moore, Charles 32
Morgan, Jonathan 137
Morgan. K.O. (Lord Morgan of Aberdyfi) 372, 390
Morgan, Rhodri 8, 20, 64, 106, 168, 332, 353
Morgan, Rhodri Llwyd 278
Morgans, Alun 255
Morley, Professor David 373, 392
Morris, Estelle (Baroness Morris of Yardley) iv, 70, 380
Mourshed, Mona 149
Moxey, Rachel 357
Murphy, Paul 125
Myhill, Boaz 94

Neagle, Lynne 103
Nelson, Fraser 187
Ng, Professor Andrew 319

Nicholas, Heather 11, 117, 293
Noble, Roy 276, 277
Nosworthy, Colin 268, 282

O'Connor, Betsan 51
O'Dowd, John 182, 194, 196, 197, 198, 200, 202, 204, 205, 396, 397
Opposs, Dennis 212
Osmond, John 293
Owen, Gwilym 277
Owen, Jano 51
Owens, Cathy 8

Parry, Sir Emyr Jones 291, 295
Parry, Nia 276
Patten, Chris (Lord Patten of Barnes) 348
Paxman, Jeremy 219
Pethick, Fiona 213, 214, 215
Phillips, Trevor 17, 389
Pierce, Gareth 207
Plaut, Rudi 305
Porter, Sarah 320
Powell, Enoch 15
Price, Adam 375
Price, Professor Patricia 320
Pridham, Simon 257, 261, 381
Pritchard, John 277
Prochaska, Dr Alice 237
Pugh, Dr Brett 45, 48, 93, 112, 133, 380
Puttnam David (Lord Puttnam of Queensgate) 154

Ravitch, Diane 233, 392
Redfearn, Joyce 51
Redwood, John 28, 129
Reece, Sarah 257
Rees, Professor Gareth 125
Rees, Geraint 51, 90, 389
Rees, Professor Teresa 332
Reid, Professor Ken 45, 50, 123, 134, 152, 200
Reynolds, Professor David 10, 50, 53, 54, 63, 74, 96, 106, 111, 113, 152, 154, 177, 379, 386
Rhys, Elin 278
Rhys, Matthew 274
Richards, Steve 223, 275
Riordan, Professor Colin 322
Roberts, Emyr 38, 39, 40, 48, 178, 192, 218, 280, 380
Roberts, Sioned Wyn 255, 277
Robins, Kevin 373, 392
Robson, Phil 51
Roderick, Vaughan 17, 178, 203, 389
Rogers, Glyn 261
Rowlands, Ted (Lord Rowlands of Merthyr Tydfil and of Rhymney) 356
Runeckles, Jane 20
Russell, Mike 168, 172, 194, 195, 204, 235, 307
Ryan, Conor 64, 386, 392

Sahlberg, Pasi 375, 388, 393
Samuel, Raphael 237, 241, 387
Sandals, Leigh 112
Sargeant, Carl 20, 27, 53, 54, 56, 87, 129, 131, 140, 360
Saunders, Professor Danny 355, 381
Schleicher, Andreas 50, 71, 102
Schlesinger, Professor Philip 373, 392
Schwarz, Barry 170, 171, 388
Seldon, Professor Anthony 214
Shanklin, Tom 94
Sharp, Mrs Justice 228
Sheen, Michael 249
Sheldon, Nicola 241, 387, 393
Siraj, Professor Iram 43, 48, 83, 247, 248, 381, 390
Skates, Ken 354, 359
Smith, Professor Dai 18, 233, 238, 242, 250, 315, 389, 390, 393
Smith, Iain Duncan 360
Smith, Professor Sir Steve 307

Soubry, Anna 17
Spielman, Amanda 220
Stacey, Dave 239, 292
Stacey, Glenys 189, 193, 200, 201, 213-215, 218, 219, 221, 222
Stainthorp, Professor Rhona 95
Stannard, John 158, 385
Steele, Bruce 255
Stewart, William 211
Stuart, Graham 116, 199, 255, 260
Surman, Neil 335, 379
Swan, Julie 219

Tabberer, Professor Ralph 51, 157
Taylor, Professor Chris 87, 391
Taylor, David 8
Taylor, Matthew 189
Thomas, Cllr Alun 142
Thomas, Gwenda 136, 360
Thomas, Rhodri Glyn 269
Thomas, Roger 43, 288, 381
Thomas, Steve 27, 130
Thomas, Viv 28, 51, 76, 95, 104, 110, 122, 131, 133, 135, 140, 247, 379, 394, 395
Thompson, E.P. 11, 18, 120, 250
Thrun, Sebastian 318
Tomlinson, Professor Sally 73, 177, 386
Tomsett, John 213, 392
Toshack, John 17
Towler, Keith 259
Tristan, Dr Dafydd 320
Tudor Hart, Dr Julian 81
Turner, Dr Caroline 272, 379
Tweedale, Chris 25, 48, 50, 103, 215, 221, 380
Twigg, Stephen 67, 116, 200

Vincent, Steve 137, 139, 380

Walton, Steve 51
Watts, Professor Terry 355
Webb, Professor Sir Adrian 33, 43, 66, 243, 306, 310, 327, 353, 355, 366, 381
Webb, Rachael 11, 250, 365, 381
Whelan, Fenton 70, 75, 108, 150, 388, 393
Whiting, Mike 223
Wiliam, Professor Dylan 68, 102, 149, 150, 157, 158, 189, 234, 376, 388, 392
Willetts, David 171, 331, 335, 342, 351, 394
Williams, Emma 104, 379
Williams, Gareth 50
Williams, Professor Gwyn Alf 315, 390, 391
Williams, Hywel 350
Williams, Professor J. Gwynn 315, 389, 393
Williams, Raymond 1, 18, 198, 233, 234, 241, 242, 244, 292, 372, 390, 393
Williams, Rebecca 47
Williams, Shane 94
Williams, Dr Tim 25, 111, 122, 133, 233, 234, 391
Williamson, David 106, 341
Willingham, Daniel T. 158, 241, 242, 388, 392
Wilshaw, Sir Michael 16, 69, 84, 210
Wilson, Mervyn 80
Withers, Matt 163
Wolf, Professor Alison 172, 194, 242
Woodhead, Sir Chris 214
Woods, Professor David 69, 386

Yassine, Ali 272, 277